INTRODUCTION BY HERBERT READ

CREATORS COLLECTORS AND CONNOISSEURS

The anatomy of artistic taste from antiquity to the present day

NIELS VON HOLST

with 405 plates, 32 in colour

THAMES AND HUDSON · LONDON

© THAMES AND HUDSON   LONDON   1967

TRANSLATED FROM THE GERMAN BY BRIAN BATTERSHAW

PRINTED IN GERMANY BY DUMONT PRESSE, COLOGNE

BOUND IN GERMANY BY KLEMME UND BLEIMUND, BIELEFELD

CONTENTS

KEY TO MARGINAL REFERENCES

Numbers in italics refer to black and white illustrations.
Roman numerals refer to colour plates.
N refers to Notes (page 368).
B refers to the numbered Bibliography (page 381).

Introduction

THIS FASCINATING BOOK is concerned with something much more complex than the history of art, or even the history of taste. It investigates, for the first time in such a complete manner, the manifestations of an obscure but persistent impulse in the history of mankind—the instinct that compels certain people in every age to collect—to collect what in English we often call 'objets d'art', using a foreign phrase to express the ambiguous nature of our pursuit. The pursuit is ambiguous because in the first place it does not necessarily serve any rational purpose. Art itself has an evolutionary function—it is concerned with the refinement of perception—and though we say that art does not 'progress' in any evolutionary sense (an aspect of art that worried Marx and Engels, anxious to relate every human phenomenon to an evolving social economy), this is only true of historical times. From the prehistorian's point of view there has been a continuous evolution in the refinement of human artifacts, from the first rough implements of stone to the sophisticated cult objects of the early Mesopotamian civilizations. But any social purpose we may ascribe to art in general is of no great interest to the collector. He is moved by obscurer motives.

A further ambiguity arises from the fact, so clearly demonstrated in this volume, that the impulse to collect has no consistency. It seizes only a minority of men, and expresses no coherent standards of judgment. It can be an expression of cupidity—works of art are hoarded for their material value; they make 'good investments'. They can express a sense of power and splendour, as in the great collections of kings and princes. They have often been the trophies of military conquerors, and even revolutionary governments, renouncing the ideals of the régimes they replace, replenish rather than disperse the possessions of their predecessors—witness the great collections in Peking, Moscow and Leningrad. But more generally the impulse to collect has a more modest scope and a less obvious motive.

To come nearer to the nature of this motive we must distinguish purposive collecting, which may be identified with connoisseurship, from the mere accumulation of miscellaneous objects. Many, indeed most, people accumulate family possessions, and possessions in general may be said to give a sense of security—not only in the sense that they are 'valuables' that can if necessary be sold, but also because they 'feather' the domestic nest. But this is an instinct (possibly very primitive in its origins) which can run away with itself, leading to those clutters of family possessions that we associate with the nineteenth century, the age of bourgeois comfort, rather than with our present ascetic tastes.

Taste is the word we use to describe the collector's criterion—taste rather than judgment, which is associated with connoisseurship. From an aesthetic point of view the taste of a collector may indeed be very vulgar. There are collections of ivory elephants and heraldic china, wine glasses and custard cups, tea-pots and paperweights, and there is an infinite variation of taste between the love of these lowly objects and the love of masterpieces of painting and sculpture. It may be doubted, however, whether the psychological motive is ever basically different in kind. What does differ is the social prestige of different types of collection. This is not, however, a question of cost—a piece of porcelain or even a paperweight may cost as much as a fine painting or a piece of sculpture. Works of art have a hierarchy of their own—

3

why otherwise do we speak of the *fine* arts? For this there are good aesthetic reasons—certain arts express a wider range or greater depth of feeling; others involve a higher degree of skill. But these are not necessarily the considerations that determine what particular kind of object is collected. As the author points out in his first chapter, the collector (at the best a man of 'independent mind and thoroughly independent judgment') can easily degenerate into a snob, and have the snob's 'pathological craving for novelty and change'. Nowadays many, perhaps most, collectors follow the fashions that are created by dealers and the glossy magazines that serve their commercial interests. But collecting would not have so much fascination for the public did it not allow for new trends and new discoveries. There is a great excitement in being the first collector to discover new ground to exploit, and often a hitherto unjustly neglected phase of art is in this way revealed and henceforth takes its proper place in the history of art ('Biedermeier' furniture in Germany, 'Shaker' furniture in the United States, 'primitive' painting everywhere). But by the same process of revaluation other phases of art lose their prestige and are either thrown on the scrap-heap or become the province of less snobbish collectors.

The author of this book is not concerned with these lower ranges of the collecting impulse, and it may be cynical to suggest that the same impulse motivates the collector of masterpieces and the collector of knick-knacks (or 'objets de vertu' as they may be more snobbishly called). It will be said that connoisseurship (that is to say, a combination of sensibility and knowledge) makes the difference, but the collecting of porcelain, for example, demands a high degree of sensibility and intelligent discrimination, and I do not see much *psychological* difference in such faculties when exercised on a bronze figure by Giovanni da Bologna and on a porcelain figure by Franz Bustelli. The *quality* of art is not determined either by size or by scarcity; indeed, where the collector's impulse is concerned, grandeur or monumentality is by the nature of things almost excluded, until we come to the quite different phenomenon of the public collection, enshrined in a museum of art.

Historically the public collection was a development from the princely collections of the Baroque period. As these collections grew in size and importance special galleries were constructed in palaces to house them—typical examples described by our author are the 'Kunstkammer' of Rudolph II and the 'Pinacotheca' of the Prince Elector Johann Wilhelm of the Palatinate. Such galleries needed curators and a new profession gradually came into being, the 'keeper' as distinct from the 'collector'. The next step was to admit the general public to these galleries and in this manner the concept of the museum of fine art was gradually realized. With the growth of industry and a public educational system in the nineteenth century, a social function was eventually imposed on these museums—they became museums of *applied* art, and in theory, if not always in practice, collections were formed with the express purpose of providing models for the designers and manufacturers of mass-produced utilitarian wares. Even museums of fine art, especially in the United States of America, were more and more conceived as educational institutions.

In conformity with such a development collecting became a science. It may be that the good museum curator is always a collector at heart, but there is an obvious conflict of interest if the museum curator is also a private collector, and in some public museums a strict prohibition is enforced. But the aims of the private and the public collector are quite distinct. The private collector, in the satisfaction of a personal impulse and a singular taste, may 'specialize' and confine himself to the work of one or two artists or to a single category of objects. The public collector must have no such prejudices: he must look on the world of art in the same spirit as a botanist looks on the world of plants, and what he collects he must arrange and categorize with Linnaean assiduity. Arrangement, or presentation as it is now called, becomes an art in itself, and 'museology' a scientific discipline.

4

The museum or art gallery is designed to educate the general public, but it also educates the collector, and collecting, as a social phenomenon, is now widespread. As a consequence not only have works of art of any great aesthetic merit disappeared from the market, but a great impetus has been given to the collecting of contemporary works of art. Great museums of 'modern' art have been founded in many cities and these again stimulate the collecting impulse. While this development is natural and inevitable, it leads to some less desirable consequences. The 'forging' of works of art, both ancient and modern, is the most obvious of these, but there were forgeries in the ancient world. What is more serious, if less evident, is a certain corruption or de-valuation of art itself. The work of art, as this book illustrates, has always, in historical times, been a commodity, but in former times it was not conceived as a 'collector's piece'. Primarily it was always the product of an activity that was socially or psychologically significant— pictures were painted and figures carved as symbols of religious beliefs or at least for a specific function (if only a decorative one) in churches or palaces. Artists usually worked for a patron, and the patron, however active he may have been in commissioning works of art, is not to be confused with the collector; he always has a practical purpose in mind. The artist, similarly, sees his work as fulfilling a purpose of a practical kind, and not as a free commodity. One might even claim that the concept of 'art for art's sake', or art as 'self-expression', indicates disinterestedness on the part of the artist: he has no design on the collector. Then gradually, but only massively and deliberately from the middle of the nineteenth century, artists began to make what we might call 'art objects', that is to say, works with a deliberate design on the potential collector. The collecting impulse was thus short-circuited; what was formerly sought with diligence and found with surprise and delight in the world at large was henceforth provided as a ready-made art object by the dealer. Art-collecting now hardly differs from stamp-collecting. All sense of serendipity is prevented.

The serious student of art, however useful he may find the collector's collection, usually has a certain disdain for the collector's motives. This attitude relates to the phenomenon of 'taste', which I have already described as ambiguous. The art historian and art critic may have their personal preferences, but if as good scholars they aspire to objectivity, they cannot afford to express these preferences in their scientific activities. Like the museum curator, they must moderate their enthusiasms in the public interest. 'Good' taste is almost as embarrassing as 'bad' taste; the snob is the counterpart of the philistine. Nevertheless, objectivity is an impossible ideal, in art no less than in science, and one must not forget one supreme service that the collector has performed—he has saved many of the greatest works of art from destruction or neglect. Looking through the four hundred illustrations in this volume (which admittedly have been selected from thousands of alternatives) one is impressed by the infallibility of the taste of the great collectors of the past. No doubt their mistakes have often been suppressed, or fallen by the way, but what has survived in the great collections of the world is witness to the highest spiritual triumphs of mankind, and the collecting impulse needs no other justification.

HERBERT READ

5

The past as a source of inspiration | how copies and imitations come into being | the divorce of art from its original purpose | the collecting impulse | the function of the collector and effects of his activities

'Every pleasure of the mind entails a certain amount of effort. We must therefore meet works of art half-way, if we are not to pass them by entirely.'

JAKOB BURCKHARDT

THIS BOOK DEALS WITH something outside the scope of ordinary handbooks of art history, though it is something without which the picture of any age would remain incomplete. Our subject is the attitudes of the different generations towards the art of the past, both recent and remote, which those generations feel to have some affinity with themselves. We shall be discussing the growth of the great collections and their influence, the theft of works of art and their migrations, the work of the dealers—and the forgers.

Unlike technology, art does not progress; there is no supersession of the old by the new. Every great work of art from the past is capable of a rebirth, of a renaissance, and so when we survey great areas of history we become aware of a polyphony of influences, of a choir of many voices. It is not irrelevant to refer here to one of those basic kinds of experience which Goethe describes and which he calls 'the sense at once of the past and the present'. He speaks of this experience in *Dichtung und Wahrheit* and tells how he himself underwent it when confronted by Le Brun's portrait of the art collector Jabach and his family. Shortly before his death Goethe once more returned to the same theme: the sight of old pictures and statues develops a sympathetic understanding for the age in which they were created; it makes a part of past life wholly contemporary and needs to be re-interpreted in the context of our own day.

Each generation's taste for the art of the past has been variously interpreted. Only a few decades ago it was generally accepted that the creative artist was invariably forward-looking, whereas the merely receptive layman was always looking back. Today the feeling is that in all late and mature periods and throughout the whole of the modern age, a sense of history is present, though varying both in strength and direction. Perhaps one can venture to say that historicism is a mark of all productive cultures. B 163

At least as far back as the days of the Medici, the intellectual élite in Europe has shown itself receptive towards the art of a previous age; and artists in particular may always be credited with a special instinct for detecting their spiritual ancestors. Before 1900, when no collector had so much as heard of El Greco, his name was already enjoying occasional mention among the studios in Paris.

The more facets to a master's art, the more frequently he comes within our view. Tiepolo, re-discovered in 1870 in Vienna, where a taste for the neo-Baroque prevailed, was an object of interest to the devotees of Impressionism on account of the brightness of his palette. Around 1900 Goya was regarded as someone who had actually anticipated Impressionism, yet his works also had significance for the Expressionists.

Once a vanished world of art has come to light again, one new aspect of it after another unfolds for us. Around 1780 the late Middle Ages attracted the generation of Blake and Flaxman, around 1820 the Romantics, about 1870 they appealed to the men of the boom years in Germany, and about 1920 to the contemporaries of Rouault. The world of antiquity, rediscovered five hundred years ago, has never been allowed to sink into complete oblivion.

We can often observe how a contemporary artist, who has discovered some master of the past, is, in the years that follow this discovery, himself more quickly eclipsed than the predecessor he has re-introduced. His act of discovery goes unrewarded: quite suddenly the world sees in him no more than the effete heir of one greater than himself. The painters of Goethe's day, from Mengs to Ingres, the men who forced their own age to take note of Raphael, were no more able to escape this fate than the English Pre-Raphaelites who chose Botticelli as their leader—or those painters and sculptors who, with El Greco as their battle-cry, sought to discover new regions of art. The Expressionists opened our eyes to the art of Africa, but are today accused of shameless plagiarism. Their 'African still-lifes' are forgotten, while Negro idols continue to be admired. And when critics speak of Henry Moore and declare with a certain air of objective detachment that it is impossible to think of certain of his sculptures without calling to mind some of the ancient American exhibits in the British Museum, we are approaching the time when this discovery could carry a much more unfriendly implication for the living artist. But such derogatory judgments are often revised by a succeeding age.

Each generation loves not only what it immediately perceives to be spiritually akin to itself; it often follows a still deeper impulse and is moved by what is apparently alien. Ages which felt themselves to be too restless, changeable and too much at odds with themselves, gazed longingly at the stiff self-contained art of ancient Egypt.

We must, however, guard against over-simplifying the relationship in which any period stands to the art of other ages, cultures and countries. Imperial Rome idolized all that was the work of Greek chisel and brush, but it also felt attracted to Egyptian art and *51* the Buddha images of Asia. In the Florence of the Quattrocento Ghiberti and Donatello favoured the antique, while their fellow citizens who were painters were eager to see the art of Jan van Eyck, so alien to their own. We know that Raphael used to admire the *Apollo Belvedere*, yet there are probably few who realize that the rigidly front-faced effect of the *Sistine Madonna* can only be explained by the assumption that the painter was in some measure influenced by the religious art of Byzantium. Rembrandt loved *155* the sculptures of the antique Baroque, yet was also impressed by the classical balance of Raphael's *Port-* *153* *rait of Balthasar Castiglione*. About 1800 the antique was decisive for Canova, the High Renaissance in Italy for the painters of Paris, the phase immediately preceding it for the German Romantics, and for Constable, the art of van Ruisdael. In the second half of the nineteenth century Feuerbach was paying homage to Titian, Manet was studying Velazquez and Frans Hals, Renoir acknowledged Boucher, and Leibl was taking Holbein as his model.

How variegated the pattern becomes as we move into the second half of our own century! People now turn their attention to the art of non-European peoples, both primitive and advanced; they discover archaic phases in periods with which they are already familiar. Yet the great masters of post-Renaissance Europe, who have been appreciated for centuries, do not fade from view as much as might be thought. Before the First World War one could have seen Nolde and Matisse in the Louvre, standing before the Titians, and Rouault in front of *The Hunt* by Annibale Carracci. Kokoschka could have been found in Venice, absorbed in the study of Tintoretto. Since 1920 there have been periods when Picasso has devoted himself with sympathetic understanding to pictures by Cranach, Raphael and Murillo. 'The higher a culture rises, the wider grows its horizon.'

A painter or a sculptor who finds that a work of art from another world and another age has something to say to him is not content to stand and look at it but seeks to come to terms with it in a wide variety of ways. The way to come closest to such a work is to copy it, and such copies represent acts of homage paid by great men to their equals. Later ages can nevertheless recognize in them a stylistic compulsion imposed on the copyist by the age in which he lived and by the dictates of his personality. Of such a kind are Rubens' copies of Titian, Delacroix's copies of Rembrandt and van Gogh's copies of Delacroix. Free variations on some theme from an older work of art—using the term 'variation' in its musical sense—is something which we encounter less frequently, though Picasso has exhibited in London some fifty works which were inspired by Velazquez' famous picture *Las Meninas*.

When minor talents familiarize themselves with the style of a great artist without being able to translate it into fresh terms, we speak of imitations. Goethe rebuked some German landscape artists of his youth for being strongly Rembrandtesque. An interesting and rather special case is presented by the playful forgeries of certain young men of genius who were chiefly moved by a desire to assert themselves. Michelangelo, for instance, while still young and unrecognized, fooled the public of his day with a piece of his own sculpture which he got up to look like a work of antiquity, but soon revealed himself as its creator when it had aroused general admiration. It is also worth recalling that in 1925 a Frankfurt connoisseur wanted to see how he and his friends would react to a Tintoretto being created, so he commissioned an artist to paint a composite picture based on elements of actual paintings by the master. In all these cases genuine creative participation may have been at a discount, and perhaps there was some measure of dishonesty too—in an artistic as opposed to a commercial sense. The case of forgeries carried out for purposes of deliberate fraud is another matter.

While the great artist, having once come to terms with the unfamiliar, returns again to creative work that is truly his own, the layman is much more likely to succumb to the spell of one particular movement or style. Ludwig I of Bavaria, for whom at one time the art of his own day—for instance the work of Canova—represented the summit of artistic achieve-

1 Great works of art are often known by the names of previous owners. The *Fugger Sarcophagus* (detail above), found in Crete in the sixteenth century, recalls Hans Fugger, the powerful Augsburg merchant. Four hundred years ago, when he owned this sarcophagus, it was the first piece of original Greek sculpture in Germany

2 In many cases, the names given to sculpture from the Palazzo Farnese in Rome, which once contained the most important private collection of classical art in Italy, refer back to this collection. Examples are the *Farnese Diadumenos* in the British Museum, and the *Farnese Jove* (right) in Naples

ment, soon turned to the sculpture of Greece and Rome to which he remained devoted. When the public feels itself to have an affinity with a particular period and sets a high value on the work of some master, it demands to see his work again and again. It is here that the collector enters the picture. Certain sets of circumstances may, however, cause a work of art to move, as it were, out of its proper sphere and away from the purpose for which it was created.

3 Rubens was not only a great painter but also an important collector. He owned this fifth-century Byzantine glass vase which even today, more than three hundred years after his death, is still known as the *Rubens Vase*

In the west, and almost two thousand years earlier in the world of antiquity, the discovery of the intrinsic value of art went hand in hand with a loosening of the religious bonds which at one time had given coherence to man's picture of the world. At such times the wishes of the art patron and collector are suited by events outside the realm of art. In the years when Europe passed from the Middle Ages to the Renaissance three factors began to operate which were due to the same historical conditions: the purely artistic interest of the governing class in altarpieces which had been newly erected in the churches, the desire of certain individuals to acquire works of sacred art and bring them into the private sphere of their own homes, and the partial release from their liturgical function, in those countries which had fallen away from Rome, of certain ecclesiastical appurtenances. From now on the Protestant states became a most promising hunting-ground for the collector: the Austrian Habsburgs acquired old German altarpieces from Wittenberg and Nuremberg, while the Spanish branch of the family filled their castles with early Netherlandish panels from the territory in which Alba and other Spanish generals were fighting those who had turned against the Faith.

The decisive element in bringing about the withdrawal of works of sacred art from their original functions is the interest of art-lovers, which at a certain point of time emerges in every culture. In post-Renaissance Europe every opportunity was used that might help to satisfy the growing demand: the tendency of works of art in churches to suffer damage, changes of taste among the faithful of either persuasion, the rebuilding or replacement of churches and finally economic crises and the consequent lack of money in clerical circles.

When they pass from the sacred to the profane sphere, works once made for the glory of God appear in the eyes of the beholder to have new emphases. The Italian Madonnas of the fifteenth century speak to the public in our museums of human types, of the discovery of the world of nature, of the Renaissance sense of composition and choice of colours. Yet in 1910 an Italian princess still threw herself to the ground in prayer before a Florentine altar in the newly built Kaiser Friedrich Museum in Berlin, moved purely by the religious power which radiated

4 Many items from Cardinal Borghese's collection, which was started in Rome at the beginning of the seventeenth century, were later sold: among them the *Borghese Hermaphrodite* in the Louvre, and the *Borghese Hera* (detail left) in Copenhagen

5 The *Arundel Homer* calls to mind the first great English collector. It was the first original Greek sculpture to reach England and is still known by its traditional name, even though it is now thought to represent a later poet, possibly Sophocles

from the painting. Apart from altarpieces and devotional pictures, innumerable other objects originally intended to serve religious purposes now fill our collections and museums—for instance, a door-panel from a sacristy cupboard by Taddeo Gaddi (in the Munich Pinakothek), the sides of a Sienese bier painted by Pacchia (in the same museum), the standard of a religious brotherhood in Siena painted by Sodoma (in the Palazzo Pitti, Florence), or the memorial tablet of a Stuttgart citizen, painted by Schaffner (in the Kunsthalle, Hamburg). In collections of applied art we find acquisitions dating back to the time of the Crusades, products in whose half religious, half magical miracle-working power men have believed for

63   centuries. The *Luck of Edenhall*, a glass vase, was recently acquired by the Victoria and Albert Museum in London where it is labelled 'Aleppo, mid-thirteenth century', and where, bearing the registration number C. 1. 1959, it shares a case marked 'Egypt and Syria' with twelve similar objects.

Since we are members of a community of nations whose religion continues to live on, the return of this or that object from the service of man to the service of God is always possible. This movement to and fro is characteristic of the way in which things have developed in Europe since the Renaissance. A *Virgin Mary* by Cranach, which a Protestant prince in central Germany removed from his collection around 1600 and presented to an archduke reigning in the Tyrol as a valuable painting from the time of Dürer, found its way back as part of a princely foundation to the high altar of the Catholic Stadtpfarrkirche in Innsbruck. In this district, the picture almost attained the fame of a miracle-working ikon. The *Annunciation* by Veit Stoss in the Lorenzkirche in Nuremberg was for a short time in the early nineteenth century the property of a museum. In Augsburg Cathedral prayers are said before altarpieces, painted by the elder Holbein, which had long been in the hands of dealers. Titian's *Assumption of the Virgin*, the high altar panel in the Church of Santa Maria Gloriosa dei Frari in Venice, could be seen by our grandfathers in the Gallerie dell'Accademia. The painting by Tintoretto set up again on the high altar of the Theatine Church in Munich in 1950, had been hanging for over a century in one of the affiliated galleries of the Pinakothek.

6 The names of two noble Italian families of the seventeenth century live on in the works of art they once possessed, even though the families themselves have long since died out. There is the *Giustiniani Apollo* in the British Museum, and the *Ludovisi Throne*, a fine piece of early Greek sculpture (detail below) which may have been used as a wind-break for an altar to Aphrodite

If a picture, a piece of sculpture or an objet d'art which had originally been intended to serve a particular secular purpose is viewed primarily or exclusively as a work of art, its character also undergoes definite changes. Let us begin with the visible symbols of state power. The imperial crown jewels in Vienna are stored in a special room of the Hofburg, the old imperial residence, and so preserve at least something of their old significance. But the French in 1789 and the Russians in 1917 acted in a much more radical fashion and condemned everything pertaining to the crown to the existence of a mere museum exhibit. The legendary sword of Charlemagne survives in the Galerie d'Apollon of the Louvre as one treasure among others. Trophies of victory which call to mind some supreme moment in a country's history lose much when they leave their place in some public building and are relegated to a museum. We feel this with peculiar intensity when contemplating the booty from the Burgundian Wars in the Landesmuseum in Berne.

In contrast, the battle standards which a Christian army captured from its Mohammedan foes seven hundred years ago are still preserved with pious gratitude in the monastery of Las Huelvas near Burgos. The antique bronze horses captured in 1204 during the Fourth Crusade would be less effective even in the finest museum hall than they are above the portico of St Mark's in Venice.

Transference from its proper place almost invariably destroys something of the effect of a work of art. The allegories of Paolo Veronese, destroyed by fire in 1945, had once imparted a feeling of high solemnity to the mercantile activities of the Fondaco dei Tedeschi in Venice, but left many a visitor unmoved when they were housed in a museum in Berlin. The same is true of the *Triumph of the Victor* by Rubens, which left its original home in the house of an Antwerp marksman's guild and is now in the Landesmuseum Cassel. As against this, however, the 'alcove pictures', representations of the loves of gods, which were common in the Renaissance and often decorated marriage beds, acquire a new dignity in the neutral atmosphere of a collection. The erotic quality which once appeared very obvious seems somehow diminished.

One could quote other examples almost indefinitely. There is the Florentine wedding chest (in the

7, 8 These two famous Madonnas remind us of eighteenth- and early nineteenth-century collections. The *Incehall Madonna* (above), probably by Jan van Eyck, went from an English country house to Australia, and Giorgione's *Tallard Madonna* (below) from Paris to Oxford

9, 10 Two Madonnas by Raphael, his early *Connestabile Madonna* (left) and the mature *Alba Madonna* (right), bear the name of an Italian and a Spanish family respectively

Hanover Landesmuseum), now far removed from those Florentine citizens who once sought to do honour to the bridal pair; and Weenix's *Still-life with Game* (in the Munich Pinakothek) which no longer has anything to say to the princely hunter; or Watteau's shop sign (in the Berlin Museums) which no longer attracts clients to the art dealer Gersaint. Runge's *Night* (in the Reinhardt Museum, Winterthur) was originally painted to fill a niche in the Hamburg house of Perthes, whose family were on terms of great intimacy with the artist. Courbet's *Asters* (now in the Basle Kunstmuseum) is another case in point. It bears the inscription 'à mon ami Baudelaire' but has a different audience from the man for whom it was intended. Yet even in the case of secular works of art the original home of a picture imparts a certain atmosphere which accompanies it on its travels. Titian's paintings gave St Petersburg, the Tsars' capital, the reflected glory of a past it had never known.

When wars occur, all kinds of art treasures, indeed whole collections, pass from the vanquished to the victor as the 'wandering prizes of power', and when this happens a newcomer among the older civilized peoples comes into possession of things which it regards only as precious trophies. Familiarity with such booty has a refining effect on the new owners and accustoms them to pleasures of which they knew nothing before. This was the effect of Greek sculpture on the Romans and of the Habsburg Correggios on the victorious Swedes in the Thirty Years War. When the rulers of some newly powerful country marry women from an older centre of civilization, the works of art they acquire by way of dowry sooner or later spread their influence. A picture by Mantegna came to France along with one of the Gonzagas before 1500 (it is now in the Louvre) and around 1530 Saxon princesses brought with them to Sweden panels by Cranach.

State presents are often chosen in collaboration with the powerful recipient and thus show that he is far from ignorant in such matters. In the seventeenth century Charles I of England received Italian paintings from the Dutch States General, and Louis XIV was given one of Veronese's principal works by the Doge of Venice. Canada in 1950 was happy to accept *The Two Watermills* by Hobbema from the Queen of the Netherlands for its National Gallery in Ottawa, the picture being taken from the Mauritshuis in The Hague.

Works of art in the possession of princely houses change their home when the dynasty ascends a new throne. It was for this reason that, about 1750, the antique statues in the Farnese collection were moved from Rome to Naples. For the same reason the Düsseldorf pictures that belonged to the Wittelsbachs of the Palatinate were later transferred to Munich.

Political crises and revolutions often cause works of art to travel to most unexpected places. When she left her native land, Christina of Sweden took the

11 One of the loveliest Greek statues in the British Museum, the *Strangford Apollo*, which dates from 490 BC, is named after an English art-lover of the early nineteenth century, the Sixth Viscount Strangford

masterpieces of the Habsburg gallery in Prague back to the Catholic part of Europe. The posthumous auction in 1649 of King Charles I's collection had similar consequences. After 1917 Russia not only lost many pictures which émigrés spirited out of the country, but also masterpieces from the Hermitage which were valuable only by strictly western standards and which the government therefore had no scruples about selling. If we take into account the purchases of itinerant art-lovers and the activity of dealers which for half a millennium have helped to keep works of art on the move, we shall hardly be surprised at the odysseys which some pictures have made, and at the area over which the pieces of an altar have been dispersed once it has been broken up. Correggio's *Leda and the Swan* in the Berlin Museums has, since its creation, been housed in Mantua, Spain, Prague, Sweden, Rome, Paris, Berlin, the United States and Wiesbaden. The separate parts of an altarpiece painted by Benozzo Gozzoli for St Mark's Church in Florence must now be sought out in Milan, Berlin, London, and Philadelphia.

As long as people still believed in the validity of the antithesis between the artist who in the nature of things was always creating something new and the art-lover whose face always turned towards the past, art collecting was not held in high esteem. A kind of marginal function was conceded to the collector. No one was prepared to regard him as standing at the centre of artistic life.

So far as the west is concerned, this older view is untenable: in the Florence of Donatello, in the Venice of Titian, in the Amsterdam of Rembrandt there was passionate collecting. Magnificent as the collections of Stockholm and St Petersburg are—or were—they are far surpassed by those of Florence, Munich and Paris. Indeed, so positive was the collector's function, so much was he the driving force behind this whole activity that a very remarkable situation resulted. While the art-lover in the metropolis could play the Maecenas and commission work, a person of similar inclinations living at a distance or

12 Michelangelo's unfinished work, the *Rondanini Pietà* (below) in Milan, still bears the name of a Roman family. The *Rondanini Medusa* in the Munich Glyptothek and the *Rondanini Satyr* in the British Museum also come from the once famous Palazzo Rondanini on the Corso

even on the periphery, could only pick up an occasional finished work in the lifetime of the artist concerned. This was the position of such rulers as Isabella d'Este in Mantua when, around 1510, she was searching for paintings by Giorgione, and of Francis I of France in regard to the majority of Florentine artists. Catherine II found herself in the same predicament when she was endeavouring to acquire the work of eighteenth-century Venetian painters.

The close connection, over a considerable period of time, between large galleries in important art centres and the actual creation of works of art gives them a less museum-like atmosphere than that characteristic of their sister institutions in remoter districts. Just how true this is may be seen in the case of Florentine art of the Quattrocento if one compares the Uffizi Gallery with the National Gallery in London, or of early German art if one compares the Germanisches Nationalmuseum in Nuremberg with the Cleveland Museum of Art in Ohio, or if in the case of works of the period of Rembrandt, one compares the Maurits-huis in The Hague with the Herzog Anton Ulrich Museum in Brunswick. For still greater contrast, one can compare the respective collections of Dutch paintings in the museums of Turin, Madrid, Stockholm, Leningrad, New York and, finally, Melbourne.

Insufficient research has been done to attempt any sociological generalizations on art collectors through the ages. This much however may be said: it is not true—though we might all too readily be led to assume it—that members of the upper classes collect merely with an eye to monetary value and decorative effect. When the Emperor Rudolph II took pleasure in gazing on Aertsen's pictures of markets and still-life and when, around 1700, German princes were buying up Brouwer's scenes of brawling, it was their own taste that was leading them along new unconventional ways. Whereas the prince or titled landowner—and in more recent times the industrialist—being in the nature of things a person used to making up his own mind, tends in these matters to form a pretty independent judgment, the commoner all too often timidly clings to traditional attitudes. In the mercantile circles of Frankfurt, Leipzig and Hamburg during the eighteenth century every man collected after the fashion of his neighbour. If pictures which depart from the prevailing realistic norm turn up in this sort of milieu, we may deduce the presence of exceptional intellectual activity, though often enough the anomaly is due to mere chance. For example, around 1800 French émigrés were transferring much of their property to Hamburg. In the Paris of Napoleon III aesthetes who yearned after the Ancien Régime would protest that 'the patronage of art has fallen to the couturières'. Their

13 The *Elgin Marbles* were named after Lord Elgin who rescued many of the Parthenon statues. This detail shows a reclining male figure, probably representing Dionysus

concern was premature. As we shall see, the last century did produce, in the Old World as well as in the New, collectors of independent judgment and thoroughly lively minds.

From the approach of the individual collector to the spirit of his age, we can distinguish the following types: the man in advance of his time who can easily degenerate into the snob and show the snob's pathological craving for novelty and change; then the great mass of the ordinary collectors who swim with the stream; and lastly, the straggler, who can never free himself from standards that have been superseded but whose judgment nevertheless often coincides with that of the snob.

Which collector is ahead of his time? That is a question which we can only answer if we have in each case exact knowledge of the prevailing conditions. It needed daring to buy an El Greco in 1900. Today it no longer represents a deviation from current taste. When we hear that around 1650 an art-lover acquired a Rembrandt in Messina, our interest is 155 immediately aroused. Today such a purchase, whether made in Europe, Latin America or Japan, would scarcely indicate an original decision. On the whole, with the growth of the number of available works of art and our greater awareness of art, it is increasingly difficult to become in any sense an independent collector. We shall observe this development when we compare the collectors of the Baroque period with their predecessors of the sixteenth century.

14 The *Raczynski Madonna*, an early Botticelli, was owned by a Prussian count of that name at the beginning of the nineteenth century (detail)

had painstakingly weeded out for her collection at the Hermitage. The conduct of the Dresden authorities is an excellent example of artistic snobbery, which, as we see, can affect an old centre of culture quite as much as a place which lacks such an aesthetic background.

We can observe this in the attitude of art-lovers towards contemporary masters quite as much as towards masters of the past. The upper strata of eighteenth-century Paris society, spoiled and wearying all too easily of their favourites, turned aside from Watteau one day and back again the next. In music we know that the people of Vienna around 1825 turned away from the aged Beethoven to cheer wildly for Rossini: 'the butterfly flew into the eagle's path', remarked Schumann.

In the higher ranges of culture innumerable people from the upper and middle sections of society busy themselves with the accumulation of works of art. Fashion turned Florentine burghers of the late Renaissance, French bankers of the Ancien Régime and noble English landowners into collectors. Which works of art these and similar groups acquired, liked to look at and bequeathed to posterity, is a question worth investigating. Sons and grandsons, themselves often quite lacking in judgment, take over the houses of their forebears with all their contents, and it then becomes an act of filial piety to share their forebears' taste in art. In conservative Russia before 1917 it was accounted good form to set a high value on all that had been acquired by those who had occupied the throne from Catherine II onwards. It was only in St Petersburg that a Viennese Baroque painter such as Platzer contrived to maintain his reputation. When the curator of the Germanisches Nationalmuseum in Nuremberg extended its department of painting in 1930, he procured Platzer's *The Concert* from the Hermitage and presented it to the German public of the late Expressionist period as an interesting new discovery.

The whole nature of the individual collector is expressed in his relationship to the work of art. The types range from the calculating accumulator of objects with a cash value to the man who simply takes enormous pleasure in collecting and who is as rare a being as the great creative artist himself. But even with the latter type of collector, the sense of possession is inseparable from the enjoyment of art. There is a story told of a Paris collector under the Second Empire who used to dream of being able to witness the auctioning of his collection on the last day of his life. He would have given much to know what material sacrifices his friends were prepared to make to obtain his favourite pictures.

A collector whose purchases range over a wide area cannot always have a personal knowledge of

It has sometimes been claimed that places pulsating with new life and not yet burdened by tradition provide a more promising venue for modern collecting than the proud old art centres. It is said that prior to the First World War, Budapest found a home for an El Greco before Vienna; that Moscow, a new centre of industry, made a better showing than St Petersburg, the museum city and imperial capital. If we examine the matter more closely, we realize that we are dealing with a phenomenon analogous to the quickly forgotten migration, in the early thirteenth century, of the Gothic style in architecture from France to Magdeburg. In the examples mentioned above, influence stemmed from the main centre, Paris. To take another instance, in about 1765 the classicizing trend was already strong and the curator of the Dresden Gallery resolved to put up for auction at Amsterdam a number of Late Baroque Venetian paintings—among them Tiepolo's *The Banquet of Cleopatra*. Catherine II, who was not au courant with artistic fashion to the same degree, acquired the paintings which Dresden

every individual work of art, and in his purchases he will often be compelled to seek other people's advice. An eighteenth-century German prince, Landgrave William VIII of Hesse, spoke of his principal adviser as 'Director-General of the delights of my eye'. But the born collector sets forth to make his own discoveries, and buys regardless of what others may think. He pays no attention to the price or the origin of the work in question or even to its ability to fit into his existing collection. Such a man in the days of the First World War was Marcel von Nemes, whose enthusiasm was at its height on the day he made his choice. He began collecting with Cézanne and ended with ancient art, which seemed to him 'greater, more mysterious, richer in hidden and fantastic treasure than the art of our own day could ever be.'

Whereas the passion of many collectors is kindled by controversial works, others love what is lasting and firmly established. He, however, who collects landscapes because he is a lover of nature or, surrounded by the portraits of great men, seeks to feel his way into the world of history, is a prisoner of the objects of his peculiar interest and desire. The collector with a truly artistic character will follow impulses that come from the deeper levels of his being. If he is sensitive to the stimulus of colour, he will be seduced by the art of Venice. If he is a man of action and a lover of movement, Rubens will capture his heart. If he is attracted by firmness of line, he will be surrounded by classical, or at least neo-classical sculpture. An active collector who is by nature strongly marked with traits in some measure akin to those of the practising artist will often find his passion cool with age. Charles I of England in his later years made hardly any additions to his gallery. As against this, businessmen with an active bent often turn to the enjoyment and acquisition of works of art only in the second half of their lives, when the urge to make money has been satisfied. An instance of this is Willibald Imhoff of Nuremberg in the sixteenth century. It frequently happens that the collector falls a victim to specialization. The wish to have a complete series—say of Rembrandt's etchings —becomes too strong to resist. Before they are aware of it, such men are listening to the voice of mere expertise, while their artistic urge grows weaker. The collector's love for his possessions sometimes expresses itself in a curious, sometimes quite eccentric, way. A Frankfurt merchant of Goethe's time collected vast quantities of pictures and yet would let no one into the over-filled rooms in which they hung. The Goncourt brothers, those men of rare sensibility, were unable to think of a more exquisite form of pleasure in the noisy Paris of the Second Empire than to secure an anonymous picture at an anonymous auction sale and then to enjoy it quietly by themselves, far removed from the acquisitive gaze of others. One can discern a kindred spirit about the middle of the present century in the collector Gulbenkian who kept the house in the avenue de Iéna in Paris that contained his treasures shut to everybody without exception. Where the true art-lover is concerned we should regard with charity this pathetic fear of being parted from his possessions, and listen with compassion to the pitiful cry of Mazarin as, close to death, he wandered through his gallery crying 'all this I must leave behind me.' Such men cling desperately to their possessions. Another good example is Sir George Beaumont, who even on his travels was accompanied by his favourite picture—Claude's *Hagar and the Angel*, now in the National Gallery, London.

Collectors of drawings and etchings tend to be singularly free from all self-assertion. These things have in themselves such an unassuming air, and in any case, mere portfolios and sheets of paper are unlikely to engender any far-reaching fame. Statues

15 For a long time the *Burgley Galleon*, originally made in France, was in the possession of the Marquess of Exeter, who lived in Burgley House

N 2

B 128

16 The *Basilewski Situla* was made in Milan around AD 980, but it is known by the name of its former Russian owner

Whoever has a sense of historical continuity will understand the affection with which people often regard a work of art which has delighted some connoisseur in the past. Names of innumerable art-lovers from forgotten generations have continued to be linked with sculpture, paintings and even with the products of applied art, and have increased their value. Some works of art seem able to transport us right into the world of those admirers of antiquity who lived in the sixteenth and seventeenth centuries. Such are the *Farnese Jove* in Naples 2 (Museo Nazionale), the *Fugger Sarcophagus* in Vienna 1 (Kunsthistorisches Museum), and the *Arundel Homer* 5 in London (British Museum). Titian's *Pardo Venus* (*Jupiter and Antiope*), now in the Louvre, recalls a palace not far from Madrid, in which the kings of Spain kept their finest secular paintings. Madonnas by Raphael bear the names of ancient Florentine families such as the Tempi (a work now in the Munich Pinakothek), and in Leningrad a Madonna by Leonardo reminds us of Count Litta of Milan. England's great collecting period around 1800 is called to mind by works of antiquity such as the *Strangford Apollo* and the *Elgin Marbles*, or by paintings 11, 1 such as the *Ince Hall Madonna* of van Eyck (National 7 Gallery of Victoria, Melbourne). Two forms of the Romantic love of art are represented by the *Lyversberg Passion* by an early painter of Cologne, and by Botticelli's *Raczynski Madonna*. We are reminded of the 14 sophisticated collectors of old Russia by the Greek *Saburoff Head* in Paris, the medieval *Basilewski* 16 *Situla*, the *Soltikoff Crozier* and the *Demidoff* 17 *Altarpiece* by Crivelli in London. An unknown early Netherlandish painter goes by the name of 'The Master of the Khanenko Adoration'. Some names take us into our own century—the *Figdor Lucrezia* and the *Thyssen Madonna* are examples. Then there N 3 are makeshift titles given to important works of art overseas; the 'Painter of the Boston Phial' and the 'Chicago Painter' are names we give to two Athenian artists who were practising their crafts two thousand years before America was discovered.

The names of great collectors live on in those of public institutions. The Albertina in Vienna, for instance, recalls Prince Albert of Sachsen-Teschen, one of the greatest collectors ever of etchings and drawings. An instruction that nothing was to be added is a sign of the founder's great self-confidence. The Musée Jacquemart-André has transmitted to our own age a type of collection that was characteristic of the late nineteenth century, but it is now in danger of becoming fossilized. On the other hand, in the Städelsches Kunstinstitut in Frankfurt, which owes its existence to a very generous will, a great number of the pictures which the founder himself looked at have been removed.

and paintings are a different matter, and successful businessmen know that the possession of works of art is the only way of displaying one's wealth permitted by good taste. We shall often encounter the phenomenon of the collector who engages in this activity as a means of indulging plutocratic vanity. In the nineteenth century the moneyed men of Paris kept a collection much as people keep a racing stable or a mistress. But even in those circles it was considered bad form on the part of Chauchard, the department store owner, to have expressed the wish that the most expensive picture in his collection should be carried in front of his coffin.

The degree to which a collection of works of art exalts its possessor was something of which Goethe had a very lively perception and which he often put into words. 'They outweigh any splendour which the richest man can gain for himself', he said of the early German paintings in the collection of the Boisserée brothers. Whatever may have been the original motive in buying them, the great masters impart a dignity to their possessors 'at first in appearance only, but finally in reality'.

The extent to which in earlier days the hoarding of works of art enhanced the esteem in which a religious centre or ruling house was held is a matter that will be discussed later. The Escorial is a good example of this, having been at one and the same time a royal residence and a national sanctuary. Philip II presented it with more than a thousand pictures, mostly representing Christian subjects. These pictures remained part of the patrimony of the crown but some later found their way into the essentially secular Prado. A jealous nationalism strove in the twentieth century to safeguard the great art museums of modern times which in Europe came into being largely through the activities of princely art-lovers of the Baroque period, through the confiscation of church property round about 1800 and through purchases by scholarly officials. Bitter experience has taught us that we can no longer share Goethe's view and look on museums as 'immortal bodies'.

The individual work of art, whose value may, as we have seen, arise from a variety of causes, can in the middle and late phases of a culture become a useful object of commercial speculation. There is, on the one hand, the collector who in the final analysis regards his pictures as something more than financial assets, and on the other, the professional art dealer, with the 'marchand-amateur' in between. The professional dealer must know his market: he must know, for instance, that higher prices are sometimes paid in the remoter places than the great centres. St Petersburg in 1750 was a better sellers' market than Paris. The trade can generally foresee a boom and can even accelerate its arrival by occasionally holding back merchandise, but it must also be prepared for slumps such as occurred around 1830 in Claude landscapes, and around 1880 in Madonnas by Murillo.

When merchandise is in short supply, substitutes become important. While conscientious collectors and curators have copies made of works they cannot obtain—plaster casts of antique sculptures in about 1800 and copies of Late Gothic figures in the mid-1920's—dealers supply their customers with those free imitations which a sense of affinity has called into being. The absence of a signature need not alarm prospective buyers since they know that many masters—Tintoretto for instance—only signed works for clients who lived at a distance and not for those

17 Like the situla on the opposite page, the *Soltikoff Crozier*, the work of a fourteenth-century south German craftsman, bears the name of a Russian collector (detail)

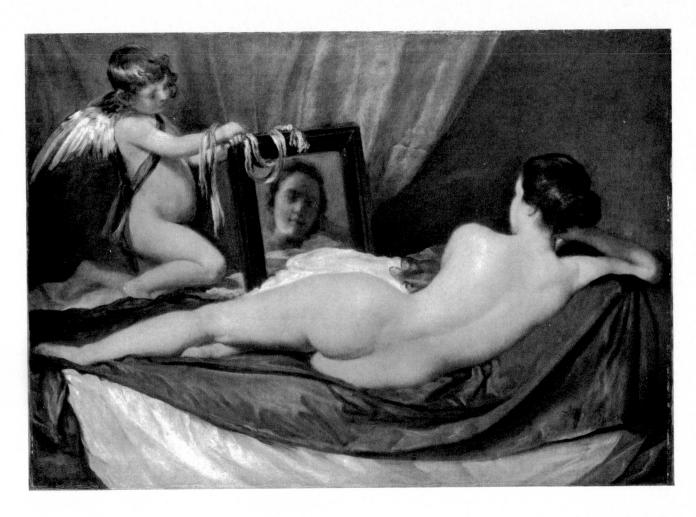

18 The *Rokeby Venus*, the finest Velazquez in a British public collection, is popularly known by the name of an English country estate

of their own city. Moreover, forgeries made simply for purposes of sale can be a profitable business. Around 1500 much money was made from small 'antique' sculptures. The same happened in about 1650 with half-length figures purporting to be by Giorgione and in about 1900 with fake Goya portraits.

One possible objection remains to be met. Many people wonder whether there is any room for art in the making, when we seem to be so exclusively concerned with the art of the past. I do not share these apprehensions. What our own time produces will most certainly find its place. What I am concerned with is continuity, the influence of the past on the present. In this sense there is neither old nor new in art and the only thing that matters is creative power. Just as we regard a major work by Kokoschka as more important than a mediocre Cranach, so we would not give up a sculpture by Michelangelo for some standardized product of today.

CHAPTER 1

Antiquity and the Middle Ages

The Oriental heritage | the aesthetic discovery | the first picture frames | the beginnings of an art market | Roman triumphs and the consecration of loot | the taste for Hellenistic and Egyptian art | destruction of heathen idols | the 'Christianization' of antiquity | Islamic and Byzantine works of art in Venice | the Habsburg, Guelph and French royal treasures

CREATORS—COLLECTORS—CONNOISSEURS: these three words describe phenomena which all act upon each other, but which in periods with strong religious ties are either altogether lacking or achieve only a shadowy existence. In the present context therefore the description of them will vary from the summary to the painstakingly detailed.

The oldest of the great cultures of man arose in Egypt. For Egypt the incarnation of the ruling god—of Horus, for example, worshipped in the falcon—was the king, and the religious task of sculpture was limited to the expression of the idea of sovereignty: hybrids, the body of a man with the head of an animal, were frequently represented. The development of art according to its own laws, the emergence of the artist from the status of an artisan and an appreciation of art for its own sake—such things never occurred in Egypt.

The faithful were assured of a life after death, a life lived under conditions more or less identical with those of the present world; they were therefore anxious that their bodily form should be preserved. The reliefs on the walls of tombs guaranteed the magical continuance of all the things with which the dead had been surrounded at the time of burial. Entire collections of precious objects accompanied the king into the life after death. When in 1922 the contents of Tutankhamen's grave were disinterred, among them articles of earlier periods and others not of Egyptian origin, people spoke of a 'veritable museum'; but this expression leads to misunderstandings. Nebuchadnezzar II of Babylon (605–562 BC) kept in his palace certain statues, reliefs and other objects, among them for example an object dating back to the reign of King Sulgi of Ur (*c.* 2000 BC).

This collection has lately been spoken of as a 'museum of antiquities', yet religious, juridical and political ideas were associated with the different articles. The fact that we might be prepared to ascribe to them a certain artistic value today is beside the point, for in Mesopotamia as in Egypt, art was a mere servant of the local cult.

The Greeks are the people without whom it is impossible to think of the development of a truly civilized life. At first all manner of treasure and equipment was gathered together in the grounds of their different temples and at the royal seats of power. The descriptions of the earliest poets, and the accounts left us by travellers at the time of the Roman Empire who were still able to see some remains of this earlier civilization, and finally the discoveries of modern archaeology, have left us a fairly comprehensive picture of this vanished world. There is a passage in Homer that shows us particularly clearly how well that world could appreciate the applied arts and the extent to which those arts were already practised. From his accumulation of treasure Priam chose a ransom for the corpse of his son Hector:

> *And he raised the lids of the lovely chests*
> *And took forth a dozen wonderful garments,*
> *And the same number of coverings and of carpets,*
> *And twelve upper garments and twelve mantles,*
> *And of gold he weighed out ten talents*
> *And he chose two tripods and four kettles,*
> *And a magnificent beaker, a gift of honour,*
> *Which he had once received in Thrace, a precious thing.*

Weapons of famous heroes were preserved by their descendants but were also brought to the temples as offerings; even in the lifetime of the Emperor Augustus the cult centre of Apollo in the Peloponnesian town of Sicyon possessed such antiquities. Objects with which great men had come into physical contact were regarded as having been endowed with mysterious magical powers and were therefore preserved and held in reverence. The same was true of unusual products of nature, of substances with the power of healing, and of rare objects from foreign countries.

708.051
1.

19 *Leagros on horseback*, a cup-painting by Euphronius about 510 BC, is one of the earliest signed works of art

20 *Dionysus on a sea-journey*, another signed work of art, was painted about 540 BC by Execias

As in Egypt and Mesopotamia, art served cult purposes in the more primitive periods of Greek civilization. Images made at first of wood and often in the form of animals—Athena, for instance, represented as an owl—dominated the temples. Here it should be noted, lest we take too supercilious a view of such practices, that similar customs also appear in Christian Europe. Until the late Middle Ages the Venetians portrayed St Mark the Evangelist, their patron saint, in the form of a lion.

In the course of the archaic period, from about 700 to 500 BC, man came to be considered the measure of all things. The gods no longer appeared as animals, let alone as half-animals as previously in Egypt, and Zeus no longer showed himself to mortals in the form of a bull. The conception of man had become so purified that it could serve as an expression of the divine without the addition of unhuman elements. So, conversely, a gleam of divinity transfigured every representation of the human form. Sculpture in the round discarded the purely frontal composition that had persisted in Egypt and Mesopotamia; the joints were emphasized and took a shape of their own independently of the torso, while body and vestments achieved an organic relation with one another. The classical age, from about 500 to 350 BC, achieved the ideal compromise between rigidity and freedom.

As early as the sixth century, during the late archaic period, a beginning was made in Athens and the Peloponnese with the creation of some kind of frame for pictures and reliefs; this is evident from funeral steles and pictures on pottery. Two-dimensional representations of scenes from actual life, in which clear expression is given to the artist's personal vision to a quite unprecedented degree, are now separated from their surroundings by having a frame as an aesthetic boundary. Thus was born the movable work of art, whose value resided wholly in its individual quality and was expected to be judged on the basis of that quality alone. In the fifth century small panel paintings were already enjoying great popularity.

B 66

It was during this period that the artist began to consider himself as an individual with a special personal contribution to make. In the Museum Antiker Kleinkunst, Munich, is a vase which has been signed both by the potter who made it, Kachrylion, and by Euphronius, the artist who painted it. In the same place is another vase in the red-figure style decorated with particularly fine drawings. Made in Athens about 510 BC, it carries an inscription reading roughly as follows: 'Euthymides painted me in a manner of which Euphronius would never have been capable.' So we can see that among those who practised this form of art an overweening arrogance was already in evidence as well as a conscious effort to win public favour. The artist's personality frequently came to the fore again when tributes were paid on vases to good-looking youths in such words as 'Onetorides Kalos' ('Onetorides is beautiful'), which we find on an amphora by Execias dated *c.* 535 BC, the subject of the painting being Ajax and Achilles at a board game.

As the artist began to take up much the same part he has played ever since through the centuries, so the trade in art began. A bowl now in Baltimore shows us a customer examining vases: it is significant that such a scene should have been thought worth recording. Apart from the ordinary market booths there were now permanent shops for the sale of works of art, both fine and applied. Such shops once stood in the harbour of Piraeus and at Olbia. Statuettes which served no purpose other than that of pleasing the beholder now had a regular place in the home.

Sacred art was not immune to the general trend. Laymen compared various examples and favoured now this master and now that. We know that a competition was organized when a statue of an Amazon was required for the temple of Artemis, and Phidias was beaten by Polycletus. It is said that on another occasion Polycletus set one of his own works beside an inferior variant which he had produced according to the comments and advice given by the public. This reaction of an artist tells us that laymen already gave their opinions in an over-selfconfident way: the artist found this extremely irritating. Aristotle was later to have little sympathy for such a point of view, and was to defend the right of any man with an all-round education to form his own opinion in matters of art.

After 330 BC in the so-called Hellenistic epoch, certain traits of the artistic life of Greece which strike us as especially modern became even more pronounced. Zeuxis charged an admission fee for allowing people to view his *Helena*, while at the court of Alexander the Great, Apelles was accounted 'an interesting personality': he was already painting pictures that were not commissioned and was in a position to wait for future purchasers.

21   The cup-painting by Phintias (c. 500 BC) of a young man buying pottery (above) is one of the earliest known representations of the sale of works of art

22   By 400 BC artists were already treating slightly erotic subjects. *The dancing Maenad* (right) is a detail from a painted vase by Meidias

23   The spread of Greek culture led to extensive export of works of art. This head of Aphrodite was found in Satala in Armenia

Even at the cult centres aesthetic considerations began to predominate. There is a delightful dialogue of Herondas that dates back to the third century BC and shows us two female art experts in eager discus-

N 7 sion with one another in the temple of Asclepius.

The great ancient temple grounds were also undergoing changes at this time, for instance the sanctuaries on Samos and at Olympia where Hera was worshipped. These changes were designed to meet the requirements of travellers who had historical and artistic interests. Keepers engaged by the priests gave talks on the different statues. Reproductions in all sizes of the images which had once served as objects of religious veneration now took on the character of souvenirs and had an essentially artistic or historical

N 8 interest.

It is significant that the *Aphrodite* of Praxiteles on Cnidus stood in a small temple open at the back as well as at the front so that the artistic quality of the work could be properly appreciated. We can be sure that the *Nike (Winged Victory)* and the *Venus de Milo*—both now in the Louvre—were originally set up in such a manner as to permit close inspection.

It was inevitable that sooner or later people should begin the actual accumulation of works of art. Archaeologists of our own day have shown quite definitely that towards the end of the fourth century BC a picture gallery was established in the town of Sicyon N 9 for the work of native painters, an event that gave occasion for art criticism and also for some research in the field of art.

Efforts of this kind in the Greek homeland were hopelessly overshadowed by the activities of the rulers of the new empires of the Greek east. Persian gold enabled the successors of Alexander the Great not only to engage in colossal building projects but to acquire works of art in a manner which excluded all rival purchasers from the field. The rulers of Pergamum were rather like Philip II of Spain, whose American gold in the sixteenth century enabled him not only to buy up the leading masters of his day but also to obtain earlier works of art. Philip ultimately found a home for his vast acquisitions in the semi-sacred precincts of the Escorial, and in much the same way works of art in Pergamum were stored in the halls of the sanctuary of Athena. Here, according to the art historian Max Fränkel, Eumenes II created a veritable museum of plastic art around 170 BC, filling it with works from the sixth to the third centuries. The oldest exhibit was probably the *Graces* group of Bupalos. Next came the colossal *Apollo* of Onatas captured in Aegina and dating from the early fifth century. There was also work by Cephisodotus the son of Praxiteles, by Theron and Silanion (fourth century BC) and by Xenocrates and the younger Myron. B 77

Just as Philip II ordered a copy of van Eyck's *Ghent Altarpiece* to be made for him when he found that he was unable to buy the original, so the rulers of Pergamum sent painters to Delphi with instructions to copy some of the famous paintings in the temple grounds—above all the works of Polygnotus. We know from inscriptions on plinths that copies of famous statues which were among the sacred objects at Delphi were to be found at Pergamum. A copy of Phidias' *Athena Parthenos* was also admired there.

Similar collections of works of art were also acquired by the rulers of Antioch and Alexandria; in the city of Cyrene which belonged from 322 BC to Alexandria there were excellent original works of Greek art to be seen as well as copies. Among these treasures was an *Aphrodite* after Lysippus (now in the Museo delle Terme, Rome) whose morbid grace shows it to be a late variant of the original. *35*

We hear of very considerable prices being obtained for pictures at the time of the conquest of Corinth by Rome in 146 BC. From Pergamum on that occasion the tempting offer of 100 talents was made to the victorious Roman general for a famous painting by Aristides, a contemporary of Apelles, which B 77 was in one of the temples of the beleaguered city.

The general view that the artist is active in the great centres and the collector in the outlying districts finds no confirmation in the history of Greece. It was not only older works of art that began to accumulate in the great new metropolis of Pergamum; the leading artists of the day were busy there and created the 'Greek Baroque'. It is they whom we have to thank for the Berlin *Pergamum Altar* and the *Barberini Faun* in Munich. A wealthy Greek prince in the Greek homeland would have furnished his palace with works of art in exactly the same way as N 10 was done by the successors of Alexander the Great.

It is well known that from the seventh century onwards there was a considerable importation of valuable Greek works—especially vases—to Tarquinia (Corneto), Vulci and other Etruscan cities. Over the last century most of these objects have found their way into the great museums of the world. It would seem that the custom of interring vases with the deceased by way of a funeral gift lasted longer in Etruria than in Greece itself. At the time of Etruria's supremacy such Greek works also reached Rome, as is shown by the finds in the district of S. Omobono. Larger works from Greece may occasionally have travelled the same road even at that early date. Indeed today it is a matter of discussion whether the Capitoline *She-Wolf* may not be an N 11 archaic Greek bronze of an animal demon.

It was only after shaking off Etruscan rule that Rome became a great power in her own right. As the number of its conquests grew, however, the Roman people with its stern moral discipline and firm religious bonds found it increasingly necessary to come to terms with the ways of foreign nations. At first the gods of such foreign nations were brought more or less indiscriminately to Rome and placed in the service of Jupiter. The helplessness of the vanquished found a particularly eloquent expression in the helplessness of their gods. From Carthage the Phoenician Queen of Heaven found her way to Rome, from Asia Minor Magna Mater Cybele, in the form of a fetish stone, and all manner of images of gods came from Hel- B 153 lenized southern Italy.

Final victory was followed by the triumph. This word originally signified a religious procession which was to cleanse the general and his soldiers of the curse of blood shed in battle. On such occasions the

24 Numerous copies of Greek sculpture were made in Rome, among them this idealized portrait head of Alexander the Great

images of gods and other symbols of foreign cults that had been brought to Italy in the war just ended were taken into Rome along the Via Sacra together with booty and prisoners of war. In the course of time the religious character of the triumphal procession grew fainter and it became a symbol of the worldly fame of the general and his army. What mattered was to stagger the people with the sheer numbers of captured statues. In 180 BC Fulvius Nobilior B 159 brought along 785 bronze and 230 marble statues in his triumph. In 168 BC Aemilius Paullus even brought paintings. In Rome the names of Greek artists remained long unknown and the more impressive statues were called after the general who had brought them back to Italy. People spoke of 'the Apollo of Socius' and of 'the Monuments of Parius' much as they speak today in Stockholm of 'the Gustavus Adolphus Booty' captured in the Thirty Years War.

25 Greek Hellenistic works of art, like this *Drunken old woman*, were imported into Rome, which became the focus of the ancient world

It has already been noted that Mummius Achaicus, the Roman general who took Corinth in 146 BC, received from Pergamum an offer for certain works of exceptional value in the beleaguered city. Mummius took great care of certain pieces, such as the *Dionysus* by Aristides, which he brought to Rome. The picture was placed in the temple of Ceres on the Aventine, and other items from this important booty (nearly all of it statues) were placed in front of marble pillars in the temple of Jupiter, a very suitable setting. In the place where this temple once stood, a number of pillars which probably date back to Augustan times remain today. They have been renamed the Porticus of Octavia.

N 12

The Hellenization of Rome was still kept within moderate bounds, but already some people recognized where things were leading. Cato, so Livy tells us, was having misgivings about the manner in which the 'signa' from Sicily—presumably statues—were finding so many admirers. As the influx of works of art continued to grow, not all the items of booty were consecrated in the sanctuaries. Many Romans were little attracted to the enthusiasm for beauty; when Greek slaves were put up for sale and their 'defects' were made known, we find that the 'love of looking at pictures' was among the 'defects' mentioned. No doubt this long continued to be accounted a typically Greek failing.

It was only in the last hundred years of the Republic that the ruling class, having absorbed late Hellenic culture, assumed a Greek attitude to art. The name of Hellas now began to imply the ultimate refinement of pleasure and the ability to derive enjoyment from a world of art whose roots lay more deeply embedded in the past than those of Rome herself. The aristocrats of St Petersburg around 1800 and the industrialists of the United States a century later turned towards earlier Western art in a similar fashion.

During the last century of the pre-Christian era Romans began to add to the names of Greek statues the names of the artists that had produced them. In the temple of Apollo on the Palatine, for instance, it was now specifically the work of Scopas that was admired. Art-lovers also searched for work that had belonged to some famous collection in Greece. Sulla was the proud prossessor of a *Hercules* by Lysippus said to have been previously owned by Alexander the Great.

Shortly before the end of the Republic Greek works of art were continuing to find their way to Rome in large numbers. Between 73 and 70 BC Verres acquired the gold and ivory doors of the temple of Minerva in Syracuse and set them up in his villa in Rome. From Tyndaris he carried off a bronze cult statue of Hermes and from a certain Heius of Regium (Reggio Calabria), a private citizen, he appropriated statues of gods by Myron and Polycletus, which Heius had kept in a 'sacrarium', a consecrated room within his house. Verres also possessed a bronze *Hercules* by Myron and a *Cupid* by Praxiteles.

In 56 BC the financial collapse of Sicyon led to the sale to Rome of all paintings publicly owned by the city. We know that about this time the cemeteries of Greek cities were being dug up in the hope of finding old bronzes and pieces of pottery, a practice carried out in the interests of collectors in Rome. This was also the time when Hortensius, a contemporary of Cicero, had a special building constructed in order to provide a worthy home for Cydias' *Argonauts* which he had acquired. The wealthy Crassus who died in 53 BC removed the oldest of his silver vessels from use, so that they should be regarded only as works of art. In Rome at this time such Greek objets d'art, which probably dated back to the fifth century, were attributed to a certain legendary 'Mentor'.

Then as now collectors occasionally over-reached themselves. It is significant that in a letter of Cicero's written in about 60 BC we find the words 'Jam sunt venales tabulae Tulli'—'Tullius's pictures are already up for sale'.

N 13 Caesar himself possessed gold-embroidered wall hangings and fine furniture from the Greek cities of Sicily, and started a number of collections of cut gems. He paid the highest prices for work by Greek painters—80 talents on one occasion for the *Ajax* and the *Medea* of Timomachus. He compelled Cleopatra to send to Rome all she had accumulated in the way of Greek art.

The coolness displayed at first by the true Roman when confronted by Greek enthusiasm for art persisted more or less unchanged for some time. When Cicero made his speeches in the courts against Verres, who was either a vain philistine or a collector driven by genuine and almost frantic enthusiasm, he thought it advisable not to give the impression before the Roman public that he himself was at all expert in matters of Greek art, while attributing just such expertise to the man he was attacking. He hoped thus to prejudice the Roman judges against the latter. Elsewhere Cicero remarks that people should not let a statue by Polycletus cause them to lose all self-control. Apart from the inherited Roman ideal of manly dignity, such a sentiment also contains elements of Stoic thought. Some decades later Horace was to make fun of those rich people who could think of no better present to give each other than some original work of Scopas or Parrhasius, and Petronius refers to excited art-lovers as 'Graeculi delirantes'.

B 153 In the reign of Augustus and his immediate successors there finally came about a definite Graeco-Roman symbiosis which in its essential features lasted right up to the end of antiquity. Virgil gave the Romans a counterpart to the *Iliad* in his *Aeneid*, while in his *Eclogues* he produced a modified version of the pastoral lyrics of Theocritus. Half of the odes of Horace are based on Alcaeus, Sappho and Anacreon. Augustus called his workroom 'My Syracuse' after Sicily's loveliest Greek city.

The feeling of the cultivated Roman for Greek art now began to take a variety of forms. As before, people continued to admire those Hellenistic works we speak of as 'Greek Baroque'. Caesar was especially fond of works in this style, and Augustus himself had similar leanings. He acquired two pictures by Apelles for his forum and the same painter's *Aphrodite* for the temple of Divus Julius. One of the pains of Ovid's exile was that he could no longer see this masterpiece. Tiberius paid 60,000 sesterces for the painting by Zeuxis of the high priest of Cybele and had it hung in his bedchamber, and there can be no doubt that the *Laocoön* group reached Rome very

26 This *Dancing faun*, like the *Drunken old woman* on the opposite page, must have reached Rome shortly after it was carved

N 14

B 264

soon after its creation. A famous passage in the *Aeneid* tells us something of its effect.

Many admired what Eduard Schmidt calls 'the dazzling fire of the *Laocoön*' but many now also turned towards the classical epoch of Greek art. The Roman must have found it comparatively easy to approach works which, by reason of a certain harshness and discipline, had some affinity with his own character, the works of Polycletus and Myron for instance. The *Doryphorus* was eulogized under the early Empire as 'vir gravis et sanctus'. The same quality is apparent in portraiture. The head of Augustus in the Boston Museum of Fine Arts is almost that of a classical Greek god. In the *Ara Pacis*, according to modern archaeology, there is a mingling of 'classical restraint' and Roman reticence and dignity. In painting under the Augustan empire the masters of Hellenistic art, with their almost Impressionistic brightness and dissolution of form, began to lose their appeal. Cicero had already on occasion praised the 'harshness' of older pictures. The *Aldobrandini Wedding* and similar works that were essentially classical in spirit may well have originated under the early Empire.

28

N 15

27, 28   In the reign of Augustus the Romans discovered the work of Greek artists like Phidias who had lived five hundred years before. The effect of this discovery can be seen in statues like this Roman copy of a Greek Apollo (detail left) and Augustus as a Greek youth (above)

It might be interesting to enquire whether the so-called 'neo-Attic' trend in Greece was not in the final analysis inspired by the artistic taste of Rome. In reviving their own classical style of the fifth century BC were the Greeks merely adapting themselves to the tastes of the great world power? Certainly in more recent times there have been cases where the artistic fashions that moved collectors in Italy and Spain were originated by art-lovers north of the Alps and even in America.

30   *Aphrodite leaving the Sea* is a detail from the *Ludovisi Throne*, which was made about 500 BC and may once have belonged to the poet Sallust

29   Archaic Greek art was admired by the Romans before the birth of Christ. This relief of a young man and a boy dating from the fifth century BC was rediscovered in Rome about 1520

The Romans first became aware of pre-Phidian Greek art probably about the time of Christ's birth. Augustus gave a place of honour at the very top of the temple of Apollo on the Palatine to archaic sculpture from the sixth century believed to be the work of Bupalos and Athenis, two semi-legendary artists from the Ionian islands. The Emperor's attempt to honour those who bore witness to a more disciplined and pious way of life, as a mark of his own age's moral and religious renewal, was in tune with a trend of artistic fashion that could ultimately be traced to the philosophy of the Stoics. As their taste for the classical had done before, so the appetite of collectors for the archaic brought many original Greek works of art to Rome, brought a number of imitations into being and no doubt also a number of forgeries manufactured with definitely fraudulent intentions.   N 16

31, 32 Rome's new interest in archaic art led to the manufacture of copies and fakes. The head of Dionysus (above) and the statuette of a girl (right) give the impression of being five to six hundred years older than they really are

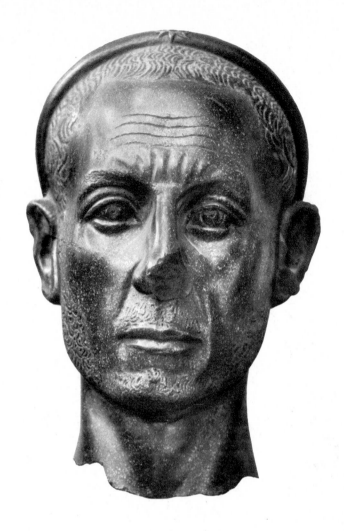

33, 34 Roman interest in Egyptian art began in the time of Cleopatra. *Isis suckling her son* (left) is most likely a Roman work based on Egyptian models, while the so-called *Caesar* (above) was carved in Egypt and probably represents a priest

When Egypt became a Roman province under Augustus, artistic influences began here and there to penetrate from the Nile to the Tiber. Already at an earlier stage under Sulla the cult of Isis had found its way into Rome, though it only obtained official recognition under the early Empire. Sculptures in a hybrid Roman-Egyptian style now became more frequent, among them representations both of the priests of Isis and of the goddess herself. 33, 34

N 17

35, 36, 37 Under the emperors that followed Augustus, Roman art dealers exported Greek works of art to all corners of the Empire. This statue of Aphrodite (left) was found in Cyrene in North Africa. The standing figure of a god (detail above), discovered in 1926, is a magnificent Greek original dating from about 460 BC. The silver coin (below) comes from Syracuse

In Augustus' time there were many collectors in the town of Pompeii near Naples. This portrait bust, a typical example of Roman realism, is of a rich citizen of Pompeii

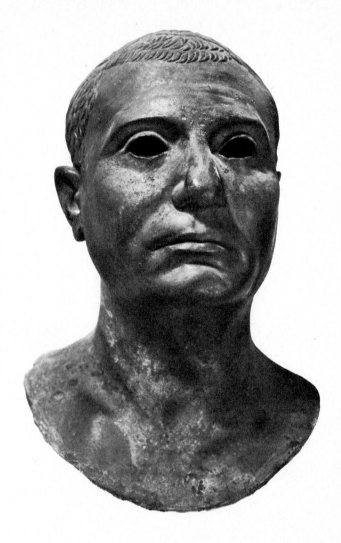

Rome had a special neighbourhood where art dealers carried on their business, just as New York has its 57th Street; whole ship-loads of merchandise came from Greece. Recently valuable original works have been salvaged from the bottom of the Mediterranean. They came from ships wrecked on the way to the market in Rome.

B 300

Auctions of works of art were nothing unusual in Rome. Suetonius describes with biting humour how Caligula forced his courtiers and dependants to bid for pictures of which he had grown weary. One poor courtier who had fallen asleep found on waking that every time he nodded his head the Emperor had treated the nod as an agreement to raise the bid.

At this time Vitruvius was designing houses in which it was regarded as a matter of course that there should be a room specially reserved for works of art. It is significant that when Tiberius removed the *Apoxyomenos* of Lysippus from a public building into his own home there was much dissatisfaction among art-lovers: they were unwilling to forego the enjoyment they derived from the public exhibition of such works.

It was another sign of the widespread zeal for art that about the time of the birth of Christ, Gaius Asinius Pollio, statesman, poet and patron all in one, threw open his house, rich in art treasures, to every educated man. Exhibitions of privately owned works were by no means uncommon. Indeed, we can regard as such the special occasions when theatres were decorated for a short time with statues from rich men's houses. In one instance three thousand pieces of sculpture are said to have been exhibited.

In the early days of the Empire we encounter a love for the arts in most diverse forms, and also an unmistakable collector's passion outside Rome as well as in the capital itself. In the wealthy resort of Pompeii, buried in AD 79, genuine Greek statues and copies as well as archaicized imitations have come to

N 18

light. The series of frescoes in the Villa of the Mysteries at the edge of the town reproduces originals dating back to the fourth century BC. Juba II, King of Mauretania and husband of a daughter of Antony and Cleopatra (his name occurs in Horace's ode 'Integer vitae'), furnished his property in Caesarea Sol (situated in present-day Morocco) with copies of

39 Art-lovers in Pompeii also owned older Greek works of art such as this silver vessel, decorated in relief with scenes from Greek mythology, which was probably made in Pergamum in the second century BC

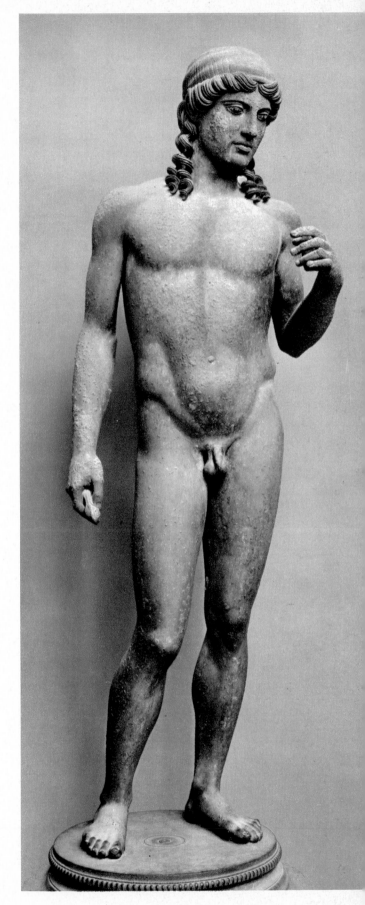

34

works representing a diversity of styles, among them an *Aphrodite* represented as Goddess of the Sea, a *Satyr* and a *Spinario*.

North of the Alps high Roman officials graced their villas with the products of past art. In the Palatinate a small Hellenistic bronze has come to light which was about four hundred years old when N 19 its owner brought it along with him from Italy. There were Romans living in Trier and Cologne who were active collectors.

Beyond the borders of the Empire, Germans of high social standing set store by the same things that the Romans prized. The original owner of the Hildesheim Silver Hoard, discovered in 1868 and now in the Hildesheim Museum, had reduced a few unimportant pieces to scrap but had left what was of real artistic value untouched, including an amphora of the Augustan period. An even more extraordinary case is that of a member of the tribe of Alemanni who acquired in the early Iron Age a painted bowl, a piece of Attic pottery which was of N 20 no value so far as its material was concerned.

In Rome under Hadrian we note an intensive preoccupation with the art of earlier ages. Whether

40, 41   Collectors in Pompeii often commissioned copies in bronze of older Greek originals. The original of *Aphrodite arranging her Hair* (far left) dates from the fourth century BC, and that of the statue of a young man (left) from a century earlier

42, 43   An excellent copy (above) of the Gorgon's head from the shield-boss of *Athena Parthenos* (completed by Phidias in 438 BC) was made in Rome. Roman silver dishes with satyrs and dancing Maenads (below) reached as far afield as England

44, 45 Hadrian was an art-lover, and for him his friend Antinous (left) was the embodiment of Greek stylized beauty. After the latter's strange death in the Nile (AD 130), Hadrian pronounced him a god. The Emperor also encouraged the cult of Isis, and busts of priests commissioned by him were carried out in a mixture of Roman and Egyptian styles (above)

a more genuinely Greek mentality than in the time of Augustus prevailed about AD 120 is something of an open question. Archaeologists speak of a N 21 particular fashion for Hellenistic art under Hadrian. Yet this emperor also held to the fifth-century type of classical Greek beauty in the young male and found the embodiment of this ideal in his favourite Antinous who sacrificed himself for Hadrian in the Nile. At that time Rome also had a market for N 22 old Greek coins, which absorbed many imitations of the coveted article.

How varied the tastes of collectors had become in the years since Augustus is shown by the growing affection for the ancient Egyptian austerity of form. On his vast estate in Tivoli, near Rome, Hadrian not only set up classical Greek sanctuaries but also laid out temple grounds dedicated to the god Serapis, which he filled with both genuine Egyptian sculptures and free imitations in the Egyptian idiom. 45 Among the latter was the bust of a priest of Isis which is now to be seen in Venice. N 23

46 Hadrian had a summer residence built near Tivoli as a kind of 'museum of architecture'. He combined adaptations of Greek and Egyptian temples, and decorated the whole complex with statues

Scholarship has conspicuously failed to trace any clear pattern in the successive changes of style in the post-Hadrianic epoch and has fared no better with the vagaries of collectors' tastes. There seems to have been a marked though temporary return to classicism around AD 200 under Septimius Severus, while shortly after this Caracalla sought out splendid examples of the mature Greek Baroque. Among these was a copy of *The Vengeance of Zethus and Amphion on Dirce, Queen of Thebes*, the three-hundred-year-old group that has been known in Europe since the days of Michelangelo as the *Farnese Bull*; it is now in the Museo Nazionale, Naples.

It is impossible to summarize all the delightful stories that Roman literature has to tell us about half-educated art enthusiasts. Furnished with guide books, Roman tourists visited the world of the Mediterranean, admired in a temple at Sicyon some clothing of Odysseus, elsewhere the bones of demigods and also of primaeval creatures, as well as the products of the crafts of foreign lands. Of course they also saw the principal works of ancient Greek art.

Returning to Rome, they could show their incredible acquisitions to their friends. Martial makes fun of the silver cups that had belonged to Achilles and similar things in the houses of the newly rich, and Petronius mocks the parvenu Trimalchio, in whose house the table silver had to be dented and scratched so that it should be thought valuable. Petronius' public, who were thoroughly at home in their Greek mythology, must have given a superior smile when they read of Trimalchio's costly relief from the days of Homer which showed 'Daedalus shutting Niobe up in the Trojan horse'! N 24

In the last phase of antiquity there is a falling off in the development of art. Weary of liberty, men took refuge in new self-imposed constraints. Earthly things lost their value. From the third century onwards, the accounts of all that touches our present theme become increasingly sparse; we hear hardly anything of private collectors in Rome. N 25

In 330 Constantine transferred the seat of government from the Tiber to the Bosphorus, was converted to Christianity and broke with the past; he sent those works of art he still valued from Rome to Byzantium, now re-christened Constantinople. Along with the imperial treasure the *Gemma Augustea* came to the east. Four magnificent bronze 101 horses which Rome must have valued very highly indeed went to the new capital, but returned to Italy in 1204; today they adorn the portico of St Mark's in Venice.

In the Hippodrome at Constantinople the Emperor surrounded a snake pillar and two Egyptian obelisks with numerous marble statues. Over four hundred monuments filled the court of Hagia Sophia and inscriptions proclaimed their various origins and historic importance. In Rome Constantine decorated his triumphal arch (still in an excellent state of preservation) with ancient pieces of sculpture. All this indicates a mental attitude that would seem to justify the use of the term 'museum spirit' in a critical sense, a term there was no reason to use in discussing what happened half a millennium before in Pergamum.

The art of the new epoch was moving along new paths which led away from Phidias and Polycletus. The harmony between body and spirit was no longer a valid ideal; even statues of the Emperor avoided physical attractiveness. In faces of mask-like rigidity the eyes, now greatly enlarged, became the vehicles of spiritual power. Recent scholarship has inclined to the view that in the creation of this new image of man the influence of Indian representations of Buddha played some part. If this is so, there seem N 26 to be grounds for assuming that art-lovers of late antiquity were already among those to whom the image of Buddha had something special to say.

47 Many late Egyptian works of art, including this Canopic jar, have been discovered in Hadrian's Villa. Most of these finds are now in museums in Rome

48, 49, 50 After Hadrian's death, the ideal of Greek classicism was gradually replaced by a new form of deliberate primitivism—a process that continued until the early Middle Ages. Ancient Greek coins (above), long prized by collectors, inspired the artists of late classical times. The portrait head of Diocletian (below) is an example of the early stages of this development, which was carried farther in the female allegorical figure of Constantinople (right), dating from about AD 400

51 Artists and collectors in the Roman Empire also took considerable interest in unfamiliar Asiatic art. This ivory Buddha, with a bronze base dating from late classical times, is now in Sweden

The caravan trade brought from the more remote parts of Asia precious stones, silk from China and drugs from India—and also small ivory figures of Buddha. Even the Teutonic tribes contrived to get hold of such things and were alive to their significance.

51

The value set on non-Greek art helped to save the Temple treasure of Jerusalem for a considerable period. When in AD 70 Titus captured the Jewish capital, the treasures of the Temple went of course to Rome. The reliefs on the Arch of Titus represent the table of the show-bread, a seven-branched candlestick, silver trumpets and the Ark of the Covenant being carried in procession. After the collapse of the Roman Empire, Teutonic tribes laid hands on this booty. We know that Alaric, King of the Visigoths, accumulated in Carcassonne some ancient Jewish vessels belonging to Solomon's Temple, which were presumably buried with him in the waters of the Busento in southern Italy. Recently it has been reported that Cogoza is being scoured for this treasure. Others came into the possession of the Vandals and were stored in Carthage until the Byzantine general Belisarius put an end to Germanic glory in Africa. These Jewish antiquities graced Belisarius's triumph in Constantinople in 535 and according to Procopius were ultimately handed over by Justinian to the Christian community in Jerusalem. To what use they were put we have not been told. Honoured as a pledge of victory, as a valuable hoard and as a collection of objects pertaining to an age-old cult, the Temple treasure passed from hand to hand after leaving its first sacred home. We seem to be back in primitive times again. The liberty-loving Græco-Roman world with its wealth of individualists, its passionate collectors, critical art-lovers and cunning dealers, has utterly perished.

Today more people are stirred by the art of the Middle Ages than at any time since the Renaissance. In the last few decades scholarship has been particularly active in helping us understand the medieval period. For the men who lived a thousand years ago there was a graduated sequence of realities leading from God and His Kingdom to the humblest phenomena of the earthly world. The work of man had no value of its own, nor had the creative work of the artist.

In the Middle Ages art was anonymous. The artist, whether monk or artisan, remained invisible behind his work and laboured for the glory of God and for the salvation of his soul; his creations were not deliberately intended for human eyes, still less to inspire either delight or criticism on the part of his own generation. The sculptures on or near the roofs of cathedrals and many precious ecclesiastical treasures were seldom looked at by anyone at all. It is true that such stern conceptions did not always prevail. The thousand years that intervene between antiquity and the Renaissance are not a closed unity; there were breaches within the unity and movements that went in a contrary direction.

In the eyes of the Greeks the sensible world had been a divine cosmos. For the Christians of the early period it was 'deceit, temptation and a fetter upon the soul yearning for its heavenly home'. Earthly objects served only as symbols in early medieval art.

The fish, the symbol of life which Christianity took from the Asiatic cult of Astarte, became the secret symbol that represented Christ. Animals were associated with the Evangelists and ultimately came to represent them; the bull which had once represented Zeus for the Greeks now came to represent St Luke. The present tendency is to look upon the style of early medieval art as a kind of return to the closed stiff patterns of pre-Greek and ultimately Egyptian culture, its characteristic features being the extensive use of plane surfaces, the frontal view and strict symmetry.

But the spirit of antiquity had not wholly disappeared. There was a tentative Carolingian and Ottonian renaissance and a definite artistic development under the Hohenstaufens. About AD 1100 there was a new awareness of organic life that led from the realistic representation of plants in ornament, to animals and human figures on portals and façades. Behind this change lay the idea which was now beginning to gain ground, that the present world was something more than a mere passage-way to the next, that it was God's creation in which man had to justify himself by action. Rather surprisingly the Gothic age once more turned to an escape from the world. Gothic statues do not stand firmly on the ground like those of the early thirteenth century, but seem to be drawn away from the earthly sphere by a superior power.

The first question the modern art-lover has to ask of the Middle Ages concerns the fate of the various works of art that survived from ancient Greece and Rome. It was noted above that in AD 330 numbers of statues were transferred from Rome to Byzantium, though the interest and care bestowed on them may not have been much more than a dabbling in antiquarianism among fashionable circles. Two generations later Augustine developed his conception of the Civitas Dei, calling the Olympian gods demons and declaring that heathen statues N 28 were demons in stone. To ensure its safety, many a temple statue was now reverently buried by the last devotees of non-Christian cults.

52 Particularly striking examples of the artistic tastes of late antiquity are the numerous representations of the Near Eastern goddess of fertility. This pillar-shaped figure of the *Artemis of Ephesus*, dating from the third century AD, is copied from seventh-century BC statues like the *Hera of Samos*, now in the Louvre. The many breasts and the relief figures of goats are allusions to the reproductive powers of nature. Thr contrast between the classical treatment of the head and hands, and the anti-classical profusion of forms in the rest of the statue, is clearly intentional

In about 1865 an over-lifesize gilt statue of Hercules was discovered in the centre of Rome buried in a deep and carefully-dug pit. On closer examination it was found that the statue, which today can be seen in the Sala Rotunda of the Vatican Museum of Antiquities, had fallen on the back of its head, but had afterwards been laid in the ground with scrupulous care. We may thus assume that the statue was first knocked over by Christians and afterwards hidden away very carefully.

53

N 29

In AD 399 a decree forbade sacrifices on pagan altars in Africa. No doubt the consequence was that cult statues were got rid of by the authorities, usually by burying them. In 407 this decree was extended to all provinces of the Roman Empire. Many well-preserved statues that have come to light since 1500 were doubtless interred intact as a result of thus being officially deposed. This is certainly true of the *Laocoön* group, which was after all a piece of religious sculpture. It had been kept secure in a chamber that had obviously been deliberately walled up to ensure the safety of the work; from there it was removed in 1506. This also applies to the figures brought to light about 1870 from excavations in the Roman theatres at Arles and Vaison.

There were of course many occasions when the authorities had no means of restraining the destructive fury that Christians all too often displayed. For the majority of the devotees of the victorious religion, all that had been produced from Pericles to Hadrian was no more than the residual rubble of a superseded past. When all intangible values had been repudiated, whether religious or artistic, there was nothing left in a work of art save the material from which it was made. The bronze Apollo went off to the melting-pot and the marble Venus to the lime-kiln.

B 194

But the great campaign of destruction was carried on with variable fervour. In many cases it was thought better to undertake the purification of images and other heathen objects. In the early Middle Ages there were set prayers in the liturgy for consecrating figures, vessels and coins that had been unearthed. An 'oratio super vasa in loco antiquo reperta' has actually survived. The immuring of stone demons with their heads pointing downwards to Hell, a practice that took place in churches and monasteries, helped to dispel the apprehensions of

53 The unrest that marked the spread of Christianity often made the adherents of the old religions carefully hide their cult statues and other temple ornaments. Such must have been the fate of this colossal statue of Hercules, rediscovered in an excellent state of preservation

54 Christians ascribed evil powers to the pagan gods and, as in the case of this statue of the goddess Isis, often walled up their carved representations in churches with their heads placed towards the ground, or Hell

55 This statue of Venus, which had been built into one of the exterior walls of a monastery in Trier, was pelted with stones until it was almost completely unrecognizable

the faithful. A statue of Isis venerated in Roman Cologne survived the Middle Ages there in the Church of St Ursula (it is now in the local Museum of Roman Antiquities). It might be added that the Germans east of the Elbe treated Slavonic idols in a similar way.

When an ancient statue was fitted into the outer wall of a church or a cemetery with the intention of rendering it harmless, the faithful would sometimes express their abhorrence by disfiguring it. A Venus in the monastery of St Matthew in Trier was regularly stoned and her nakedness must have inspired the pious folk with particular ill will. Sentiments of this kind have continued to present a danger to works of art right up to our own day. Even as late as 1800 a bigoted Spanish king wanted to have Dürer's *Eve* (in the Prado) committed to the flames.

In the middle of the fourteenth century there were strange happenings in Siena when a figure of Venus was found. Though a few enlightened artists such as Ambrogio Lorenzetti set about drawing the statue, the citizens insisted that they were being confronted by a shameless object which should in no circumstances be exposed to public view. Although the primary objection was to the statue's nakedness, the old idea of disaster-bringing demons was re-awakened, and in the end the people of Siena destroyed the diabolical thing and secretly strewed its fragments over the territory of a neighbouring state with which they were in conflict. At the beginning of the fifteenth century two antique statues were discovered in Guntramsdorf in Austria, and promptly placed behind iron railings in St Stephen's Church in Vienna so as to hold in check the dangerous powers that might still inhabit them.

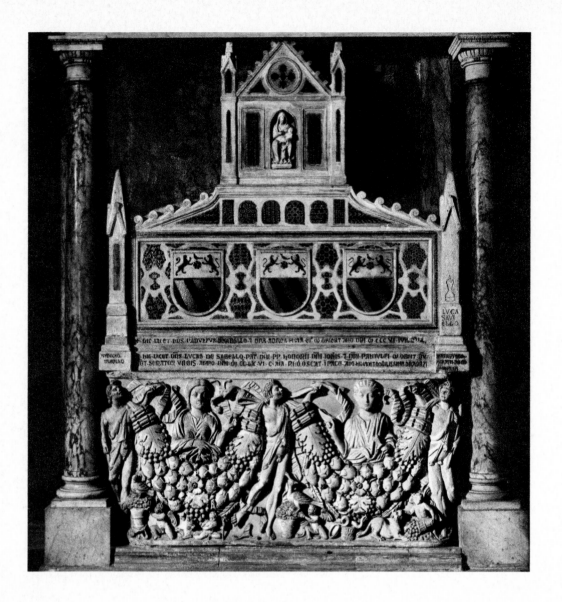

56 In the Middle Ages, Christians began to recognize classical works of art as being rare and valuable. Often they also, quite wrongly, gave them a Christian interpretation. The Bacchus relief on Luca Savelli's tomb in the Church of Santa Maria in Aracoeli was taken to represent the return of the messenger sent by Moses to Canaan

What probably contributed more than anything else to the preservation of antique works of art in the Middle Ages was the 'interpretatio christiana'. The best-known example of this is the great equestrian statue of Marcus Aurelius on the Piazza del Campidoglio in Rome. Till 1471 it was venerated in the neighbourhood of the Lateran, the favourite papal residence in the Middle Ages, as representing Constantine, the first Christian emperor. Not far away from it there were to be seen the *She-Wolf* and the

Spinario, both apparently on high pillars, according to the accounts of pilgrims. In what way Christians interpreted these works, which are now in the Palazzo dei Conservatori, we do not know. N 30

In other parts of Rome, visible above ground, were the recumbent statues of gigantic river gods, among them the so-called *Marforio*. In many obscure cases of this sort, people in the early Middle Ages undoubtedly thought of the words of St Augustine: 'If we use them [works of art from the temples] for the honour of God, then the same thing happens to them which happens to men who are brought from godlessness to the true faith'.

The Church was ready to read a Christian meaning into even the most pungent of the fables of Ovid and to transform innumerable pagan reliefs, sarcophagi and other serviceable works of art into illustrations of biblical events. A few deft touches and Messalina could become a Christian saint. The

44

churches of Italy were—and are—full of baptismal
fonts, altars and marble sculptures, all of which once
served some purpose other than that to which they
are now ostensibly dedicated.

In the Church of St Mark in Rome the marble
body of a chariot ('biga') was used till 1780 as a papal
throne (now in the Vatican Museum of Antiquities).
The sarcophagus with representations of the Orestes
myth, now in the same museum, came originally
from the church of Sta Maria in Aracoeli; the marble
font with Bacchic reliefs in the Villa Albani came
originally from the Church of St Francis in Trastevere
and was in the sixteenth century in the Cesi collection, which between 1521 and 1550 was enriched by
six other antique works of art from the churches of
Rome. The two reliefs representing *The Triumph of
Marcus Aurelius*, now in the Palazzo dei Conservatori
on the Capitol, came originally from the Church of
Sta Martina. In Gaeta Cathedral a marble Attic urn
with scenes from the life of Bacchus was used
57 until 1800 as a baptismal font. To this day in the
Church of Sta Maria sopra Minerva in Rome,
one can still see a relief representing Hercules strang-
ling the Nemean lion, which has obviously been
59 accepted as a representation of Samson's similar feat.
In Florence the best-known example of a large piece
of antique marble sculpture in a church is the sarcophagus in the Baptistery with a representation of a
N 31 boar hunt.

There can be no doubt that on account of their
material value many antique objets d'art were in fact
never buried. It was the practice of the kings and
queens of France on their coronation day to drink
from an onyx cantharus called the *Coupe des Ptolemées*
(now in the Cabinet des Médailles at the Bibliothèque Nationale, Paris). The use of this vessel was
part religious, part secular. The agate bowl in the
Schatzkammer in Vienna was used at the baptism
of the infant sons of the House of Habsburg.

An antique alabaster vessel used as a reliquary has
outlasted the centuries in a Westphalian monastery
3 (now in the Berlin Museums). The *Rubens Vase* in
the Walters Art Gallery, Baltimore, can be traced
back with a high degree of certainty to a medieval
church treasure, as can the onyx vessel from the time of

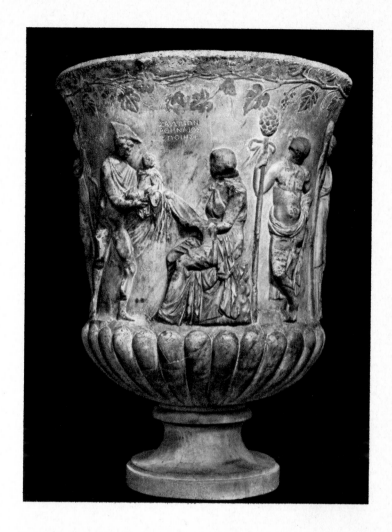

57 This large marble vase decorated with scenes from
the childhood of Bacchus (above) was regarded as
commemorating the birth of Christ in Bethlehem, even
though one side of it showed dancing Maenads (below).
Until about 1800 the vase was used as a font in the
Cathedral of Gaeta, north of Naples

Caracalla, now the property of the Herzog Anton Ulrich Museum, Brunswick. From the monastery church of Montier-en-Der in France a small ivory relief with a carving of a priestess of Bacchus has found its way to the Victoria and Albert Museum, London; 61 possibly this female figure had been thought to represent one of the women at the grave of Christ. In a number of European churches—in Genoa Cathedral, for instance—there are some particularly fine thick-walled glass vessels of late antiquity, originally intended for purely secular use, which are even now held in honour as 'grail-beakers'. N 32

A whole chapter could be written on the fate of antique cut stones. Two superb examples formed part of the imperial treasure which Constantine transferred from Rome to Byzantium, where they were adapted to use as reliquaries, despite the fact that they had originally been created to glorify the Julian imperial house. The *Gemma Augustea*, to 101 which reference has already been made, and the

58 A pure gold head of unknown origin has, since the tenth century, formed part of the statue-reliquary called 'Majesté de Sainte Foy' in the abbey of Conques in southern France. The fact that this head dated from the late Imperial period was discovered only in 1964, when the statue was being cleaned and repaired

59 A magnificent Greek relief of Hercules fighting the lion, carved around 500 BC, was preserved as part of a tomb in a church in Rome because of its identification with Samson's feat in the Bible

60 From the ninth century onwards, a cameo with the profile of the Emperor Augustus has formed the centrepiece of a new cross donated by the Emperor Lothar to Aachen Cathedral. The cameo was regarded as an idealized representation of a ruler

61 This late classical ivory relief of a priestess of Bacchus preparing a sacrifice was at one time in the shrine of St Bercharius in the Church of Montier-en-Der in France

so-called *Cameo of the Sainte Chapelle*, had already returned to the west in the Middle Ages as sanctified objects of the highest value. A gem with the profile of Augustus, representing the reigning Christian emperor, was fitted into a reliquary cross that *60* was set up in the cathedral at Aachen. The noble creation of Augustan classicism contrasts strangely with the barbaric splendour of the gold and jewels *B 265* of the arms of the cross.

Whether it is always permissible to speak of a 'Christianization' of the gems is a matter still disputed. Can we really enter into the mind of a cleric who engraved a Hebrew inscription upon a cameo showing the dispute between Poseidon and Athena, thereby turning it into a representation of the fall of Adam and Eve? Perhaps some cultivated prince of the Church sought to save the works of art he admired from destruction by fanatics by using them to embellish holy appurtenances.

Here we touch upon the phenomenon of the medieval renaissance movements. The view expressed by recent scholarship is that the Carolingian epoch was in many respects a 'counter-movement' to the medieval trends. Much can be cited in support of this. As a kind of counterpart to the statue of Marcus Aurelius which had been reverently set up on the Lateran as the Emperor Constantine, Charlemagne, the restorer of the Imperium Romanum, had a great equestrian statue brought from Ravenna to Aix—also a *Dancing Satyr* and a *She-Bear*, perhaps of Hellenistic origin. We can detect a reverence for antiquity when Charlemagne's body was laid in a sarcophagus showing a number of representations of Persephone, the ancient Greek goddess of the Underworld, which had been brought from the south. The passion for antique gems in Charlemagne's day had reached such a pitch that in many places efforts were made to produce imitations. Whether the term 'forgery' can be applied to these is something of a question. It is only in our own day that the art-historian's skill in judging styles has enabled us to distinguish false cameos and gems in reliquaries and on book bindings from genuine ones.

It is not easy to form a clear conception of the nature of the 'Ottonian renaissance'. This return to antiquity synchronized with yet another movement which endeavoured to take over some of the characteristics of Byzantine art. On the processional cross of Archbishop Heriman of Cologne is a head of Christ from the time of Hadrian carved out of lapis lazuli—probably originally a head of Venus (Diocesan Museum, Cologne). The *Bernward Cross* in Hildesheim is decorated with twelve antique gems, among them an onyx with a Bacchus.

The renaissance phenomena of about 1200 have long been the subject of research. To form part of the monastery treasure of St Denis, Abbot Suger had a chalice decorated with particularly fine antique 239 gems (now in the National Gallery in Washington) and by setting a bronze on top of a porphyry vase he transformed it into an *Eagle of St John* (now in the Louvre). An ancient Roman onyx vessel is presumed to have been repaired for use in Bamberg Cathedral (the vessel is now in the Historical 128 Museum, Stockholm).

In those days both knights and clerics used antique gems as seals. In 1189 a dean in Soissons used as his seal a carving of Leda and the swan. On the Shrine of the Three Kings in Cologne Cathedral is a gem which shows Mars standing before a seated Venus. The carving corresponds to the traditional theme of one of the kings doing reverence to Mary. An unmistakable revival of the ancient art of gem-cutting was started at the southern Italian court of the Emperor Frederick II.

As the sculpture of the thirteenth century ripened into its 'Greek moment', attention was again directed to large pieces of antique sculpture outside Rome. In various parts of Europe religious statues were being made which bore witness to the study of the draped figures of ancient Roman works. Frederick II had inherited a lively interest in antiquity, and ordered excavations on the east coast of Sicily north of Syracuse. Slaves transported all sorts of statuary from various places in southern Italy to the imperial residences in Apulia and presumably to Bari, Barletta and Castel del Monte. N 33

In the more northerly parts of Italy we also find during this period a slowly awakening interest in antique sculpture. The merchants of the trading centre of Pisa brought into the cloisters of their Campo Santo not only the sarcophagi in which they were laid to rest, but also other antique marbles, while at the same time they spread out in the midst of their magnificent churchyard shiploads of 'holy earth' from Palestine.

North of the Alps, Bishop Henry of Winchester was regarded in his day as one of the leading collectors of antiquities. He acquired 'idols in the curia', i.e., in Rome, no doubt small works of art, and B 149 special mention is made of a portable altar set with cameos, valuable stones (probably cut stones), a candlestick which probably dated back to classical times, and vessels 'in effigie hominis'. N 34

Considerable widening of the artistic horizon resulted both from the warfare waged by Christian knights against the Infidel in Spain, southern Italy and Asia Minor, and from peaceful exchanges of all kinds that occurred during the period of the Crusades.

I Among the most beautiful vases to reach Italy from Athens is this amphora, signed by Execias, which shows Ajax and Achilles playing at dice

A great quantity of beautiful Byzantine art of the early Middle Ages accompanied classical works of art to the west during the Fourth Crusade. This included some religious objects such as the 'Staurotheke' or receptacle for the Cross, a reliquary dating back to the tenth century that was taken in 1204 from Hagia Sophia in Constantinople. It was bequeathed to the cathedral in Limburg by Heinrich von Uelmen where together with its Greek name of 'Staurotheke' it has been carefully preserved to this day. In 1200 another knight, Conrad von Krosigk, bequeathed some reliquaries from Constantinople to the cathedral in Halberstadt where they have likewise been preserved. The Basilica of St Mark in Venice acquired a veritable hoard of Byzantine objets d'art, since many who returned from the Crusades in a Venetian galley, and could not find money for their fares, pledged some precious object and were then unable to redeem it.

Of course many purely profane luxury goods also came to Europe from Byzantium—ivory hunting horns, for instance, with carved representations of the hunt. These 'oliphants' were often bequeathed as reliquaries to churches and monasteries. Examples of such horns which once belonged to the Swiss monasteries of Muri and Rheinau and also to Brunswick Cathedral can now be seen in public museums.

In many parts of the Mediterranean area Islamic works of art fell into Christian hands. Superb examples of such products are still to be found in the monasteries of Spain. An explanatory notice in the chapter-house of the Abbey of Las Huelgas near Burgos reads 'Trofeo conquistado al enemigo en la Batalla de las Navas de Tolosa'—'Trophies captured from the enemy at the Battle of las Navas (1212) by force of arms'.

Another example is the bronze griffin captured in the Balearics by the citizens of Pisa. Inspired by a sudden fear of demons, they placed this on the roof of their marble cathedral, and today it is in the Pisa Museum. The finest ceremonial robe that the Norman kings of Sicily had fashioned for them by Islamic

craftsmen was in 1220 handed over by the Emperor Frederick II to the imperial treasure as a coronation robe.

From the Egypt of the Fatimid dynasty precious vessels of glass and rock-crystal found their way to Palestine, where crusaders and afterwards pilgrims sought to acquire them. These relics from the Holy Land, originally nothing more than purely secular pieces of tableware, often ended up in Christian churches. A glass decorated with a stylized heart-shaped pattern carried out in high relief was set aside for sacred purposes by Elisabeth of Thuringia, who was later canonized. Towards the end of the Middle Ages this vessel, the *Fatimid Glass*, became the property of the Schloßkirche in Wittenberg, and is now in the Coburg Museum.

62

Particularly fine examples of Islamic glass-work were produced in Syria, probably in Aleppo. In northern France a tall glass beaker coming from this part of Asia Minor was fitted with a metal foot and served as a chalice in Chartres Cathedral. The alleged 'Beaker of Charlemagne' today graces the local museum.

62 Just as Greek and Roman works of art were given a Christian interpretation, so Islamic objets d'art were often consecrated because they contained holy relics brought from Palestine. This glass once belonged to St Elisabeth of Thuringia

II The eruption of Vesuvius in AD 79 preserved many Pompeian wall-paintings, among them some showing the activities of a secret cult. This example is in the building known today as the Villa of Mysteries

The most famous item of this glassware is the *Luck of Edenhall*. Its leather case, a piece of thirteenth-century French workmanship, is marked with the IHS for Jesus. Its first Christian owner must have been a French Crusader. In Protestant England after 1500 this Christian vessel became a kind of talisman of the families that lived in Edenhall in Cumberland. The friends of Sir Walter Scott sang of 'The Luck of Edenhall'. This well-preserved glass vessel, now more than 700 years old, passed in 1959 into the possession of the Victoria and Albert Museum in London for the sum of £5,500.   63

Pilgrims to Palestine in the fourteenth and fifteenth centuries occasionally brought home the products of Far Eastern craftsmanship. A Chinese celadon vessel was so highly valued by the Katzenellenbogen Counts of the Middle Rhine that they   64 provided it with a silver framework. This object is now in the Landesmuseum, Cassel.   N 37

In the late Middle Ages north and south for a time went their separate ways. The role played by Venice as the gateway to distant worlds—to Asia Minor, Egypt and China—has already been hinted at. It was inevitable that in this place, the market for all kinds of worldly goods, men should have started at an early date to make a hobby of art collecting. We know that Marco Polo possessed many objects of Asiatic origin, while the Doge Benedetto Dandolo gathered together in his apartments things that were both rare and beautiful. A doctor, Oliviero Forzetta, who had come from Venice's northern neighbour Treviso, also belonged to this circle of collectors. Around 1350 he set up a little 'antiquarium'—a collection of antiquities—and hunted for drawings and acquired Christian works of art, for instance 'una tabula in qua est imago S. Georgii', possibly a Byzantine work.

The age of the Gothic style north of the Alps tends to be regarded as the expression of a renewed longing for Heaven; the ascetic features of Christianity, which now come to the fore again, are wholly in harmony with such a conception. In the fourteenth century it was not only precious objects from the east that were given over to the churches and adapted to their use; many luxury articles produced by contemporary western craftsmen underwent a similar fate in token of penance and to signify the owner's turning away from the world. Jewel boxes, mirrors, toilet articles and other knick-knacks found their way to the sacristies. A gaming board made in Venice with representations of knights and their ladies, of players, sirens, and centaurs, was made to serve as the binding of a liturgical book: it was presented by the Guelph Duke Otto the Mild to Brunswick Cathedral in 1339.   65

63   A crusader returning to France brought with him as a reliquary this particularly fine example of enamelled glassware, made in Syria about AD 1250. It later belonged to the family that lived at Edenhall in Cumberland and came to be known universally as *The Luck of Edenhall*

Five of the thirty-odd squares underwent transformation; next to dallying couples were placed the symbols of the Evangelists and splinters of wood from the hill of Golgotha. The board which its worldly creator had made a temptation for weak characters was transformed into a 'Staurotheke'. In those regions where the Gothic reigned without a rival, there also died the passion for gems mentioned above. It was only around 1500 that a cameo with a Roman emperor's head was again used in Minden to adorn a processional cross.

In this connection, a word must be said about the treasure chamber of the Vienna Hofburg, the Guelph treasure, and the former French royal treasure. The Middle Ages believed that Christ, Lord of the World and of the Heavenly Jerusalem, had suc-

64 Pilgrims to the Holy Land were able to purchase Chinese ceramics like this celadon bowl which was made into a goblet in Germany in the fifteenth century

ceeded the Roman Emperor. The Holy Roman Emperor was Christ's representative on earth. More than any other person he had a claim on the remains, the 'Reliquiae', that were connected with Christ's earthly life, together with the other insignia they were the guarantors of the lawfulness of his rule. Crown and orb, moreover, had been traditionally accompanied by the Holy Lance which Otto the Great had carried before the Christian army at the Battle of the Lechfeld. There also belonged to the imperial treasure—as we call all these objects—the Sword of St Maurice, the Imperial Cross which was covered with relics, and the Bursa of St Stephen containing the earth which had been soaked with the saint's blood. When Charlemagne was canonized in 1166, all the insignia and garments that were in any way associated with his person became relics: for instance, the Crooked Sword of Charlemagne.

The more personal quality of Christianity in the late Middle Ages gave this imperial treasure a somewhat different significance. The pious Christian claimed the right to contemplate as many relics as possible in order to win both spiritual blessings and aid in his temporal affairs. This claim was behind Emperor Sigismund's decision in 1423 to abandon the practice of carrying the treasure along with him wherever he went; from then on it was kept in custody at Nuremberg and under the solemn form of 'Heiltumsweisung' was shown on special occasions to the assembled people from the gallery of Our Lady's Church. In 1524, however, the council turned Protestant and forbade this 'papist practice'. Somewhat later the imperial treasure found its final home in the Hofburg in Vienna.

The Habsburg emperors (who from 1423 could preside over the imperial insignia only once in their lifetime, on the day of their coronation) accumulated a treasure of their own which, as in the previous case, accompanied them from one place to another. Emperor Maximilian, 'the Last Knight', had a particularly rich collection, which contained reliquaries, silver busts of saints and a chalice now in the Vienna Museum. The Emperor commissioned Dürer and other artists to commemorate the accumulation of all these precious things in the woodcut called *The*

N 38   *Triumphal Arch.*

Whereas items from the Vienna treasure continued to serve their original purpose at imperial coronations up to 1917, the Burgundian royal treasure which had dazzled all Europe in the later Middle Ages changed its whole character two generations after it first came into being and became a mere accumulation of valuable objects. Around 1400 a prince of the House of Valois had founded a short-lived duchy between the French crown lands and the German imperial domain. Its rulers, perpetually concerned with further conquests, carried their entire treasure with them on their campaigns. The ducal insignia, together with relics in precious settings, luxurious carpets and gold tableware, were meant to strengthen the confidence

B 62   of the troops. Yet in 1476 at Grandson and at Nancy in 1477, the Swiss peasants defeated the Burgundian knights and captured vast booty on the field of battle. Since that day the citizens of the little town of Liestal near Basle preserve in their

town hall the gold drinking bowl of Charles the Bold, Duke of Burgundy. What his enemies failed to capture was brought to the House of Habsburg by his daughter when she gave her hand to the man who was afterwards to become Emperor Maximilian. Among these treasures was the Unicorn Sword, now in the treasure chamber of the Hofburg in Vienna.

At one time the Guelph treasure was of hardly less artistic if not historic importance than the imperial treasure. In the course of time, however, it has sustained severe losses, and today, apart from the Imperial Robe of Otto IV, its chief contents are reliquaries of various kinds. In 1218 the son of Henry the Lion decided on Brunswick Cathedral as the place in which to keep the treasure; even then it was a very extensive one. In the centuries that followed, its contents increased still further. According to an inventory of 1482 most of the items stood on altars, and the remainder were kept in a secure cupboard. After the Reformation in Brunswick it devolved upon the Hanoverian line of Guelphs who had remained Catholic, and after the Prussian victories of 1866 the treasure was expressly recognized as the private property of the King of Hanover who had fled to Austria. In 1869 it was lent to the Museum für Kunstindustrie, Vienna, where the individual items were exhibited as valuable examples of medieval craftsmanship. During the world economic crisis of 1929–30 a group of art dealers took over the treasure. A considerable part of it went to the Cleveland Museum of Art and to various American collectors. The essential part, however, was sold to the Kunstgewerbemuseum, Berlin. After the Second World War the breaking up of Prussia had the curious consequence that the Guelph treasure, though greatly reduced, returned to Brunswick after wandering from place to place for three hundred years. As a token of gratitude for the care and protection which had been bestowed on works of art from the Berlin museums between the years 1944–1955 the

65 Non-religious western European luxury goods, such as chess-boards, were donated to churches from time to time as symbols of penitence. In 1340 Duke Otto of the Guelphs made a present of this elaborately decorated board, made in Venice about 1300, to be used as a cover for a liturgical book

55

66 Emperors and princes in the Middle Ages possessed articles of gold and silver, reliquaries and other precious objects in hoards which already had some of the characteristics of actual collections. Maximilian's treasure, shown here, was probably kept in a Habsburg fortress in either Innsbruck or Wiener Neustadt

treasure was handed over in 1956 'in trust' to the authorities of Lower Saxony. Its present manner of exhibition, in the castle of Dankwarderode built by Henry the Lion in Brunswick, avoids the usual coldness and reserve of a museum atmosphere and may indeed be considered exemplary.

Whereas the imperial treasure and the Guelph treasure are shown to the public today in a manner which does justice to their original character, the royal treasure of France was rather less fortunate when the Ancien Régime collapsed. We cannot say just how much was lost under Robespierre. Only a few isolated items which the French kings had placed in their court chapel, the Sainte-Chapelle on the Ile de la Cité, or in the Cathedral of Nôtre Dame, the seat of the Bishop of Paris, but most of all in the Abbey of St Denis, escaped destruction. We find them exhibited as examples of ancient craftsmanship, though without any reference to their original purpose, in the Cabinet des Médailles of the Bibliothèque Nationale and in the Galerie d'Apollon of the Louvre.

CHAPTER 2

The Fifteenth and Sixteenth Centuries

Renaissance artists' collections set the lead | the 'Garden of Antiquities' in the Vatican | Puritanism, iconoclasm and confiscations | the collections of Dürer, Margaret of Malines, Cardinal Albert and the Fuggers | the creation of Fontainebleau and the Escorial | the magical 'Kunstkammer' | the connoisseur Rudolph II in Prague

FROM THE POINT OF VIEW OF RELIGION and intellectual development, of sociology and art, the fifteenth and sixteenth centuries are a period of cross-currents and transition. In the Netherlands and Florence the middle classes first became persons of importance: men concerned with property and with earning money but who also took intellectual possession of the world around them. Religion lost its ideal quality. The golden background, which in painting had represented the next world, disappeared. Scenes from the Bible were enacted in the home town of the artist and his patron.

North of the Alps Jan van Eyck acknowledged the new ways as early as 1430; in his *Ghent Altarpiece* Adam and Eve are depicted in their natural nakedness. In the *Madonna of the Chancellor Rolin* (in the Louvre) the donor kneels before us as large as the figure of the Mother of God herself and apparently full of self-assurance. In Germany about this time Konrad Witz and Hans Multscher with their coarse handicraft art take their places beside older painters who still hankered after the Gothic, such as Stefan Lochner. Towards the end of the fifteenth century realism was modified by the curious Late Gothic style. Angular twisting forms, broken falls of drapery and furrowed yet deeply expressive faces give the sculpture of that day its unmistakable quality. The woodcarvers Bernt Notke and Riemenschneider, the engraver and painter Schongauer and also, in their early work, Dürer and Cranach belong to this Late Gothic phase.

In Florence and other cities in Italy the realistic trend of the fifteenth century was enhanced by a gradual return towards the spiritual world of antiquity. While Jan van Eyck was painting his *Ghent Altarpiece* Donatello was doing what had not been done since the days of antiquity; he was shaping a naked bronze figure. *Putti* appeared in a Christian and sacred context for the first time on the tomb of Onofrio Strozzi in the sacristy of Santa Trinità. The eagles of Zeus graced the tomb in Santa Croce of the humanist Bruni who died in 1444. In Italy, as well as north of the Alps, the pattern of style grew more complicated, for instance in the work of Botticelli, through the reintroduction of certain elements of form which were somewhat Gothic in character. The urge to give Christian themes a contemporary context was so strong that banality and even desecration often resulted. In the epoch of the High Renaissance this danger was recognized and faced. Leonardo da Vinci, Raphael and Michelangelo strove for the grand manner of antiquity. They gave dignity to their figures, an expression both grave and restrained. The lively or violent touches of Early Renaissance art disappeared. The preference was for calm and well-balanced compositions, often with a strictly symmetrical character built around some central point. The High Renaissance also found a renewed understanding of the solemnity of early medieval art. We often find a frontal composition in altarpieces and occasionally even in portraits. Raphael's *Sistine Madonna* has not only the mighty physical form of an antique Juno, but also the wide eyes of the Byzantine saints of Ravenna.

Added to these developments in Rome and Florence, in Venice and the adjoining parts of northern Italy there was also the Oriental taste for the decorative tapestry-like quality of a work as a whole, as well as an instinct for the refined play of colour and a certain poetic mysteriousness in the manner of representation.

North of the Alps, it was impossible for a new, 'classical' level of maturity to be achieved on its own. Dürer's journeys to Italy were really due to a desire to escape from the Late Gothic maze. In Italy such German artists sucked in no 'sweet poison', as romantic historians were inclined to believe. Sooner or later all the peoples of Europe were compelled to come to terms with the classical art of Italy, much as the ancient Romans were unable to ignore the art of Phidias and in the Middle Ages Germany and England could not overlook the French Gothic.

Apart from Dürer, members of the Augsburg bronze-founding family of Vischer and the younger Holbein had been in Italy before 1520, while Cranach got to know the style of classical Italian paintings in the Netherlands in 1508. In works produced in northern Europe during the time of Dürer, the striving for strict composition and for the 'Italian beauty' of the human form encountered several cross-currents, especially the lingering and vestigial pattern of the Late Gothic style.

After the deaths of Raphael in 1520 and Dürer in 1528, there is a turning away from classical ideals which would be incomprehensible without a knowledge of the general historical position. As a result of its debate with Lutheranism, Catholicism underwent a renewal. The educational ideal of Humanism proclaimed by Erasmus of Rotterdam was

67 North of the Alps, even as late as 1400, the antipathy of the Middle Ages towards portrayal of the naked human figure was still evident. This medallion from northern France shows a semi-nude Venus, an allegory of sinful lust, averting her gaze from the fountain of life and the Holy Cross, while a more decently clad figure, representing the Church, looks on

rejected by both schools of ecclesiastical thought and lost its vitality. After the disappearance of the bishops in the Protestant territories, the princes increased their power. In Austria, the Netherlands and Spain—the latter with its newly-won colonies overseas—the Habsburgs founded an empire on which the sun never set. Florence, once a city of bourgeois, was transformed into the capital of the Grand Dukes of Tuscany. While Christians were divided by religious differences, new dangers threatened from without. In 1529 the Turks stood before Vienna. In 1571 Italy defended herself against them with difficulty in the naval battle of Lepanto. Gloomy cares weighed down the peoples of Europe.

The harmony between body and spirit that had characterized the High Renaissance no longer existed. In Florence a large number of artists devoted themselves almost exclusively to problems of form. Value, independent of things seen in nature, was placed on construction, spoken of as 'the divine spark'. The figures of the Mannerists are often elongated and stand irresolutely on the ground. Violent alternations of light and shade and a glittering play of colour replace the majestic reserve developed during the period of Raphael. In Rome the aged Michelangelo was chiselling his *Rondanini Pietà* (now in the Castello Sforzesco, Milan) which, far from expressing that corporeal beauty cultivated by the Renaissance, is concerned with the mystical transfiguration of the medieval style.

In Venice Titian, now also approaching old age, was turning his back on the ideals of his early manhood and devoting himself to the somewhat solemn works of his late manner. His younger fellow-citizen Tintoretto was, meanwhile, so transforming the component elements of Renaissance style that in his ecstatic pictures this world and the world above simultaneously become objects of sensory experience. The Greek Theotocopoulos, born within the Venetian colonial empire of the eastern Mediterranean, was surpassing the effects which Tintoretto had sought to achieve. Ultimately, as 'El Greco', he found his true home in Counter-Reformation Spain and there achieved widespread success.

In the first chapter of this book it was shown that in about 500 BC art had woken to freedom in the city states of ancient Greece. In the Florence of the Medici this process was repeated. The new importance that was now attributed to all earthly things, the slackening of religious bonds, the transition from the natural economy of feudalism to the capitalist economy of cities—these and other factors from roughly 1430 onwards brought about

68 It was in Italy, and above all in Florence, that the process which had taken place in Greece 2000 years earlier repeated itself, and works of art were once again prized in their own right. Furniture was richly decorated, and displayed in parts of the house specially arranged for such show-pieces. This *cassone* belonged to a Florentine family

the same transformation of artistic life in Tuscany as had occurred in Hellas two thousand years previously. To the great painted altarpiece in the church was now added the small devotional picture in the home. One species of painting was particularly popular in Florence, the so-called 'quadri da spose', pictures that were presented to the bride. These provided an opportunity for a secular treatment of religious subjects. Representations of

the Madonna became family scenes; those of St Sebastian, studies in the nude. The 'cassoni', or clothing chests, had pictures fitted into them on which Biblical themes gradually gave place to the myths of the ancient gods or to scenes from the stories of Boccaccio. Around 1460 these pieces of luxury furniture were transferred from the bedroom to the principal room of the house, so that visitors could appreciate their artistic merits. B 322

From about 1430 painted portraits and busts were produced in Florence in increasing numbers. Historical painting celebrated its first triumph with the battle pictures of Uccello ordered by Cosimo de' Medici in 1456. Nude recumbent couples such as Piero di Cosimo's *Venus and Mars* (now in Berlin) 232 decorated the backs of marriage beds and are noteworthy as the earliest examples of what may be called alcove-painting.

The changed attitude towards the nude human form is particularly evident in a medallion commissioned from Niccolò Fiorentino or one of his assistants in 1486. It shows on the obverse the head of Giovanna Tornabuoni and on the reverse an antique group of the three naked Graces, already well known at that time. The heads of the three figures show the features of the beautiful Giovanna. *70*

70 In 1486 a medallion was cast in Florence in honour of Giovanna Tornabuoni. The obverse shows her head in profile, but the reverse alludes to her physical beauty by comparing her to the three Graces. To make this comparison quite clear, the Graces bear her profile

69 The Italian Renaissance affirmed its belief in the value not only of man's soul, but also his body. Ancient statues, which were discovered from time to time, were now greatly admired. Cardinal Francesco Piccolomini granted these three Graces a place of honour in his house in Rome

While representations of Christian subjects tended, as already indicated, to suffer from secularization, allegories whose source was the new system of philosophical and humanistic ideas almost attained the rank of religious works. A painting of Pan, the goat-footed god of nature, together with his retinue of naked nymphs, satyrs and shepherds, was painted by Signorelli for Lorenzo de' Medici (formerly in Berlin, now destroyed); Signorelli here used the compositional scheme that was customary for the enthroned Mother of God with attendant saints. Botticelli's *Primavera*, a programme picture of the Neo-Platonist philosophy, shows the extent to which new spiritual forces were narrowing the scope of religious life.

B 289 The framing of pictures and reliefs in the age of Phidias was a matter of great significance. This was equally true in the early Florentine Renaissance. At one time every work of art in a church had a place in the greater context and required no isolating frame. When around 1430, however, the eternal was made temporal and Christian themes received a realistic portrayal, the idea of the cathedral as a picture of the Heavenly Jerusalem began to disappear. The frame now began to stress the independent existence of a painting or relief, which had by this time come to be regarded as something mobile, and enhanced its purely individual relation to the beholder. This self-contained quality is particularly evident in the circular paintings. Pictures for domestic devotion and portraits—both had already begun to travel far and wide—were quite frequently composed in the form of a round 'tondo'. It seems as though wide and richly ornamented frames, which separated the picture sharply from its surroundings, were used especially for paintings and reliefs which sophisticated patrons and self-conscious artists regarded as important and unique creations. In the case of more ordinary works for churches, frames were more modest.

N 39 As in Athens at the time of Pericles, the artist in the Florence of the Medici emerged from his anonymity and took up a position beside his work. Signatures became familiar, and along with his name the personal style of the individual master, his 'handwriting', became known. When Giovanni Ruccellai died in 1481 he set a fashion. Instead of identifying the various works of art in his possession by their contents or by the purpose for which they had been created, in his will he simply listed the works after the artists' names.

After about 1430 interest began to be aroused in the maquette for sculpture executed in cheap material and in the unpretentious drawing on cheap paper. The Medici at that time possessed reliefs of the Madonna in plaster that were valued up to 10

71 It was in Florence that pictures dealing with Christian themes were first painted small enough to be moved from room to room at will. The perspective in Botticelli's *Adoration of the Kings* draws the onlooker's gaze and yet at the same time the wide decorative frame isolates the picture from its surroundings and lends it importance

gulden, then a considerable sum. These may well have been original preliminary studies from a famous hand, of a kind that can be seen in the museums of Florence, Berlin and London. When Uccello died in 1475 he left whole boxes full of drawings. B 289

The immense importance attached by certain Florentines to artistic value can be seen from the story dating back to 1492 according to which a dying man asked to be given a more beautiful crucifix to kiss than the one that was offered. A few years later something which would have been quite unimaginable hitherto was asked of the nuns of St Clare: an admirer of Perugino wanted to acquire the *Entombment* (now in the Palazzo Pitti in Florence) and offered three times the sum which the convent had originally paid the artist. Art-lovers of Florence and of the neighbouring Tuscan republics did not confine their interest to the work of native sculptors

72 There was a broadening of artistic taste in Italy during the fifteenth century. Collectors bought paintings by Jan van Eyck, Rogier van der Weyden and Hans Memling, whose *Bathsheba* (left) existed in Genoa before 1500

and painters. Artists from Lombardy and Venice carried out commissions in the region of the Arno. Older samples of art, for instance small Byzantine panels and works to which the great name of Giotto was attached, were now mentioned in domestic inventories.

Though it was three generations before Italian art began to be thought of as something desirable in the regions north of the Alps, members of Italian merchant families had been quick to understand the true quality of Netherlandish art, different as this was from the art of the south. The delicate reproduction of reality was no doubt particularly prized. Jan van Eyck's Madonnas, now in the Städelsches Kunstinstitut in Frankfurt and the Dresden Gallery, *141* were originally painted as domestic devotional pictures for Italian clients. Many of the pictures of women bathing, by van Eyck and his successors, which have since been lost, were in the fifteenth century in the possession of Italian art-lovers as, we have reason to believe, was Memling's *Bathsheba*. *72* Towards the end of the fifteenth century a curious competition took place. An Italian and a Netherlandish painter did a portrait simultaneously and the foreigner won.

About fifty years after the scene described earlier, in which an antique goddess was hacked to pieces by the Sienese, a marble statue representing a female figure in the attitude of 'Venus pudica' was admired in Florence in a private house. About 1439 the sculptor Ghiberti possessed a small collection of antique works, among which were a satyr torso (now in the Uffizi), a winged spirit, two statues of Venus, a representation of Venus and Vulcan—the famous *Bed of Polycletus*—and some painted vases. Shortly before 1440 Poggio Bracciolini the humanist placed some antique sculptures in the garden of his country house in Terranuova. For the most part they came from Chios. About the same time Donatello fitted an antique bronze head of a bearded man, together with a companion piece which he himself had fashioned, into his Cantoria (now in the Museo dell'Opera del Duomo, Florence). Like Ghiberti, he probably possessed a few pieces of antique art. Gentile da Fabriano is the first painter we know of to make drawings of ancient statues. N 40

A new trend in collecting often appears first among artists and those whose work is in some way related to the arts. Only later does it assert itself among the propertied and cultivated members of the public at large. Much as in Paris, around 1900, it was a handful of painters who first discovered El Greco while the collectors simply followed them, so around the middle of the fifteenth century the Medici only appeared as collectors of antiquities after the sculptors and humanists. Once their appetite had been excited, the Medici used every effort to accumulate the leading collection of antique sculptures. Among others, the little collection of Poggio Bracciolini, mentioned above, became their property. Lorenzo the Magnificent, grandson of the great Cosimo, accepted from Pope Sixtus IV in Rome in 1471 two

73   In the second half of the fifteenth century, Lorenzo de' Medici, il Magnifico, built up a superb collection in Florence. He kept in touch with art-lovers throughout Italy and in 1471 gave Count Carafa an antique bronze horse's head, probably in exchange for some other item. Donatello based the head of the horse in his equestrian statue of Gattamelata on this antique bronze

74   The most famous portrait of Lorenzo de' Medici is this bust by Verrocchio. As an art-lover and patron and, above all, as an intellectual, Lorenzo surpassed all his contemporaries

marble busts, an *Augustus* and an *Agrippa*. He also possessed a head of Scipio and two statues of Marsyas. Of the two gigantic horse's heads Lorenzo owned, he presented one to Count Diomede Carafa in Naples (now in the Museo Nazionale there); the other head remained in Florence and is now in the Museo Archeologico. In 1489 the collection had grown so large that Lorenzo created a 'Garden of Antiquities' not far from the monastery of San Marco (which incidentally contained plastic studies by Donatello who had died in 1466). It was at this place that the young Michelangelo began to work.

Around 1490 Lorenzo de' Medici kept in his palace, together with other precious objects, numerous gems and cameos. For some time now they had begun to be removed from the bindings of medieval manuscripts and had found their way into the hands of

73

To satisfy the newly awakened Italian interest in Roman art, there appeared a number of small copies in bronze and other materials as well as imitations. Doubtless there also existed at this time some outright forgeries. Small-scale bronze reproductions of the equestrian statue of Marcus Aurelius and of the *Spinario* in Rome began to be manufactured, presumably in Florence, soon after the middle of the fifteenth century, and were highly valued in that city. The *Cavalry Battle* by Bertoldo, who was employed by Lorenzo de' Medici, has recently been recognized as a fairly exact copy of a marble sarcophagus in Pisa. It was about this time that the relatively large reproduction of the *She-Wolf* was made. It later found its way from Dresden to Vienna and ultimately reached Washington. The bronze *309* statuette with broken arms of a *Young Bacchant* (now in the Kunsthistorisches Museum, Vienna) is the work of a late fifteenth-century Tuscan master. The *77* artist endeavoured to create the semblance of an antique bronze which had survived in a fragmented state—possibly with deliberate intention to mislead.

76 Artists were granted free access to Lorenzo's collection for the purpose of study. A small carved cornelian provided the subject for this marble relief of Apollo and Marsyas, which was discovered in Florence in 1880 and has been attributed to the young Michelangelo

75 Lorenzo's most precious possession was the superbly carved *Tazza Farnese* which he bought in 1471. It is probably an allegory of the Nile's fertility, and was most likely the work of an Alexandrian craftsman of the second century BC. It reveals a combination of Egyptian and Roman formal styles and may well have belonged first to a member of the House of Ptolemy. In the sixteenth century it passed into the Farnese collection

art-lovers. Three antique gems or perhaps imitations bearing the inscription LAUR MED (Lorenzo de' Medici) are today in the British Museum. The inner court of the Palazzo Medici was decorated with free copies of similar cameos and gems. A copy of a cameo representing Apollo and Marsyas, which had long been in the possession of the Medici and which may have been executed by the young Michelangelo, was acquired some time ago by the National Gallery *76* in Washington. A vessel with a representation of the Nile god, a masterpiece of Hellenistic carving, was valued by Lorenzo at 10,000 ducats, that is to say a thousand times higher than a panel by Botticelli. This, the famous *Tazza Farnese*, so called after the family to which it later belonged, is now in the Museo *75* Nazionale, Naples. Antique stone jars once the property of Lorenzo can be seen in the Palazzo Pitti in Florence.

Lorenzo de' Medici and possibly his father Piero might well be called art collectors, while the elder Cosimo was predominantly a founder and spent more money on the monastery of San Marco which he established than on his own house and its contents. Unfortunately no accurate description survives of the art treasures in the Palazzo Medici in Florence, which was long ago emptied of its contents but is still well preserved. Guests of Lorenzo were occasionally allowed to see certain pieces after a banquet, but nobody else enjoyed this privilege. Besides works of antique and contemporary art mentioned earlier, there was a small Byzantine mosaic *Christ in Benediction*, now in the Bargello, Florence, and a *Deposition* by Giotto. One could see long rows of Flemish tapestries; above them battle scenes by Uccello (now in Florence, Paris and London); elsewhere a *Madonna with Four Saints* by Rogier van der Weyden (now in the Städelsches Kunstinstitut, Frankfurt), and an *Adoration of the Magi* by Filippo Lippi (now in the National Gallery, Washington). There were portraits, medallions and objets d'art

77 Collectors who could not obtain original antique statues had small copies made in bronze. Art dealers were faced with this shortage even before 1500, and they commissioned copies, in a fragmented state to prove their authenticity—like this *Young Bacchant*

78 Italian princes occasionally sent paintings by living masters abroad as special gifts. That was how Raphael's *St George and the Dragon* (detail above), the first valuable Italian painting to reach England, came to be included in Henry VII's collection

and no doubt, behind silk curtains, paintings of naked couples. All this constituted a loosely connected unity, a colourful array of the various arts.

The subtle and secularized artistic culture of the Medici circle was confronted by a resurgence of the spirit of the Middle Ages. In his penitential addresses Savonarola inveighed against the fashionable finery of Botticelli's Madonnas. The Mother of God, he proclaimed, was no whore. Discussions in the churches about the purely formal merits of newly erected altarpieces were dismissed as un-Christian. Savonarola insisted that the representations of naked gods should be consigned to the flames, as should playing cards, jewellery and all other earthly baubles.

Even more disastrous for Florentine art than this invective was the temporary expulsion of the

79, 80 Northern Italian collectors of antique works of art had to rely even more than their counterparts in central Italy on small bronze replicas. There was also a ready market for fakes like the relief of a nereid on a sea-ram (above) and the purposely mutilated statue of a satyr (below)

Medici family soon after Lorenzo's death. According to an old tradition, some of the antique statues were put up for auction in 1494. Some five years later the French marshal Pierre de Rohan accepted from the city of Florence nine antique busts which the Medici had originally owned. How the works which once belonged to Lorenzo came to be scattered all over the world is something about which we have only fragmentary information. N 42

In other centres of central and northern Italy art played a similar though less clearly defined part. Federigo da Montefeltro fitted out 'studioli' or places of study in his two Renaissance castles at Urbino and Gubbio. What remains of the pictures they contained—allegories of the arts, ideal portraits of heroes and the like—are today in the Louvre and the Metropolitan Museum, New York. It was his son who sent to Henry VII of England Raphael's *St George and the Dragon*, the first major Italian painting to reach that 78 country. We know that Cromwell sold the picture on the Continent. It travelled to France and Russia and was ultimately sold to Andrew Mellon for $747,500 (now in the National Gallery, Washington).

In the second half of the fifteenth century the d'Este family in Ferrara owned antique works of art and early Netherlandish devotional pictures. We can be fairly certain that the pictures did not hang in their domestic chapel but in a small room devoted to secular purposes, which implies that it was their artistic value that was paramount. Presumably the small statues of Hercules ascribed to Bertoldo in the Frick Collection, New York, once belonged to Prince Ercole d'Este.

Around Venice there was a greater number of antique works of art. They were brought from the Venetian colonial empire in the eastern Mediterranean. In Mantua the painter Mantegna owned a collection of antiquities which Lorenzo de' Medici made a special journey to see. Cardinal Ludovico Gonzaga, in Gazzuolo Castle near Milan, possessed some genuine antique sculpture to which he added numerous plaster casts. Padua, one of the chief centres of Humanism, was the place where Squarcione, painter and

III Spain provided a second home for Netherlandish painting. Isabella of Castile owned a large number of important paintings by artists from Bruges and Ghent. Four hundred years later one of these paintings, Rogier van der Weyden's *Christ appearing to his Mother*, the third panel of a triptych of which the other two panels are in the Capilla Real in Granada Cathedral, came into the possession of the Metropolitan Museum of Art, New York

lover of antique art, enjoyed most influence. When he died in about 1470 he left behind a considerable collection which had partly been accumulated on a journey to Greece. The German humanist Ulrich Gossenbrot in 1460 made lead castings in Padua of medallions for collectors more interested in their artistic than their financial value. In Venice the painter Gentile Bellini believed that a torso in his possession was that of the *Aphrodite* of Praxiteles. From 1495 onwards we find in Venetian interiors, as represented by Carpaccio, small antique sculpture or sculpture in the antique style, for example above the doors.

Rome's great period in this respect did not begin until after 1500. The home of the popes, a wretched town of only moderate size when compared with Florence and Venice, was at first only remarkable through the slowly increasing number of large antique pieces of sculpture discovered there. Around 1435 the Colonna family already possessed a *Hercules* in a somewhat fragmented state which was placed after 1530 in the Belvedere Court of the Vatican. In the eighteenth century this *Belvedere Torso* was greatly admired by connoisseurs. Pope Paul II was an art-lover with tastes similar to those of Lorenzo de' Medici. He possessed gems, cameos and a number of pieces of large antique sculpture. In 1467 he had the late antique sarcophagus of Constantia removed from the church of Santa Costanza and set up in the square in front of the Palazzo Venezia. His successor reversed this measure and it was not until 1778, in the age of neo-Classicism, that this work (now in the Museo Pio-Clementino, Vatican) was finally transferred from the sacred sphere to the profane.

In 1471 something happened in which a feeling for art, a humanist outlook and pride in the ancient greatness of the 'urbs aeterna', all played a part. The bronze statues which throughout the Middle Ages had stood in the open air under the protection of the Lateran Palace were handed over by Sixtus IV to the citizens of Rome to be placed upon the Capitoline Hill. Shortly afterwards, in 1498, the emperor's statue was recognized as being that of Marcus Aurelius and was scrupulously restored. The *She-Wolf* was presented with a pair of baby boys, Romulus and Remus, while the *Spinario* was no longer allowed to stand on top of a high pillar

B 145

81

81 A collection of antique bronze sculpture was kept by the popes in the Lateran Palace or its surroundings throughout the Middle Ages. In the Renaissance this collection was placed on the Capitol so that this centre of Rome might be restored to its previous majesty. Included was this equestrian statue which has been recognized since 1498 as representing Marcus Aurelius

(as the patron saint of Venice still stands in the Piazzetta in front of the Doge's Palace). A drawing by Mabuse dating from the winter of 1508–9 seems to indicate that the *Spinario* was set up fairly close to the ground and so could be seen in detail much more easily.

N 43

In the late fifteenth century Cardinal Piccolomini, then resident in Rome, possessed a *Standing Hercules* and the *Three Graces* group which has been drawn and copied so many times subsequently. He presented the latter in 1502, along with his collection of manuscripts, to the cathedral in Siena, where it was placed in a side chapel. More than four hundred years later misgivings began to be felt about the presence of three nude goddesses in the cathedral. In 1930 the group had to be moved to a museum.

N 44

IV Hieronymus Bosch was among the Dutch painters most highly esteemed by art-lovers in southern Europe, especially in Venice. Many of his masterpieces, such as the *Adoration of the Magi* (detail), went to Spain. This painting remained in the Escorial until 1839

82 From 1480 onwards a number of cardinals showed an interest in the antique statues that were being discovered in and around Rome. Pope Julius II was the original owner of a statue of Apollo, which came to be known throughout the world as the *Apollo Belvedere* (see Ill. 187), after the Belvedere Court in the Vatican where it was put on display early in the sixteenth century

Naples belonged from 1442 to the Spanish Royal House of Aragon. The still undecided struggle against the Moors on the Iberian peninsula had sustained the forces of Christianity in every country under Spanish rule. If this hardly induced a receptive atmosphere for statues of antique gods, Netherlandish devotional pictures for domestic use were highly valued, on account of their sincere piety. There is an unmistakable Netherlandish element in the works of the southern Italian painter Antonello, and until recently it was thought that this could only be explained by a journey to Bruges. Today, however, the view is taken that the source of Antonello's art was the large collection of pictures by Jan van Eyck and his successors, which belonged around 1450 to Alfonso of Aragon in Naples. An older contemporary of Antonello's, the Neapolitan Colantonio, came so close to the Netherlands in style and general conception that even his contemporaries were deceived.

Spain in the fifteenth century was a kind of artistic colony of the Netherlands. Between 1427 and 1428 Jan van Eyck visited both Barcelona and Compostella, and his *Fountain of Life* was presented to a monastery in Segovia in 1455. In exchange for the wool of Castile innumerable altarpieces and devotional pictures came to Spain from the ports of the Netherlands. The Spanish painter Gallegos was an imitator of van Eyck, and as late as 1900 his paintings were still being mistaken for originals by the master himself. When a real passion for early Netherlandish painting began to develop around the turn of our century, it was found that the Iberian peninsula was the richest reservoir. In 1914, the *Adoration of the Magi* by Hugo van der Goes, still in its well-preserved original frame, travelled from a remote monastery in Spain to the Berlin Museums.

Queen Isabella of Castile, who together with her husband Ferdinand of Aragon at last contrived to expel the Moors from the Iberian peninsula, had a magnificent collection of paintings. Though she had innumerable Netherlandish devotional pictures there were only two Italian paintings—Botticelli's *Christ on the Mount of Olives* and Perugino's *Resurrection*. Obviously Florentine painting was too worldly for the taste of the Spanish court. On her death in 1504 Isabella bequeathed 38 selected devotional pictures to the as yet unfinished Cathedral of Granada, the capital of Andalusia, which had only recently been liberated. To see these pictures in the Royal Chapel is to be transported to Bruges and Ghent at the most glorious period of their history. Many other panels from Isabella's collection were sold, among them works by the court painter Juan de Flandes. About 30 of them have now been traced. Four hundred years after Columbus had discovered the New World while serving Queen Isabella, a picture from her collection, Rogier van der Weyden's *Christ Appearing to His Mother*, entered the Metropolitan Museum, New York.

As early as 1480 Florentine painters who were decorating some of the chapels of Rome were being better paid there than they were in Tuscany. A generation later, artists were hurrying from all parts of Italy to the residence of the popes, which was enjoying a sudden access of splendour. Once Donatello could have been seen standing in his working clothes in front of his studio in Florence; now Raphael rode splendidly dressed through the streets of Rome, and Michelangelo too was one of those who made a fortune. The truly great artist was looked on as 'the pencil of God' and was accorded immense fame. The products of mature antique art were reflected in the new artistic ideal of monumental dignity and heroic pose. The heavy mantle, the rich Roman toga, the pride so visibly expressed in the posture of gods and emperors, made priceless the finds of ancient statuary that now came to light in Rome. Raphael's generation attained a gloriously equal relationship with these works. The popes of the early sixteenth century and their contemporaries took no exception to the fact that they were dealing with the bequests of a heathen culture. When a statue of a youth from the circle of Polycletus was found on the Adriatic coast of central Italy, it was given the affectionate nickname of *Idolino* or 'Little Idol', by which it has been known ever since (now in the Museo Archeologico, Florence).

The two most famous statues of Rome have become permanently associated with the name of the great cardinal from the House of Rovere, later Julius II. Already as Grand Confessor, Julius II had set up a Garden of Antiquities close by San Pietro in Vincoli. Statues from this collection later came to the Belvedere Court on the Vatican Hill. Between cedars, myrtles, cypresses and orange trees there were rows of niches, and for the first time works of non-Christian art were given a definite relationship to a building. Banquets accompanied by music occasionally took place in the open air. When Titian visited Rome he was allowed to live in the Belvedere. It was here that he painted his glorious *Danaë* (now in the Museo Nazionale, Naples), while Michelangelo stood by and watched.

The Belvedere Court was later rebuilt and worked into the great complex of the Vatican, but today it still contains statues erected there in the early sixteenth century. From the Garden of Antiquities near San Pietro in Vincoli had come that lovely Apollo which for more than four hundred and fifty years has been known as the *Apollo Belvedere*. The *Laocoön* group, discovered on 14 January 1506, was

330

82
83

83, 84 The *Laocoön* group, which Virgil himself once admired, was rediscovered in 1506 and within a few weeks it had been brought to the Belvedere Court, where it has remained ever since. The fame of this Greek statue of the first century BC spread so quickly that immediately it reached the Belvedere, an engraving was made of it (above). The engraving of the three monkeys (below) was probably intended as a reproach to those who placed too high a value on the *Laocoön*

acquired by the Pope a few weeks afterwards; its finder received a post in the Curia as his reward. Of equal importance to the contemporaries of Raphael was the so-called *Venus Felix*. A kind of attendant 85 court for these three pieces of sculpture, which were set up in the niches, was partly formed by indifferent copies dating from late Hellenistic and Roman times. In addition to an *Emperor Commodus*, there was an *Ariadne* which was also known as *Cleopatra*, a *Mercury*, the wrestling *Hercules and Antaeus*, a copy of the *Aphrodite* from Cnidus and a number of recumbent river gods. 'Procul este, profani' read an inscription over the entrance of the Belvedere. It was reserved for an élite of humanistically trained art-lovers, men without prejudice of any kind. A number of earnest B 97 Christians felt that they were here in a kind of pagan grove, set up in honour of the goddess of Love, and looked upon the place as a symbol of moral corruption. Such was the view of the young Pico della Mirandola, who in 1512 was observing conditions in the Curia with a critical eye. N 46

Apart from the papal 'Antiquario delle Statue' in the Belvedere Court—the word 'statue' at that time also designated busts, heads and reliefs—there were, during the first half of the sixteenth century, about twenty other places in Rome with Gardens of Antiquities or indoor rooms with statues of Græco-Roman origin. In 1503 Cardinal Cesarini described one of the rooms of his house as a 'Statuaria'. This has somewhat pointedly been called the oldest museum room in Rome. All manner of finds

85 The *Venus Felix* which Julius II set up in the Belvedere was particularly admired in the sixteenth century. Small replicas of it were bought by collectors living some distance from Rome; the one shown here went to a collector in Mantua, and was later owned by Charles I of England

86 The practice of putting antique sculpture out of doors in gardens came to Rome from Florence. Lorenzo Galli collected old statues of the gods of antiquity. He bought Michelangelo's *Bacchus* because he was not able to obtain a statue of the god from any other source. Before Michelangelo became famous, most of those who saw Galli's collection accepted this as a genuine classical original

came to light while the palace of Cardinal Domenico Grimani was being built. To these the Cardinal added other works which he bought. He later bequeathed the whole collection to his native city of Venice where today it is in the Archaeological Museum. Raphael, as has recently been shown, used the *Grimani Apollo* as a model for a figure in his *School of Athens*. The *Grimani Trajan* is today regarded as a forgery from the hand of Cristoforo Romano, who died in 1512.

In 1508–9 Mabuse drew the *Boy with a Goose* which belonged to the Savelli family. The recumbent *Ilioneus Son of Niobe* in the Munich Glyptothek and the *Icarius Relief* in the British Museum were in the Palazzo Maffei in 1510. At that time Lorenzo Galli, treasurer to Julius II, added Michelangelo's *Bacchus* to the Græco-Roman statues in his Garden of Antiquities. One of the hands was accidentally broken off Michelangelo's work and for some time the damage was not repaired. This caused admirers to toy with the idea that they were looking at a piece of antique statuary. In 1513 Cardinal Andrea della Valle embellished the triumphal arch which he had erected for the entry of Pope Leo X with antique statues from his own collection, among them a *Ganymede* and a *Venus* which some think was the Medicean one. In 1520 Raphael's pupil Giulio Romano acquired the antiquities of the Ciampolini collection and sold them again at a profit.

Whereas in Rome intensive building activity brought new marble statues to light almost every day, lovers of antiquity in other parts of Italy had to content themselves mostly with plaster casts and particularly with small reproductions in bronze. North of the Apennines there were three artists at work whose chief source of income was copying and reproduction but who now and then engaged in imitations of antique works which were for all practical purposes forgeries. Alari Bonacolsi, who called himself 'Antico', lived chiefly in Mantua; he was a restorer of statues and produced numerous small bronzes. A little statuette of Venus now ascribed to him was recognized only in 1937 by the Museum Antiker Kleinkunst, Munich, as a work of the early sixteenth century (it is now in the Bayerisches Nationalmuseum, Munich). Andrea Riccio of Padua offered his customers the *Spinario* as a boy with a torn pair of trousers. For the upper part of his censer, now in the Brunswick Museum, he used a genuine small

87 In 1572 the Medici, who now ruled Florence again, managed to buy Michelangelo's *Bacchus* for 240 ducats. This statue by the city's most famous son was immediately given a place of honour in the Uffizi. In 1873 it was transferred to the Bargello

Etruscan statuette which until recently was believed to be an imitation. From Tullio Lombardo in Venice, himself the possessor of a draped antique statue, came a mock antique bust of an emperor, now in the Bayerisches Nationalmuseum. His *Venus without Arms*, now in the Vienna Museum, displays in her slender figure and the uncertainty of her stance stylistic elements which still belong to the dying early Renaissance epoch. No doubt it was accepted in Venice as a genuine antique, though in Rome by 1510 it may well have been already recognized as an imitation.

N 48

As we have seen, the artistic enthusiasms of the upper classes in Rome were chiefly for large, often over-lifesize and even colossal pieces of sculpture. The *Ignudi* or 'Naked Men' on Michelangelo's ceiling in the Sistine Chapel and the naked figures in Raphael's wall paintings in the Vatican and the Villa Farnesina revived the classical love of the beautiful body. In Venice there was an almost total lack of antique monumental sculpture, and this deficiency could only partially be made good with small bronzes, as in the house of Andrea Odoni from Milan. Fresco painting was not successful in the damp climate. There was also a lack of commissions on the scale of the popes; on the other hand, the tradition of the moderate-sized picture was still alive and contemporary painting was the substitute for sculpture. The Arcadian scenes by Giorgione and Titian and Correggio's pictures of gods may have compensated their first owners for the antique sculptures which they could not obtain. Posterity valued these creations among the highest of earthly goods.

B 102

Rome had lain dormant till the end of the fifteenth century, but Venice was by then already full of treasures which previous generations of art-lovers had accumulated. This is the first time that we encounter in the west a set of circumstances where works of art conforming in some special way to the particular taste of an individual, together with other works bequeathed to their owners, and new acquisitions admired by their possessors, can no longer be distinguished from one another, as in the case of the Foscarini, Venier and Vendramin families. Around 1525 in Venice there was already talk of previous possessors of works of art. In the first quarter of the sixteenth century self-portraits by Rogier van der Weyden and Memling are mentioned as being in the palaces on the Grand Canal, but three pictures of the contemporary painter Hieronymus Bosch are also cited. An illuminated manuscript prior to 1530 passed from hand to hand and was regarded as a possession of high artistic value. Paintings with large nude figures by living artists were usually concealed by a curtain but 'their out-

lines must as it were have penetrated right through the walls'. And it is worth noting that around 1500 in the official residences of the clergy, of brotherhoods and in monasteries, pictures not actually used in connection with divine worship were not removed but sometimes, as in the Scuola di San Giuliano, were set up simply to be admired.

B 37
N 49

In the important princely capital, Mantua, the development of the Early Renaissance did not end as in Florence with a sudden break. Isabella d'Este, who transferred her home from Ferrara to Mantua when she married Giovanni Francesco Gonzaga, had already by 1491—that is to say, while Lorenzo de' Medici was still alive—designed her 'Paradiso', a succession of small choicely furnished rooms of a kind favoured in Florence. In 1504 she commissioned some older masters, among them the 74-year-old Mantegna and the 57-year-old Perugino, to paint for one of her 'studioli' allegories and representations of Olympus and Parnassus (now in the Louvre). From 1510 onwards, however, the Princess surrendered more completely to the new fashions. She acquired a cast of the *Laocoön* which she revered as 'cosa divina'. Her court artist, that same 'Antico' referred to before, produced to order some particularly fine little bronze copies of the statues in the papal Belvedere Court (now in the Vienna Kunsthistorisches Museum). When Giorgione died Isabella let it be known in Venice that she was interested in making purchases from his estate. We are fairly certain today that Titian in his capacity of working partner and heir to Giorgione, who was 33 years old at the time of his death, on this occasion sold her the painting now in the Louvre which we know under the title of *Concert Champêtre*. For centuries it has competed with Leonardo's *Mona Lisa* for pride of place as the most beautiful Italian painting on French soil.

85

After her husband's death, Isabella went to live in a different part of the castle in Mantua and in 1522 began to arrange her 'Studio della Grotta', where she hung her finest pictures. Her son Federigo Gonzaga II now also began to surround himself with works of art. A story dating back to the year 1524 tells us how little he cared about the contents of such works. In this year he sent a message to an unidentified Venetian painter to the effect that he liked 'qualque pitture vaghe e belle da vedere'—handsome pictures pleasing to the eye. However, they must not be 'cose da santi'—Christian themes. It was this prince who recommended Titian to Charles V and who commissioned Correggio to paint for an intimate room the unparalleled series of *The Loves of Jupiter*. Jupiter approaches Danaë as golden rain, Leda as a swan and Io as a cloud and, in a

124
130

88 The passion for collecting antique works of art also affected rich Venetian merchants in the course of the sixteenth century. This portrait, which has long been part of the British Royal Collection, shows Andrea Odoni surrounded by sculpture of every kind, while on the table in front of him are ancient coins

sudden access of paederasty, visits Ganymede in the shape of an eagle.

North of the Alps the arrival of the new age in the realm of art was a less consistent process than in Italy. It was only in the sixteenth century that it began to develop by regular stages. In 1479 the

Lübeck merchant Dunkelgut had some paintings among his merchandise, presumably small devotional pictures. A little before this, all sorts of works of art were offered for sale at Our Lady's Fair at Antwerp. Sometimes there were lotteries, for B 73 instance in 1490 in Schwäbisch-Gmünd near Stuttgart. In such cases there was no relationship between the person acquiring a work and the individual artist. Production for individual clients was beginning to give way to production for the market. N 50

Towards the end of the fifteenth century the practice of coin-collecting, fashionable among the humanists of the south, began to spread northwards. The Emperor Maximilian is usually regarded as being the founder of the Habsburg Coin Room, the priceless contents of which are now in the Kunsthistorisches Museum in Vienna. About this time an art-lover of Cologne was painted with a gold coin in his hand (portrait by Bruyn in the museum at Bonn). At various periods the portraits of collectors give indications of their special interest—around 1750 antique vases, around 1880 Japanese woodcuts and around 1920 African idols.

In 1502—shortly after the rediscovery of the *Apollo Belvedere*—there came to light under the floor of a late Roman sanctuary in Carinthia the classical bronze statue of a naked youth. As in Rome, so here too in the Alps, a humanistically-minded prince of the Church immediately came forward as purchaser. He was Matthäus Lang, administrator of the bishopric of Gurk and Provost of Augsburg. When he became coadjutor of the Archbishop of Salzburg in 1513 this bronze, the *Ephebe of Helenenberg*, found its way to the castle of Hohensalzburg and in the nineteenth century passed from there to Vienna. Dürer in his drawing of a *Naked Man with a Club* followed the outlines of this supposed representation of Antinous.

In 1500 a stone statue of Mercury (now in the Augsburg Museum) was dug up from the Roman settlement there. Some years later the humanist Peutinger boasted of his *Hercules*, probably a small Italian bronze. Woodcuts of these statues dating from the year 1534 show us how long, north of the Alps, the classical formal language of the south was felt to be neutral and inexpressive, and underwent a process of marked stylization with leanings towards the late German Gothic.

Around 1510 interest and understanding for small objets d'art began to increase. There arose a fashion for collecting medals, and reliefs began to be produced in box-wood and in Solnhofen stone. Small bronzes were cast at the court of Ludwig of Bavaria in Landshut which was open to Italian influences, and in Nuremberg too. Goldsmiths preserved for art-lovers the wooden models of their work. The first effects of the great antique statues of Rome can be traced from 1515 onwards. Dürer made use of the *Apollo Belvedere* in a drawing, and Peter Vischer the Younger was inspired by the *Hercules* today known as the *Belvedere Torso* when modelling a small figure on his tomb of St Sebaldus in the church in Nuremberg dedicated to this saint.

So far we have only been describing phenomena which are part of a development similar to that which took place in Italy. We can also look upon them as the effects of an influence which radiated from the south. With the spread of Protestantism all this is changed. It will be remembered that around

89

B 118

90

89 Around 1500 the same interest was shown in the antique statues discovered in Austria and southern Germany as was shown in those that came to light in Italy. This statue of a young man entered the collections of Matthäus Lang, coadjutor of the Archbishop of Salzburg, soon after it had been discovered

90 The woodcut (below) represents the statue of Mercury dug up in Augsburg around 1500. It is still in Augsburg, but in a bad state of preservation

91 The statue opposite was held in great regard by artists. It inspired Dürer's *Apollo* (right), in which the arm positions have been reversed

1500 a citizen of Florence offered the nuns of St Clare a large sum of money for an altarpiece. German art-lovers now had fewer difficulties than this Florentine. In 1521 'popish' pictures of saints were destroyed in Wittenberg while a clearance of treasures was made in all the churches of Ulm. Zwingli inveighed, much in the tones of Savonarola, against the wanton appearance of Mary Magdalene and the Junker-like air of St Maurice. In a letter of 12 May 1529 Erasmus described to his friend Pirckheimer in Nuremberg the iconoclastic activities that had taken place in Basle. 'Of the sculptures nothing remains. The paintings on the walls have been daubed over while the movable ones have been consigned to the flames'. N 51

How far did this destruction really go? Just as around AD 300 the devotees of the ancient pagan religions hid their cult images and pictures in

94 Art-lovers who had been converted to Luther's doctrine were often so attached to old paintings and statues that they kept in their houses works of art which they had banned from their churches. At the beginning of the Reformation, Dürer's *Lamentation* (detail right), painted in 1500, was taken to the safety of Hans Ebner's house in Nuremberg ▶

some secret place, Roman Catholics of the sixteenth century often succeeded in a similar way. Even in the catastrophe at Basle, which Erasmus himself witnessed, many works of ecclesiastical art managed to escape damage. The fragments of Holbein's *Last Supper*, painted on wood and hacked in pieces by the mob, were reverently pieced together again. Some decades later the collector Amerbach, a convinced Protestant, managed to acquire this picture, now in the Basle Kunstmuseum. From the Predigerkirche in Nuremberg, where the monks had been forbidden in 1525 to say Mass, Dürer's votive picture (now in the Munich Pinakothek), painted for the goldsmith Glimm, came into the possession of the Nuremberg patrician Hans Ebner. The famous 'Wittenberger Heiltum', the collection of relics in precious settings belonging to the Wettin dynasty, was last exhibited before the faithful in 1522. Some years later most of the objects that were made of precious metals were melted down.

N 52
92
B 208

94

92 The spread of Protestantism north of the Alps led to waves of iconoclasm. A panel of *The Last Supper* by Holbein was smashed by the mob but the fragments were saved and the panel was carefully restored

93 In this engraving from a pamphlet by Eberhard Schoen one can see devotional statues, which in Germany were mainly of wood, being taken out of a church and burned

The *Fatimid Glass*, however, which is associated with the name of St Elisabeth of Thuringia, came into the possession of none other than Luther himself who without any misgivings used to show it to the guests in his house.

The best insight into artistic life north of the Alps after 1500 is gained by examining important representatives of the various grades of society. While still a young man, Dürer, the opponent of Altdorfer and Baldung and indeed every kind of gothicizing tendency in German art, already called a small collection of Italian engravings his own. In 1507 he wrote his name as owner of a drawing from northern Italy, which is now in the Berlin Kupferstichkabinett. Some ten years later he made a note on a drawing in red crayon to the effect that it had been sent to him by Raphael as 'an example of his hand'. Today this drawing is in the Print Room of the Albertina, Vienna. On his return from his journey to the Netherlands, in the course of which he visited various churches of Cologne to see altarpieces dating back to about 1430, Dürer brought with him a great number of varied acquisitions. Among them was a small panel by Patenier, *Lot's Flight from Sodom*, which found its way in 1936 to the Ashmolean Museum, Oxford. In Malines Dürer vainly sought to lay his hands on drawings by the painter Jacopo de' Barbari, who had moved from Venice to Nuremberg in 1500, then on to Wittenberg and finally Brussels. He managed to get hold of a few objects from America, some Indian weapons, for instance. From this incomplete evidence we can get some idea of the nature of his collection. It was of a kind which no artist north of the Alps had ever possessed before Dürer.

95   In the Netherlands, Margaret of Austria was an active collector. She once owned one of Jan van Eyck's major works, *The Marriage of Giovanni Arnolfini and Giovanna Cenami*. For the past hundred years this painting has been among the prize possessions of the National Gallery in London

96   The love of art in miniature found its expression, north of the Alps, in numerous medals, like this one from Nuremberg which shows the Emperor Charles V as a young man

In the Netherlands the Regent Margaret of Austria, daughter of the Emperor Maximilian and N 54 Mary of Burgundy, was another collector. Two inventories in French inform us that in addition to tapestries and many fine examples of the applied arts, her palace in Malines was a treasure house of early Netherlandish painting. Here was the double portrait of Giovanni Arnolfini and his wife by 95 Jan van Eyck, now in the National Gallery, London, B 223 as well as paintings by Rogier van der Weyden, Memling and Bosch, precious illuminated manuscripts, numbers of small bronzes of Italian origin in the classical style, a copy of the *Spinario* in marble, no doubt on a somewhat smaller scale than the original, some sketch-books of Jacopo 97 de' Barbari and some small statues by Konrad Meit, a sculptor who had originally come from Worms and had been in Margaret's service since 1512. Among these small statues was a portrait of the Regent herself, now in the Bayerisches Nationalmuseum, Munich. Margaret also possessed the first examples of pre-Columbian art to come from America—a particularly high value was placed on N 55 these. On her death her nephew Charles V was sole heir, but ultimately the possessions were divided between the German and the Spanish Habsburgs.

Halle was the favourite residence of Cardinal Albert of Brandenburg, Archbishop of Magdeburg and Mainz. On the eve of the Reformation this prince of the church, following medieval usage, gathered together a quite unusually magnificent collection of relics in precious settings. This contained, as we can see from drawings that have been made of it, one Byzantine, four Norman-Sicilian, eleven Romanesque, thirteen Early and Late Gothic items together with about three hundred pieces of the fifteenth and early sixteenth centuries. All that now remains is a standing reliquary cross of about 1420 which fell into the hands of the Swedes in the Thirty Years War and is today in the Historical Museum in Stockholm. Albert, who was sympathetic to Humanism and showed an astonishing delicacy of perception in his assessment of contemporary painters, must have deeply enjoyed the nobility of form and the richness of the precious objects which made up his wealth. One particularly fine work was the crown of Emperor Otto II which Albert took from a Saxon monastery and added to his collection, though he had no proper authority for doing so. In his building activities Albert first introduced Italian Renaissance forms into central Germany. For the church which he founded in Halle he had altarpieces painted by Grünewald and Baldung (these are now in the Munich Pinakothek and the

97 Margaret of Austria, Charles V's aunt, bequeathed to him her collection which included this *Judith*, by the German artist Konrad Meit

Germanisches Museum, Nuremberg). Cranach, even after turning to Protestantism, continued to enjoy the Cardinal's favour.

Albert of Brandenburg was known as 'the most worldly of all the princes of the Church'. In 1530 he set up a 'pleasure bath' in his palace in Halle. We also hear of 'pictures and portraits' hung in his rooms. When the progress of the Reformation drove the Cardinal out of Halle and forced him back into the second of his spheres of ecclesiastical authority, the archbishopric of Mainz, he took all his movable art treasures along with him. In his will of 1545 he bequeathed his *Ecce Homo* panel by Dürer to 'Mainz Cathedral for St Michael's Chapel or wherever there is room for it and where it will receive the best light.' (The panel is now in the

98 In the early sixteenth century German collectors were fond of small carvings in general, and of small reliefs in particular. The master I. P., whose *Adam and Eve* is shown here, probably worked in Salzburg, and was influenced by the paintings and woodcuts of Altdorfer

gallery of Pommersfelden Castle). The Cardinal owned Grünewald's *Small Crucifixion* (now in the National Gallery, Washington), Cranach's *Ecce Homo* (in Freiburg Cathedral) and his *Christ on the Cross* (in the Munich Pinakothek), Baldung's *Nativity* (also in Munich) and his *Small Crucifixion* (in the Aschaffenburg Gallery, Munich) and Hans Sebald Beham's painted table-top showing scenes from the life of David (now in the Louvre). Of the portraits kept in Halle Jacopo de' Barbari's so-called *Portrait of the eighteen year old Albert of Brandenburg* (who was at that time a canon in Magdeburg), has recently come to light and is in a private collection in Stuttgart.

Albert of Brandenburg's junior by about ten years was Ottheinrich of the Palatinate. When he was young Ottheinrich lived as a Count of the Palatinate in Neuburg on the Danube. He ended his life as Prince Elector in Heidelberg. This Palatine Wittelsbach knew all the princely courts of his time from Malines to Ferrara. He cultivated a Latin correspondence with the princes in Mantua and Florence. In return for a weapon of particularly splendid workmanship, the Duke of Tuscany presented him with a pair of live lions. From Mantua Ottheinrich received 'antiquas res', probably little bronzes in the antique style. He collected imperial Roman coins which were used as models for the architectural decorations in Heidelberg Castle and constantly had sent to him the latest etchings of the 'courts of antiquities in Rome' (these etchings are now in the university library at Heidelberg).

Ottheinrich's affection for living art was more varied than that of Cardinal Albert. He loved tapestries and finely decorated weapons as well as devotional pictures and objets d'art. He kept up with contemporary Italian painting and wrote to Ferrara that he took a special pleasure in good pictures. In 1540 he received from Mantua a portrait of Federigo Gonzaga II by Titian, the first picture by that artist to cross the Alps. During this period Ottheinrich displayed an interest in the work that Hans Sebald Beham had left in his studio on his death, which shows that he was not averse to acquiring unfinished work commissioned by others. Even after he had gone over to Protestantism in 1542 he owned carved panels suitable for altars which must certainly have been older works made for churches before the Reformation.

The scope of Ottheinrich's interests is in the main attested by sound historical evidence; but even so it may be wider than is generally supposed. There are certain pictures which came to light at a later stage in his residences at Neuburg and Heidelberg which we may confidently associate with him. Only an art-lover with a real capacity for personal choice would ever have decided to acquire the *Still-life with Game* by Jacopo de' Barbari (now in the Munich Pinakothek), a picture that at first sight appears curiously insignificant. The portrait of Columbus by Sebastiano del Piombo (now in the Metropolitan Museum, New York) can definitely be proved to have been in Heidelberg Castle in the seventeenth century. It must have been moved to some remote place north of the Alps fairly soon after being painted, for there are no older copies extant.

N 57

99

Augsburg's leading merchant family, the Fuggers, owned houses that strike us as being more Italian than German in character. From 1506 to 1510 the younger Ulrich Fugger lived in Venice. Raimund Fugger was in Mantua in 1511 and later also frequently in Venice, and Anton Fugger stayed in Rome from 1517 to 1522. Around 1525 Raimund Fugger had his portrait painted by Catena in Venice (the picture is now in the Berlin Museums). Older Fuggers of importance in their day had churches built and endowed them. But about 1530 the Fuggers became art-lovers and started collecting in the Italian manner. Raimund Fugger, whom the Emperor Charles V raised to the rank of count, had very considerable means at his disposal and not only possessed numerous devotional pictures but was also, according to the words of the old family chronicle, 'a particular lover of antiquities'. He collected a number of pieces of classical statuary, principally from Greece and Sicily, which he kept in two 'studioli' in his house in the Kleesattlergasse in Augsburg.

About the middle of the sixteenth century the great house of the Fuggers on the Weinmarkt became the scene of events which deserve some mention here. Charles V, who had just defeated the Protestant princes of northern Germany in the Schmalkaldic War, was the guest of Anton Fugger in this house. The Habsburg Emperor had grown up at the court of his aunt Margaret in Malines and it was she who had first drawn his attention to Netherlandish painting. Since then he had widened his artistic horizon. At his coronation in Bologna he received from Federigo Gonzaga II Correggio's series of pictures, *The Loves of Jupiter*. In 1532 he first met Titian, from whom he never withdrew his favour. Charles V brought the aged master, who was already over sixty at the time, to Augsburg in 1548 and again from 1550 to 1552. There Titian painted him mounted on an Andalusian stallion and wearing the armour that he wore on the day of his victory at Mühlberg. The armour was the work of Desiderius Helmschmied of Augsburg who made it in 1544. Both the painting and the armour went to Spain and are today in the Prado Museum and the Armeria in Madrid. Another

B 67

99 Ottheinrich, Prince Elector of the Palatinate, who built Heidelberg Castle, was a collector in the manner of the Italian princes of his day. He owned valuable Italian paintings like this idealized portrait of Columbus by Sebastiano del Piombo

portrait of the Emperor, of which Titian probably completed only the head, remained in the house of the Fuggers and is now in the Munich Pinakothek. The pictures of the imperial counsellors Alba and Granvella were also painted at this time, as was probably the *Reclining Venus* now in Berlin. The Emperor's prisoner John Frederick of Saxony, stripped of his Electoral dignity, had to sit for his portrait by Titian (the picture is now in the Vienna Gallery).

Titian brought with him to Augsburg a number of devotional pictures he had painted in Venice, among them a *Mater Dolorosa* (now in the Prado). At this time the imprisoned Wettin prince, John Frederick, in the hope of bettering his lot in custody, presented the influential Granvella with Dürer's *The Martyrdom of the Ten Thousand Christians* (now in the Vienna Gallery), a picture at that time more than forty years old and which had been commissioned for the 'Wittenberg Heiltum'. Cranach, on a visit to his captured sovereign in Augsburg, found the opportunity to paint a portrait of Titian which unfortunately has been lost.

In the literature dealing with French art we keep encountering a certain merchant named Jacques Duché, who is spoken of as 'the first Parisian art collector'. According to one account, the authenticity of which has recently been questioned, he possessed in the early fifteenth century wall hangings, costly furniture, musical instruments and many examples of the applied arts. One room of his house was spoken of as adorned with various paintings.

In Bourges, several days' journey south of Paris, Jean Duc de Berry held his court around the year 1400. Treatises on art-collecting mention him with more justification than Duché. His position as 'Prince des Bibliophiles' is unchallenged. He had a passion for illuminated manuscripts. Once when on a campaign he made an arrangement with an enemy of similar tastes, the Duke of Bedford, which enabled the pair to look peacefully at a new Book of Hours while war continued to rage around them. Jean de Berry was the owner of Oriental textiles, Persian miniatures, gems, cameos and medals representing Roman emperors, which had been produced in northern France but which for several generations were thought to be genuine antiques.

B 106

B 44

N 58

While for the Habsburgs and for the Fuggers the Venetian Titian became the principal star of the Italian firmament, it was the Florentine, Leonardo, who enjoyed the highest regard of Francis I of France and those about him. Leonardo's fellow citizens, Raphael and Michelangelo, also attracted French interest at an early date. Florimond Robertet, the financier and royal state secretary, acquired probably in 1506 a painted panel by Leonardo, the *Madonna with the Distaff* (now lost). This work caused such a sensation at the French court that efforts began immediately to invite its creator to France. It was ten years before these efforts were successful.

Leonardo moved to France with half a dozen pictures dating from all periods of his life. Francis I granted him a house not far from the Château d'Amboise. In it he received such personalities as the Cardinal of Aragon, who visited him on 10 October 1517 and whose secretary has left us a description of the meeting. The painter appears at this time to have been in possession of the following pictures which were subsequently acquired by Francis I: the idealized portrait of the Florentine lady *Mona Lisa*, the *Virgin and Child with St Anne*, the *St John the Baptist*, the *Bacchus*, the portrait of an unknown woman called *La Belle Ferronnière*, and *Leda and the Swan*. Except for this last, which was probably destroyed as obscene in the seventeenth century, all the above-named pictures have survived and are well known to visitors to the Louvre; they became the core of the royal French collection of pictures.

B 1

100

In due course four paintings by Raphael entered the collection of Francis I, including the well-known Madonna that later came to be known under the Rococo name of *La Belle Jardinière*. The collection also included the *Caritas* by Andrea del Sarto and the *Annunciation* by Fra Bartolommeo. All these paintings are now in the Louvre.

In the entourage of Francis I, Florimond Robertet owned around 1530 a bronze *David* by Michelangelo, which has disappeared since 1633, while the Duc de Montmorency set up in the niches of his palace at Ecouen two *Slaves* (now in the Louvre) from the unfinished tombs for Julius II by Michelangelo.

100 Although Venetian art first reached Vienna and Munich, French collectors soon became aware of the worth of artists working in Milan and, above all, Florence. Leonardo da Vinci's *Mona Lisa* was incorporated in the French royal collection when the artist died in France. For centuries it has been one of the most famous paintings in the world

101 The exquisitely carved *Gemma Augustea*, which King Francis I appropriated from a French monastery, is one of the masterpieces of classical art. It shows Tiberius descending from a chariot in the company of Augustus and a figure representing Rome. It was almost certainly made shortly after Tiberius' triumph in AD 12

and the paintings. Philip II acquired the *Death of the Virgin* by the Master of Flémalle (now in the Prado Museum as are all the pictures named below unless otherwise stated). He also acquired a copy of Jan van Eyck's *Ghent Altarpiece*, Rogier van der Weyden's large *Deposition*, painted for the Louvain chapel of

the Fraternity of Crossbowmen (this was transferred from the Escorial to the Prado only in 1939) and a panel by Ouwater. Of the Netherlandish painters of the early sixteenth century, the King paid special regard to Orley, Scorel, Mabuse and Patenier. Around 1560 in Spain the abstruse allegories and Christian devotional pictures of Hieronymus Bosch, of which three are known to IV have been in Venice immediately after the artist's death, were accounted among the most sought-after works of the Netherlandish school.

There has been much discussion about a hidden meaning behind the pictures of Bosch which is anything but Christian or devout. José de Siguenza, the author of a history of the Escorial which appeared in 1599, described the *Garden of Delights* and similar pictures to his contemporaries as sermons in morality to mankind persisting in sin and therefore threatened with the pains of Hell. It is clear from this that the expression 'sueños de bosco' used in Spain at this time must not be translated as 'dreams' or 'free wanderings of the imagination', and used to give the pictures of Bosch a lascivious and un-Christian interpretation. In the time of Philip II the expression 'sueños' usually meant nothing more than compositions which treat of some theme not strictly defined. We know that at about the end of the sixteenth century pictures by Bosch were distributed between the sacristy, the chapter-houses and other apartments of the Escorial, and could therefore be seen by any visitor. The table-top with the *Seven Deadly Sins* had its place in the King's bedroom, the room in which he died.

102 After the death of Charles V, the House of Habsburg divided into the Austrian and Spanish branches, both of which included a number of collectors. Many paintings by Dutch artists, like this *Last Judgment* by Hieronymus Bosch (detail), now entered Habsburg collections

As to Italian art in the Escorial, in 1574 Philip II had the pictures by Titian with Christian themes, which Charles V had desired to see on his deathbed, transported from the monastery of San Yuste to the Escorial. These consisted of the *Holy Trinity* (also known as *La Gloria*) which had been commissioned in Augsburg, and the *Ecce Homo* and the *Mater Dolorosa*. Two large altar pictures, Veronese's *Annunciation* and Tintoretto's *Nativity*, were hung in the 'aula' of the Escorial, a term which should probably be taken to mean the sacristy. In 1810 some of Napoleon's officers took a number of exceptionally fine pictures from the sacristy, among them Titian's magnificent *Seated Madonna* (now in the Munich Pinakothek).

The question arises whether Philip II, who had such a deep affection for early Netherlandish painting, also appreciated Italian art prior to the period of Titian's maturity. Around 1810 small Italian devotional pictures by Raphael and his contemporaries were particularly liable to seizure by French officers and left Spain in large quantities: for instance, Raphael's *Madonna della Tenda*. Shortly after 1600 the Duke of Lerma acquired, from a church near Florence, Fra Angelico's *Annunciation*, painted about 1440 and today in the Prado, and it is not too rash to infer that the Spanish Habsburgs had similar tastes. It should be noted that of all the graphic work of Dürer, Philip II had a particular affection for the Late Gothic series of woodcuts of the *Apocalypse*. Apart from religious paintings, there came into the Escorial relics in precious settings, medieval church furniture, illuminated manuscripts, tapestries, and a number of pieces of sculpture.

About the middle of the century a member of Philip's II's entourage, Philip de Guevara, picking up the threads of certain ideas then current in Italy, suggested that pictures of a bygone age which were being kept in various royal residences should be open to view 'for people of artistic sensibility'. They should be housed 'in places where they could be frequently seen by many people'. The Escorial, a monastery rather than a royal palace, satisfied these requirements more than any other princely residence in Europe. Whereas Leonardo's *Mona Lisa* was hardly seen by anyone for generations after the death of Francis I, there passed through the Escorial not only foreign ambassadors and travellers of high rank, but also artists and more humble visitors. These people, it appears, could often enter even the royal apartments.

Philip II treated his profane works of art in the manner of other princes. His winter residence in the great Pardo Forest was described as a second Fontainebleau. This hunting seat was built at about half a day's journey from Madrid in 1547 and must not be confused with the Prado Museum which

103 Both the Austrian and Spanish Habsburgs liked the work of the Venetian masters. Titian, who had been ennobled by Charles V, sent Charles' son, Philip II, this picture of a sleeping nymph. It came to be known as the *Pardo Venus* after the palace near Madrid where it was kept

was built in the capital itself about 1800. The Pardo Palace housed 117 paintings. Titian's *Jupiter and*
103 *Antiope*, a painting now in the Louvre and which still bears the name *The Pardo Venus*, was affixed above one of the doors. In another room there was a double row of paintings, the lower ones being representations of the battles of Charles V and portraits of court dwarfs, while in the upper row were portraits of princes alongside self-portraits of the King's favourite painters. In 1604 fire destroyed the Pardo Palace and a great part of the art treasures it contained.

Philip II also gathered together some 350 paintings in the old Alcazar at Madrid. In the topmost room of the Golden Tower were freely conceived representations of mythological subjects; among these half a dozen pictures from the hand of Titian,

for instance a late version of his *Danaë and the Shower of Gold* (now in the Prado). Baldung's *The Three Graces* (now in the Prado) was also probably in the Alcazar, together with Jan van Eyck's *The Marriage of Giovanni Arnolfini and Giovanna Cenami.* 95 Jan van Eyck's masterpiece was just small enough so it could leave Spain in the baggage of one of Napoleon's officers around 1800. It is now in the National Gallery in London.

There was a considerable number of art-lovers in Philip's II entourage. Paintings by Bosch were owned, among others, by Philip de Guevara and an illegitimate son of Alba, whose paintings, as was customary in the Netherlands, were ultimately auctioned. The royal secretary of state, Antonio Perez, later disgraced, had managed to gain possession of Correggio's *The Loves of Jupiter*. Philip II's preference for early Netherlandish and Venetian paintings had represented a kind of epitome of the tastes of several of his ancestors, but farther from the court, artistic life now tended to follow other paths. The ecstatic style of El Greco, who had emigrated from Venice to Toledo, was not to the taste of Madrid, but this painter nevertheless won the goodwill of the Toledo aristocracy from 1575 onwards. For his altar picture *The Burial of Count Orgaz* in St Thomas'

Church in Toledo, El Greco received the exceedingly high fee of 13,200 reals. El Greco was further permitted to hang thirteen of his pictures, which are still there, in the sacristy of the cathedral at Toledo alongside the early Netherlandish devotional pictures. It was not till the twentieth century that so high a value was again placed on the works of this Spanish-Greek painter.

The Counter-Reformation in Spain was virtually a continuation of the Middle Ages, but in Italy it met with the forces which Humanism and the whole Renaissance movement had released. This led to a confused situation in which both trends had their own adherents. While Tintoretto was representing as timeless religious experiences those very Biblical themes that around 1500 had been regarded as historical fact, in Rome a classical statue of an empress was being transformed by means of additions and alterations into a *St Agnes*, and in Florence a statue of Hercules became a *Moses* and in Venice Titian's *Sibyl* (now in the Munich Pinakothek) became a Christian allegory of the vanity of all earthly things. Many older domestic devotional pictures found their way into churches and monasteries by gift and endowment. Precious vessels which had once been used by Lorenzo de' Medici and his free-thinking table companions were turned into reliquaries and handed over to a church in Florence.

The naïveté which the age of Raphael displayed towards the naked human body was lost again in Italy under Spanish influence. Whereas Giorgione had presented his Venus innocently sleeping (the picture is now in the Dresden Gallery), Tintoretto fascinated his contemporaries with deliberately erotic scenes: *Venus and Mars Surprised by Vulcan, Hercules Throwing the Faun out of Omphale's Bed, Joseph and Potiphar's Wife*. In an age whose attitude towards the nude vacillated between indignant rejection and lascivious enjoyment, the popes looked with misgivings at the Renaissance frescoes and the antique statues in the Vatican. Loincloths were painted on Michelangelo's naked figures, and Pius V went so far as to give away numerous statues to foreigners and to have the niches in the Belvedere Court shut off with wooden doors. The *Apollo Belvedere* and his companions once more disappeared from sight.

In an Italy now politically impotent and wholly given over to private life, the events which have just been described and which remind us so much of the Middle Ages were accompanied and in part counteracted by considerable activity on the part of artists, art-lovers and collectors, a company which was soon joined by art critics and artists' biographers. In Florence from 1561 onwards the most respected artists and those laymen who were particularly interested in

art used to meet for discussion in the Accademia del Disegno. When travelling, such people never failed to visit celebrated works of art in churches and private houses. Everyone spoke about art; read his Vasari; bought here and bought there—even if it was only a matter of drawings or little waxen models of the Medici tombs by Michelangelo. N 62

Despite all that the popes might do, antique statues continued to be coveted objects. In Rome, Cardinal Alessandro Farnese was the first to begin systematic excavation. In the Baths of Caracalla was found the *Farnese Bull*. Fifty years after the discovery of the *Laocoön* there were as many as 1,500 ancient statues above ground in Rome; the learned Aldovrandi described them and punctuated his descriptions with cries of delight. Those who possessed such treasures could enjoy a life of 'serene happiness'.

In the latter part of the sixteenth century, thanks to the economic trends of the day, more and more statues were coming into the hands of a few wealthy people. At the same time, Rome began to run out of supplies. The Grand Duke of Tuscany acquired the statue which from then on was known as the *Venus de Medici*. The d'Este family in 1572 carried off *Ilioneus Son of Niobe* to Ferrara. Meanwhile the Patriarch of *123* Aquileia, Giovanni Grimani, brought the *Praying Boy* (now in the Berlin Museums) from Rome to a palace on the Grand Canal. The supply of available antique statues was ultimately insufficient to meet the general demand.

Pictures now became the collector's prime concern; the masters of the Raphael style, which Lomazzo described in 1590 as exemplary, enjoyed a particular esteem. The connoisseur's horizon was no longer N 63 confined to his own city or his own landscape. Antonio de' Medici acquired in 1600 a triptych by Mantegna of Mantua while the Gonzagas, having come to the conclusion that the solitary work of Perugino which they possessed was not enough, had a second picture by this 'valent' huomo'—excellent man—sent to them from Umbria. The Florentines Andrea del Sarto and Fra Bartolommeo also enjoyed great favour in Mantua at this time.

The fact that a picture was situated in a church did not in the least deter really passionate art-lovers. Andrea del Sarto's altar painting of *The Transfiguration of The Virgin* passed from Cortona Cathedral into the possession of a private individual (now in the Palazzo Pitti in Florence). Raphael's *Deposition* was taken with the knowledge of the monks but to the indignation of the citizens from San Francesco in Perugia to the palace of a cardinal.

Sometimes an energetic ruling prince would bring pressure to bear on a subject. The Borgherini family, for instance, had to sell to the Grand Duke of Tuscany the series of the *Legend of Joseph* which had been

104 In the late sixteenth century, Mannerism led to the placing of a high value on the more abstruse works of previous ages. This Etruscan chimaera entered the Medici collections in 1555, and has remained in Florence ever since

painted by Andrea del Sarto in 1511 to decorate the marriage bed of an ancestor and which till then had been jealously guarded (now in the Palazzo Pitti in Florence). With demand so strong for works of the 'Golden Age', the forgers found plenty to do. Even at the home of Cardinal d'Este in Rome one could see drawings allegedly by Raphael which were simply copies of certain pictures of the master's by the skilful Fleming, Calvaert.

As the collections continued to grow, a place was also found for works with an anti-classical stamp. On the whole more tolerance was shown than at the beginning of the century. In Mantua, apart from the masterpieces of Italian painting already mentioned, the onyx vessel from the time of Caracalla was treasured as a relic of the Temple of Solomon, and ulti-

mately found its way to Brunswick. In Mantua one could also have seen a head painted by Dürer which a Gonzaga had personally acquired in Munich in 1591, as well as numerous Netherlandish paintings from all periods of the sixteenth century. The Medici in Florence accounted a panel by the early Netherlandish painter Gerard David among their most precious possessions, and placed the early *Etruscan Chimaera* in the Palazzo Vecchio shortly after it *104* had been dug up near Arezzo, and boasted of the Chinese lacquer work which they possessed. In Parma around 1600 Count Masi owned two pictures by Pieter Bruegel the Elder (now in the Galleria di Capodimonte, Naples).

Works of art began to multiply in the course of the sixteenth century and it gradually became possible to establish series of works with similar themes. From the earliest days of Humanism people liked to balance the twelve Christian Apostles with the sequence of the twelve ancient Roman emperors. Titian had to paint these again in 1537 for the Gonzagas, while

105 In the age of Mannerism collectors prized anti-classical group sculpture with contorted figures often arranged to form a single composite shape, as in Giovanni da Bologna's *Rape of the Sabine Woman*, of which a small replica in bronze is shown above

in Rome it was found possible in 1566 to dispatch to the Habsburgs the desired number of antique portrait busts.

Portraits of ancestors increased endlessly in the courts of many princes. The Gonzagas organized a special room around 1600 containing the 'most beautiful women in the world'. The strongest influence was however exerted by the 'viri illustrissimi' of the historian Paolo Giovio, Bishop of Como, in whose house on Lake Como there were gathered together several hundred portraits ranging from Aristotle to Leonardo da Vinci. Originals by Mantegna, Bellini, Raphael and Titian mingled with second-rate portraits, with completely idealized representations. When Giovio died in 1552, copyists were actually busy reproducing all the portraits in a standard size for the Florentine court.

The collection on Lake Como has long since disappeared, but the name 'Musaeum' which its founder had given to it has entered every language in the world. Until then a collection of pictures was given its collective name after the type of room in which it was housed, such as 'studiolo', 'camerino', 'anticamera' or simply 'guarderoba'. The humanist Giovo had revived an ancient Greek word which had been used in Pergamum and Alexandria as the name of a place of study. B 252

The growing practice of collecting in this systematic manner harmonized with the tendency of the artists to observe 'più di maniera che di natura'—style rather than nature. In Tintoretto's later work 'individual form and spatial depth resolved themselves into a calligraphic play of line'. The most N 64 famous group by Giovanni da Bologna was first conceived as an artistic idea and was only later given its name *The Rape of the Sabine Woman* (now in the Loggia dei Lanzi, Florence). While, however, *105* artists and sculptors treated the content of their work in any manner which their sovereign will might dictate, collectors, guided and supported by architects, arranged their possessions according to certain fixed formal principles. In the early part of the sixteenth century the popes in the Belvedere had placed important pieces of statuary next to one another and treated them as being of equal importance but the Court of Antiquities in the palace of Cardinal Valle ushered in a new phase. An engraving dated 1536 shows *106* it in its then unfinished state. As on the triumphal arches of late antiquity, which were decorated with statues and reliefs, so here sculpture and architecture combined in a complicated network of forms. The B 272 no longer existing Court of Antiquities on the first floor of the Palazzo Valle had a long and far-reaching influence. In Rome itself there is still evidence of this in the court of the Palazzo Maffei and the side of the Villa Medici that faces towards the garden. N 65

Around 1500 people had still respected the actual form in which a piece of antique sculpture came to light, but now began the great period of restoration. Marble was smoothed over, torsos were supplied with heads and limbs, and there was little hesitation in the fitting of missing parts. Only statues that were entire or apparently entire were to be used.

106, 107 Collectors who liked complex group statues often arranged their collections of antique sculpture on the same principle. Statues were now no longer simply displayed next to each other, but were placed in niches and incorporated in the general architectural layout. The courtyard of the Palazzo Valle-Capranica (above) and the back of the Medici villa in Rome (detail below) illustrate this trend

108 In the Uffizi, the most valuable items from the Medici collection were placed in the Tribuna and displayed there according to the taste of the time. By the early nineteenth century, as this detail of a painting shows, the style of presentation was already much freer

109 An autocratic attitude towards art was characteristic of the age of Mannerism, and this expressed itself in the restoration of antique works of art. Cellini incorporated fragments of a Roman statue of Apollo in this Ganymede

Whether among the public of the latter part of the sixteenth century there was any conscious enjoyment of the tensions arising between old and new parts seems rather doubtful.

N 66

Collectors of the late sixteenth century organized the interiors of their houses as they did their Courts of Antiquities. In Florentine houses around 1570 medium-sized pictures, bronze statuettes on pedestals and possibly also vessels and drawings were arranged in three rows, one on top of the other, and were grouped together in a complicated artificial system. This was the appearance presented by a number of halls built on a centrally symmetrical ground-plan and which were equipped with lantern windows, such as the main apartment of the villa of Giovio, the little 'Antiquario' of Cardinal Cesi in Rome, which has now been degraded to a wine store, and the 'Tribuna' in the top storey of the Uffizi, the State Chancery in Florence.

B 119

110, 111 The Mannerists' desire for energetic and nervous movement led to the construction of rooms that resembled long corridors. When Tintoretto painted *The Miracle of St Mark* (left), architects were designing galleries like the one in a former residence of the Gonzagas in Sabbioneta (below). Even though it has lost all the works of art it once contained, this gallery remains important because it was one of the first in this style

As the number of works of art in the possession of princes continued to multiply, people began to close in the open loggias with glass and to use them for the exhibition of statues and pictures. Thus there came into being in Italy promenading rooms of a kind that could have been seen on a smaller scale in French castles and palaces before 1500. In his palace at Fontainebleau Francis I planned a long and roomy 'galerie', as the French called it in those days, but apart from a few statues there were apparently no works of art there. In Florence and in Mantua about the middle of the sixteenth century, the Italian 'loggia' developed into the French 'galerie'. The Italian word, even today, only denotes a particular kind of room, whereas the word 'galleria', borrowed from the French, has become a synonym for an art collection. In a small forgotten residence of the Gonzagas at Sabbioneta, there has been preserved a gallery, now emptied, dating back to 1560, which received light from two sides. Its length, which had a strangely disquieting effect on those who entered it and seemed somehow to urge them forward, was in harmony with the vitality of the Tintoretto epoch and set the fashion. After the Tribuna of the Uffizi and the neighbouring rooms had been filled, the Grand Dukes of Tuscany also had the adjoining East Loggia covered with glass and thus made a 'Galleria delle Statue'. Later the West Loggia of the Uffizi was similarly treated, as was the short stretch that united the two. In Mantua there had been talk

111

B 337

110

112

from about 1570 onwards of a 'grande galleria', but building did not start till 1594. When about 1600 Scamozzi wrote his work on architectural theory, people had already had so much experience with the so-called 'galleries' and had learned so much about their use as places for hanging pictures that the author insisted on the necessity of a north light.

N 67
N 68

Northern Europe attained in the latter part of the sixteenth century the same stage of development as Italy. In the history of the cult of antiquity, a significant interlude took place in Augsburg and Munich. In the ageing metropolis of trade on the Lech the Fugger family had continued to rise. They controlled mining undertakings, were concerned with the trade with Venice and also with banking; now came the farming of the Spanish taxes. The Emperor had granted them the right to coin money and to bear the title of count. Little more than halfway through the century, Count Johann Jakob Fugger made something of a stir. Born in 1516, the son of Raimund Fugger, he added to his inherited collections, acquired old manuscripts and subsidized historical and antiquarian research. In 1563 Johann Jakob's debts had reached such a figure that he had to flee from Augsburg. He left the firm and looked about for buyers of his artistic treasures and rare books.

B 114

Count Hans Fugger, who was Johann Jakob's junior by some fifteen years, was a different and much more prudent person. He had enjoyed a diversified education and had serious artistic interests, but he combined all these with successful business activity. In good years Hans Fugger enjoyed an income of 240,000 guilders. On his table there were oysters from Venice, honey from Spain, and malmsey wine from Greece. He had parrots sent him from Antwerp and jewels from Peru. He bred falcons and, after the manner of princes, kept a court jester.

The third person in this affair was Duke Albert V, who resided in Munich and who had married the daughter of the Habsburg Emperor in Vienna. Her younger sisters had been married to reigning princes in Mantua, Ferrara and Florence. There were thus ties of kinship between the most important art centres in Italy and the court in Munich. The guiding principle of Albert V was to grace his Bavaria from both within and without. His love of art was equal to his appetite for pomp.

The fourth man was Jacopo de Strada, a humanist and lover of antiquity but also a capable agent, art dealer and general adventurer. In Mantua, where he was long active, Jacopo had acquired from the son of Giulio Romano several drawings by Raphael. In Rome he was well-known among art dealers and patrons and had promised Titian commissions from German princes. Titian in return for this painted Jacopo with some ancient coins before him and with a small copy of Praxiteles' *Pseliumene* in his hand, but Titian spoke of the 'doppiezza di questo galant'uomo' —the duplicity of this man of honour—who, he said, was severely overcharging the Germans.

VII
N 69

Their common interest in antiquities brought these four people together. Johann Jakob Fugger and Strada had known one another since 1545 and from Rome Strada acquired antique coins and statues for the passionate collector. When the insolvent merchant had to leave his native city, he found a new sphere of activity in Munich and became the ducal Hofkammerpräsident (President of the Exchequer), while Albert V took over his works of art. Johann Jakob Fugger was soon so firmly in the saddle in Munich that he was able to indulge his passion for antique art with the Duke's money. The merchant turned courtier introduced his old factotum Strada to Albert V and shortly after this the foundation stone of an 'Antiquarium'—a great collection of antique statues and busts—was laid. Strada obtained from Mantua sketches of the rooms in which collections were housed, while from Venice there came a drawing of the 'Antiquarium' of the Patriarch of Aquileia. The possessions of Johann Jakob Fugger were the nucleus of the Munich collection of antiquities. It was increased by a great number of purchases, many of them rash.

In Augsburg, meanwhile, Count Hans Fugger had decided to become a collector of antiquities himself; he despised the kind of thing that was going on in Munich. All he cared for was 'cose rare'. He was far from submitting passively to the middlemen in Venice. 'I believe', he says in a letter which he sent to the Rialto, 'that the Seleuco is a cast and "moderno" whatever Juan Sculptor may say'.

In 1567 a positive race began between the agents of Albert V and those of Hans Fugger. On 7 June of that year we find the first mention in the correspondence between the mother house in Augsburg and its Venetian depot, of an 'altfrenkisch Sepultura' (an antique sarcophagus). Right under the nose of Strada, who was then in Venice, Hans Fugger immediately arranged for the object to be bought for the high price of 250 ducats, and gave instructions that the disappointed agent should be left free to acquire the Loredan collection which came up for sale at the same time. 'I would be glad', wrote Hans Fugger to his agent, 'if you would make it plain to Strada that the antique sarcophagus belongs to you. Be firm in this matter and draw his attention to "das Loredanisch Studium". The principal [Albert V] understands nothing of these things.' Strada had no choice but to buy the Loredan collection for 7,000 ducats. The transport of the sarcophagus caused Hans Fugger a

112 The most famous sixteenth-century galleries still in use are those in the Uffizi in Florence. This painting by John Scarlett Davis shows the first gallery as it was in the early nineteenth century

degree of concern that might appear exaggerated to us today. He instructed his agents to be very cautious when moving it 'damit es nit unterwegs im Bairland uffgeholt werde'—so that it would not be intercepted on its journey through Bavaria. The sarcophagus arrived at last in Augsburg in good condition, the first example of Greek art in full flower to come to light in the sixteenth century. It is known as the *Fugger Sarcophagus* in the Vienna Museum, and dates

back to the fourth century BC. The place where it was found is today believed to be Silos on Cyprus.

In Rome Hans Fugger also acquired a statue of Venus. The antique statues in the house on the Weinmarkt were set up in a colonnade in the courtyard, in two vaulted rooms on the ground floor and in a larger banqueting-room on the main floor. A pupil of Titian painted the walls and ceilings which were accounted one of the sights of the town.

Meanwhile in Munich 'il Palazzo da metter le anticaglie', as Strada called it, had been completed. 'Sacrae Vetustati dedicatum' is the inscription over the inner side of the entrance gateway. Presumably it derives from some stock phrase of the Ingolstadt humanist circle of 1530. A traveller declared in 1611 that he had never seen so many antiquities 'even in Rome and Florence themselves'. Similar comments are recorded right up to the time of J. J. Winckelmann, the eighteenth-century art historian.

In spite of the changes made by Albert V's successors and the restoration carried out in 1950, and in spite of the fact that all the best items have been given to the Glyptothek, Albert V's 'Antiquarium' in Munich remains an invaluable example of the sixteenth-century collection. We can no longer grasp the system of arrangement, probably based on portraits of emperors and 'Viri illustres'; and we must overlook the fact that heads (genuine, imitations and forgeries) brought from the south were attached to busts made in Munich. The whole of the 'Antiquarium' presents a creation that has no equal today. In regard to the general architectural layout the halls in the palaces of the Gonzagas and in the Vatican and the Escorial may have played the role of godparents. In the manner in which the statues fitted into the sharp and often interrupted relief of the wall system, the Munich 'Antiquarium' followed the ideas

N 70 of collectors in Rome, Florence and Venice.

As in Italy collectors in the middle and latter half of the sixteenth century spared no pains to get hold of paintings by Perugino, Raphael, Andrea del Sarto and Fra Bartolommeo, so north of the Alps the search began for native artists who were their contemporaries. In Bavaria and Austria it was Dürer who was all the rage, in Switzerland Holbein and in northern Germany Cranach, while in the Netherlands it was Quentin Massys. Earnest Christians, both Catholic and Protestant, were no doubt influenced amongst other things by the fact that they could not hope for truly pious devotional pictures from living artists. This was a view to which Philip II and the Italian critic Gilio both subscribed. It was N 71 also expressed by Hans Fugger in regard to an altarpiece of his own day which he considered too bold ('zu frech'). The artist, he complained, was only concerned with displaying his skill. Pious Protestants had no misgivings about hanging pictures of the

113 The 'Antiquarium' of the Wittelsbach Residenz in Munich provides a splendid example of the overall appearance of a late sixteenth-century gallery of antiquities. The most valuable sculpture was transferred to the Glyptothek in 1830

114 The return to Raphael and his contemporaries, which took place in Italy during the second half of the sixteenth century, was paralleled north of the Alps by a return to Dürer, Cranach (whose *Venus* is shown right), Massys and other early sixteenth-century masters

99

Virgin from Cranach's early Catholic period in their private chapels.

The general popularity of the masters of the early sixteenth century embraced not only devotional pictures, but also portraits and every other kind of work down to the most modest sketch. This interest caused imitations, variations and forgeries to flourish which posterity has often experienced much difficulty in distinguishing. The *Crucifixion* in the Dresden Gallery was believed as recently as 1900 to be one of Dürer's major works; at an even later date the *Virgin and Child (The Madonna with the Iris)* from the Cook collection in Richmond, which today bears the caption 'Style of Dürer' in the National Gallery in London, was believed to be an original work of the master's. It was in fact painted around 1580. Both the above pictures were to be found as late as 1820 in Vienna, where around 1600 the demand for works by Dürer was particularly lively. Many Dürer experts profess to recognize the master's brush-stroke in the case of the *Virgin and Child with St Anne* in the Metropolitan Museum, New York, while others see

in it the affected character of the archaicizing trend around 1600. Much as in the Netherlands fake Bosch pictures were in circulation, so from Mainz to Vienna there was a regular trade in painted panels which professed to come from Dürer's own hand. The work of art was now only one among many kinds of merchandise and was the subject, whether forged or genuine, of business transactions.

In Germany about the middle of the sixteenth century, numerous small collections came into being. In Nuremberg Willibald Imhoff stood out as a distinguished collector. He was given the name of Willibald after his grandfather, the famous Pirckheimer. Imhoff served his apprenticeship in Lyons and Antwerp, knew Spain, having travelled there on business, and enriched his firm by trade in saffron. His house was the favourite visiting-place of princes in Nuremberg. In 1573 he started to make a sort of catalogue of the works of art in his possession. From this record we know that in many of the great museums from Vienna to New York there are early German paintings which hung in his house four hundred years ago. Imhoff also compiled a 'Kunstbuch Albrecht Dürers' (now in the Albertina in Vienna), a volume into which etchings and drawings, among them the *Arion*, have been stuck. After his death his heirs, who were excellent businessmen, sold all his possessions. This was also the occasion for some forgery, such as the addition of the Dürer monogram.

With Imhoff, the Nuremberg collector of Dürer, one might well compare Basilius Amerbach, the admirer of Holbein whose place of business was Basle. He began his purchases so soon after the Basle period of the great Swabian that his determined efforts to acquire the master's works were highly successful. Amerbach even managed to bring back to Basle works of Holbein that had gone abroad. In 1570 he was the owner of 29 paintings and 1,068 drawings, which he later arranged according to their schools and dates. As conditions in Switzerland continued to be politically and economically calm, the 'Amerbach Cabinet' remained in the place where it had first been created and ultimately became the nucleus of the city's Kunstmuseum.

115 Paintings by Dürer were particularly in demand. This naturally resulted in numerous copies and fakes, among them this *Crucifixion*

V Dürer's *Madonna of the Rose Garlands* was bought by the Habsburgs from the Church of San Bartolommeo in Venice. Unfortunately it is not in a good state of preservation

Towards the end of the sixteenth century the efforts of various princes to obtain works of Dürer and his contemporaries increased in intensity. Not only was this the death knell for collectors who were mere commoners, but also a threat to town halls, hospitals and churches of both Catholics and Protestants. In 1588 the Elector of Saxony acquired seven little panels by Dürer which had found their way into Cranach's studio from a church in Wittenberg. The Habsburgs got possession of Dürer's *Adoration of the Magi* from a Saxon church (the picture is now in the Uffizi), but thanks to an adviser, whose identity is unknown, Dürer's great rival Grünewald also came within the Emperor's field of vision. In the Vienna archives is a draft of some written instructions dated 1597 regarding the negotiations for the purchase of a painted panel which had been 'made with great art by a high ranking master'. Although the efforts by the Habsburgs to obtain the altarpiece of the Antonite Monastery in Isenheim (now in the Colmar Museum) remained unsuccessful, one of the Wittelsbachs of this time, William V of Bavaria, managed to gain possession of two of the works of the greatest pictorial genius of Dürer's age, despite the fact that the master's name was unknown to him. The *Mocking of Christ*, which ultimately reached Munich and is today in the Pinakothek, probably came from a church in Aschaffenburg. Grünewald's *Small Crucifixion*, too, must once have been situated somewhere in the Rhineland. In the early seventeenth century an engraving was made which shows it to have been the property of William V of Bavaria. Some decades later Joachim von Sandrart, the artists' biographer, had expressed his admiration for it, after which the picture disappeared for more than two hundred and fifty years. In 1922 it turned up quite by chance among some old lumber in a private house in the Ruhr district. Today Grünewald's *Small Crucifixion* is the outstanding example of German art in XVI America; it is in the National Gallery, Washington.

VI Titian painted the portrait of Jacopo de Strada in 1566. This Italian art dealer exercised considerable influence on the collecting activities of German princes towards the end of the sixteenth century. He not only supervised existing galleries but also gave his advice on the construction of new ones. It was also in 1566 that Tintoretto painted Jacopo's son, Ottavio, as a companion-piece to Titian's portrait

It is necessary to mention briefly the German 'Kunstkammer' (cabinet of curiosities), an expression that conjures up the image of a 'Faustian' universality in collections, something peculiar to that sombrely reflective age, the late sixteenth century. At the time when Shakespeare was writing *Hamlet*, his contemporaries were assembling all kinds of objects in a 'Theatrum mundi'. Here there were early scientific and pre-scientific stirrings, and 'with a rare appreciation of spiritual values an attempt was made to catalogue the whole field of knowledge'. The B 19 'Kunstkammer', however, also served as an arsenal

116 A particularly charming painting in the style of Dürer is the *Virgin and Child*, fomerly in the Cook Collection in Richmond, England. Its authenticity was questioned by Friedländer in 1906 and Glück in 1909. Pictures of this kind were generally painted around 1600 in Prague, Vienna and Munich

of alchemy and housed materials with magical powers: the 'bezoars' which were the gall-stones of camels and were reputed to banish melancholy; adders' tongues; the teeth of fossilized sharks, used to *118* detect poisons; and 'unicorn', whose origin from the walrus was still unknown and which was supposed to have the power of transmuting harmful materials. In these surroundings the belief in the magic power of precious stones, which had come down from late antiquity, was still alive. One of the Habsburgs saw in his crystals revelations of the power of the Almighty, even the reflection of Godhead itself. In certain unusual older works of art, the *Gemma Augustea* for *101* instance, the key to secret astronomical knowledge was discovered. As in the works of El Greco, an air of magic infused the whole.

A somewhat more restricted application of the word 'Kunstkammer' has been resorted to by certain art-historians to denote special kinds of small

118 This credence vessel from the Emperor's Kunst-kammer in Prague owes its strange appearance to the use of fossilized sharks'-teeth

117 Collections which combined 'the wonders of nature and art' were in keeping with the spirit of the late sixteenth century. Frans Francken the Younger gives us glimpses of such 'Kunstkammern' or 'chambres de merveilles' (detail)

119 Giuseppe Arcimboldo's peculiar heads proved very popular among contemporary collectors. In *The Allegory of Fire* (right) the chain of the Order of the Golden Fleece indicates that this is probably a portrait of one of the Habsburgs. Arcimboldo became court painter to the Emperor and was elevated to the peerage

works of art which are called 'Kunstkammerstücke'. A characteristic example of this special category of the applied arts in the sixteenth century may be seen in the Metropolitan Museum in New York. It is a miniature memorial grave slab for the Archbishop of Mainz, Daniel Brendel of Hohenheim, who died in 1582. Similar pieces are to be found in large numbers in the Victoria and Albert Museum and the Louvre, to take two further examples. It has sometimes been said that a certain hankering after the bizarre, evident in these cabinets of art and among certain artists of the time, represents a primitive German trait, but this contrast between Germany and the south should not be overstressed. Arcimboldo, who came from northern Italy, far surpassed the most fantastic

creations of Bruegel with the heads which he built up out of roots and plants and other abstruse constructions. The 'Galleria della Mostra' in the castle at Mantua contained both works of art and 'rarità naturali', while the ancient *Etruscan Chimaera* received a place of honour in the 'Guardarobe' of the Palazzo Vecchio and a high value was placed on examples of pre-Columbian art both in Florence and Rome. As late as 1670 an English traveller saw in the Tribuna of the Uffizi alleged results of transformations by alchemy and monstrous 'products of nature' alongside the paintings of the great masters.

Among the most important of these cabinets of art was the one in Vienna. Many of the works already described found their way to that city when Charles V

119

104

N 72

120 The late sixteenth-century interest in the unusual and the exotic resulted in a reappraisal of many of the items sent back from America by Cortez. Among them was this feather headdress which once belonged to Montezuma, the last Emperor of Mexico

moved to San Yuste and the House of Habsburg split into two separate lines. In Vienna, where the word 'Kunstkammer' seems to have been coined in 1555, a number of Roman finds and medallions were added to the inherited treasures. The Grand Duke of Florence made gifts of contemporary statuettes. After the death of Ferdinand in 1564 the various possessions were divided among his sons. Archduke Charles of Styria (founder of the Lipizza breeding stables, from which come the horses of the Spanish Riding School in Vienna) received a valuable share which he housed in a long hall in his castle in Graz and which became the heart of his 'Kunstkammer'. Ferdinand II, the reigning archduke in Tyrol, kept his inheritance in the castle at Innsbruck until 1580 and afterwards in the neighbouring castle of Ambras. His morganatic marriage with the rich Augsburg woman, Philippine Welser, the first example of a sentimental misalliance in the House of Habsburg, put him in a position to make purchases on a grandiose scale.

Magnificent armour from the days of Charles V, in particular, pieces that had belonged to generals and famous warriors, formed in Ambras a kind of knightly pantheon. The Archduke no doubt set a special value on those items that had come down to him from the collection of his great-aunt, the Regent Margaret in Malines—her portrait bust by Meit for instance (now in the Bayerisches National-museum, Munich). In Ambras there were antique pieces of statuary, pre-Columbian curiosities, medieval manuscripts, Dürer's 'Kunstbuch' from the house of Imhoff and the famous Cellini salt-cellar, rich in allegorical allusions. Archduke Ferdinand may have been moved to start a collection of miniature portraits by Giovio's treatise on the Como 'Musaeum', a dissertation which the author had dedicated to Ferdinand's father in 1551. Of these portraits, to-day housed in Vienna, 53 are copies from Giovio's series; in many other cases Ferdinand himself obtained models to be worked from. An imperial ambassador who was travelling to Russia was instructed to obtain portraits of the Russian tsars, but whereas Protestant princes possessed portrait series in which Luther and Zwingli, or Coligny and Egmont, held places of honour, Ferdinand of the Tyrol would suffer no heretics. The names of the persons portrayed were painted in gold, silver or yellow, according to the importance ascribed to them. The humanist Erasmus had to be satisfied with silver. Dürer's name, however, shone forth in gold letters, while Flemish painters such as Floris ranked somewhat lower.

In Munich the 'Kunstkammer' of the Wittelsbachs acquired its own building (later the mint), some years before the 'Antiquarium' was erected. As has recently been shown, it was modelled on the Vienna Stallburg where Emperor Ferdinand had housed his collections. Important works of art that it contained before 1600 can be found today in considerable numbers in the Bayerisches Nationalmuseum, Munich—for instance, Multscher's *Model of a Tomb for Louis the Bearded*, Peter Vischer's *Branch-Breaker* and the *Minne Casket* from the Upper Rhine dating back to the thirteenth century. Among the Wittelsbachs there was a particularly keen interest in medieval manuscripts which were now rapidly giving place to printed books in churches and monasteries. Duke Albert V of Bavaria acquired a papyrus codex dating back to the tenth century from the archbishopric of Ravenna and his successor acquired a late Carolingian prayer-book.

In Augsburg, that flourishing centre of every form of applied art, Philip Hainhofer was the most influential patron of all activities connected with the 'Kunstkammer' movement around 1600. Although a Protestant, he had studied in the universities of Padua and Siena and having no fortune of his own worked as a political correspondent for several courts. He combined with this the work of an agent and art dealer and owned some valuable drawings, including one by Jan van Eyck (now in the library at Wolfenbüttel). From Dutch merchants who came to the Frankfurt fair, Hainhofer obtained Chinese porcelain bowls, and besides these he owned a store of various objets d'art and miniatures. The adroit Augsburger specialized in display cabinets which found purchasers not only in Germany but in Sweden and Italy. These fine pieces of furniture, which in Hainhofer's own words inspired pleasant thoughts, might be called 'chambers of art' on a small scale; they contained in drawers and secret compartments, musical instruments and handicraft tools, playing cards, surgical instruments, a prayer-book, a home pharmacy, a compass, a musical clock, and some small cooking utensils.

N 74

In southwest Germany the Stuttgart 'Kunstkammer' enjoyed particular fame. Its creator, Frederick I of Württemberg, visited Florence shortly before 1600 and saw the studio of Giovanni da Bologna. He was familiar with collectors in Holland and knew England. The Stuttgart 'Kunstkammer' contained the finds which had come to light during the first systematic excavation north of the Alps, in the Roman fort near Benningen. From the Württemberg 'Kunstkammer' the Stuttgart Landesmuseum still preserves a late Gothic set of cards and a Chinese porcelain vase with a silver-gilt mount. Not far from Stuttgart, in Schloss Neuenstein, which belongs to Prince Hohenlohe, there still remain the complete contents of an old 'Kunstkammer'.

121

The Dresden 'Kunstkammer' of the House of Wettin, the leading Protestant power within the Empire, was founded in 1560 and could claim to be the oldest in existence after the imperial 'Kunstkammer' itself. It entirely resembled those in south Germany. Statuettes with an affectation of antiquity, ranging from a bronze copy of the *Marcus Aurelius* which had been made for Piero de' Medici in 1460 to the *Venus and Faun* group by Giovanni da Bologna, mingled with Chinese Ming porcelain and all sorts of other attractive objects.

N 75

In 1591 an inventory of the Hohenzollern 'Kunstkammer' was begun in Berlin, but unfortunately has been lost. Further to the north the Duke of Pomerania, a pious Protestant, was also active as a collector. He knew all the cabinets of art in Vienna and Munich and in 1596 visited the 'Musaeum' on Lake Como. From Hainhofer he acquired a particularly splendid display cabinet (now in the Berlin Museums). Michelangelo and Aristotle had a place in his various portrait series, as did Spanish conquistadors and Roman popes. He kept his treasures in his summer house, built after 1612 on the border of Stettin. One description runs: 'Your serene Highness

121 Prince Frederick of Württemberg had a base made for this Chinese porcelain bowl in about 1600

dined once with princes and served up nothing but antique and foreign plate, made of unicorn, rhinoceros, crystal, jasper, mother of pearl, porcelain and other such materials, to the astonishment of your guests.'

Emperor Rudolph II comes at the end of this epoch. When speaking of his enormously rich collection he simply referred to it as his 'Kunstkammer'; it included a number of important paintings that were kept in special galleries. Rudolph II was a few years younger than El Greco and Cervantes; he died in 1612, four years before Shakespeare. From his eleventh to his nineteenth year this German Habsburg prince was brought up at the court of his kinsman Philip II. He was younger than twenty-five when he ascended the throne and chose Prague as his place of residence. An inborn melancholy afflicted him, and a fear of human society often reached pathological proportions. 'Sono certo del diavolo' (I am assuredly the devil's), the servants heard him cry. It often happened that even foreign ambassadors could get a sight of the Emperor only if they were disguised as grooms. He was happiest when consorting with his valets, painters with whom he happened to be familiar and his concubines (among these was the daughter of Jacopo de Strada, who had died in 1588 in Prague as imperial antiquarian).

B 314

Rudolph II won the deepest respect of his contemporaries as an art collector; his knowledge was almost overpowering. An alleged Dürer which had been sent from Besançon was immediately recognized by him as a fake; if pictures arrived in a damaged state, it was he himself who directed how they should be repaired. When two still-lifes by contemporary Flemish painters were presented at Prague as a gift, he astonished his courtiers by studying them for an hour and a half, without so much as moving. Sometimes Rudolph would throw open one of the great rooms of his palace to art dealers.

122

122 Thanks to the efforts of Rudolph II, Prague became an important art centre and attracted artists and craftsmen from all over Europe. From time to time the Emperor allowed art dealers to carry on their trade in the Wenceslas Hall of his palace (detail)

When Adriaen de Vries glorified him as the protector of the arts on a relief, which today is in the Royal Collection in Windsor Castle, he was surely saying no more than the truth.

The Emperor sat in Prague like a spider in its web; he knew the histories of all the pictures and statues in which he was interested and waited for the opportune moment. He received from Nuremberg Dürer's *Adoration of the Trinity*, which he had 'striven very hard' to obtain and which is now in the Vienna Gallery. The Duke of Ferrara presented the Emperor with the *Ilioneus Son of Niobe*. The famous *Bed of* 123 *Polycletus*, of which there is only one copy, executed in the early sixteenth century, made its way from N 76 central Italy to Prague. Rudolph II also paid the enormous sum of 12,000 ducats for the *Gemma* 101 *Augustea* which shortly before had been stolen from the King of France. From the church of San Bartolomeo in Venice he acquired Dürer's *Madonna of the Rose Garlands*, declaring at the time that he would V pay whatever was asked for it. Strong men had to carry this altarpiece the whole way to Prague, where it is now in the National Gallery. From the heirs of the Spaniard Granvella, Rudolf acquired important works of art, including *The Martyrdom of the Ten Thousand Christians* by Dürer, pictures by Titian and a bronze bust of Charles V; the Emperor had a portrait

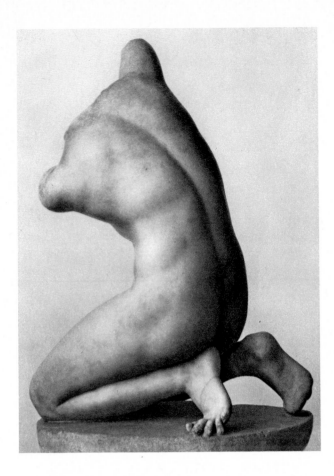

1,500 ducats. The pictures are today in public galleries in Berlin, Rome and Vienna.

From his castle in Prague the Emperor also looked towards the Netherlands. From there he received early ecclesiastical pictures of the kind that were prized by Philip II, but also such novel works as Bruegel's *The Land of Cockayne* (now in the Munich Pinakothek) and, by the same artist, *The Tower of Babel, The Massacre of the Innocents, The Conversion of Saul* and probably also *The Peasant Dance*. These four pictures are now in the Vienna Gallery.

124 Rudolph II managed to acquire Correggio's series of paintings, *The Loves of Jupiter*, which had once belonged to Charles V. *Jupiter and Io* (below) is one of these (see Ill. 130)

123 Rudolph II was among the most successful and perceptive collectors of all time. He acquired an enormous number of antique pieces including this famous statue of Ilioneus

126 bust of himself made by one of his court artists as a companion piece to this work. From Augsburg Hainhofer sent him two small wooden portrait busts of a Burgundian courtier and his wife, a work by Meit (presented by a member of the Rothschild family to the British Museum in 1900). On the other hand, he failed to persuade the Fugger family to part with N 77 the *Fugger Sarcophagus*.

Rudolph was acquainted, from his Madrid days, with Correggio's *The Loves of Jupiter*, which in some inexplicable manner had disappeared from the apartments of the King of Spain. After negotiations which went on for years, the Emperor was able to bring back into Habsburg possession all four pictures, *124* namely *Leda, Danaë, Io* and *Ganymede*, for a total of

125 Rudolph II shared his ancestors' predilection for the work of Venetian artists; he greatly admired Tintoretto and purchased several of his major works, including *The Origin of the Milky Way*. In the course of its travels the lower portion of the painting was lost

N 78 In 1602 or thereabouts the painter and artists' biographer Karel van Mander, whose home was in Haarlem, was given the opportunity of seeing the Emperor's works of art. He saw both the new gallery 'where the Germans and Netherlanders are hung' and an older gallery which probably contained chiefly Italian works. Van Mander did not hesitate to speak of the Emperor as 'the greatest art-lover of our time'. This estimate is confirmed by a dispatch from the Ambassador of Ferrara. When Rudolph received from northern Italy the picture of a *Satyr with Nymph*, he gazed at it for a long time and then said that he would very much like another work by the same artist, 'whether it showed figures nude or clothed and whether it was religious or profane'. The Emperor valued a work of art for its own sake without paying any attention to the content. In the memory of posterity Rudolph II lives on as one of the greatest art collectors of all time.

The Age of Baroque

THE CENTURY OF THE Thirty Years War brought an unparalleled increase of wealth and influence to the sea powers of Holland and England, while Spain was already preparing to abdicate her position in the grand manner. France, under Louis XIV, acquired a marginal strip of the Spanish Netherlands and, in conjunction with the new power of Protestant Sweden, prevented the Habsburgs in central Europe from tipping the political balance in their own favour. Both Amsterdam and Stockholm now enter our field of vision. In the early eighteenth century the stage widens again. After the victories over the Turks, Vienna came to the fore as the metropolis of a semi-eastern military state, while in eastern Germany, Dresden and Berlin became the residences of ambitious royal houses eagerly striving for power. In the marshy estuary of the Neva, St Petersburg had been spreading in feverish growth since 1703, fed by the immeasurable forces latent in the huge Russian empire. Yet in those places where the strongest battalions stood, there was no corresponding immediate flowering of culture. Politically impotent, Italy remained a great power in art alone. The dome of St Peter's was imitated both within and without the Catholic world: for instance, in St Paul's Cathedral in London, in the Frauenkirche in Dresden and in the churches of St Petersburg. It was the Italians who laid the foundations of Baroque painting which flourished all over Europe. The spiritualizing tendency of the late sixteenth century, which found its culmination in Tintoretto and El Greco, was followed around 1600 by Caravaggio's harsh naturalism. He represented evangelists and saints as coarse people from the suburbs of Milan and Rome. In his religious pictures the direction of light helps to bring out the plastic modelling of men and objects. The colours reveal the particular character of the skin of a face, or of a piece of clothing or furniture. The paintings of the High Baroque fused Caravaggio's realism with the form of the High Renaissance; and as Peter Meyer says, 'in this process the divine was represented as a natural summit of reality.' Masters, or, to be more exact, schools of painting, made use of tradition in various ways. Titian and, indeed, all that diffuseness of the pictorial image that characterized Venetian art, was an ideal education not only for the painters of northern Italy, but also for Rubens and van Dyck. Tuscan clarity, with its greater insistence on precision of line, found imitators in Bologna and also among certain French and Spanish painters. The collectors distributed their favours in a similar way.

Maximilian of Bavaria was one of the foremost collectors of this period. In the 'Kunstkammer' of the Wittelsbachs previously mentioned, a number of early German paintings had been gathered together during the second half of the sixteenth century; for instance Altdorfer's *The Battle of Alexander on the Issus River* and Dürer's *Lucrezia* (both now in the Munich Pinakothek, as are all the paintings mentioned below where not otherwise stated). Maximilian had travelled through Italy in 1593 and resolved to group the most valuable pictures of his old 'Kunstkammer' together with newly acquired works in a long room of his palace. This room, which has since fallen victim to rebuilding, was in fact a 'Galleria' after the Italian fashion. Completed in 1612, it included a north light, according to the latest Italian ideas. Maximilian owned a number of Italian paintings, among them one by Raphael which was destroyed by fire during the eighteenth century, and several works by contemporary painters. For his country seat at Altschleissheim, four hunting pictures by Rubens were commissioned in 1617, but the Elector's real preference was for the early Germans, above all Dürer. He made no efforts to acquire Grünewald's *Isenheim Altarpiece* when he learnt that it was not a work of Dürer's; he acquired Cranach pictures from time to time only, whereas he eagerly sought altars by the Master of Messkirch and paintings by

126 The Thirty Years War gave ample opportunity for the plunder of works of art. In 1648 the Swedes took back with them from Prague a large part of the Imperial collection. Among the numerous items was this bronze portrait bust of its founder, Rudolph II

Aldegrever, whose style he had doubtless come to know through the study of the artist's engravings. When the occasion arose, Maximilian was ready to open his purse wide and after the outbreak of the Thirty Years War used his position as head of the Catholic League to satisfy his collector's appetite.

Maximilian was fully informed of Rudolph II's failure to purchase certain works of art, and he prided himself on being more successful. The Nuremberg authorities told Maximilian that Dürer's *Paumgartner Altarpiece*, which the Emperor had already tried in vain to purchase, was not in fact a genuine Dürer at all. But he was not put off by such subterfuges and at length acquired the work. He also acquired from the Tucher family in Nuremberg the *Virgin and Child with St Anne*, a picture believed in the nineteenth

century (when it travelled from Munich to Russia) to be the work of a pupil of Dürer. It has been among the most precious treasures of the Metropolitan Museum in New York since 1913. For the early *Lamentation* Maximilian paid the Imhoff family 1,000 guilders, apparently ten times the sum that Willibald Imhoff had had to pay for the panel. When Dürer's *Dominican Altarpiece* (subsequently destroyed by fire) arrived in Munich from Frankfurt, Maximilian, with typical collector's pride, wanted to know what princes had endeavoured to obtain this work before him and what they had offered. When there was any doubt as to the merits of a picture, the Elector insisted on judging the matter himself, declaring that it was the same with pictures as with horses; you can't buy them without actually seeing them. When a *Martyrdom of St Lawrence* was sent from the Rhineland he returned it, saying that neither he nor other experts recognized it as being from Dürer's hand nor in his manner of composition, although it was the work of a good Old Master. On the other hand Maximilian made the most determined efforts to acquire the centre panel of the altarpiece from Maria Lysskirche in Cologne, with the support of his brother Ferdinand, who was Archbishop there. There was some reluctance to allow the picture to leave the church, and Maximilian suggested that, until a copy of the picture was available, the wings should be closed so that nobody would notice that anything had been removed. As compensation, the people of Cologne were offered an altarpiece in the Italian manner. In the correspondence of Maximilian's brother it is stated that such a picture would take less time to complete than a carefully executed copy. Thus the authorities of the Catholic Church and the Elector of Bavaria, the head of the Catholic party in the Empire, made common cause in the midst of the great war of religions to remove an altarpiece from a place of divine worship to the gallery of a secular prince.

When, during the course of the fighting, the Catholic League moved forward into Franconia and central Germany, Maximilian of Bavaria made his greatest scoop. He notified the council of the independent Protestant city of Nuremberg that he set great store on Dürer's *Apostles* and that a refusal of his request would be treated as an act of great disrespect. These words admitted of no misunderstanding and the *Palladium of Nuremberg*, which Dürer himself had bequeathed to the town hall, was transferred to Munich. The troops however were ordered not to enter Nuremberg territory. In Munich Maximilian ordered the offending titles with their references to the word of God to be sawn off. Otherwise he was not worried by the acquisition of a work in which Dürer, shortly before his death, had expressed his belief in Protestant doctrine. The high value he set upon the painting simply as a work of art outweighed all other considerations.

In 1627 the Bavarian Elector gave precise instructions to his troops as they moved northwards, telling them to enquire where old paintings, particularly by Dürer, were to be found in Brandenburg and Lower Saxony. For the benefit of the inexpert, an elaborate description was given of Dürer's manner of writing his initials, and it was made known that a *Last Supper* said to be in a house in Prenzlau, north of Berlin, was specially desired. 'A request by officers of the Imperial Army is not likely to be refused': these words occur in a letter of 24 December 1627 to General Aldringer. To prevent their being damaged, captured paintings were to be carried by strong men, but, if in enemy territory, the roads were first to be carefully reconnoitered and transport was to be accompanied by 'sundry musketeers'. Dürer's *Lamentation* (now in the Munich Pinakothek) arrived from Wittenberg, as did Burgkmair's *St Sebastian Altarpiece* (now in the Nuremberg Museum).

The fortunes of war, however, did not remain permanently favourable to the Roman Church. Almost before anyone was aware of it, Swedish armies under King Gustavus Adolphus appeared on the Middle Rhine and in Bavaria, and for a time even Munich itself was occupied. Whereas Maximilian, fastidious connoisseur that he was, would seek out this or that work of art in order to make his 'Galleria' more complete, the Swedes were less eclectic. They found justification for their actions in the Biblical command to the Israelites to despoil those that despised Jehovah. To the northern devotees of the pure word of God, who looked upon themselves as the chosen people, the Papists on the Rhine and in Bavaria were unbelievers.

As the Swedes approached, the Elector Maximilian just had time to hide away the greater part of the paintings of his 'Kammer-Galleria' in a safe place outside Munich. The old 'Kunstkammer', however, fell into the conqueror's hands. A German partisan of Gustavus Adolphus, the Duke of Sachsen-Weimar, looked it over and understood something of what he saw. Maximilian protested that he allowed much to be plundered which even the King of Sweden refrained from taking. The Munich booty of the Weimar prince has been preserved for us in Gotha. Here today are paintings by Amberger and Beham, statuettes by Meit and the fruit of Jacopo de Strada's life work, the long sequence of his manuscripts on coins. When the Swedes left Bavaria Maximilian's troops contrived to recapture some of the booty, including Burgkmair's *St John Altarpiece* (now in the Munich Pinakothek).

127 Christina of Sweden, daughter of Gustavus Adolphus, came into possession of the Habsburg collection. When she renounced the throne and was converted to Catholicism, she took the most valuable items in the collection with her to Rome

In Bamberg and Würzburg, in the castle of Aschaffenburg and in Mainz itself the Swedes captured further rich booty. One of their transport ships sank in the Baltic with three Grünewald altarpieces from Mainz Cathedral. At the very last moment, shortly before the armistice came into force, the Swedish general Königsmark scored a remarkable success. While besieging Prague he captured a part of the contents of the imperial Habsburg picture gallery that had not been rushed off to Vienna. Not until the time of Napoleon were works of art of comparable value captured in war.

The victorious Swedes clearly knew how to value the rewards of their success in arms. The works of art from Prague, accompanied by their inventories and custodians, were stored in the fortress of Dömitz and thereafter in the harbour town of Wismar. Hardly 127 was the winter over when Queen Christina, who had followed her father onto the throne, immediately ordered the commandant to put everything in a strong ship and to send it to her.

It will be remembered that in the year 146 BC the Romans carried away many pieces of Greek sculpture from the temples of Corinth, and at that time began the Hellenizing of Rome and the identification of native deities with Zeus, Hera and Apollo. Around 1650 the contrast between 'the barbarians of the north' and the inhabitants of the civilized districts between the Main and the Alps was hardly less than that between the Romans and the Greeks in the second century BC. The homeland of Gustavus Adolphus was contemptuously referred to in Germany as

128 This reliquary, dating from the late classical period, with later additions, was taken by the Swedes from Bamberg to Stockholm

'the land with ten stone houses, one religion and one physician'. There existed only a single picture in the castle of Stockholm when the Swedes began to take part in the great war; a few years later, a collection of art treasures had been gathered here that surpassed any other north of the Alps.

In addition to late antique and early medieval manuscripts, among them the *Codex Argenteus* captured from Prague, containing Bishop Wulfila's West Gothic translation of the Bible, dating back to the fourth century (now in the university library in Uppsala), there were 'sacred papistical objects', set with jewels, from south German cathedrals. From Bamberg, presumably, there came the reliquary already mentioned which 128 obtained its final form in Goslar in the twelfth century. In Würzburg the Swedes had captured the skull-reliquary of St Elisabeth of Thuringia which had been made in 1236 from a chalice, and the crown of the Hohenstaufen Emperor Frederick II. In Aschaffenburg the remainder of the sacred treasure of Halle, belonging to Cardinal Albert, had fallen into Swedish hands, including a standing reliquary cross of the early fifteenth century (all these objects are now in the Historical Museum in Stockholm). N 80

The Swedes probably appreciated the numerous paintings of the early German school more than any other works. The churches of Stockholm still possessed Late Gothic altars from Lübeck, and everybody knew the great *St George* group by Bernt Notke. The Grünewald altarpieces from Mainz, however, which owed so much to medieval art, could not be used in Protestant churches. Since people were willing to go to the labour of transporting them we can argue that there was a certain amount of appreciation on grounds of artistic merit alone. In the National Museum in Stockholm a number of excellent early German paintings have been preserved, among them Ruprecht Heller's *Battle of Pavia*, an authentic representation of the important victory of Emperor Charles V over Francis I of France. The elder Holbein's *Fountain of Life*, part of the Munich booty, later travelled from Stockholm to the Lisbon Museum. A curious fate befell the *Entombment* by the Bavarian pupil of Altdorfer, Hans Muelich. This panel was previously in the Munich 'Kunstkammer', and therefore had already been withdrawn from religious usage. Although of 'papist' origin, it obviously B 100 did not offend the susceptibilities of a pious Swedish Protestant who obtained it from the collection of Queen Christina. Ultimately it was incorporated into his own memorial tablet in the church at Solna where it still remains. N 81

When the opportunity occurred, the Wittelsbachs bought back from the descendants of Swedish officers panels that had been captured from Munich in 1632. Among these is the *Story of Lucrezia* by the

Augsburg painter Jörg Breu (now in the Munich Pinakothek).

The thirty panels, mostly early German, taken from the Bavarian Elector, proved not altogether repugnant to Swedish tastes. The 425 paintings of different schools from Prague were not appreciated to such an extent. The chief works by Dürer in the collection of Rudolph II had been tranferred to Vienna just in time; only *Adam* and *Eve* represented the art of the great Nuremberg painter at Queen Christina's court. Important works of Netherlandish artists of the middle and late sixteenth century now graced the castle in Stockholm, among them Bruegel's *The Land of Cockayne* (now in the Munich Pinakothek) and the relief by Adriaen de Vries of *Rudolph II as Protector of the Arts* (now in Windsor Castle).

Among the Prague pictures, the masterpieces of the great Italians held a dominating position: for instance several Madonnas by Raphael, among them in all probability the two famous *Cowper Madonnas* (now in the National Gallery in Washington) and two of *The Loves of Jupiter* by Correggio which had already passed through many hands and could not be got away to Vienna in time: namely the *Danaë* (now in the Borghese Gallery, Rome) and the *Leda* (now in the Berlin Museums). Among other painters at Stockholm, Veronese was represented by *Mars and Venus united by Love* (now in the Metropolitan Museum in New York), and the four glorious *Allegories* which have a place of honour in the great Venetian room of the National Gallery, London. Also at Stockholm was Tintoretto's superb *The Origin of the Milky Way* (now in the National Gallery, London).

In contrast to her fellow countrymen, Queen Christina had a strong personal enthusiasm for the art south of the Alps. She wrote (probably in 1650) to a member of the Roman family of Orsini concerning her pictures and spoke of 'an infinite number of items, but apart from thirty or forty original Italians I care nothing for any of the others. There are some by Albrecht Dürer and other German masters whose names I do not know...I swear that I would give away the lot for a couple of Raphaels'.

130

125
N 82

B 22

129 Christina took with her to Rome two Dürer panels, *Adam* and *Eve* (right), which, since 1587, had been among the prize possessions of the Imperial collection in Prague. In 1664 she presented them to Philip IV of **Spain**

Some years later the daughter of the victor of Lützen resolved on a step which made it possible for her to live permanently in that Italy which she worshipped and gave her the opportunity of continually looking at the art of the south. In male attire, under the name of Count Dohna, she left her home in the company of her favourite pictures, renounced the throne and in Brussels went over to the Catholic faith. This step was taken in the house of the Spanish Viceroy, a brother of that emperor whose pictures General Königsmark had seized for the Swedish crown. When the extravagant Swedish queen—a reckless huntress and the unscrupulous heroine of many scandalous love affairs—arrived in Innsbruck, her conversion was publicly announced; the Pope

travelled to meet her and in Rome she occupied the Palazzo Farnese. All over Rome it was confidently believed that she appropriated a number of smaller works of art from the palace. Later Christina moved to a palace of her own on the left bank of the Tiber near the Vatican. Here her guests could admire the principal works of Correggio, Titian and their contemporaries, pictures which had once belonged to the Emperor. With a grand gesture the daughter of Gustavus Adolphus presented Dürer's *Adam* and *Eve* (now in the Prado) to the Spanish line of the *129* Habsburgs. After an equivocal life and an equally equivocal conversion, Christina found her last resting place in St Peter's, Rome. N 83

The short sojourn of the masterpieces of Italian art upon Swedish soil has a counterpart in the cultural history of England under the first Stuarts. Mention has already been made of the fact that in the early sixteenth century Raphael's *St George and the Dragon 78* found its way into the possession of the English Crown as a gift from Duke Guidobaldo da Montefeltro of Urbino. When Holbein was court painter to Henry VIII, 63 portraits and a number of other pictures were gathered together in Westminster Palace. N 84 Under the long reign of Elizabeth, England laid the foundations of her sea-power and began to build up a social system which brought political rights and prosperity to large sections of the nation. But before this development matured, the country for a time became the scene of princely glory of a kind with which the Continent had grown familiar and which made such a mark in the history of art-collecting.

Evening after evening, in the first years of the seventeenth century, the London public that witnessed the dramas and comedies of Shakespeare was transported to the Mediterranean, to the Rome of the Caesars, contemporary Venice and her subject cities of Vicenza and Verona. In Shakespeare's *Love's Labours Lost*, Antonio Perez, who had fled from Spain to England, appears on the stage as Armado. This man had once owned two of Correggio's *Loves of Jupiter* (which had since then gone to Prague); Shakespeare makes a mysterious allusion to one of these pictures, the *Jupiter and Io*, 'as lively painted *124* as the deed was done' (now in the Vienna Gallery). The poet had become estranged from his Puritanical family when shortly before his death he returned to Stratford from London. In 1623 the folio edition of Shakespeare's plays appeared in London, and here three men were active as collectors whose ambition it was to find a home upon their own island for the artistic culture of the south.

Thomas Howard, 2nd Earl of Arundel, a wealthy *131* country nobleman, highly cultured and of independent judgment, is the first of those travelling English-

130 *Leda and the Swan* from Correggio's *Loves of Jupiter* (see Ill. 124) was brought to Sweden from Prague with the rest of the Imperial booty, and this was one of the paintings that accompanied Christina when she went to live in Rome (detail)

131 The first major collector in England was Thomas Howard, Earl of Arundel. He displayed his antique sculpture in an Italian-style 'galleria' in his London house

men (whom Goethe wished to have as guides) to attract our attention. It seems likely that his desire to become an art collector began while he was on a journey on the Continent between 1613 and 1614. Accompanied by the architect Inigo Jones, Arundel paid a visit in Venice to Dudley Carleton, the English ambassador who was particularly interested in antique art. Arundel was also very well acquainted with the imperial collection in Prague and was personally concerned when the city council of Nuremberg, which had so often been under pressure from the Habsburgs and the Wittelsbachs, was compelled to part with two paintings by Dürer to the House of Stuart. A true collector's passion speaks to us from a letter in which Arundel tells his most important agent, Petty, how he had found some drawings while rummaging around in Habsburg territories. He found this country 'not so empty of drawings as was thought' and adds, 'but I hope, by your help, we shall make it emptier'. Arundel remarked about a Dürer which had been purchased in Würzburg, possibly *The Madonna with the Siskin*

B 103

N 85

N 86

Tho: Moor L'Chancelour

(now in the Berlin Museums), 'though painted upon an uneven board... it is more worth than all the toyes I have gotten in Germany, and for such I esteeme it, having ever carried it in my owne coach since I had it'.

It was natural enough that an Englishman fond of the old German masters he had seen in Prague and Nuremberg should seek to acquire portraits by Holbein. Arundel owned, amongst others, the portrait of Southwell (now in the Uffizi), that of Chambers (now in the Vienna Gallery), four other portraits (now in the Louvre) and *Christina of Denmark, Duchess of Milan;* he also had a small signed picture of an elderly man by Jan van Eyck (both the last-named pictures now in the National Gallery, London). While Arundel's feeling for early German painting was shared with the Emperor Rudolph II, his activities as a collector of the drawings of this school suggest that he should be classed with men like Amerbach in Basle. In 1619 Arundel confessed his 'foolish curiosity' for Holbein's art, which in this context should be understood as an interest in drawings and possibly engravings. In 1625 Arundel owned some of the finest Holbein drawings now in the British Royal Collection. It is probable also that the heirs of Imhoff, the Nuremberg collector, sold a number of important Dürer drawings through a middleman to the English collector.

VIII

N 87

B 296

Like Rudolph II, Arundel's liking for old German art and his interest in both the old and new art of the Mediterranean roughly balanced each other. All the sumptuous elegance and romance of sixteenth-century Venice were revealed to the visitor to Arundel House by Titian's *Tarquinius and Lucrezia* (now in the Museum in Bordeaux); yet it is worth noting that one could also see a panel from Quattrocento Venice, namely the *Martyrdom of St Sebastian* by Antonello da Messina (now in the Dresden Gallery). Arundel was particularly successful as a collector of drawings from the golden age of Italian art. In this activity he was assisted by Nicholas Lanier, the first Englishman to adopt the

132, 133 Besides Greek and Roman sculpture Lord Arundel also built up an extensive collection of drawings by the great sixteenth-century masters, part of which was later incorporated in the British Royal Collection. He owned Holbein's *Sir Thomas More* (above) and Leonardo's *Neptune* (below), both of which were exhibited in the Queen's Gallery in Buckingham Palace in 1963

VII   In the seventeenth century the Spanish crown was generally represented in the Spanish Netherlands by an archduke from the Austrian branch of the House of Habsburg. Many of these archdukes were patrons and collectors, but of particular importance were Archduke Albert and his wife Isabella, one of Philip II's daughters. Rubens' *Ildefonso Altarpiece* shows them kneeling before the Virgin

.X°. IVLII. ANNO.   ETATIS ·SVÆ
.H. VIII. XXVIII°.   ANNO XXXIII.

practice of stamping drawings with a mark, and Daniel Nys, a resident of Venice. Arundel possessed among others the drawings of the *Antique Sacrifice* by Mantegna (now in the British Museum), the *Head of St James the Greater* by Leonardo da Vinci (now at Windsor Castle) and *SS. Jerome and Francis in Conversation* by Parmigianino (now in the Ashmolean Museum, Oxford). Distinguished engravers were employed in order to preserve the most important of the drawings in copies.

It is customary nowadays to evaluate Arundel's activity as a collector only according to the actual results which can still be demonstrated today. Thus historians place great value on the sixteenth-century items from northern and southern Europe in the Arundel House collection, now long dispersed, while the antique sculpture in the same collection (now in the Ashmolean Museum, Oxford and the British Museum) is usually dismissed in a few condescending words. It must be emphasized, however, that in those collecting propensities already enumerated, Arundel had been anticipated by others on the Continent, whereas the means by which he obtained antique sculpture, not only from Rome but also from the eastern Mediterranean, opened new paths, later to be trod by Lord Elgin. Arundel may have received the inspiration for this branch of his collecting activity in Venice. In England before 1600 there seems to have been considerable Puritan feeling against the exhibition of statues of heathen deities. Arundel, a passionate friend of southern art, suffered no such inhibitions. He sent his valued agent Petty into the heart of Turkish territory; Greek sculptures now came to him by ship from Constantinople, Smyrna, Rhodes and the Greek mainland, and the English Ambassador in Turkey was one of those whose help was enlisted.

Following Italian models of the kind we have encountered in Florence, Mantua and Sabbioneta,

Arundel built a gallery in which the statues stood on pedestals carefully arranged at regular intervals. In this first 'galleria' on English soil and in neighbouring rooms, his contemporaries—among them Sandrart—were able to admire 37 statues, 128 busts, 250 inscriptions, parts of sarcophagi and so forth. Henry Peacham added a chapter to his book *The Compleat Gentleman* after seeing these rooms at Arundel House. 'The study of statues is profitable for all ingenious gentlemen,' Peacham declares, after which he makes a sort of bow to Arundel, saying that '[to him] oweth this angle of the world, the first sight of Greek and Roman statues'. Arundel is believed to have set a specially high value on his bronze *Homer*, a Hellenistic piece which he obtained in Constantinople, and with which he had himself painted by van Dyck sometime between 1638 and 1641 (the bronze head has been in the British Museum since 1760; the painting is in the Vienna Gallery). Among the marble statues in Arundel's possession was an Aphrodite torso dating from the fourth century BC and the so-called *Sappho* bust from the same period (both are now in the Ashmolean Museum, Oxford).

134 Arundel once owned these drawings by Parmigianino of two saints in conversation (possibly St Jerome and St Francis). They were studies for the famous *Madonna with the Long Neck* in the Uffizi

VIII In the early seventeenth century Holbein was accepted throughout Europe as one of the greatest artists of the past. When in 1621 Lord Arundel presented the Grand Duke of Tuscany with Holbein's *Sir Richard Southwell*, he could not have given anything of greater value

135 The second important English collector in the early seventeenth century was George Villiers, Duke of Buckingham. He was chiefly interested in the great Venetian masters and owned major works by Titian and Veronese, including the latter's *Rebecca at the Well*

Next to Arundel, the amateur savant, comes George Villiers Duke of Buckingham, who was slightly his junior. He was handsome and very much a ladies' man. As minister of two Stuart kings he did all he could to ensure the absolute power of the monarch as it was understood on the Continent. Compared with Arundel, Buckingham may have had a more spontaneous attitude to art; he possessed a few works of the Dürer period but loved best of all the great Venetians and in particular his own contemporary, Rubens, whom Jakob Burckhardt called their 'heir in chief'. Buckingham owned nineteen paintings by Titian, among them the great *Ecce Homo*, which he acquired in Venice in 1620 and which he was unwilling to sell even when offered £7,000 (now in the Vienna 135 Gallery). Presumably the painting *Rebecca at the Well* by Veronese (now in the National Gallery, Washington, D.C.) comes from Buckingham's collection.

We know for a fact that the *Parable of the Sower of Tares* by Fetti, a pictorial jewel which after a long stay in the imperial castles of the Habsburgs has again returned to England (now in the Count Seilern collection in London), once belonged to Buckingham. B 270 Buckingham acquired dozens of paintings by Rubens, among them the *Head of Medusa* (now in the 162 Vienna Gallery). From the same artist he also commissioned the *Apotheosis* for the ceiling of a 136 room in Osterley Park. N 90

It was from Arundel, an older man and a more cultured collector, that Buckingham at the end of his life acquired an interest in antique sculpture. N 91 However, when writing to the English Ambassador in Constantinople, whose aid he was soliciting, he expressed a certain reserve: 'Neither am I so fond of antiquity as to court it in deformed or misshapen stone; but where you shall meet beauty with antiquity together in a statue, I shall not stand upon any cost your judgment shall value it at.' When in 1627 N 92 Rubens found himself temporarily in financial difficulties, he made over to his English protector some antique sculptures and modern statuettes in antique style, and Buckingham placed these objects in one of his houses in the Strand. Here were now to be seen 'the galleries and rooms ennobled with

the possession of these Roman heads and statues which lately belonged to Sir P. P. Rubens'. Since 1932 the Ashmolean Museum in Oxford has been in possession of an ivory statuette by Georg Petel, which in composition imitates antique models and which on the occasion of the above named sale passed from the hands of Rubens into those of Buckingham.

136 Among contemporary artists Buckingham preferred Rubens. This preparatory study for a ceiling in Buckingham's country seat, Osterley Park, deals with an allegorical subject. War raises the statesman (i.e., Buckingham) on high, Peace crowns him and Calumny tries in vain to drag him down. The study has been in the National Gallery, London, since 1843

B 215

137

The third and youngest of the three great English collectors was Charles I. At an early age he became acquainted with Arundel's treasures as well as the pictures that Buckingham possessed. When he was twenty-three, Charles spent a few months at the Spanish court, where at this time the reigning king, Philip IV, was only eighteen years of age. The unsuccessful attack of the Spanish Armada on England was thirty years behind and the two young princes, both of them passionate art-lovers, got on excellently together.

137 Buckingham also purchased from Rubens works of art which were not by the master himself. In this way he acquired a number of antique statues as well as this ivory Venus by a contemporary German artist, Georg Petel, whose work was highly valued at that time

In the Escorial and the castles of the Spanish Habsburgs, the young Stuart's affection for the great Venetian painters grew stronger than ever. Mention was made earlier, in connection with the Pardo, of Titian's great composition *Jupiter and Antiope*. In *103* 1609 this picture had come within a hair's breadth of being destroyed in a fire. People whispered in Madrid—alluding to the auto-da-fés of worldly luxuries—that it was 'heathen enough to deserve death by fire'. When the King, Philip IV's father, N 93 heard that the *Pardo Venus* had been saved, he exlaimed 'All is well! Everything else can be replaced'. This picture made a great impression on the young English prince in 1623. He asked for it and received it as a gift (it is now in the Louvre). He was also given Titian's *Woman in a Fur* (now in the *138* Vienna Gallery). Charles's request for a portrait of Charles V, the founder of Habsburg greatness, was probably intended as a delicate flattery of the reigning House in Spain. It was successful, for he received the full-length portrait of the Emperor which Titian had painted in Bologna in 1532 (now in the Prado). 'Monsieur le Prince de Galles est le Prince le plus amateur de la peinture qui soit au monde', said Rubens of the young Stuart, even N 94 before he ascended the throne.

When Charles I began his reign he had the means to buy pictures on a grand scale. Following the example of the Habsburgs, he made Venice his artistic Mecca; from there he brought over the important private della Nave collection, in which the Venetian school was brilliantly represented by Antonello, Giorgione, Titian, Palma, Lotto and Veronese. Charles even contrived to acquire Veronese's *Deposition* from SS. Giovanni e Paolo, one of the principal churches of Venice (the picture is now in the Hermitage, Leningrad). When the Dutch States General wished to show its good will on the occasion of the birth of a daughter to the King, it presented to him not works by native artists but four paintings by Titian and Tintoretto.

Charles was equally interested in works of the great masters of other Italian schools dating from about 1490 to 1530. He sacrificed Holbein's *Erasmus*

138 Charles I of England began collecting even before he became king. While visiting Philip IV of Spain he received paintings by Titian, including the *Woman in a Fur*. The same model sat for the *Venus of Urbino*, now in the Uffizi

of Rotterdam in order to acquire Leonardo's *St John the Baptist* (both paintings now in the Louvre) and exchanged a volume of Holbein's drawings for Raphael's *St George and the Dragon* which had been presented to Henry VII and was at that time the property of Lord Pembroke (now in the National Gallery in Washington). In 1630 Raphael's cartoons for the series of tapestries in the Vatican came into his possession (now on loan from the Crown to the Victoria and Albert Museum). But Charles's greatest triumph was the acquisition of the art collections of the Gonzagas. Only the handing over of a hundred of the principal pictures of the gallery of Modena to the Saxon dynasty in 1746 and the sale of a selection of masterpieces to America by the Hermitage in 1930 can compare in importance with this great event in the history of art dealing.

The last princes of the House of Gonzaga, politically incompetent and personally unamiable though they were, continued to play the proud role of Maecenas. Their name figures in the history of the opera and they never ceased adding to the art treasures they had inherited. Rubens, who in his youth served them as a court painter, was an intermediary in the acquisition of Caravaggio's altarpiece, the *Death of the Virgin*, which the members of a monastery in the Roman district of Trastevere rejected as irreverent and vulgar. Vincenzo Gonzaga did not hesitate on that account to pay 280 gold ducats for the picture. In 1607, at the request of the artists of Rome, it was exhibited for a few days in the house of the Mantua agent for free inspection before being despatched to its destination. In 1625 Mantua was faced by state bankruptcy, even though only shortly before the painter Fetti had been active in Venice as a buyer for the ruling house. It was at this moment that, by means which are still unknown today, Cardinal Richelieu managed to secure the pictures (now in the Louvre) which Isabella had had painted for her 'studiolo' by Mantegna and others around 1500. The Gonzagas sought to turn the great mass of their works of art into money in a foreign country, in order to conceal the financial disaster for as long as possible in Italy. At this time Daniel Nys, the financier and art dealer, who had apparently already served Arundel and other English art-lovers, was active in Venice and Antwerp. In 1627 Charles I

139, 140 In the early seventeenth century Dürer and his contemporaries were almost as highly prized as the great Italian masters. Charles I's collection included, among a number of Dürers, this self-portrait of 1498 (detail above), as well as Cranach's *Cuspinian* (below)

141 One of the most momen-
tous events in the history of art
dealing was Charles I's acquisition of the Gonzaga collection
of paintings. Apart from masterpieces by Italian artists the
collection included the small
Giustiniani Altarpiece by Jan van
Eyck. For some time this
painting was attributed to
Dürer

acquired for 110,000 ducats (£80,000) the larger
pictures and statuettes. The drawings were diverted
—probably secretly—by Nys, who handed them
over to Arundel. A number of older paintings also
failed to come to the King; these turned up in 1640
B 269 in the hands of Antwerp dealers.

Around 1640 the Palace of Whitehall alone
contained 102 pictures, 28 by Titian, 11 by Correggio,
9 by Raphael and his pupils and 7 by Tintoretto; there
were several paintings by Dürer, Cranach and the
early Netherlandish masters as well as portraits
which Holbein had painted in England. Flemish
contemporaries, among them the King's court painter van Dyck and his teacher Rubens, were also
represented and three paintings by Rembrandt, a
Dutch Calvinist, were allowed into this distin-
N 96 guished company.

IX Charles I was forty years old when his star began
to set. The predominantly Puritan country refused
to accept the rule of a Stuart married to a Catholic
and it also refused to tolerate his Catholic courtiers any longer. The absolutist form of government
was felt to be an importation from the Continent,
even more so the culture of the London court.
Voices were heard saying that the King had been
deceived to the detriment of the country through
gifts of paintings, antique idols and trumperies
brought from Rome. Parliament, after facing the B 116
King with some hesitation, ventured ultimately
on a trial of strength, and among other things
shut the theatres. Arundel anticipated what was
coming and fled abroad with his family and part of
his collection. After a short stay in the Netherlands
he travelled to his beloved Italy and died not far

142 After Charles I's execution most of his paintings were sold. Prosper Henry Lankrink, a landscape painter from Antwerp, bought Rubens' *Landscape with Gallows* (left)

from Venice four years later. The family of the murdered Duke of Buckingham managed to get 193 of his most valuable paintings into the Spanish Netherlands. This choice collection was taken over by a pupil of Rubens and an English financier for a modest price, said to have been 30,000 guilders; the pictures were then auctioned and scattered. But the King could save neither his works of art nor himself. In 1649 he was beheaded.

A resolution of Parliament, moved by the radical Puritan elements, provided for the immediate burning of all pictures of the Blessed Virgin in the royal gallery. This, however, did not come about. Cromwell endeavoured to arrest the campaign of universal destruction in regard to both the late King's pictures and other works. The series of Mantegna's *Triumphs of Caesar* which had come from Mantua (now at Hampton Court Palace), and Raphael's great cartoons for a series of tapestries representing the Acts of the Apostles (acquired on the advice of Rubens), seem to have been regarded as inoffensive by most Puritans, as were a number of early German portraits. But numerous Catholic altarpieces and alcove pictures of the Italian Renaissance artists

were put up for sale. All the efforts of the curators of the National Gallery over the last hundred years have been unsuccessful in recovering that nucleus of first-class works which in Cromwell's day returned to the Continent and found permanent homes in Paris, Madrid and Vienna.

Sales from 1649 to 1653 disposed of 1,387 paintings and 399 other pieces at Somerset House, Hampton Court, Greenwich and other places. Many a work of art which was not too highly priced was bought by some art-loving commoner, for example the *Landscape with Gallows* by Rubens (since 1928 in the Berlin Museums). Only some of the antique sculpture, which had been over-valued, could not be sold. A few items went to people to whom the State owed money. The most noteworthy purchases, however, were made by the great collectors on the Continent.

Philip IV was still reigning in Spain, and must have been anxious to get back the magnificent portrait of Charles V by Titian which he had presented to the young Stuart prince. The price would not be too high—of that Philip was sure—especially if the bidder's identity remained unknown. Humble tailors and timber merchants, so the old accounts say, acquired the paintings which were to round off the great collection of the Spanish Crown. Thanks to the auctioning of the Duke of Buckingham's collection two years before and the consequent glut on the market, the prices obtained for Titian's works around 1650 were extremely low; the full-length portrait of the Emperor Charles V standing returned to Madrid for a mere £150. The *Address of the Marchese del Vasto* fetched only £250 (both are now in the Prado). Titian's early altarpiece *St Peter with Pope Alexander* (now in the Antwerp Museum) was once more made to serve its original religious purpose and was handed over to a convent in Spain.

Much better prices than those fetched by Titian's works around 1650 were paid for great works of Raphael's maturity. The painting known to us as *La Perla* or *The Holy Family* fetched £2,000; it was given a place of high honour in the Escorial over the altar of the sacristy (now in the Prado).

A number of important works by Mantegna, Andrea del Sarto, Correggio, Veronese and Tintoretto also found their way to Spain; today they are reckoned among the most important pictures in the Prado. Dürer's early self-portrait of 1498, which travelled to London in 1636, found a permanent home in Madrid (now in the Prado Museum). A particularly fine Correggio, the *Mercury instructing Cupid before Venus*, was acquired in London by the Duke of Alba for his palace in Madrid (now in the National Gallery, London).

A further group of masterpieces travelled in the middle of the seventeenth century from England to France. Walking through the Grande Galerie of the Louvre we often pause before what may have been one of King Charles's favourite pictures.

In the sixteenth century, rivalry with the House of Habsburg had led the kings of France to ignore the art of Venice, which was allied with the emperor, and to turn exclusively to the Florentine school. Meanwhile Titian had risen from his role as personal painter of Charles V to become a fixed star in the artistic firmament. The dispersal of the collection of the English King brought to Paris some major works of Titian and of his immediate predecessors and contemporaries in northern Italy. Mention might be made of Giorgione's *Concert Champêtre*, the principal possession of the Gonzaga gallery in Mantua, Titian's *Pardo Venus* as well as the *Entombment*, the *Young Woman at her Toilet* and the *Man with a Glove*.

The lion's share of the treasures which the English Civil War now spilled over the Continent was acquired by the German Habsburgs. The transfer of the Prague 'Kunstkammer' to Stockholm had involved a painful loss of prestige which the Habsburgs were anxious to make good as quickly

143 Charles I also owned several Rembrandts, among them this self-portrait of the artist in middle age which the King received as a gift

and as ostentatiously as possible, and the sale of Buckingham's pictures and of those belonging to the late King presented them with an opportunity which they used with skill.

An invaluable bastion of power from the days of Charles V was still firmly in Habsburg hands: the southern Netherlands. Since the beginning of Philip II's reign this had belonged to the Spanish line, although the viceroy in Brussels was usually an archduke from the German branch of the House. In 1646 Leopold Wilhelm, a younger brother of the then reigning Emperor, had taken over this post. He managed to get hold of the best of Buckingham's paintings when these were auctioned, among them Titian's *Ecce Homo*, the sequence of eight Biblical scenes by Paolo Veronese and the *Head of Medusa* by

Rubens. Of the paintings and other treasures of Charles I, Leopold Wilhelm bought almost half. A part of this acquisition went immediately to Prague, where towards the end of the seventeenth century even a Swedish traveller had to admit to having seen 'a "Kabinett", three galleries and a great hall full of pictures'. In his Brussels palace Archduke Leopold Wilhelm set up a gallery with more than 1,300 paintings (most of them now in the Vienna Gallery). Here in 1654 Christina, daughter of Gustavus Adolphus, went over to the Catholic faith. The total effect of the Archduke's gallery, which the guest on this occasion must have seen, was intended to

N 99

XI

144   Like Charles I of England, collectors in the Spanish Netherlands were interested in the work of fifteenth-century artists. Cornelius van der Geest, a collector in Antwerp, once owned *A Woman Bathing* by Jan van Eyck. The picture itself has been lost, but we can see what it looked like from this detail of a painting of van der Geest's gallery by its keeper, Willem van Haecht

blot out the memory of the famous collection taken from Prague, and which at that very time was following Christina from Stockholm to Rome.

Before the collection of Archduke Leopold Wilhelm is described in greater detail, certain observations should be made about artistic life in Antwerp and in other centres of the Spanish Netherlands. This was last referred to when Rudolph II acquired pictures by the elder Bruegel. Soon afterwards, to quote Burckhardt, Rubens 'took it upon himself to carry on his gigantic shoulders the whole weight of southern greatness to the north'. In the Spanish Netherlands, where a new spirit was beginning to inspire Catholicism, the painting of the High Baroque reached its crowning achievement in the great pictures which came from Rubens' Antwerp studio. The pathos of these martyrdoms and transfigurations, the allegories so replete with life, the immensely moving rhythms of the scenes of abduction and hunting, evoked enthusiastic approval from art-lovers in every part of Europe.

During the happiest years of Rubens' creative life a predecessor of Leopold Wilhelm, Archduke Albert, was living in the viceroy's palace in Brussels. Albert   B 183
had been sent at the age of eleven from Austria to Spain and at the age of eighteen became Archbishop of Toledo, but abandoned his ecclesiatical status when King Philip II sent him as viceroy to the Netherlands and gave him his daughter Isabella in marriage. Rubens' finest ecclesiastical picture, the *Ildefonso Altar-*   VII
piece (now in the Vienna Gallery), shows us Albert and Isabella in solemn devotion before the Virgin Mary.

Archduke Albert's affection for old pictures remained with him when he came to the Netherlands; when Maximilian of Bavaria was chasing after works of Dürer, Albert and Isabella were eagerly seeking paintings by his Flemish contemporaries. In the house of the Antwerp collector van der Geest, who   B 122
had commissioned Rubens to paint the *Battle of the Amazons* (now in the Munich Pinakothek), the vice-regal couple in 1615 saw a *Virgin Mary* by Quentin Massys and asked if they could acquire it; but the owner was bold enough to refuse. In the same year Archduke Albert paid the very high sum of 2,000 guilders to the Abbey of St Adrien in Grammont for an *Adoration of the Magi* by Mabuse, while Rubens at the same time received 300 guilders for a half-length portrait of Isabella.

Let us compare a few other well attested prices given for paintings around the year 1600. At that time Gillis Mostaert received 98 guilders for two pictures which had just been completed, while a *Vision* by Bosch fetched 106 guilders and an important painting by the elder Bruegel 320 guilders. In the viceregal palace in Brussels, which no longer

145 The portrait of van der Geest by van Dyck is now in the National Gallery in London

N 100

exists, there were at that time three galleries, as well as long promenades, which contained numerous pictures. Albert and Isabella refused to allow into their palace any representations of heathen gods or goddesses that lacked decorum. In the land in which Alba had stamped out heresy the king's representative had to be beyond criticism.

It was not the quiet distinguished Brussels but the great trading metropolis of Antwerp that was the real centre of the country in the first half of the seventeenth century. Riches were accumulated here just as in Venice, Madrid, or Paris, and art-lovers

filled their houses with paintings of the first rank. Next to contemporary works and works of the period of Dürer, that is to say the period of Massys and Mabuse in the Netherlands, early Netherlandish masters were also highly valued. The collector van der Geest owned *A Woman Bathing* by Jan van Eyck 144 (now apparently lost).

The country's successful painters themselves boasted of considerable collections. Rubens, who never tired of copying the works of Titian, acquired eleven original paintings by the great Venetian. King Philip IV was later to pay 900 guilders for Titians from

Rubens' estate, but he paid 1,800 guilders for copies of Titian by Rubens, which means that he regarded them as new creations possessing artistic merit of their own. The Vienna Gallery considers itself fortunate in having at least a copy by Rubens of a vanished portrait of Isabella d'Este by Titian, and the Nationalmuseum in Stockholm is proud of its copy by Rubens of Titian's *Bacchanal* in Madrid. Rubens painted his lovely second wife Hélène Fourment in a picture which was really a free variant *138* of Titian's *Woman in a Fur*. He himself liked to refer to the picture as 'The Little Fur Coat'. Titian's original and the Flemish variant both came ultimately into the imperial collection (now in the Vienna N 101 Gallery).

After Titian, Tintoretto held the second place of honour in Rubens' collection and was represented by six pictures. Among contemporaries there were works by the German Elsheimer and the Dutch Brouwer; nor was there any lack of the older Netherlandish names, such as Jan van Eyck and Hugo

van der Goes. The most costly part of Rubens' collection consisted of some antique marble sculptures which were set up in a small round room lit from above. He acquired some of these in 1618 from the N 102 English art-lover Dudley Carleton in exchange for some of his own works, which in certain cases Rubens had to buy back from private owners. A large composition, *Achilles with the Distaff*, which for

146 'Painted galleries' were a speciality of seventeenth-century Antwerp painters. Frans Francken the Younger painted interiors of the house of Rubens, who was also an active collector and owned antique sculpture as well as many works by other painters

147 The largest collection of paintings in the Spanish Netherlands was assembled in Brussels by Archduke Leopold Wilhelm, a younger brother of the Emperor (portrait by Peter Thys) ▶

purposes of the exchange was valued at 600 guilders, is described by Rubens himself in the following words: 'Achilles dressed as a woman by the best of my pupils and gone over entirely by my own hand. A beautiful picture full of very many pretty N 103 girls'. The pupil in question was van Dyck.

3 A year later Rubens discovered in the Market of St Germain in Paris a late antique porphyry vase for which he had to pay 2,000 gold scudi. The difficult years 1626–28 compelled him to sell part of his collection. The antique statues, as we already know, came into the hands of Buckingham. The B 247 vase was to be sent by a dealer to India.

Van Dyck's successful career enabled him also to start a collection in his last years. Among other works he owned some of the most important of Titian's paintings, for instance the *Vendramin Family* (now in the National Gallery in London), *Laura and Alfonso* (in the Louvre) and probably also the grandest creation in the 'ultima maniera', the *Crowning with* N 104 *Thorns* (now in the Munich Pinakothek).

The fate of Caravaggio's *The Madonna of the Rosaries* (now in the Vienna Gallery) throws light on the relationship between the Antwerp painters and contemporary Italian art. It will be remembered that in 1607 Rubens was involved in the Gonzagas' acquisition of Caravaggio's *Death of the Virgin*. In those years another altarpiece by Caravaggio, *The Madonna of the Rosaries*, incurred the censure of the clergy in Naples. This was brought by a Fleming to Antwerp, where ten years after it had been painted it aroused the warmest admiration from the local artists. Rubens, however, decided not to include it in his own collection but persuaded the Antwerp Dominicans to set up the picture that had been condemned in Italy on an altar of their own church.

Antwerp, with its exchange and far-reaching economic connections, became for a time in the seventeenth century the most important art market in B 287 Europe. Its success began when travelling Netherlandish merchants offered paintings on canvas and similar objects for sale at the markets and fairs. We B 129 hear of the first of these merchants in Cologne in B 135 1546, in Danzig in 1577, and in Riga in 1633. In the meantime firms well supplied with capital were being developed in Antwerp. They watched the market, adjusted supply to demand and guided artistic taste. The Forchoudts had branches in Paris, Cadiz and Vienna. The firm enjoyed a good reputation and in Vienna counted the families of the Princes Liechtenstein and the Counts Harrach among their B 58 customers. Other firms in Antwerp were less scrupulous in the matter of business ethics. Around 1640 there was considerable faking in Antwerp after engravings of the Rubens school for customers from Germany and Poland.

Since 1646 Archduke Leopold Wilhelm had been gathering his collection in close connection with the Antwerp art market. Rubens and van Dyck had recently died and their collections had already been scattered, but thanks to political developments in England and through the exploitation of other opportunities that offered themselves, the adaptable Archduke was able to build up a nucleus of paintings within a few years which even today sets its stamp upon many rooms in the Vienna Gallery. If the Emperor Rudolph II had been more diversified in his tastes and even more passionate as an art-collector, Leopold Wilhelm's prudence in watching his chances made up for any lack of instinctive judgment.

Leopold Wilhelm's constitution was weak and he died before he reached the age of fifty. As the second-born son of the Emperor he had been brought up in Madrid and lived from his earliest years true to the ideal of a Spanish Catholic prince. In the Escorial and in the castles of his Spanish relatives the Archduke was so entirely at home that his own later collections bore a strong family likeness to the royal treasures in Spain. Shortly before the end of the Thirty Years War Leopold Wilhelm—Bishop of Olmütz, Passau and Strasbourg and at the same time Grand Master of the Teutonic Order of Knights— was in command of an imperial army in southern Germany. At that time he saw in Neuburg on the Danube three altarpieces by Rubens (now in the Munich Pinakothek) on which he passed a very significant judgment. He liked the 'lively breadth of invention and the superb quality of the colouring' but he took exception to certain individual figures where the drawing did not seem to him sufficiently 'devout and correct'. This could only N 105 be the judgment of a collector who valued Titian and the Italians of the sixteenth century above everything else.

Even though Leopold Wilhelm had resided in Brussels for ten years only, he could claim ownership of 517 Italian and Spanish paintings, 880 German and Dutch paintings, a further 542 pieces of sculpture and 343 drawings.

Titian's *Portrait of Jacopo de Strada*, Bruegel's *Tower* VI *of Babel* and probably a number of other pictures had already belonged to Rudolph II; and the Archduke occasionally sent paintings to his brother Ferdinand III in Prague, for which he may well have received some compensation in the form of other paintings. In the viceregal palace at Brussels the Archduke found many paintings acquired by his predecessors. The younger Teniers, who had immediately been taken into service as court painter, was charged with their care. Purchases already mentioned from among the pictures left behind by Buckingham and Charles I at their deaths enabled the Archduke to widen his artistic horizon, and this process was intensified by discussions with Antwerp art-lovers. Some examples of more recent Italian and Dutch painting were now introduced into the Archduke's collection, while the classical Raphael joined the Venetians of the Giorgione circle and the fifteenth-century precursors of Massys and Mabuse, who were entered in the inventory as 'van Eycks'.

N 106

A rapid survey of the collection of Leopold Wilhelm in 1656, when it was completed, must begin with the Venetians. At that time the name of Titian had almost been overshadowed by that of Giorgione, whose *Three Philosophers* the Archduke possessed (this is now in the Vienna Gallery as are all the other pictures mentioned below unless otherwise stated). A contemporary of Leopold Wilhelm's, the Venetian Pietro della Vecchia, painted in the manner of Giorgione; his pictures, accepted as free variations on themes by the favourite master of the Venetian Renaissance, found purchasers both north and south of the Alps though quite often they were sold as 'originals by Giorgionio', as we learn from the well-informed Italian author Boschini. According to Sandrart, Leopold Wilhelm also held the art of Pietro della Vecchia in high esteem. The Archduke possessed about forty paintings by Titian of which twenty are still regarded as wholly by the artist's own hand. A quarter of these have left Vienna but can still be traced.

N 107

N 108

Leopold Wilhelm did not refuse paintings of nude or semi-nude Venetian courtesans for his gallery; he was a generation later and more tolerant in this matter than his predecessor Albert. He possessed an excellent selection of works by Veronese. Of later Italian painters the Archduke acquired numerous pictures by Fetti but would have nothing to do with the Caravaggio altarpiece from the collection of Charles I. Only five of the Rubens pictures in the Vienna Gallery can be traced to Leopold Wilhelm. But on the other hand he looked upon it as his duty as regent to ensure that living artists in the country he ruled should not starve; sixty-five painters received commissions. Paintings have survived which show the Archduke out hunting and shooting birds, praying in Antwerp Cathedral or as a spectator of skating, and even watching a burning house in the night. He had his portrait painted thirty-four times.

N 109

It is Leopold Wilhelm who was responsible for the small but well-chosen early Netherlandish section of the Vienna Gallery, which contains paintings by van Eyck, Hugo van der Goes, Geertgen, Memling and Gerard David. The Archduke paid marked tribute to the taste of Philip II of Spain when he purchased *The Last Judgment* by Hieronymus Bosch (now in the Academy of Fine Arts, Vienna). About

102

148 In his gallery in Brussels, Archduke Leopold Wilhelm had several excellent paintings by old Dutch masters, like this portrait of Cardinal Albergati by Jan van Eyck

ten paintings by the elder Bruegel were found in the viceroy's palace at Brussels and incorporated in the collection; one of these, *The Harvesters*, was removed from the imperial Habsburg gallery during the Napoleonic Wars by a French officer (it is now in the Metropolitan Museum, New York).

N 110

Occasionally, and not fortuitously, paintings by Calvinist Dutch painters entered the Catholic Archduke's collection. The little cabinet pictures of Frans van Mieris and Gerrit Dou became a speciality in the middle of the century and were quickly taken up even in Italy. Leopold Wilhelm is said to have paid as much as 2,000 guilders for a picture of

this type. The inventory of the collection also refers to paintings by Saftleven, Wouwermann and Poelenburg, though these have since disappeared. There was, however, no interest in Dutch landscape painting.

Thanks to Leopold Wilhelm a picture by Rembrandt, the *Astronomer*, travelled via Brussels to Vienna. No doubt it was an unimportant picture of his early years which could not be authenticated at that time. According to recent Dutch scholarship the Archduke purchased shortly after their completion Rembrandt's *Self-portrait* of 1652 and also his *Boy Reading*, two works of his last years. The House of Habsburg made no further serious effort to acquire the works of the great Calvinist painter; even to-day he is inadequately represented in the Vienna Gallery.

Whereas Rudolph II had regarded his passion for art as something personal, Archduke Leopold Wilhelm stressed the official side of his artistic appreciation and his function as a patron. After morning Mass and dealing with the most important items

149 This allegorical painted gallery, called *Friends and Enemies of Art*, by Frans Francken the Younger, shows art-lovers on the left and enemies of art on the right in the period of the Thirty Years War

IX After the execution of Charles I, Cromwell sold the bulk of the Royal Collection. Most of the paintings, including van Dyck's portrait of the deposed King, found buyers on the Continent

of state business, audiences held in the picture gallery were part of the recognized ceremonial of the day, and even commoners who were fond of art were occasionally allowed to visit the pictures. In Venice Boschini composed rapturous verses on the 'bel erario del archiduca'—the lovely treasure house of the Archduke—while the French traveller Patin praised the 1,500 pictures—the number was hardly exaggerated—which he himself had seen as the most beautiful in all the world.

B 285 In the Netherlands the Archduke found a species of picture which had been developed particularly in Antwerp since about 1600: the 'painted gallery'. In collectors' circles it was the practice to commission views of interiors in which there were statuettes, Persian faience, drawings and other objects distributed over a number of tables in the foreground. In the middle distance the space was filled by the family of the owner of the house or by an art dealer and his clients, or even by figures from ancient mythology or the Bible, for instance Joseph and Potiphar's wife. In some of these paintings a companion scene is represented out of doors, near the interior that contains the works of art: cavaliers with asses' heads, for instance, are shown smashing a statue of Venus 149 or some other precious object. There was no doubt sufficient reason for scourging the intolerance of the philistines at the time of the Thirty Years War.

B 286 The chief value to art-lovers of 'painted galleries', now as in the seventeenth century, is the fact that they show us the walls of the rooms, densely covered with paintings from top to bottom. A comparison between the early and late examples of such 'painted galleries' reveals a steadily increasing symmetry and a tendency to work the individual picture into the general layout of the wall. This last stage was exemplified by a painter who was working in Antwerp up to 1684 and who used the hispanicized name Gonzales Coques.

It was the fairly loose form still prevailing in the 'painted galleries' in the middle of the century that XI was employed by Teniers the Younger in his dual capacity of court painter and curator to the Arch-

duke. He had to paint pictures of this kind repeatedly; they were sent to important visitors or to friendly courts and represented (in a manner suited to the taste of the recipient or possibly as thanks for a present received) individual pictures mounted on an easel. This is how a portrait of an Infanta by Velazquez, which has since disappeared, is still known to us. N 112

In order to make clearly discernible copies of as many paintings as possible, Teniers did not show the actual rooms in which the pictures were housed in the old Coudenberg Palace, but arbitrarily combined a number of selected pictures which differed as each particular case might require, and presented them as housed in wholly fictitious rooms. In the middle distance we often see the Archduke himself, who wears his hat in his own house according to the etiquette on official occasions. He is pictured examining drawings which Teniers is handing him, and one also sees the court chaplain and flower painter Antonius van der Baren, a figure easily recognized by his dwarf-like size, as well as a few visitors and servants.

To enhance the glory of the House of Habsburg, Leopold Wilhelm resolved to make his finest paintings better known through engraving. This was the origin of the first 'Gallery Book' in Europe. In this work about one-fifth of the Archduke's paintings were reproduced, the choice being made exclusively from among those which came from Italy; no doubt he was more attached to these than to any others, and they had been by far the most costly. N 113

It is in Brussels, and in connection with the collecting activities of Archduke Leopold Wilhelm, that we encounter on several occasions the word 'Pinacotheca' in its Latin form; the use of this term illustrates the affection of the Baroque period for rather strange and high-sounding borrowed Greek words. Whereas we can tell with a considerable degree of exactitude when the Greek 'Mouseion' became an accepted term under the form 'Musaeum' in modern Europe, we are in the dark regarding 'Pinacotheca'. In the second half of the seventeenth century this word, which had been coined in the Athens of Pericles, was in use over areas as far apart as Italy and Sweden as a rather pretentious synonym for 'Kunstkammer' or for a collection of any kind of works of art. Later its meaning was B 278 again narrowed down and around 1800 it denoted, as originally in Athens, simply a collection of pictures. N 114

In the northern Netherlands, at that time usually called the United Provinces, a Calvinistic form of Protestantism had taken strong root since 1550.

X   The most beautiful Italian painting in Charles I's collection was the *Concert Champêtre* started by Giorgione and probably finished by Titian. In the sale of the King's collection, it was bought by Jabach, the Paris banker, from whom it passed on to Louis XIV

After desperate fighting, the harbour cities of Rotterdam, Dordrecht, Haarlem and Amsterdam, and the country immediately behind them, managed to free themselves from Spanish rule. The heroic age in Dutch history was followed by a flowering of national painting which displayed an astonishing wealth of talent but only lasted a few decades. It was inspired by pride in victory and a growing economy, by the Christian love of 'God's nature' and by the burgher's affirmation of his way of life.

There is a certain unity about Baroque art wherever the Catholic faith was supreme—which means from Seville to Antwerp and from Naples to Paris. Within the Roman sphere great altarpieces filled the churches with spectacular representations of sin and remorse, of martyrdom and ecstasy, but no pictorial representations of any kind were tolerated in the churches of Holland. Here Christian art withered away in favour of the picture designed for domestic edification, a picture that contained often rather prosaic genre elements. While the Catholic was moved to self-examination by a meditating Jerome or a converted Magdalene, a modest 'Vanitas' still-life had a discreet message for the Calvinist and reminded him of the transitory nature of all earthly things. Holland lacked that aristocratic upper class which could be found within the Catholic area. Artists were not invited to paint reality in grandiose terms or even, as in the case of Rubens, to make use of the powerful symbolism that mythological allegory could convey. In Amsterdam the vehement rejection of what was in the final analysis a southern and Roman conception led to what has been designated as anti-Baroque extremism: Asselyn painted a swan attacking a dog that is swimming towards its nest as an allegory of national resistance (now in the Rijksmuseum, Amsterdam). The first revolt against the world of the Baroque with its feudal overtones brought a

150 From about 1600 onwards, Antwerp was fast becoming one of the main centres of the European art market. This painting by Frans Francken the Younger shows the shop of the art dealer, Jan Snellinck (detail)

151 *Dutch Market* by David Vinckeboons. In the northern part of the Netherlands paintings were almost over-produced. At markets even farmers bought pictures in simple black frames (detail)

variety of moods; with Rembrandt it was a personal inwardness, with the great mass of artists it was an essentially bourgeois conception of life. The fashion was now for pictures with moral lessons: for instance, Metsu's *Justice Protecting Widows and Orphans* (now in the Mauritshuis, The Hague) and other pictures which praised the ideal conditions of Holland.

In all the different phases of seventeenth-century Dutch painting the portrait played an important part, expressing the unfailing self-assurance of merchants, doctors, preachers and scholars. The Dutch, proud of their fleet, brought marine painting into prominence, a form of art which sometimes degenerated into mere portraiture of ships. Willem van de Velde, the naval chronicler in paint, had to be present during sea battles. The landscape painters never tired of their subject. Paulus Potter gained fame with a life-size picture of a bull (now in the Mauritshuis) while painters of still-life placed hams, grapes, pastry and goblets of wine before people who did not yet take such delights of the palate for granted.

B 305 But artistic life, which seemed so vigorous in the newly enriched harbour cities, was not without its darker side. In Holland during the age of Rembrandt phenomena which appeared elsewhere only at a much later stage became evident. From about 1620 onwards economic freedom led to anarchy in art and to over-production. This caused an artist-proletariat to come into being. Patrons capable of independent judgment were rare in bourgeois society and those who existed were not venturesome. It was the truly great artists who most often lacked recognition or, if they received it, found it to be capricious and grudgingly given. Many could only keep their heads above water by earning money on the side: Jan van Goyen dealt in tulip bulbs, Hobbema became a tax collector, Adriaen van der Velde managed a tap room, Jan van de Capelle a dye works. After his bankruptcy Rembrandt occupied himself with plaster casts of antique statues, and Steen once offered to paint three pictures for the ludicrous price of 27 guilders. Adriaen van Ostade valued some pictures in a collection as follows: one by Pieter Lastman at 120 guilders, one by Frans Hals at 28 and one by N 115 Rembrandt at 16 guilders. At the end of the century Vermeer's *The Lace-makers* (now in the Louvre) fetched 28 guilders at an auction. As against this, Frans van Mieris, whom fashion once praised to the skies, received as much as 2,600 guilders for some of his pictures and thus was in the Old Master class so far as prices were concerned. During Rembrandt's lifetime 3,000 guilders were paid in Amsterdam for Holbein's *Burgomaster Meyer's Madonna* (now in the

152 In Holland in the seventeenth century, paintings by Holbein obtained such high prices that it became worthwhile for art dealers to have an apparently genuine copy made of a Holbein Madonna, such as this one by Sarburgh

possession of the Hesse-Darmstadt family). For such a price it was worthwhile to have a copy of the picture made with deliberate fraudulent intent (the copy is now in the Dresden Gallery). *152* N 116

The over-abundance of pictures of a manageable size encouraged speculation despite the modest prices fetched. In 1641 the diarist John Evelyn saw farmers buying genre pictures and landscapes. In *151* the houses of humble inn-keepers, millers and small tradesmen as many as two hundred pictures at a time could be found with a total value of 3,000 guilders or more. This can hardly be called art-collecting: the pictures were regarded as merchandise and passed from hand to hand. Whereas in Antwerp the scroll mouldings of picture frames were related to the panelling of the rooms and made possible their permanent allocation to particular places, in Holland people preferred modest flat black frames: every picture was completely self-contained and exchangeable, and there was thus no need to hang it in a particular place.

Compared with contemporary native painting, foreign art played a relatively small part in the Netherlands of Rembrandt's day, at least so far as actual numbers were concerned. During the course of the century the increase in the size of rooms and improved lighting brought about a certain demand for Flemish pictures from the Rubens circle. A number of big collectors shared the general European predilection for works of the age of Dürer. The pharmacist Abraham Francken possessed for a time a small carved altar which probably originated in Antwerp around 1520, and this particular piece can be seen next to a Chinese figure *154* on the portrait etching which Rembrandt made of

153 Just like Rubens, Rembrandt had his own collection. When Raphael's *Portrait of Balthasar Castiglione* was being auctioned in Amsterdam, Rembrandt took the opportunity of making this sketch of it

him. Far Eastern porcelain was a favourite import which Dutch art dealers handled on a large scale. Frederick William of Brandenburg, the Great Elector, acquired in 1685 a Chinese porcelain statuette of the eighteen-armed goddess Kuan-Yin (now in the Berlin Museums). N 117

The art of the Mediterranean region—antique statues and Italian Renaissance painting—was represented by good examples in at least some Amsterdam houses. The collector Rheynst had aquired the Andrea Vendramin collection from Venice. This contained the antique copy of a clas- B 150 sical Greek head of a youth (now in the Berlin Museums), several works by Giorgione and a portrait of a youth by Sebastiano del Piombo N 118 which has since disappeared. Rembrandt possessed a head of Homer from the Hellenistic period, a small 155 reproduction of the Christ Child from the *Bruges Madonna* by Michelangelo and a number of paintings of the Venetian school, among them one by Palma Vecchio. When the splendid collection of the Dutch merchant van Uffeln, a resident of Venice, was auctioned in Amsterdam in 1639 and fetched 60,000 guilders, Rembrandt took the opportunity of sketching Raphael's *Portrait of Balthasar Castiglione* (now 153 in the Louvre). He attached to the drawing a note that the picture had been sold for 3,500 guilders. It should be remembered that the highest price he himself had ever obtained for a portrait was 500 guilders. About this time Rembrandt admired Titian's *Flora* (now in the Uffizi in Florence) which was then in the house of Lopez, the dilettante dealer who was temporarily resident in Holland. Some years later Dou painted a self-portrait, with a small modello of Michelangelo's group *Samson slaying the Philistines* in his hand (the picture is in the Dresden Gallery; the statuette cannot be traced).

Close relations existed between the Dutch trading centres and Protestant northern Germany. Here the Thirty Years War had devastated large stretches of territory. 'Germania saw her palaces graced with glorious pictures go up in flames, and the desire for art was betrayed and extinguished', wrote Sandrart. This referred not to galleries of expensive pictures such as existed in London and Brussels, but to the institution of the 'Kunstkammer', which was still alive.

In the century of the Thirty Years War there began in Germany that liberation of secular interests which was ultimately to lead to the Enlightenment of the Lessing period. At first, however, older ideas still continued to influence men and the belief in relics penetrated from the south into the very heart of Protestant territory. In Eisleben people pointed B 134 out a picture of Luther that had been miraculously

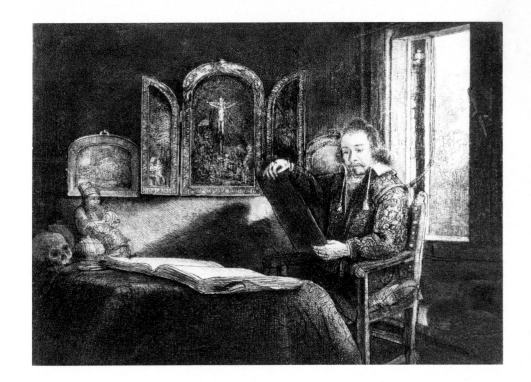

154 This etching by Rembrandt shows Abraham Francken, who lived in Amsterdam, looking at a painted panel. On the table there is a seated figure of Far Eastern origin, and on the wall a carved altar made in Antwerp about 1520

155 Rembrandt's most valuable antique sculpture was a Hellenistic head of Homer, which he included in his *Aristotle contemplating the bust of Homer*, painted for Marchese Vincenzo Ruffo. Though the original of the bust has disappeared, several copies exist

156 In Germany, Scandinavia and Russia collections in which works of art were displayed next to natural objects such as shells and skulls persisted into the eighteenth century. This collection once belonged to a citizen of Hamburg. The ivory goblet is now in Copenhagen

preserved from a fire. Leipzig possessed the so-called Magic Sword of Gustavus Adolphus. Protestant pastors liked to start 'Kunstkammern' on a small scale in which a mood of edification mixed oddly with the spirit of early scientific enquiry. 'Let every man be cut to the heart with the Word of God, which penetrates body and soul; then his heart will be translated to the everlasting Kunstkammer': thus an appeal of the year 1674 to those who visited one such collection.

It will be remembered that around 1600 unicorn horn and bezoar, precious stones and rare natural products were admired in the 'Kunstkammer'. It is true that even after 1700 a definition of the word 'Kunstkammer' could still be found in which it was stated that the curiosities of nature were added to the other contents. Nevertheless at that time the products of nature and products of art were already often separated. The latter were beginning to be systematically arranged in separate cabinets.

The progressive evaluation of all things by reason led in the late seventeenth century to the more dispassionate estimate of works of art from the 'papist' Middle Ages. Protestants had ceased to destroy old altars, and instead handed them over to country churches, where around 1900 they were to be rediscovered; even towards reliquaries a more tolerant attitude was adopted. In 1680 in a church at Linköping in Sweden, chalices and reliquaries were discovered that Catholics had hidden there when the Reformation came to Sweden. This treasure was not destroyed but regarded as a rarity (it is now in the Historical Museum in Stockholm).

In the Scandinavian countries and between the Baltic and the Erzgebirge attention was paid to 'sepulchral antiquities of the ancient pagans' (prehistorical finds); even forgeries of the Bronze Age golden wind instruments, which had been dug up in Denmark in 1639, were offered around 1700 to collectors in northern Germany. From the Dutch ports examples of pre-Columbian art reached as far as Riga.

In the course of the seventeenth century active trade relations developed between Russia and the European states. Germany paid for her imports from the east partly with precious metals in the form of table silver. A large silver eagle (now in the Kremlin Museum) from one of the Nuremberg Jamnitzer was taken by sea along the Norwegian coast to the port of Archangel, and from there by land to Moscow. In 1911, 96 per cent of all the old goldsmiths' work in Moscow's ecclesiastical or 'Patriarch's Treasury' was of German origin, as was 75 per cent of that in the secular treasury of the Tsars. B 133

Russia, the newcomer among the nations of Europe, went at a rapid pace through the various stages of social evolution that the west had undergone since the end of the Middle Ages. Tsar Peter the Great soon became thoroughly acquainted with the 'Kunstkammern' of northern Germany. He visited the rich collection in the upper storey of the castle at Dresden almost immediately after his arrival in that city and studied it throughout the whole night. From the Berlin 'Kunstkammer' he requested and received a classical statuette of Priapus. At the Brunswick Gallery the Tsar in 1713 was interested only in two paintings of ships; the door to the great art of Europe remained closed to him. Occasionally Peter the Great himself made small ivory reliefs, such as the one he presented to the Landgrave Carl von Hesse-Cassel as a contribution to the latter's 'Kunstkammer' (now in the Landesmuseum, Cassel).

B 63

A bare ten years after the founding of the new Russian capital, St Petersburg, the basis was laid for a comprehensive collection. Peter the Great took over the German word 'Kunstkammer' to describe it, a term which incidentally was also current in Amsterdam and the Scandinavian countries. For the post of architect he managed to engage Schlüter, the inspired builder of the town palace of the Hohenzollerns, who had fallen out of favour in Berlin. The palace-like structure on the Neva, which housed the 'Kunstkammer' and the Tsar's library, now serves as the Academy of Sciences.

157 Joseph Arnold's painting of 1668 shows an extensive collection assembled by an art-lover in Ulm

Peter's collection, though conceived on a grandiose scale, was essentially a copy of earlier German 'Kunstkammern' and possessed all the ingredients which had become associated with them. Just as enlightened Protestants exhibited with a superior smile 'papist curiosities' in their collections, there was a section in St Petersburg called 'Frivola', exhibits illustrating the history of superstition. In it were placed miracle-working ikons from the ancient Russian churches of Moscow. Nearby stood a beautiful late Gothic monstrance of 1474 (now in the Hermitage), which one of the Tsar's generals had brought from the conquered Hanseatic city of Reval. When on a visit to Danzig Peter asked the town officials—unsuccessfully—for Memling's altarpiece in the Marienkirche. He may have had in mind an addition to the 'Frivola' section of his 'Kunstkammer'; the artistic value of early Netherlandish panels showing angels and saints, the gate of Heaven and the mouth of Hell, was something wholly beyond his comprehension.

B 129

In the princely 'Kunstkammern' of the north, the first breath of the Enlightenment could already be felt, but south of the river Main was an antiquated feudal world whose thoughts and beliefs were determined by the Rome of the popes, which had now

regained its strength. The Catholic regions were a long distance from progressive Amsterdam, where Descartes and Spinoza formulated their doctrines. The art of the age of Dürer, for which there was at least a modicum of affection everywhere in Europe, was felt in Frankfurt and Cologne to be particularly pious; small, delicately painted devotional pictures in particular seem to have had this effect and were placed on altars, much as in Spain. The merchant Eberhard II Jabach acquired for the chapel of his Cologne house a panel from Dürer's *Altar of the Three Kings* which had been painted for Wittenberg (now in the Cologne Museum). The Catholic line of the Zähringer family used a graceful and very decorative *Virgin Mary* by Cranach as an altarpiece in one of its private chapels (now in the Kunsthalle, Karlsruhe). From the residence of the Wittelsbachs, Grünewald's *Mocking of Christ* came to the Carmelite church in Munich and a Burgkmair altar was presented to the church of the Jesuits in Augsburg (both pictures now in the Munich Pinakothek). A few pictures of the Virgin originating in fifteenth-century Florence and designed for domestic devotion were also in the seventeenth century used for religious purposes north of the Alps. Examples are a relief by Rosselino in Ambras Castle (now in the Vienna Museum) and a painting by Lorenzo di Credi (now in the Kunsthalle, Karlsruhe).

In the period of the Thirty Years War certain works of art from the time of Dürer even rose to the rank of miracle-working objects. Leinberger's bronze statuette of the Virgin was presented to the Pilgrim Chapel in Altötting as being effective in exorcism. A *Virgin Mary* by Cranach which a Protestant Wettin had taken from his 'Kunstkammer' and presented to a Habsburg archduke, was handed over in the Holy Year 1650 to the Stadtpfarrkirche in Innsbruck; as a votive picture of Mary it has enjoyed popular veneration ever since through copies that have been distributed as far afield as Vienna. About this time a number of medieval religious manuscripts were transferred from the Ambras 'Kunstkammer' to a Tyrolean convent. In 1671 the Catholic branch of the Guelphs removed the treasure of the Protestant cathedral in Brunswick and placed it in a reliquary chamber of the castle chapel in Hanover, where Catholic rites were still observed.

No man in the seventeenth century knew the world of art-lovers and collectors both in the north and the south better than the painter, engraver, art-dealer and painters' biographer, Joachim von Sandrart. Sandrart was born in Frankfurt in 1606; here as in Aschaffenburg and Mainz the churches were still filled with the works of Dürer and Grünewald, which were moved only later to Munich and Pommersfelden. Sandrart had received an impression as a youth in Prague of the rich artistic life which had flourished under Rudolph, and managed to collect some facts concerning the old German masters. In London, Sandrart saw the art treasures of Charles I and Arundel. In Amsterdam in 1639 he sat beside Rembrandt at van Uffeln's auction and took part in the bidding for Raphael's *Portrait of Balthasar Castiglione*. In Rome he drank with Poussin and accompanied Claude to the waterfalls of Tivoli. When he was just on seventy, Sandrart retired to Nuremberg and began the publication of his 'Teutsche Akademie', which still contains source material of the highest importance.

Sandrart himself had a small collection of early German panels and Venetian paintings, landscapes by his French artist-friends Poussin and Claude, and van Dyck's *Portrait of the Sculptor Petel* (now in the Munich Pinakothek). He owned outstanding drawings by Dürer, for instance the *Orpheus* (now in the Kunsthalle, Hamburg), and commissioned a cemetery memorial to Nuremberg's greatest son, following, no doubt, the example of the Antwerp collector van der Geest who had honoured Massys in a similar fashion. As a painter and man of letters Sandrart was not in the position of a wealthy merchant who could enlarge his art collection according to some systematic plan; instead he bought and sold as a 'marchand-amateur', a type that became steadily more numerous during the seventeenth century. He offered three paintings by Rubens to Prince Liechtenstein in Vienna and passed on an antique statue to the Swedish King. Of his four volumes of drawings he sold two to a foreign diplomat for 3,500 guilders.

Sandrart was particularly fulsome in praising the collections of the Hohenzollerns and of the Wittelsbachs of the Palatinate. In Brandenburg the Great Elector's victory at Fehrbellin had put an end to the idea of Swedish military invincibility. Here in 1678 there were 'not only arsenals and armouries with weapons but "Kunstkabinette" and rooms full of books with every imaginable rarity and treasure of art'. Therefore, says Sandrart, 'the honorary title of a German Phoebus and Apollo would be more apt than that of a German Mars' for the Great Elector of Brandenburg.

According to an Italian source the Great Elector had indeed set up in his Berlin palace a 'galleria' more than fifty paces long. Here could be seen the *Portrait of a Woman* by Mabuse, the *Bearded Young Man* by Titian, the *Lamentation* by van Dyck (all now in the Berlin Museums) and many Dutch pictures. In his taste the Hohenzollern followed the example of the great merchants of Antwerp and of the Dutch collectors, to whom he was bound through a common profession of the Calvinist faith. Recent research has revealed that the Great Elector acquired the collection of a young member of the artist Merian's family from Frankfurt, among them masterly drawings by Altdorfer, Baldung and Cranach (now in the Kupferstichkabinett of the Berlin Museums).

N 120

In 1679 Sandrart visited Heidelberg. The elderly son of Frederick V of the Palatinate and of Elizabeth Stuart, sister of Charles I, resided there at that time. Shakespeare had written *The Tempest* in honour of their wedding, celebrated in London. In his castle in Heidelberg the Elector Palatine possessed a sort of small sketch copy of what had once been the proud gallery of his royal uncle in London. So strong was the impression which Sandrart received

158 In the seventeenth century the Counter-Reformation often resulted in religious works of art being restored to churches and monasteries. The Guelph treasure, which had for some time been in the possession of a Protestant branch of the family and included this twelfth-century reliquary, was reclaimed by the Catholic branch and placed in the sacristy of the Schlosskirche in Hanover in 1671

159 In 1604 the Spanish ambassador negotiating a peace treaty between England and Spain was given the Royal Cup of the Kings of France and England. This remarkable piece, decorated with scenes from the life of St Agnes, is thought to have been made for the Duc de Berry in about 1380

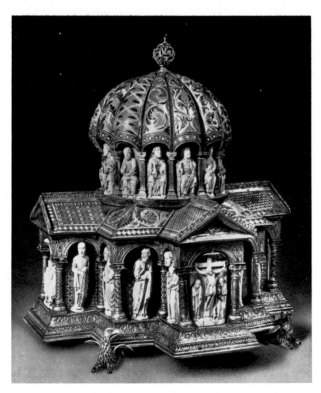

that he expressed his feelings in Heidelberg in verse which celebrated the castle as 'Parnassus'. Sandrart gave individual descriptions of early German paintings, among them a portrait of Frederick II of the Palatinate by Dürer which has since disappeared. In an inventory of the year 1685 we find references to other paintings, among them no doubt heirlooms from the former collection of Ottheinrich. Next to the early Germans, among whom Holbein, Cranach, Amberger and Pencz were represented, the Venetians of the early sixteenth century were obviously objects of particular pride in the Heidelberg gallery. There was a portrait by Jacopo de' Barbari of a duke of Mecklenburg (now in the Mauritshuis, The Hague) and the idealized portrait of Columbus by Sebastiano del Piombo (now in the Metropolitan Museum, New 99

160 In large collections such as the Uffizi, busts and reliefs were grouped symmetrically around a centrepiece. This drawing, made in about 1710, shows the wall of a room in the Uffizi. The centrepiece is part of the *Ara Pacis* which dates from the time of Augustus. It was transferred to Rome in 1937

York). Among the masterpieces of the early seventeenth century was a *Death of the Virgin* by Saraceni (now in Ampleforth Abbey in Yorkshire); there were also, of course, works by Rubens and van Dyck in the Heidelberg collection.

Some years later the male Palatinate-Simmern line of the Wittelsbachs died out. Princess Liselotte,

the daughter of the prince whom Sandrart visited, had meanwhile become the wife of the Duke of Orleans and the sister-in-law of Louis XIV. Before French troops destroyed Heidelberg Castle in the war of the Palatine succession, the paintings which had been housed there came to France as an inheritance of Princess Liselotte. In her letters, she makes occasional mention of certain pictures from the 'Heidelberg Gallery' which were honoured after 1690 by gilt borders in the Palace of St Cloud near Paris.

N 121

In Italy there was a characteristic change in the relation of the Roman art world of the seventeenth century towards antiquity. Bernini made the classical *Apollo Belvedere*, which had been idolized in the epoch of the High Renaissance, acceptable to his own contemporaries by transforming its restfulness into movement in the *Apollo and Daphne* group (now in the Borghese Gallery in Rome). The collectors of the Baroque period were generally inclined to Hellenistic art. Copies of statues full of classical

161, 162   The Renaissance had favoured above all the restrained harmony of antique statues, but in the seventeenth century artists and collectors alike preferred Hellenistic sculpture which may justifiably be called 'antique Baroque'. Bernini (above) and Rubens (below) both chose the head of Medusa as a subject

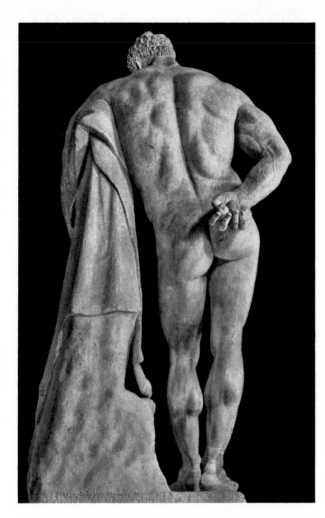

even St Christopher himself. French artists preferred N 122 a rather more slender younger brother of the *Farnese Hercules*, the *Vatican Hermes*, at that time known as the *Belvedere Antinous*. Duquesnoy gained great success in 1625 with a small replica of this statue. *165*

The bearded heads of staunchly masculine gods like the *Farnese Jove* and the head of the tortured *2* *Laocoön* were a revelation for artists of all nations then staying in Rome. Schlüter's *Dying Warriors* in the courtyard of the Berlin Arsenal are variations of the *Laocoön* head; Bernini declared his particular love for the *Belvedere Torso* and the *Vatican Cleopatra*. N 123 Besides the older collections of antique art in the Vatican and in the Palazzo Farnese the newly created collections of Marchese Giustiniani and of the papal nephews Borghese, Barberini, and Ludovisi gained fame. The *Borghese Fencer* (now in the Louvre) was particularly well attuned to the taste of the Bernini epoch, as was the *Barberini Faun* (now in the Munich Glyptothek), which was found in 1630 at the base of the Castel Sant'Angelo. As the vital impulses of the High Baroque died away, the *Farnese Hercules* and similar works lost something of their great reputation. There now began an age which preferred more subtle qualities, when connoisseurs admired 'the Love Goddess of Phidias', the *Venus de Medici* in the Uffizi. This famous statue, which

163, 164 The massive and perhaps excessively powerful statue of Hercules (above), which had belonged to the Farnese family since about 1540, was particularly admired in the Baroque period. Annibale Carracci made a sketch of the statue (right) which stood in the courtyard of the Palazzo Farnese, and Rubens based several of his figures on it

repose had once been popular: the *Marcus Aurelius* and the *Venus Victrix* in the Belvedere, for instance. Susini now gained a great following with his little bronze copies of the *Farnese Bull*, which at that time could be seen in the courtyard of the Palazzo Farnese at Rome. Here also stood the *163* muscular *Farnese Hercules*, who was drawn from every possible angle; for Rubens this work became the prototype for legions of gods and heroes, hunters and soldiers built on a Herculean model, and unites classical with Hellenistic elements of style, was praised by English travellers around 1700 as 'beauty itself'. But some decades later the 'antique Rococo' of the Naples *Venus Kallipygos* had its peculiar message for the contemporaries of Boucher.

166

As in London and Brussels, so now in Rome and Florence the great Venetians became the decided favourites of art-lovers: Cardinal Scipione Borghese who collected during the Bernini epoch on a more grandiose scale than anybody else, preferred to receive presents of pictures by the Venetian masters; thus the Patriarch of Aquileia sent him two paintings by Veronese. In 1608 Cardinal Borghese acquired one of the finest masterpieces of Titian's early 'Giorgionesque' period: a nuptial picture that came from the old Venetian family of Aurelio, representing Penelope and Calypso and containing an allusion to the mythical origin of the family of Odysseus. At the end of the seventeenth century the

166 The French sculptor Duquesnoy became famous as a result of his small copy of the Hellenistic *Vatican Hermes*. He commissioned Jacques Blanchard to paint this portrait

166 The most versatile and successful collector of the seventeenth century was Cardinal Scipione Borghese in Rome. This portrait bust of him is by Bernini

name *Amor sacro e Amor profano*—sacred and profane love—was attached to it for the first time, and the title has clung to the picture ever since (the painting is now in the Borghese Gallery, as are all the other acquisitions of Cardinal Borghese here named). At this time there also came into the possession of the Borghese family *The Education of Amor*, a late work of Titian. Van Dyck was permitted around 1625 to sketch this painting in the family's town palace and could not resist the temptation of writing on the breast of one of the servants of Venus 'Quel admirabil petto'.

When in 1598 the d'Este family were compelled to hand over Ferrara to the Pope they just managed to save Titian's *Tribute Money* (now in the Dresden Gallery) and got it to their new residence in Modena. They were unable to prevent the Roman grandees from requisitioning their remaining Titians. *Bacchus and Ariadne* went to the Aldobrandini (now in the National Gallery, London); the *Feast of Venus* was studied by Poussin in 1630 in the Ludovisi Palace. About this time the Grand Dukes of Tuscany became heirs to the princely House of Urbino, which had died out. They promptly gave places of honour in the Tribuna of the Uffizi to the Titians that were brought to Florence, the *Venus of Urbino* for instance (now in the Palazzo Pitti in Florence).

Besides Titian himself, his contemporaries and immediate predecessors were also held in high regard. Cardinal Pietro Aldobrandini brought Bellini's *Feast of the Gods* in 1598 to Rome (now in the National Gallery, Washington, D. C.); the Marchese Giustiniani had a preference for portraits by Lorenzo Lotto (now in the Berlin Museums); above all Giorgione was a recognized star of the first magnitude. His *Concert Champêtre* (finished by Titian) came to Florence in 1654 (now in the Palazzo Pitti). Dosso Dossi of Ferrara is a painter of whom nothing has yet been said. The dream-like mood which his pictures express and their glowing colours gave him a place by the side of Giorgione; in 1598 the *Bacchanal* which had been originally painted for the studiolo of Alfonso d'Este came into the possession of the popes (now in the Castel Sant'Angelo in Rome). Shortly after this Cardinal Borghese acquired the *Circe* (now in the Borghese Gallery, Rome).

The honour in which Raphael was held—already noted when dealing with Charles I of England—naturally had its consequences among Italian collectors, although the number of available pictures was limited. Correggio was now discovered as 'the Raphael of Parma' and the d'Este family found ways to remove his altarpieces from churches in order to grace their great gallery in Modena. The Medici would not rest until they too possessed a painting by Correggio, the *Rest on the Flight to Egypt* acquired from Modena in 1649 by way of exchange (now in the Uffizi Gallery).

Whereas the collections of the north contained works of an earlier date than 1500, this was very rare south of the Alps. A guide for art-lovers travelling in Italy which appeared in 1671 and of which an English translation had been made within eight years, does not mention any painter born before Raphael. Nevertheless Leopoldo de' Medici added the *Bust of a Girl* by Desiderio da Settignano (1428-64) to his collection (now in the Bargello in Florence). Before 1700 Botticelli's *Adoration of the Magi* (now in the Uffizi Gallery) was taken from the Church of Santa Maria Novella to the Medici villa at Poggio Imperiale.

While Tintoretto was represented on a considerable scale north of the Alps, his fame seems to have been less extensive in Italy, with the exception of Venice. So far as the second half of the sixteenth century was concerned, Scipione Borghese favoured the painters of Emilia, Tuscany and Rome. We have already encountered the contemporary art of Italy in the north in the works of Caravaggio. When the *Madonna dei Palafrenieri*, the altarpiece of the papal stablemaster, was rejected as irreverent by the cardinals in charge of the architectural administration of St Peter's, Scipione Borghese, the Pope's nephew, had no misgivings about taking the work into his gallery. Marchese Giustiniani also acquired Caravaggio's *Altar of St Matthew*, which was regarded as unsuitable for religious purposes (this picture was destroyed by fire in Berlin in 1945). If any proof is needed of the genuine artistic feeling among Italian collectors of the Baroque age, there are four cases in which the rejection of an altarpiece by Caravaggio on the part of the clerical authorities was immediately followed by the purchase of the work in question by art-lovers who appreciated its value.

Cardinal Borghese also showed considerable sympathy for the 'classical line' in the painting of his time; from the Roman studio of Domenichino he removed, almost by force, the artist's *Hunt of Diana*. The mildly anti-Baroque element was represented by Guido Reni, Dolci and Sassoferrato and also by the French painters Poussin and Claude. It was only exceptionally that these French artists enjoyed any considerable success among the great collectors of the epoch; the eccentric Cassiano del Pozzo owned some forty paintings by Poussin, whereas the art-loving Barberini family had only a few of his works, among them *Augustus and Cleopatra* (now in the National Gallery in Ottawa).

Paintings from the north generally played an unimportant part in the Baroque Italian collections. Around 1630 a number of Dürer panels came into the Tribuna of the Uffizi as a present from Vienna. The Barberini family possessed *Christ and the Scribes* (now in the Thyssen collection at Lugano). Scipione Borghese acquired a *Venus* by Cranach.

Little Flemish landscapes with figures, by the school of Bruegel, were very popular; we still find them in the Pinacoteca Ambrosiana in Milan and in old Roman collections. This kind of painting on a miniature scale could not be found amongst the Italians at that time and was the cause of the high regard in which Flemish painters like Metsu and Mieris were held after 1630, for instance in Florence. Rembrandt's etchings reached Italy fairly early. Four of his paintings were commissioned by the Marchese Antonio Ruffo in Messina.

Among the most important collectors in Rome the Cardinals held the dominant position, though some of the old noble houses and certain families which had migrated to Rome from northern Italy endeav-

167 Cardinal Valenti-Gonzaga commissioned from Pannini a free Roman adaptation of the Flemish type of painted gallery. Many of the paintings in the picture were never owned by the Cardinal: their purpose is merely to indicate his general taste. The arrangement of the pictures corresponds to Late Baroque theories

N 129 oured to keep up with them. The artistic treasures in the palaces of the Borghese, Spada, Barberini, Aldobrandini, Doria-Pamphili, Colonna, Giustiniani, Massimi and Pallavicini-Rospigliosi offered artists and travellers from the north an excess of delight.

Exhibitions had already begun to play a certain part in the artistic life of Rome in the seventeenth century. Among works by Roman artists, Velazquez exhibited the portrait of his servant Pareja in the B 113 vestibule of the Pantheon on 19 March 1650. B 115 On 29 October for many years one could have seen in the courtyards of San Giovanni Decollato parts of the famous private collections, and once even pictures from the collection of Christina of Sweden.

In Florence, the ruling House contrived to engross all the separate collections of younger princes and illegitimate descendants. In the middle of the seventeenth century there came into being the room of artists' portraits as a late outcome of the 'Gallery of Copies' and in the manner of Giovio's

168 The picture gallery of the Palazzo Colonna in Rome, which was completed in 1703, has managed, in spite of alterations, to preserve much of its original form. Sculpture and paintings were combined for overall effect

'Musaeum'. This, next to the Tribuna, aroused particular interest among visitors after 1681. In the Palazzo Pitti, the liberally expanded residence of the Grand Dukes, five picture-rooms were arranged which till today have maintained their original character. 'The best collection that ever I saw', was the comment made in 1670 by the well-informed

N 130 Englishman Lassels.

Next in order of magnificence after the collection of the Medici in Florence, in Lassels's estimation,
N 131 came that of the d'Este in Modena. Eighty years later one hundred of its best pictures were removed to Dresden. In Parma the Farnese possessed nearly a thousand paintings. In Bologna, Venice, Milan and Genoa there were numerous smaller private collections. Two of the important collections in southern Italy were those of Gaspard Roomer,

who had migrated from Antwerp and had about fifteen hundred paintings in Naples, and the B 43 Marchese Ruffo in Messina, a small but extremely choice collection.

During the course of the seventeenth century the centre of gravity moved more and more towards the north. Italy had to pay for its economic weakness by a decline in the quantity of the artistic treasures it possessed. Spain, itself slowly sinking into decay, continued for a time to absorb Italy's riches. It was then that, under Louis XIV, France began to appear as a purchaser. After the repulse of the Turks, who had pressed forward as far as Vienna, Germany attained a degree of prosperity which encouraged

XI Of the paintings of this kind that have survived more are by Teniers the Younger than by any other single artist. Teniers painted this idealized representation of the collection which Archduke Leopold Wilhelm had built up while viceroy in Brussels (detail). Many of his paintings are now in the Kunsthistorisches Museum in Vienna

artistic life and facilitated the creation of new collections not only in Bavaria and the Rhineland but also east of the Elbe.

After Charles I of England had acquired the collection of the Gonzagas, Philip IV of Spain set his heart on increasing the fine collection that he had inherited. The great Venetian painters, who since the days of Charles V had particularly attracted the Habsburgs, found special favour in Spanish eyes. Two of the Titians, which in 1598 had been moved from Ferrara to Rome, went to Madrid forty years

N 132 later. There is a tradition that Domenichino broke into tears when in 1638 he saw for the last time the *Feast of Venus* in the Palazzo Ludovisi (now in the Prado as are all the paintings mentioned below). Philip IV, the great art-lover and dilettante painter, sent his court painter and friend Velazquez to purchase pictures in Italy in 1649; three Venetians headed the list of painters whose works he particularly wished to acquire—Titian, Veronese and Bassano. Velazquez on that occasion acquired a particularly fine Veronese, *Venus and Adonis*, and also Tintoretto's

B 113 *Gloria. The Virgin and Child with St Anthony of Padua and St Roch* by Giorgione, the favourite of the seventeenth century, came into the royal collection by another route. Around 1660 the inventory of the royal collection mentions 102 Titians and a great abundance of other sixteenth-century Venetians. Even today we get a better impression of the great century of Venetian painting in the Prado Museum than anywhere else in the world.

On that list of painters whose work Velazquez was to acquire, Raphael came fourth. Clearly the King of Spain regarded a certain number of his works as indispensable. Around 1650 three of Raphael's altarpieces, which had been partly painted by others working in his studio, came into the possession of the Spanish Crown. These came from Naples, from Palermo and, after the execution of Charles I, from London.

The attitude of Philip IV towards contemporary art was marked by greater reserve than that of such a man as Cardinal Scipione Borghese. Not a single picture of the great revolutionary Caravaggio came to Spain. On the other hand the King could not have enough Rubenses. In 1638 alone, 120 pictures by the great Flemish artist (who was after all a Spanish subject) were hung in the palace at Buen Retiro and a further 32 pictures by the master were acquired by Philip from Rubens' estate.

At the end of the seventeenth century 5,539 paintings are recorded as being in the possession of the Spanish Crown, of which 1,622 were in the Escorial. Neither in Vienna nor in Paris, let alone any other city, was there any comparable accumulation of works of art. Several fires and the plundering of French officers during the time of Napoleon were to reduce these numbers considerably.

Research has failed to discover much about the collections of Spanish grandees. Don Gasparo de Haro y Guzman, the viceroy in Naples, owned in 1650 Velazquez's *The Toilet of Venus* (the so-called *18 Rokeby Venus* now in the National Gallery in London). Through the agency of the Duke of Medina, a moderate-sized altar painting by Guercino came to Spain (now in the Denis Mahon Collection in London). A small *Madonna* by Raphael was acquired by the ducal family of Alba and has borne their name ever since (now in the National Gallery in Washington).

The barely two hundred pictures, which in 1630 were hanging in the French royal castles, included the basic masterpieces by Leonardo and his Tuscan contemporaries acquired in 1530, but these were overshadowed by the great collections of other dynasties that had emerged since then. For this reason the French were not slow to use the opportunity presented by the sale of Charles I's London collection. The collection of Leopold Wilhelm in Brussels, which had become famous overnight, stimulated the ambitions of Louis XIV and his advisers to a very high degree. When the 'Gallery Book' with engravings of that collection aroused widespread comment, the Roi Soleil immediately arranged for a similar publication of reproductions of his finest pictures. In Louis XIV there was embodied a state under a royal mask that was perfectly conscious of its goal. How close the personal relationship of the monarch was to this or that painting it is impossible to say, since Louis let others do his collecting. The throne was surrounded by servants of the Crown who had grown rich overnight and whom their master from time to time relieved of their works of art for a very small amount of money. In such transactions collectors, it was said in Paris, were treated 'not like Christians but like Moors', and many a courtier or financier preferred to stake and lose a picture in a game with the King or even in certain circumstances to make him a present of it.

XII In the first thirty years of the eighteenth century the fame of Watteau spread from Paris throughout central and eastern Europe. Many of his most beautiful paintings were bought by princes in Berlin, Dresden and St Petersburg. After the revolution of 1917, the Soviet government sold Watteau's *Mezzetin* to the Metropolitan Museum in New York for $150,000

As in Antwerp and Amsterdam, people in Paris looked upon works of art as capital investments. 'Pictures are like bars of gold; you sell them at any time for double the price you gave for them', wrote a collector in 1675 to Madame de Sévigné. In the fine houses of bankers and ministers you could see paintings by the great masters which the owners were always ready to sell immediately if a visitor made a sufficiently high offer. Even expert opinions were already given in writing on particular pictures; during his stay in Paris in 1665 Bernini, describing a picture by Albani, ended by saying, 'Mi piace assaissimo'—I like it very much indeed.

N 133

The *Livre commode des adresses de Paris* which appeared in 1691, names 134 'fameux curieux parisiens'. The energetic activities of these people, the interest of society in questions of art and the mounting influence of art criticism, led with ever increasing speed to changes in the trends of taste. From 1670 onward there were periodic full-scale slumps in the price of works of art as particular items suddenly went out of fashion.

169   At the court of Louis XIV paintings were carefully arranged in accordance with aesthetic principles of the time. This applied even to temporary displays such as this exhibition of paintings by members of the Royal Academy

Certain typical collectors of the French Grand Siècle can be briefly described. At the auction of van Uffeln's property a distinguished Spanish Jew, Alfonzo Lopez, acquired Raphael's *Portrait of Balthasar Castiglione*; as a dealer in arms and also in art Lopez shortly after this migrated to Paris. The 'Seigneur hébreu', as Cardinal Richelieu called him, now became a Catholic and drove about the city in a coach and six. His finest picture, that same *Castiglione* by Raphael, later found its way into the French royal collection (now in the Louvre).

Two other foreigners who had moved to Paris made their appearance when the collection of Charles I of England was broken up—the German Everard Jabach and the Italian Mazarini (Mazarin). No doubt they had intended to make over their works of art to Louis XIV from the beginning. Jabach, the manager of the Royal French India Company and the supplier of the army, had his portrait painted by van Dyck, Le Brun and Rigaud; for a time Giorgione's *Concert Champêtre* and some of the principal works of Titian could be seen in his palatial house. Jabach suffered financial reverses, which he was fortunately able to survive through the sale of his paintings to the Crown, whereupon he immediately undertook new acquisitions. From his drawings, about which Bernini expressed warm appreciation, Jabach passed over no less than 5,542 to Louis XIV in 1671.

B 75

X

N 134

Cardinal Mazarin, the successor of Richelieu, engaged in collecting, exchanging and dealing on an even more grandiose scale than Jabach. He rented

B 329

the Hôtel d'Estrées for the purpose of holding auctions there. The opinion in Paris was that Jabach, who came from the Rhineland, was open-handed in his dealings in works of art, whereas the Italian Mazarin was an obstinate haggler. The palace of the Chancellor contained two galleries, one for antique statues and one for paintings. The general character of the contents was Baroque in the Roman sense with the stress on brilliance and luxury; there were also plenty of works with a distinctly erotic intention. NeverN 135theless Mazarin also owned a painting by Poussin (now in the Detroit Institute of Arts). The Cardinal's secretary, the Duc de Brienne, who was also a collector, surprised his sick master one night in front of his pictures. 'Il faut quitter tout cela; je ne verrai plus ces beaux tableaux où je vais', Brienne heard him say. Just before his death Mazarin offered Louis XIV a part of his possessions. Louis chose eighteen large diamonds and a number of pictures. When the remainder of Mazarin's collection was auctioned after his death part of it again went to the Crown.

The dominating position of the art of central Italy in France derived at first from close political relations with Florence and the hostile feelings entertained towards Venice which was in sympathy with the Habsburgs. It may well be that certain basic traits in the French character—the feeling for strict form and a luminous clarity of reasoning—made the Florentine manner particularly acceptable to Parisian painters, sculptors and collectors. As against this, the cloudy and irrational character of many Venetian artists, such as Tintoretto, seemed confused to the French, while the peculiarly Roman pathos of the High Baroque struck them as bombastic. In Italy itself there was in the seventeenth century a frequently mentioned 'classical line'; the Frenchmen Poussin and Claude, who worked in Rome and were regarded highly by Parisian collectors, tended to associate themselves with this. Poussin several times copied the classical painting which we know as the *Aldobrandini Wedding* (now in the Vatican). Until 1665 the King, the big collectors and a number of prominent Paris citizens—officials, doctors, merchants—were all eager to acquire paintings by Poussin; perhaps they found stylistic features in them which resembled those in the dramas of Racine.

About 1660 public opinion in Paris underwent a considerable change; Rubens was favoured at Poussin's expense. Prices for paintings by Poussin fell sharply, though not all collectors lost their heads. Claudine Stella, a collector of paintings who lived in Paris, advised her heirs in 1693 not to sell; the slump in Poussins would not last long.

The principal works of Venetian painting which the Italian Mazarin and the German Jabach had

170   Like Cardinal Borghese, Louis XIV commissioned Bernini to make a bust of him (see Ill. 166)

brought over from London began to have their effect from 1660, and in 1684 the name of Tintoretto was mentioned in Paris for the first time. The art N 136 critic, Roger de Piles, visited the Spanish Netherlands and there saw Venetian paintings and works by Rubens; he even continued his journey to Amsterdam, where the late work of Rembrandt had a great effect on him. In the period of the Late Baroque the anti-classical slogans in Paris grew more intense. Roger de Piles, in his *Dialogue on Colour*, took the side of the Venetians. Basically it was the traditional taste of the Habsburg collectors that now began to influence the French court, a taste exemplified in the *Pardo Venus*, the favourite picture of the Spanish 103 Kings which, since the death of Mazarin, belonged to the French Crown.

The change of taste is clearly apparent from recent research concerning the extension of the 'Cabinet du Roy', as the royal painting collection was called. In 1660 the Doge of Venice, presumably having made preliminary enquiries, sent to Paris Veronese's highly ornate *The Feast in the House*

171 When the Turkish threat had been averted, the House of Habsburg became one of the most powerful families in Europe. The Imperial gallery, with Leopold Wilhelm's collection as its nucleus, was restored and re-opened in 1728. This sketch for an ideal representation of the scene is by the Neapolitan artist Solimena

of Simon the Pharisee; in 1671 a late self-portrait by Rembrandt was acquired; and in 1681 we find a record of fourteen paintings by van Dyck. Three paintings by Rubens were bought before 1685, among them the lusty *Country Fair;* around 1690 Venetian paintings such as Veronese's *Disciples at Emmaus* obtained the place of honour in the Palace of Versailles which had just been completed. The Duc de Richelieu, a nephew of the Cardinal's, bore striking witness to the change in taste. He sold his Poussins and acquired in their stead some fifteen

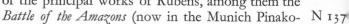

of the principal works of Rubens, among them the *Battle of the Amazons* (now in the Munich Pinakothek).

After the death of Louis XIV there was yet another change. The place of the 'grand goût', the great style, was taken by 'grâce'. The Baroque was followed by the various motifs of eighteenth-century style: 'Régence', 'Louis XV' and so on. Watteau, in his 'fêtes galantes', reproduced Titian and Rubens in boudoir size. 'Le petit tableau et la petite curiosité' were much desired. Chardin illustrates the nearness of the bourgeois world with his genre pictures that owe so much to Dutch art. He was 'discovered' on the feast of Corpus Christi in the year 1728, when he exhibited at the Place Dauphine in the open air.

At the beginning of the eighteenth century Pierre Crozat was the leading Paris collector. His father had acquired an immense fortune by trade with the French colony of Louisiana in North America. In the Palais Crozat where Watteau lived as a kind of court artist, there were 400 paintings, but Crozat's real passion was for drawings, of which he had gathered together 19,000. The witty sketch lightly thrown off became the 'morceau de choix' for the French collectors of the Rococo period. In these years Italian artists such as Piazzetta are known to have earned more with their drawings, which were deliberately done to suit the market, than with their large paintings. Mariette acted as a kind of 'savant-amateur' and curator for Crozat, and after Crozat's death acquired his employer's finest drawings. The finest collections of pictures at that time were in the possession of the Orléans family, the Duc de Choiseul, Randon de Boisset and Julienne.

Madame de Verrue must not be left out of any description of Paris in the early eighteenth century. As a 'nymph'—that was the word used at this time—she made a fortune and probably received paintings from her lovers. She despised the great canvases of the Baroque period and surrounded herself with paintings by Watteau, Lancret, Boucher and Chardin, but was also prepared to have some Dutch landscapes of the Rembrandt period in her house.

In Germany the consequences of the Thirty Years War had at first delayed any flowering of Baroque culture and art. In 1683 the advance of the Turks on Vienna brought the whole of central Europe face to face with its greatest danger. This was overcome, and the proud series of Prince Eugen's victories gave to the generation that lived around 1700 a sudden burst of vitality. When the Spanish Habsburgs finally died out, the German line of the

House received the southern Netherlands, Milan and Naples. A new golden age began for large parts of Germany. Apart from the imperial city of Vienna, Munich, the seat of the Wittelsbachs, attained a new importance, as well as three rising Catholic courts north of the Main: the new residency of the Elector Palatine at Düsseldorf; Brunswick, whose Duke Anton Ulrich had embraced the Catholic faith; and Dresden, where for Augustus the Strong the Polish crown was worth becoming Catholic. To these five princely courts we should also add Pommersfelden near Bamberg, the residence of Franz Lothar Schönborn, Archbishop and Elector of Mainz. At these focal points of the German Late Baroque, which had more of an Italian than French air, music as well as all the visual arts flourished.

171 The apotheosis of the Baroque prince was not confined to the throne-room. In the court library at Vienna the marble statue of the Emperor was placed in the middle of the principal room. In the Spanish Court Riding School at Vienna the riders had to pay their respects to a picture of the Emperor which was hung on one of the side walls. In the 'Caesarea Pinacotheca', the imperial picture gallery, a painting by Solimena (now in the Vienna Museum) was prominently displayed showing an eminent court official presenting the Emperor with the inventory of the collection. The fresco of the ceiling of the great hall that housed the Brunswick collection represented Apollo with the Muses grouped around the bust of Duke Anton Ulrich.

N 140 The rigid presentation of paintings with emphasis on symmetry, a development which culminated in Vienna, the centre of Late Baroque architecture, began to relax from 1730 onwards. Already in the galleries of the Palazzo Pitti superb carved and gilt frames established a close connection between the paintings and the decoration on the ceilings. The relief of the Virgin Mary by the early Renaissance master Rossellino (now in the Vienna Gallery), part of the dowry that Claudia Medici brought to Innsbruck, was also distinguished by such a Baroque Florentine frame.

Annibale Carracci's *The Hunt* (in the Louvre) and the equestrian portrait of Count Olivares by Velazquez (in the Prado) are still furnished today with fine Baroque frames. Unfortunately we do not know in what fashion Velazquez decorated the picture halls of the Escorial with paintings in 1656. In the great South Gallery of the Madrid palace thirty Titians were at that time outfitted with black frames in the Antwerp manner.

Towards the end of the seventeenth century the style of the period demanded the maximum of closely-packed content and a great wealth of forms.

172 Storffer painted exact representations of the Caesarea Pinacotheca in the Stallburg in Vienna. On this particular wall can be seen the self-portrait of Rubens in middle age which was put into an oval frame at this time

Even during the exhibition of the Royal Academy in the Grande Galerie of the Louvre for three weeks in September 1699, paintings were hung as closely together as possible on top of tapestries. 169 Shortly after 1700 in Vienna, the collection of the Archduke Leopold Wilhelm, which was bequeathed to the imperial House, was placed in the 'Stallburg', an older part of the imperial Residenz. 172

Now it was considered a matter of course that the walls, to quote a contemporary writer, 'were not to be hung with anything save paintings, so that one painting should touch the frame of the other'. The entire wall space was organized according to the fashion of the time. Large central areas were decoratively surrounded by smaller shapes. Oval pictures were regarded as producing a pleasant effect if placed high up. The paintings of the Italian and Flemish masters of the seventeenth century provided an adequate supply of large-scale pictures for the centre of a wall. For the rest of the area, pictures were ruthlessly 'formatized', i. e. were cut down or had something stuck on to them and oval pictures were produced out of what had originally been rectangular ones.

This so-called 'formatizing' was applied to about forty per cent of the pictures in the Vienna Stallburg. In the Wittelsbach collection, then housed in the Palace of Schleissheim near Munich, at least a third of the pictures were treated in this fashion. Further north, in the region of Frankfurt, the Dutch conception of the intrinsic value of every picture began to gain ground. Franz Lothar von Schönborn wrote to his nephew, the Imperial Vice Chancellor

173 The gallery in the castle of Pommersfelden near Bamberg, which had been founded by the Elector Franz Lothar von Schönborn, was accepted in the eighteenth century as one of the most delightful collections in southern Germany. The engraving is by Salomon Kleiner (detail)

in Vienna: 'As to taking off much from the good pieces or for the sake of uniformity adding something to them—nobody shall move me to do this, as it is very prejudicial to the pictures and to their painters'. This lively exchange of letters between uncle and nephew from the year 1715 shows us the keen interest with which these exalted gentlemen themselves settled all the details that affected their collections. On the question whether a ceiling picture would not provide unpleasant competition with paintings on the wall, Franz Lothar von Schönborn had very determined views; he said he would 'have very little, perhaps nothing painted in the gallery "in fresco" but only some light stucco work put in by an admirable artist' in his service. When finally the hanging of the paintings was to begin in Pommersfelden, the Elector would not let anybody take this work out of his hands. In August 1715 he was at last able to report to Vienna: 'Over two hundred and fifty pieces have been hung between Monday and Friday evening, that is to say five days, and in such a manner that the most sensitive enthusiast could hardly find much to correct in what I have hung'. B 70

The room where the pictures hung has long been destroyed as a result of alterations; Dürer's *Portrait of Muffel* belongs now to the Berlin Museums and Rembrandt's early picture *Rembrandt's Mother as the Prophetess Hannah* to the Amsterdam Rijksmuseum. Dürer's *Man of Sorrows* which was once in the collection of Cardinal Albert in Halle, and a number of Italian pictures from about 1700 remained undisturbed. Franz Lothar von Schönborn, who according to his own words was plagued 'by the worm of painting', had not only acquired paintings of bygone artists but was also proud of the fact that at the time there was no major artist in Italy from whom he had not purchased fine pieces.

The method of fitting each individual painting into a general decorative scheme, which was practised more frequently in Vienna than anywhere else, suited the arrangement of antique sculpture at that time. Miniatures and porcelain figures, originally designed to be seen at close hand, were grouped together in cabinets which covered the walls from top to bottom. Drawings also lost their individual existence. They were stuck together in large volumes and framed with delicately coloured edges, thus also becoming constituent parts of a greater whole. In the early eighteenth century, especially in southern Germany, it was the practice to arrange books in a purely decorative fashion. N 141

One should not, as was often done in the past, immediately speak of 'the violation of the individual

174 By 1700 the Habsburgs in Prague had restocked their picture gallery, but chiefly with second-rate works. Nevertheless, even these were symmetrically arranged. The painting is by Johann Bretschneider

168 work of art' in connection with the Late Baroque creation of galleries. A perfectly preserved ensemble of the highest order, such as the Vienna Stallburg, no longer exists. The painting rooms of the Palazzo Pitti and the gallery of the Palazzo Colonna still offer a faint reflection, despite rehanging and the use of unsuitable frames of a later period.

The visual sense of the early eighteenth century was highly cultivated. Just as the effect of porcelain was enhanced by the use of mirrors, so contrasts were deliberately made between dark pictures and light ones, according to contemporary accounts. The remark of a collector that 'an Asselyn could be B 131 destroyed by the proximity of a Jan Both' implies an extremely high degree of artistic discrimination. As far as possible, pictures with different horizons were not placed next to each other, nor those with large figures near those with small ones.

In Vienna at the time of the Turkish Wars, the 'Caesarea Pinacotheca' was not promoted by any particular emperor, and yet it slowly expanded. From Venice pictures were continually coming into the possession of the Habsburgs, so that, as in Milan and Naples, there were complaints about the purchasing power of German thalers. The great N 142 Flemings—van Dyck now in addition to Rubens— enjoyed considerable esteem. Finally, the art of Holland, a country which had stood by the Habsburgs against Louis XIV in the War of the Spanish Succession, also attracted notice; around 1720, paintings by Frans Hals and Backhuysen became imperial property.

At the same time the Vienna palaces of the great nobles and the *nouveaux riches* began to be filled with paintings whose total number has been assessed as high as 6,000. The great majority of these paintings remained undisturbed in the houses of Viennese art-lovers till 1918; since then, with few exceptions, they have been scattered all over the world. The connoisseur Christian Ludwig von Hagedorn wrote in 1740 that 'in Vienna there is more Italian painting "in obscuro" [i. e. hidden] than in the whole of Holland'. Apart from Italian paintings there was a distinct demand for the merchandise put up for sale by the Vienna branch of Forchoudt, the Antwerp art dealers.

175 In Vienna in the early eighteenth century collecting was not restricted to the nobility, and ordinary citizens as well as artists amassed extensive collections. Platzer shows the interior of a house belonging to an artist who was evidently also an art dealer

Karl Eusebius von Liechtenstein is generally reputed to be the founder of the 'Galerie Liechtenstein'. He left his heirs, who seem to have followed the taste of Leopold Wilhelm in their purchase of pictures, a sort of memorandum dealing with the duty of the nobility to collect works of art. He wrote that 'anyone can have money but not anyone can have paintings'. Germany, he said, was only just beginning to start collections, whereas the 'magnates' in England and many commoners in Italy were most zealous in this matter. Karl Eusebius von Liechtenstein urged

his successors to purchase 'originals of the excellent old masters who attained great perfection'. A special 'galleria' should be devoted to paintings and statues; works that were proved to be copies were to be put in 'an inferior place'.

Up to 1939 the collection of the Liechtenstein Princes in the family's summer palace in Vienna was admired as the leading private collection in the world. Since then many of the principal works have been sold to the National Gallery in Ottawa and other places. The considerable remainder can be seen in Vaduz, including Rubens' *Victory and Death of Decius Mus*, a picture sold to the Liechtenstein family in 1692 by the firm of Forchoudt.

The second oldest of the Vienna private collections which has survived almost unimpaired and has recently been opened once again to the public is that of the Counts Harrach. Its founder, Count Bonaventura Harrach, travelled many times to Spain during the closing decades of the seventeenth century as ambassador extraordinary. He saw the altarpieces by El Greco in Toledo and by Murillo in Seville. In the Palace of Buen Retiro, he saw several of Bosch's fantasies of hell which Philip II had originally acquired. The impression made by these led him to buy a picture of the Bosch school. Harrach was particularly interested in the great Spanish painters; he made purchases at the auction of the Marquis de Aguilar's collection and ultimately took back to Vienna a respectable number of Spanish paintings of the sixteenth and seventeenth centuries.

One generation later a younger member of the family, Count Aloys Harrach, was sent to the Kingdom of the Two Sicilies (southern Italy and the neighbouring island of Sicily) which had recently come under the Imperial Crown. The Count, who resided as Viceroy in Naples, and from there transplanted the cult of St Januarius to Vienna, received gifts of paintings from officials in his own government and also from petitioning merchants; the subject city of Cava handed over a picture by the much-prized Solimena. When Harrach returned to Vienna in 1733 he was able to enrich the existing collection of paintings in the town palace on the Freyung with Italian paintings of contemporary as well as bygone masters.

Two smaller Austrian collections which have remained almost intact came into being in the early part of the eighteenth century at some distance from Vienna. The Imperial General, Prince Eugen of the House of Savoia-Carignano, crammed pictures into

176, 177 Prince Eugen was brought up in Paris and became rich and famous as a military commander in the service of the Habsburgs. He included a small, select picture gallery in his Belvedere Palace in Vienna. The sketch (below) by van den Berghe shows the Prince selecting paintings. The best likeness of the Prince is the sculpture by Balthasar Permoser (detail above)

two rooms of his great summer palace in Vienna which we now call the Upper Belvedere. The early Flemish masters, of which Leopold Wilhelm had thought so highly—Jan van Eyck, Petrus Christus, Memling—were represented, as were Rembrandt and Gerard Dou, who at that time enjoyed an enormous vogue. This collection went by inheritance to the line of the House of Savoy which ruled in Piedmont; today it forms one of the most interesting component parts of the Pinacoteca

N 143 Nazionale in Turin. Two fine paintings, however, Rembrandt's *Visitation* (last in the possession of the English branch of the Rothschilds in Halton Manor) and Dou's *Dropsical Woman* (now in the Louvre) travelled roads of their own. The Vienna collection of Count Gotter, who was considered in that gallant age as one of the most charming and frivolous of Germans, was sold in 1736 for 24,000 thalers to the Duke of Württemberg; roughly a hundred and twenty pictures in the present Stutt-

72 gart Staatsgalerie, among them Memling's *Bathsheba*, originate from this sale.

During the Turkish Wars the young prince Max Emanuel of Bavaria had distinguished himself as a very dashing officer at Budapest and Belgrade. Half a century after Leopold Wilhelm, he resided for a short time as Viceroy of the Spanish Netherlands in Brussels and later became acquainted with the court of Louis XIV at Versailles. Max Emanuel was a passionate art-lover. His happiest acquisition occurred in 1698, when Gisbert van Ceulen in Antwerp handed over 105 high-quality paintings to the House of Wittelsbach for 90,000 Brabant guilders. Among these pictures were ten by Rubens, thirteen by van Dyck and eight by Brouwer. The close trade connections between the two art centres of Seville and Antwerp had brought a number of pictures by Andalusian artists into the Netherlands. Van Ceulen sold Max Emanuel a particularly fine example of Murillo's art—the *Beggar Boys playing Dice* (all the pictures referred to here are in the Munich Pinakothek).

In the War of the Spanish Succession Max Emanuel of Bavaria fought on the side of France and could not prevent the imperial troops and their English allies from occupying Munich. On this occasion the Duke of Marlborough obtained

178 Rubens' *Venus and Adonis* (now in the Metropolitan Museum, New York) and van Dyck's large *Charles I on Horseback*, which Cromwell had sold to Antwerp (now in the National Gallery in London). When, after the conclusion of peace, Max Emanuel returned from France, he completed the 'Bavarian Versailles', the Palace of Schleissheim. Here, brought together in the great gallery, were the most valuable works of art he possessed, from Titian's *Charles V* to the

Rubens paintings. In his bedchamber, whose walls were covered with purple velvet, hung Rubens' *Massacre of the Innocents* and van Dyck's *Rest on the Flight*. In the adjoining oratory a place was also found for Dürer's *Four Apostles* (all these paintings are now in the Munich Pinakothek).

Around 1700 in the new Palatine residency of Düsseldorf, influences from the south were at least as strong as in the Main region. Johann Wilhelm of the Palatinate had visited Vienna and Italy in his youth; his sister was the wife of the last sickly Spanish Habsburg, and he also maintained excellent relations with the German branch of the Habsburgs. In 1691 he married a Medici princess who, as part of her dowry, brought with her from Florence Raphael's *Canigiani Holy Family* (now in the Munich Pinakothek). If some of the Habsburgs at that time mastered seven languages—those of the four great nations of the Continent and in addition Latin, Hungarian and Czech—Johann Wilhelm did almost as much. His remarkable brilliance, which was denied any political field of activity, found scope in the creation of a much admired gallery and in 1711 he had himself named on the plinth of his equestrian statue as 'Fundator Pinacothecae'. The Düsseldorf paintings, almost without exception, went to Munich around 1800.

Johann Wilhelm wanted to include only works of the first order in his collection. He wrote to an agent in Madrid: 'We are glad to hear that you have received a draft with which you are to buy good, rare and, as far as possible, large pictures, but capital pieces, even if with all the money you are able to purchase only a single one'. It must N 14 have been pleasant to serve a master of this character. Douven the painter who, under instructions from the Prince, had examined the collections of Frankfurt citizens, reported in a rather supercilious tone that he had found nothing that was in any way extraordinary or worth more than a hundred ducats. For decades the prices paid or offered by Johann Wilhelm provided a scale for the assessment of the value of pictures. The same thing had happened a hundred years previously in the case of the Emperor Rudolph II and his entourage.

Although educated by the Jesuits and a strict Catholic, Johann Wilhelm had no misgivings about robbing the churches of his country of origin—the Upper Palatinate—of their altarpieces. In order to obtain the necessary permission from the Pope for the removal of Rubens' altars, the Prince engagingly pointed out 'the nudities' of the paintings. From the Franciscans of Liège Johann Wilhelm acquired an altar by Douffet, a pupil of Rubens; after half the purchase price had been paid the monks regretted their bargain and took steps in Rome to annul the

178 In the early eighteenth century the Duke of Marlborough commanded the victorious allies of the Emperor. The Emperor gave him Rubens' *Venus and Adonis*, which remained in Blenheim Palace until 1886. In 1937 it was bought by the Metropolitan Museum in New York

transaction. 'They lie', protested the Prince, 'if they say that the picture is an object of religious veneration. I am only waiting for them to say that it works miracles'. In confidential letters to his intermediaries at the Vatican he gave way to his rage at these 'sfacciati fratacci'—the shameless rabble of monks—and finally achieved his object. The service of God and the service of the Prince now had to carry equal weight where art was concerned.

Already in Paris—for instance in the case of the Duc de Richelieu—and also in the taste of Franz Lothar von Schönborn, there was a preference for Baroque painters, which reduced even the great Venetians to a somewhat inferior place. Johann Wilhelm subscribed to the same set of values. He most certainly did not share the slight misgivings expressed by Leopold Wilhelm about the not too 'correct' drawing of Rubens, and ultimately acquired forty pictures by the master—among them the *Battle of the Amazons* from the Richelieu collection—together with a great quantity of other Flemish works. Rembrandt was principally represented by the series of scenes of the Passion which owed so much to southern Baroque art.

The Guelph Duke Anton Ulrich of Brunswick became acquainted, while still young, with the art

167

centres of western and southern Europe; later he liked to travel to Venice for the Carnival. He allied himself by marriage with the German Habsburgs and went over to the Catholic faith.

In rural Salzdahlum, which in keeping with current fashion was some way from the capital, the Duke of Brunswick erected a cheap, half-timbered, sprawling palace which has long since disappeared. Here he brought together many pictures and asked his heirs not to disturb them. This collection became the most important element in what is today the Brunswick Anton Ulrich Museum. Anton Ulrich had at first a considerable feeling for the cult of the 'Kunstkammer'. The upper storey of the Brunswick Museum still reflects these interests very powerfully, and indeed preserves certain pieces of the furnishings of Salzdahlum, for instance, consoles for displaying majolica. But the centre of all the duke's interests was more and more his collection of paintings, which was to impart a splendour to his court that would place it on a level with Düsseldorf, Munich and Vienna. This purpose was to be further served by a Gallery Book, perhaps the fifth of its kind, under the title 'Theatrum Artis'; the first (and last) volume was published around 1710.

Anton Ulrich of Brunswick possessed at this time some 800 paintings, Johann Wilhelm of the Palatinate only 343. Though the Düsseldorf collection was smaller in numbers, it held many more important works. Anton Ulrich had been less well advised and less cautious in spending money; he had a great many copies and works of only middling quality passed off to him under high-sounding names. The Venetians—from Titian to Bassano—held a dominant place in his taste as did Rubens and van Dyck among the Flemings, and Cranach, Dürer and Holbein among the Germans. Owing to the geographical situation of the Duchy of Brunswick there were many examples of Dutch painting in Salzdahlum. Although not assessed at their true value, many of the 'pearls' of the present Brunswick Museum were already in Salzdahlum in 1710: Rubens' *Judith*, for instance. Among the old German pictures one of the finest is *St Jerome in his Study* by Cranach; this work was removed from the collection during the Napoleonic era and is now in the Ringling Collection in Sarasota, Florida.

After the restoration of the monarchy, Charles II of England made a point of accumulating art treasures for the Crown again. The disastrous fire in Whitehall Palace in 1697, however, destroyed many of the paintings which had been inherited or newly acquired, so that it is difficult to estimate his success as a collector. The most important collection of an English nobleman was at that time at Wilton House in Salisbury. To the collection of pictures he inherited the eighth Earl of Pembroke added, about 1680, some antique sculptures—among them certain items from the former Mazarin collection.

In London, artists and citizens collected eagerly and there was great activity at auctions where high prices were sometimes paid. In 1684 Sir James Oxenden paid £250 for *Christ among the Doctors* by Bassano (now in the Ashmolean Museum in Oxford). Four years later at the auction of Lely's collection of drawings, a drawing of Constantine haranguing his troops by Raphael fetched the sensational price of £100 (now in the collection of the Duke of Devonshire at Chatsworth). In 1693, at the London auction of the goods of P. H. Lankrink, some excellent pictures by Titian, Tintoretto, Rubens, Rembrandt and Murillo came on the market.

CHAPTER 4

The Age of Enlightenment

The galleries of German princely courts | the cult of Venice and the Mannerists | the return to Raphael and the classical tradition | the 'Temple of Antiquities' at Sanssouci | Catherine II and the Hermitage | the 'discovery' of Ruisdael | German picture cabinets and bourgeois taste: Städel | English imports of antique statuary | public admission to the galleries | historical arrangement of the Museo Pio-Clementino

IN DEALING WITH THE EIGHTEENTH CENTURY, one cannot speak of a dominant style. The French use the term 'Dixhuitième' and give names such as 'Louis Quinze' to shorter periods without emphasizing stylistic analysis. Yet reference must be made to specific trends: powerful Late Baroque, delicate Rococo, enthusiasm for China, the playful early-Romantic 'Gothic Revival', 'Sturm und Drang' in the sphere of plastic art, as well as the early stages of neo-Classicism.

B 48

These conflicting forces had a particularly strong effect on the artistic life of Dresden in the mid-eighteenth century. In 1698 Augustus the Strong, acclaimed by his contemporaries as 'the Saxon Hercules', had acquired the crown of the kingdom of Poland. It was to remain in the possession of his House only till 1763, yet this brief period was used to great purpose. Augustus did not hesitate to sacrifice the traditional Lutheranism of the Wettin dynasty to the idea of a great Saxon-Polish power, and he accordingly became a Catholic. Dresden represented for western Europeans a kind of parallel to the rise of the new capital of St Petersburg out of lowlying marshland. The splendid edifice known as the Zwinger, the Catholic royal chapel built by the Roman architect, Gaetano Chiaveri, and the new pleasure-palaces of the ruler and those of the court favourites and the aristocracy, all aroused general admiration. Through its gallery Dresden finally became 'the Athens for artists'—as it was called in Saxony in 1760. The well-informed French traveller Fortia de Piles described the Wettin gallery as the most beautiful collection in Europe.

146
147
148

In the early eighteenth century Augustus the Strong developed a collector's taste which corresponded roughly to that of Johann Wilhelm of the Palatinate, yet it remained within modest limits. The truly great collector of the House of Wettin was his son, Augustus III. In certain character traits he was not unlike Emperor Rudolph II. He assumed power in 1733 but affairs of state occupied only a small portion of his time. By nature he was indolent, and the contemplation of paintings put him into that 'condition of sybaritic well-being' in which he particularly delighted.

179

B 221

Augustus III's energetic Prime Minister, Count Brühl, insisted on the enlargement of the royal gallery by every possible means, so that 'the lustre of the Saxon-Polish court might strike the eyes of the ambassadors and other distinguished foreigners.' The decisive acquisitions were made in the period of prosperity between 1740 and 1756, when, in Voltaire's words, 'trade flourished from Cadiz to St Petersburg'. In 1741 the agent Ventura Rossi sent seventy paintings from northern Italy. Two years later his rival, the Venetian man of letters, Francesco Algarotti, was assisted by Tiepolo in making purchases for Augustus from the Delfino, Sagredo and Cornaro palaces in Venice. In 1744, while staying in Modena, Rossi, using a false name and disguised by the mask that was customary during the Venice Carnival, visited the gallery of Prince d'Este and purchased a hundred of the best pictures for 100,000 zechini. 'My monarch has won a great battle against poor Italy', was his comment in the report of the sale which he sent to Dresden. Five years later Empress Maria Theresa was ready to sell 69 outstanding paintings from the imperial Habsburg gallery to the House of Wettin. In 1754 Raphael's masterpiece from the Church of San Sisto in Piacenza was purchased for the exorbitant price of 20,000 ducats. It is said that on the arrival of the *Sistine Madonna* in Dresden Augustus III pushed aside his throne with the words 'Make way for the great Raphael'.

182

Soon the whole of Europe knew that lavish prices were being paid in Dresden for pictures. Archdukes and ambassadors, clerics and men of

179 The neo-Classical taste which followed the Baroque era was particularly evident in the Dresden Gallery founded by Augustus III

learning, hairdressers and ladies' maids took up the business of art dealing. Brühl, the King's adviser, and Brühl's agent, the cunning Heinecken, kept their master busy with reports and offers. New acquisitions, if they were reasonably small in size, were often sent on to Augustus III at Warsaw, the second capital of the Saxon-Polish Kingdom, when the King happened to stay there.

As a sort of overflow from the royal gallery, Count Brühl's collection took on considerable proportions. At his death it included 844 paintings valued at 148,000 guilders. It was sold by his heirs to B 230 Catherine II of Russia. Algarotti, who of all those that stood in the wings at Dresden strikes one as the most honest of brokers, recommended himself to B 169 Brühl by a piece of flattery of a very subtle kind. In

the year 1743 he handed over to Brühl a picture which Tiepolo had painted according to his directions, *Maecenas presenting the Arts to Augustus* (now in the Hermitage, Leningrad). In the background of B 17 this scene are the superb gardens of the 'Saxon Richelieu' (as Brühl enjoyed hearing himself called), of which only 'Brühl's Terrace' survives.

The change in collectors' tastes from Late Baroque to neo-Classicism can be followed particularly well in Dresden, if one considers only Italian schools. The taste of Johann Wilhelm of the Palatinate was followed by Augustus the Strong in his collecting, and this continued for a time in Dresden under Augustus III. When the great purchase was made at Modena, Venetian paintings were chosen in large numbers; between 1741 and 1754 no less than

180   The Dresden Gallery, painted by Belotto in 1749
(above), was one of the first to be provided with a
building of its own and to be opened to the public

seven works of Tintoretto came into the gallery,
among them the painting *Naked Women making
Music*, originally from the Habsburg gallery and
probably the picture which Count Khevenhüller
had sent to Rudolph II from Spain under the name
The Nine Muses a hundred and fifty years previously.
In the period when the Baroque style was coming
to a close the same pictures often enjoyed as high
regard as at the beginning of the period.

In Paris in the early eighteenth century Watteau
had refined the large lush Venetian manner of his
moderate-sized pictures to suit the taste of Rococo
society; the fiery southern wine had been transformed into a piquant liqueur which could still
stimulate even jaded palates. In Munich and Vienna,
people felt so close to Italy and so familiar with it

that the art of Watteau was unable to obtain a
footing. In Dresden, however, the King acquired
two pictures by the subtle painter who had died so
prematurely in 1721, and Count Brühl did likewise.
While Augustus III, who knew Italy and its art well,
refused to recognize in the art of Watteau anything
more than a sort of marginal Parisian comment on
the painting of Venice, Frederick the Great gave
himself over entirely to French Rococo. For the son   B 125
of 'the Soldier-King' who had never been allowed
to see Italy, the name Watteau became the epitome
of Latin artistic beauty. 'Hors de Paris point de
salut', was a Berlin expression at the time. Approx-   N 149
imately half of all Watteau's paintings, roughly
thirty in number, found their way from Paris to
Berlin (most of them are now in the Berlin Museums). The French Bourbon, Philip V, who had
occupied the Spanish throne since the War of the
Spanish Succession, also acquired two pictures by
Watteau in 1730.

About 1745 Watteau was overshadowed in
Dresden itself by numerous paintings of the Italian
Late Baroque. Tiepolo, who was to decorate some

181 Because Dresden's preference was overwhelmingly for Italian rather than French art, Frederick the Great was able to obtain almost half of the pictures Watteau ever painted, including *L'Enseigne de Gersaint*

ceilings in the Bishop's Palace in Würzburg a few years later, sent in 1744 the superb *Banquet of*
183 *Cleopatra* (now in the National Gallery in Melbourne). Other excellent works by living Venetian painters, among them Piazzetta, Pittoni and Zuccarelli, came into the possession of Augustus III at
B 136 this time, mostly through the agency of Algarotti.

But the great days of Venetian art were over by the middle of the eighteenth century. Titian and that innumerable company of painters who had dipped their brushes in his palette, lost the first place they had held so long in the hearts of collectors. New masters came to the fore, heralded by Correggio and acknowledging Raphael as uncrowned king. In an English handbook for travellers to Italy printed in 1722 veritable hymns are already
N 150 sung to Correggio. His art appealed to the European élite who admired antique statues of the type of *Venus Kallipyge*. In 1728 the Saxon court painter, Ismael Mengs, gave his son the Christian name of Anton—after Antonio Allegri da Correggio—followed in the second place by the name of Raphael.

According to an old record, the five masterpieces by Correggio were the decisive factor in the purchase of the hundred paintings from Modena for the Dresden Gallery. In the neighbouring town of Parma, the Saxon agents were credited with a still unsatisfied appetite for the paintings of the master and in 1750 the *Madonna with St Jerome* (now in the Parma Pinacoteca) was brought from a small church to the cathedral so that it should not be secretly sold. When in 1753 copper engravings of the most valuable paintings in the Dresden Gallery began to be made, the first were not Titian's *Tribute Money* or Giorgione's *Sleeping Venus* (which at that time was still ascribed to Titian), but, at the express wish of the King, the works of Correggio. When the young Anton Raphael Mengs was satiated with the pictures of other great artists in the Dresden Gallery 'it was his habit to kiss one of the Correggios like a lover and to whisper as it were into its ear, "You alone please me"'.

XIII In the period of transition from Rococo to neo-Classicism collectors throughout Europe rediscovered the graceful work of Correggio. Frederick the Great bought this artist's *Leda*, and some decades later his *Madonna of the Basket* (right) came to England from Spain

From about 1750 onwards Frederick the Great submitted completely to the House of Wettin in matters of taste. Offered ten pictures by Lancret and other pupils of Watteau in 1754, he answered drily, 'Je ne suis plus dans ce goût-là'. Frederick wished to acquire 'des tableaux des grands maîtres'. In 1755 he made his most memorable purchase, Correggio's *Leda and the Swan* (now in the Berlin Museums), among whose previous owners had been Charles V, Rudolph II and Christina of Sweden. Shortly before this William Hogarth had included *Leda* (then in a private French collection), among his satirical series *Marriage à la mode* where it figures as the epitome of a frivolous wall decoration. The free-thinking 'philosopher of Sanssouci' had no such misgivings. On more than one occasion during the Seven Years War Frederick visited the gallery in Dresden, which at that time was occupied by his troops. In the course of these visits he arranged for the copying of only two pictures, both by Correggio, out of all the masterpieces that could be found there.

A number of painters from the immediate circle of Correggio, above all Parmigianino but also Dosso Dossi and Niccolò dell'Abbate, found favour with collectors during this period of transition from Rococo to early neo-Classicism. At a very early stage they enjoyed the honour of appearing in the volume of etchings of the Dresden Gallery. In the pictures of the Dutchman Adriaen van der Werff, who had lapsed completely into the Italian manner and was highly prized both in Dresden and at Sanssouci, the eighteenth century admired the Correggio-like style, though this now appeared in a rather artificial form. The same holds true of the art of Boucher, who stripped the paintings of Watteau's successors of all residual Venetian influence and, with his increasingly cool colours, gave the admirers

of Correggio exactly what they sought. Frederick the Great acquired one of Boucher's principal works; the Swedish ambassador in Paris half a dozen of his pictures (now in the Nationalmuseum in Stockholm); but in Vienna, Munich and at this time also in Dresden, people remained unreceptive towards the French interpretation of an Italian theme.

In Dresden, Algarotti, apart from his habit of promoting living Venetians for reasons of local patriotism, displayed in his appreciation of earlier art a stricter conception of Classicism than had so far been encountered. His particular enthusiasm was N 151 for the Venetian High Renaissance of the period from 1510 to 1525, and after that for the seventeenth-century painters in central Italy who had cultivated the anti-Baroque tradition. A Dresden list of requirements, which had been inspired by Algarotti and was intended to serve as a guide to the smaller agents, began with Fra Bartolommeo, followed by Raphael, while Correggio held only third place. Algarotti had a high regard for the well-balanced Palma Vecchio, whom he regarded as a Venetian Fra Bartolommeo. He acquired his *Three Sisters*, which had been painted about 1520, and commented in enthusiastic terms on the features of the central figure, saying that they were 'correct, elegant and Greek'.

Ever since the *Burgomaster Meyer's Madonna* had been housed in a palace on the Grand Canal where it was much admired, it had become the custom to place Holbein on the same footing as the classical Italians. This picture was in fact an excellent copy 152 carried out in Amsterdam about 1635 with thoroughly dishonest intentions, though nobody in Venice realized it. The original (now the property of the Hesse-Darmstadt family) shows a less markedly Italian style. The forger, by a slight smoothing of the forms, had weakened the German characteristics. Algarotti was therefore not so far wrong when, in purchasing the Venetian copy for Dresden, he stressed in enthusiastic terms its relationship with works by Raphael and Leonardo da Vinci. Tiepolo and his friends were already showing a lack of confidence in their own art which was characteristic of the mood of the age. When Algarotti once again led them to the Holbein *Madonna*, they cried: 'Those are faces—we have been painting masks'.

In the years 1742–46 three paintings by Carlo Dolci came to Dresden, among them the *St Cecilia*. In 1743 Algarotti sent from Venice two pictures by Maratta, which were followed by two more in 1744 and 1749 respectively. In 1744 two paintings by Sassoferrato were acquired and before 1754 a further picture by this artist. To such examples of work in the classical tradition by Roman and

XIV The return to Classicism resulted in an extraordinarily high value placed on the landscapes of Claude. In England around 1800 higher prices were paid for his paintings than those of any other artist—with the sole exception of Raphael. Claude's *Cephalus and Procris reunited by Diana* was, in about 1820, one of the most valuable items in the Angerstein collection and became one of the foundation pictures of the National Gallery, London, in 1824

182 By the middle of the eighteenth century the Dresden Gallery valued the work of Renaissance artists above all others. Raphael's *Sistine Madonna* was bought for the highest price ever paid for a painting in Europe up to that time (detail)

frescoes in the Vatican. From central Italy the revival of his fame spread across the Apennines and caused the *Altarpiece of St Cecilia* in a church at Bologna and the *Madonna with St Barbara and Pope Sixtus (The Sistine Madonna)* in Piacenza to be regarded as important show-pieces. In 1711, before he came to the throne, Augustus III of Poland had been deeply impressed in Piacenza by the altarpiece in the Church of San Sisto. A generation later he paid the high price of 20,000 gold ducats for Raphael's *Madonna*. If we take into account the purchasing power of money prevailing at that time this must have been the greatest price that had ever been paid in Europe for a single painting. The enthusiasm aroused in Dresden by the *Sistine Madonna* was expressed by Johann Joachim Winckelmann in 1755 in his first published writing. He praised the 'more than feminine greatness' of the Mother of Christ and the 'attitude of serene repose in that stillness which the Greeks allowed to dwell in their gods'. N 152

Many a painter received a reflected glory from the power of Raphael's name. The rise, zenith and decline of lesser stars depended constantly on the course and intensity of the great sun at their centre. Whereas in the seventeenth century Blanchard had been held in high honour as the 'French Titian', he was now overshadowed by Le Sueur, the 'French Raphael' of the Grand Siècle. In Dresden people sought in vain for pictures by Le Sueur, but they were more fortunate with Murillo, 'the Raphael of XV Seville', who first achieved international fame in 1738 when the Bourbon Philip V and his clever second wife, Isabella Farnese, discovered, during a protracted stay in Seville, that Velazquez, the friend of the Venetians, was not the only Spaniard to have engaged in painting. The royal pair returned to Madrid with no less than 29 paintings by Murillo and his school. Accounts of the newly discovered master spread northwards from the Spanish capital to the great collectors beyond the Pyrenees. As early as 1755—shortly after the purchase of the *Sistine Madonna*—a *Madonna* by Murillo entered the Dresden Gallery, and was followed by three more of his works.

It was in line with the new classical trend that there should also be a shift of emphasis in the assessment of seventeenth-century landscape painting. Claude, 'the Raphael of landscape painting', XIV became one of the most sought-after painters of the second half of the eighteenth century. Poussin also benefited from this revaluation, and the third member of this group admired by the contemporaries of Winckelmann was the Italian Salvator Rosa. By 1754 three paintings by Claude and seven by Poussin had entered the Dresden Gallery, as well as the *Wooded Landscape* by Salvator Rosa.

Florentine masters of the seventeenth century there were added numerous pictures of the Bolognese school which had pursued similar aims.

The return to classical clarity and strength was finally brought about by the arrival in Dresden of Raphael's *Sistine Madonna*. Something has already been said of the high regard in which collectors such as Philip IV of Spain held the late work of 182 Raphael when they encountered it, yet the pathos and extravagance of the Baroque had to fade away before Raphael's middle classical period could shine forth victoriously again. At the beginning of the eighteenth century Roman art-lovers were once more inspired to enthusiasm for Raphael by the

183 Dresden's rejection of Rococo was so complete in the years around 1765 that a major work by Tiepolo, *The Banquet of Cleopatra*, which had only recently been purchased, was quickly resold

This shift from Titian to Raphael, from Venice to central Italy, soon led Dresden art-lovers to criticize painters who only a short time previously had been venerated as demi-gods. As yet, nobody dared actually find fault with Titian, but the Venetian painters who succeeded Palma Vecchio (d. 1528) fell into disfavour. Veronese's 'faults' were forgiven because of the clarity of his composition and his cool luminous colours, though Carl Heinrich Heinecken took exception to the 'carelessness and extravagances' of Tintoretto. Hagedorn, in his *Betrachtungen über die Malerei* (Reflections on Painting), which appeared in 1762, nowhere so much as mentions the name of Tiepolo. When Winckelmann spoke of the 'impudent fervour of the cheerful humbugs of art', it was taken for granted that he was thinking in particular of the Venetians of the Late Baroque.

N 153

N 154

In Dresden this trend reached such a pitch that shortly after 1760 the group of important pictures by Tiepolo, Piazzetta, Pittoni and Zuccarelli, which had been painted some fifteen years previously, were regarded as a blot on the Gallery's reputation. This is the first example of important works being eliminated from a great collection because of a change in artistic taste. On 22 May 1765 all the newer Venetian pictures of the Late Baroque were auctioned in Amsterdam, where they fetched moderate but not excessively low prices. Tiepolo, who was admired by many, was still alive and the well-known picture dealer Yver unhesitatingly paid 495 guilders for his *Banquet of Cleopatra*.

N 155

The paintings of Watteau and Lancret, which Frederick the Great had possessed from his youth, benefited by the circumstance that they hung unnoticed here and there in palaces, and had found no place in the 'Galerie des grands maîtres' formed at Sanssouci in 1755. A number of French Rococo pictures, which had been affected by this trend and which the King had presented to his brother Henry,

184 The new taste for Classicism led to a particularly high evaluation of Holbein's later work. Count Schönborn bought the *Portrait of Hans Wedigh* which Holbein had painted in London in 1532

were in fact auctioned as valueless around 1800. At that time even the name of Watteau was no longer known in Berlin.

In the inventory of the Duke of Brunswick's gallery in Salzdahlum in 1744 the name of Tintoretto is the one that occurs most frequently; next after him is Titian. In 1767 the hereditary prince, Carl William Ferdinand, was staying in Rome and was in touch with Winckelmann. He personally acquired one of the principal classicizing works of Palma Vecchio, *Adam and Eve*, and with this definitely put an end to the chapter of Late Baroque development in the gallery's history. In Cassel the Landgrave William VIII started about the middle of the century to found a gallery of Italian works. His tastes underwent a change towards the classical almost at

B 69

N 156

N 157

the same time as those of Augustus III of Saxony and he acquired the full-length portrait of Count Aquaviva by Titian (now in the Landesmuseum, Cassel) and also the *Virgin and Child with Saints* by Andrea del Sarto (now in the Hermitage in Leningrad). The seventeenth century was represented by works of Guido Reni, Sassoferrato, Dolci, Poussin and Claude's four *Periods of the Day* (now in the Hermitage), all wholly alien to the Baroque in spirit. In about 1770 a *Madonna* by Dolci in the Düsseldorf collection was regarded by many visitors as the most beautiful piece in the gallery, while Raphael was exalted as 'the Apollo of painting' and the highest honours were paid to Claude, Poussin and Salvator Rosa.

On the Upper Rhine the princely House of Baden started by following the taste of Parisian collectors and acquired pictures by Boucher (now in the Kunsthalle in Karlsruhe), but soon changed over to Albani, Dolci and Batoni. In Zweibrücken the acquisition of Boucher's *Nude on a Sofa* (now in the Munich Pinakothek) was followed by the purchase of landscapes by Claude. A Murillo entered this gallery in 1756, one year later than Dresden. Further to the east the French Rococo was not adopted. In Munich, the Venetian school continued to enjoy the same respect as before: the Gonzaga cycle by Tintoretto was brought there at some time prior to 1748. In 1768 pictures by Murillo were being purchased according to a definite plan.

In the second half of the eighteenth century the House of Habsburg, which since the Renaissance had been unwaveringly faithful to the art of Venice, underwent a decisive conversion towards the classical school. About 1730, paintings by Tintoretto and also by the Baroque painters of Italy and Spain were being procured by the imperial House and by Viennese art-lovers, but as early as 1746 or even shortly before that date Dolci's *St Catherine reading a Book* (now in the Residenzgalerie in Salzburg) was   *185* acquired for the collection of Count Schönborn, three years after Holbein's *Madonna* reached Dresden. Count Schönborn, too, was boasting of the possession of a particularly classical Holbein portrait, that of a member of the Wedigh family (now in the Metropolitan Museum, New York). Count   *184* Kaunitz, the all-powerful imperial minister, contrived to get hold of a *Madonna* by Raphael (now in the Museum of Fine Arts, Budapest), Poussin's *Destruction of the Temple in Jerusalem* (now in the Vienna Gallery), and paintings by Guido Reni and Murillo. Count Czernin was anxious to find French seventeenth-century paintings with a classical bent and here an example of the 'French Raphael' Le Sueur, *Iphigenia and Orestes* (now in the Residenzgalerie in Salzburg) had at all costs to be included.

In 1770 the Emperor Joseph II removed Raphael's *Holy Family* from a church in Milan to the imperial gallery. About this time the *Madonna in the Meadow* was also placed there, together with three pictures by Maratta and (about 1790) one by Dolci.

The exchange of pictures between Vienna and the Uffizi Gallery in Florence in 1792, a matter that has hitherto been insufficiently explained, becomes intelligible when certain facts are taken into account. Archduke Leopold II, born in 1747, reigned until 1790 as Grand Duke in Tuscany, at that time a dependent state of the Habsburgs. This enlightened prince had already had himself painted by Batoni in 1769, and was very actively concerned in the completion of the Uffizi Gallery in a manner that conformed to the new trends of taste. In 1781 he acquired from a church an altarpiece by Fra Bartolommeo, a favourite master of the Winckelmann epoch and one whose works were eagerly sought for in Dresden. When Leopold II became Emperor he was anxious to have Fra Bartolommeo represented in his Vienna Gallery, together with sixteenth-century Florentine painters of a similar tradition. Hence the importation of Bartolommeo's smoothly painted altarpiece into Vienna, along with a *Holy Family* by Bronzino, hard as metal in its drawing, as well as a picture strictly symmetrical in its composition by Andrea del Sarto (now regarded as a schoolpiece), a noble *Lamentation* by Cigoli, a cool

picture by Allori, a very Raphaelesque *Holy Family* by Vasari and a most classically conceived portrait by Barocci. The pictures included a major work by the highly admired Salvator Rosa, *The Goddess of Justice fleeing to the Country-People*. In exchange Florence received masterpieces of the Venetian school, then considered second-rate. Among them, under the name of Giorgione, was the fine *Allegory* by Giovanni Bellini, Titian's magnificent *Flora* and an excellent painting by Veronese. People in Florence felt that they had had the worst of the bargain and this idea only changed around 1850 when the Venetians again began to be respected.

With her habitual energy the Tsarina Catherine II, who came to the Russian throne in 1762, revived all the past trends of art collecting of the century and anticipated all those that were yet to come. She acquired, presumably around 1766, Tiepolo's *The Banquet of Cleopatra*, which had fallen into disfavour in Dresden, and in 1769 the whole of Count Brühl's collection as well as six paintings by Watteau, five by Lancret and one by Boucher, after which she let herself be guided by the new fashions. Works by outstanding representatives of early Classicism were acquired for the Hermitage: six Murillos between 1768 and 1779, paintings by Raphael, Reni, Annibale Caracci and Poussin in 1772, Maratta and Salvator Rosa in 1779, and at about the same time, Anton Raphael Mengs.

B 141

N 158

183

N 159

N 160

185 From about 1750 onwards the major European collectors demonstrated their preference for those seventeenth-century masters, like Poussin, Claude and Dolci, who had favoured quiet classical harmony. In 1746 Count Schönborn bought Dolci's *St Catherine reading a Book*, a painting which at that time received admiration bordering on idolatry

Whoever looks at paintings by Bronzino, Dolci, Maratta and similar painters held in high regard since 1750, will recognize the hard precise modelling of the human body as one of their principal characteristics; an age for which a painting by Bronzino was more important than a Titian was bound to have an intimate feeling for the linear quality of antique sculpture. In Rome itself, the love of antique sculpture had endured in new forms over the Baroque period, though in many other places the Halls of Antiquities became covered with dust. The *Ephebe of Helenenberg* stood unnoticed as a figure on a fountain in one of the courtyards of the Fortress of Hohensalzburg, and the Swedes in 1648 did not consider the *Ilioneus* worthy of so much as a glance. Where, north of the Alps, there was a special interest in antique sculpture, as in the case of Arundel, direct influences from Italy were at work.

At the start of the eighteenth century art-lovers again began to take notice of antique statuary. The Elector Johann Wilhelm of the Palatinate who for twenty-five years had delighted in the sensual figures of Rubens, turned at the age of fifty towards sculpture. The first example of large-scale antique sculpture that came to be selected and set up in Düsseldorf was a splendid copy of the *Farnese Hercules;* this was followed by the *Laocoön* group, the *Borghese Fencer* and the *Belvedere Torso*. Johann Wilhelm even toyed with the idea of setting up a copy of Trajan's Column at his residence on the Lower Rhine.

The Elector was primarily interested in pieces of antique sculpture which the Baroque had honoured and which Rubens himself had admired in Rome. Plaster copies with their smooth brightness lacked the living charm of marble. The century of Winckelmann had begun, at the end of which Schiller was to stand before Rubens' paintings and regret that they were so rich in colour and not simply great drawings on a white surface. Johann Wilhelm was also interested in statuettes by Giovanni da Bologna; this was—if one may illustrate the matter in terms of painting—a step on the road from Rubens back towards Correggio.

Augustus the Strong in Dresden became interested in antique sculpture at the same age as Johann Wilhelm in the Palatinate. While the latter, however, loved certain specific works and preferred to set up casts of them instead of buying whatever chance happened to put in his way, Augustus was less fastidious, although he did in fact look around for antique originals. In 1728 two Roman collections of antique statues from the Albani and Chigi families were bought for 81,000 thalers.

Whereas for the young princes of the Houses of Wettin, Brunswick, Wittelsbach and Habsburg, the 'Grand Tour' to the south was a matter of course,

people had other ideas in the Calvinist court of the Hohenzollerns. Frederick the Great was allowed in his youth to go neither to Paris nor to Rome and was in the habit of saying—when it was already too late—that he would gladly give a rib for a ride on the Via Appia. In the cool air of northern Germany he experienced art and antiquity only through the medium of his formal education. Horace, Virgil and Marcus Aurelius were the first to familiarize the young prince with antiquity, and his knowledge of Roman buildings depended on such engravings as happened to be published. Frederick, who had never set eyes on the Arch of Titus or the Pantheon, caused the Brandenburg Gate in Potsdam and the French Church there to be erected as free copies of these Roman monuments. He was acquainted neither with the Forum Romanum nor with the Grotto of Egeria but he embellished the surroundings of his palace at Sanssouci with artificial ruins and a grotto of Neptune.

In purchasing pictures Frederick had proceeded very cautiously. He once remarked when rejecting the offer of an expensive Italian picture: 'What I can pay a reasonable price for I will buy, but when it is too dear I will leave it to the King of Saxony and Poland for I cannot make money, and it is not my way to impose taxes'. However, these prudent principles were abandoned when it was a matter of acquiring antique art. In 1742 Frederick paid 80,000 livres for Cardinal Polignac's collection of sculptures, which was exactly four times the amount he was later to spend on Correggio's *Leda and the Swan*. Herr von Stosch received as much as 30,000 ducats for his collection of carved gem-stones, one and a half times what Raphael's *Sistine Madonna* had cost the House of Wettin. At the auction of the famous Paris collection of Julienne which took place in 1767 in the 'Salon Carré' of the Louvre, the Prussian King ordered the purchase of the famous head of Caesar in green basalt (now in the Berlin Museums). For the *Antinous*, once in the collection of Prince Eugen, Frederick paid Prince Liechtenstein in Vienna 5,000 thalers.

At the beginning, the antique sculptures were scattered about in the entrance hall of the palace at Charlottenburg near Berlin and distributed among the new buildings of the park of Sanssouci. Later a number of large decorative statues formed a half circle in front of 'Das Neue Palais' in Potsdam. It was not in Dresden, but when looking at the sculptures that Frederick the Great had acquired, that Winckelmann received his first strong impressions of antique art. 'I have seen Athens and Sparta in Potsdam', he cried delightedly.

After the end of the Seven Years War the King resolved to set up the greater part of his sculptures

186 The neo-Classical era rediscovered Greek and Roman art. In the second half of the eighteenth century galleries of antiquities were founded throughout Europe. This painting by Per Hilleström is of the gallery of ancient sculpture in the royal palace in Stockholm. In the foreground is *Endymion asleep*, a statue that was highly esteemed in the eighteenth century

in a specially constructed Temple of Antiquities in the park of Sanssouci. In picture galleries, the individual work of art around 1700 had been worked into a strict composition which governed the whole interior decorative scheme, and statues were arranged symmetrically on similar principles. Since then there had been a certain amount of relaxation; the individual works gradually recovered their individuality. At the time when the Temple of Antiquities of Sanssouci received its final arrangement, taste was moving roughly halfway

between strictness and freedom in this matter. Presumably certain buildings in England, which Frederick the Great admired, acted as guides here.

The King could not bring himself to introduce into his Temple of Antiquities the antique sculptures of which he was particularly fond. As examples in a moral and spiritual sense and as guiding stars of his life, Homer and Socrates were present in his library, the *Caesar* from the Julienne Collection in his study and the *Emperor Marcus Aurelius*, the Stoic philosopher, in his bedroom. Immediately next to the palace of Sanssouci and at the end of the arboured walk, the King had the *Antinous* set up, so that his gaze always rested upon it when he was at work in the library. This ephebe (now in the Berlin Museums), who certainly is not the imperial favourite Antinous but probably Ganymede, the favourite of Zeus, is now regarded as a Greek original from the circle of Lysippus, that is to say, from the phase of style in antique art which corresponded to that of Correggio in more recent times.

After the middle of the eighteenth century the spirit of Classicism overcame the waning Baroque not only in Brandenburg and Saxony but also in Italy. Two Germans in Rome uttered the new shibboleths rather more loudly than the rest. From 1754 Anton Raphael Mengs was the head of the new Academy of Painting. The artist was followed by the art historian Winckelmann. It was only now, when artistic sensuality was on the decline, and a more literary appreciation of art was coming to be accepted, that Germans, as well as Danes, Swedes and Englishmen, could appear south of the Alps not only as recipients but as initiators.

As far back as 1756 Winckelmann declared that 'the new ones are donkeys compared with the old, and Bernini is the biggest donkey among the new ones'. Interest now began to decline in the antique Baroque; the *Farnese Bull* was valued less highly than before, while the *Apollo Belvedere* and similar *187* classical works came once more to occupy a place of honour. Countless copies found their way to the north. Next to statues of spiritualized and idealized gods the general public of the age of *Werther* loved heads with a sentimental expression.

From 1758 Winckelmann, who had been converted to Catholicism, guided the sons of German princes and young nobles who came to Rome in their study of antique art and advised them in their purchases. Count von Wallmoden, an illegitimate offspring of the Guelphs, acquired a small collection of antiquities (now in the Kestnermuseum in Hanover). Carl William Ferdinand of Brunswick had himself painted with antique vases from the Mengs collection by the Roman Classicist, Batoni. *188* Under the influence of the early Classicist trends antique vase paintings—products of an art which confined itself to outlines on a plain surface and dispensed with modelling and colour—were now declared the most perfect works of art of all time.

Towards the end of the eighteenth century Mannheim became for a time the place to which lovers of antiquity made their pilgrimage from all countries north of the Alps. During the Seven

187 Goethe echoed the general opinion of his time when he called the *Apollo Belvedere* the most beautiful statue of antiquity (see Ill. 82)

Years War the Elector, Carl Theodore of the Palatinate, who was residing in Mannheim, had caused the paintings and plaster casts which Johann Wilhelm had gathered together in Düsseldorf to be brought to Mannheim for safety. When peace had been concluded he sent the picture gallery with its great wealth of Rubenses back to Düsseldorf, but kept the casts in Mannheim. He had the collection enlarged and exhibited it for everyone to see. The austere white of the plaster and its even smoothness appealed to a generation which had been surfeited with the flickering unrest and the magic of colour displayed in late Baroque art.

In 1777 Lessing wrote that 'the time spent in this hall of antiquities is of greater benefit to the artist who studies its contents than a pilgrimage to the originals in Rome, for these are often placed too high or in darkness or even hidden among inferior N 161 work'. In 1785 Schiller spoke of the 'warm love of art of a German sovereign' who 'had gathered together the noblest monuments of Greek and Roman sculpture in a small but tasteful selection'. 'Everyone, whether native or foreigner', he added, 'has complete freedom to enjoy these treasures of antiquity'. In the eleventh book of *Dichtung und Wahrheit* Goethe described in his old age the impressions which on his return from Alsace he had received in Mannheim in 1771. 'Here I stood exposed to the most wonderful impressions in a square and roomy hall with the most glorious statues of antiquity, ... a forest of statues ... After I had submitted for a time to the effect of this irresistible mass, I turned to those figures which attracted me most, and who can deny that the *Apollo Belvedere*, through his moderated immensity, his slender build and free movement, his victor's look, is beyond all the rest, and also victor over our feelings!'

188 Interest in Greek red-figure vases can be said to date from about 1750. The prince of Brunswick, who was completing his aesthetic education in Rome (Winckelmann acted as one of his advisers), commissioned Batoni to paint a portrait of him with several of these vases

In modern museums it can often be observed that visitors who have had no preliminary preparation like to spend time looking at Dutch pictures which satisfy the desire for close observation. It was the same two hundred years ago. 'The ordinary taste of the rich Paris public inclines towards the Flemish and the Dutch; a Teniers will certainly find fifty purchasers, a Titian or a Correggio at the most six', wrote a Saxon agent from Paris to Dresden in 1741.

North of the Alps in the eighteenth century the markedly stylized art of the Mediterranean area appealed to an élite who had made its acquaintance fairly early. Most people were chiefly interested in pictures which put nature to shame by their closeness to reality. Since about 1740, the cultural life of the leading countries of Europe had more and more tended to conform to bourgeois standards, and at the same time there was a definite turning away from the princely Rococo culture.

This led in Paris and London, in Dresden and St Petersburg, to collectors' tastes becoming increasingly similar to those of the merchants of Antwerp and Amsterdam. Not only were the Italian classics paraded against the last followers of Watteau, but also (though on a different level) the Flemish and above all the Dutch. It was in the Dutch that one found objectivity of representation and sincerity of feeling. This trend was particularly evident, partly through the influence of bourgeois advisers, among some of the princely collections.

The most impressive example of German collectors' affection for the Dutch was the gallery in Cassel; its creator, Landgrave William VIII, spent the decisive years of his life at the court of his godfather William II of Orange. In place of the self-glorification of Saxon-Polish 'Rois-Soleils' or the wilfulness of the philosopher of Sanssouci, he possessed the quiet dignity of the House of Orange.

William VIII had seen many collections in Holland, had enjoyed talking to collectors and connoisseurs, and had already acquired paintings in those years. In Cassel he found hardly anything left by his predecessors, so that the gallery can be viewed as his own personal achievement. It is helpful in describing it to group its contents under various themes.

As a practising Protestant, William VIII had a dislike for all definitely Catholic themes; only a single altarpiece entered the Cassel gallery, but there are seventeen portrayals of Old Testament subjects, among them Rembrandt's powerful *Jacob's Blessing*. The New Testament was represented by 36 *190* pictures, to which must be added Rembrandt's *Descent from the Cross* (now in the Hermitage, Leningrad) and his *Christ as the Gardener* (now in the Royal Collection, Windsor Castle). William VIII

189 In the course of the eighteenth century the Baroque complex presentation of works of art was rejected in favour of a freer system. In 1936 the main room of the Cassel Gallery, which housed all kinds of works of art was temporarily arranged to show how it had looked in 1749

had a particular liking for those Latin authors who were favourites in Holland's humanistic bourgeois circles. Here particular attention was paid to early Roman history in which the virtues of patriotism and manliness were given a high place. William acquired 23 pictures dealing with these subjects and 47 dealing with the world of antique gods and heroes.

These seventy pictures constitute approximately a quarter of his acquisitions. He could not see enough of any paintings which recalled his stay in Holland. Accurate and objective views of cities were given an important place. About seventy portraits of known and unknown Dutchmen and Flemings reached Cassel; these included nineteen portraits and *191* studies by Rembrandt and seven works of Frans Hals. In this collection the ordinary happenings in towns and villages were brought to life on canvas; one could see bourgeois Amsterdam houses and their occupants, the activities of countryfolk in the open air and at the tavern. There were still-lifes to remind one of the rich pleasures of the table, floral pieces to bear testimony to the love of gardens. William preferred these peaceful masters to any others.

The Landgrave of Hesse wrote pleasing, forceful German and corresponded about his purchases with art-lovers in Frankfurt and other bourgeois cities. When the 64 outstanding pictures of the well-known collection of the Dutch family Reuver, which had been acquired for about a third of the price of the *Sistine Madonna*, arrived in Cassel, the old gentleman could hardly control his pleasure, for this was 'the only pure and good collection left in Holland'. Among the pictures, wrote William, 'there were eight Rembrandts of such perfection as I have never seen. Some are of the rough thickly impastoed kind of painting, others are hardly less fine than a Gerard Dou or a Mieris'.

In the eighteenth century, outstanding Flemish and Dutch pictures were also collected in the Brunswick ducal gallery, in the residencies of the Palatine Wittelsbachs on the Rhine, in Karlsruhe, Dresden and Potsdam. Known or deducible dates of purchase enable us to observe the changing assessments of individual masters in these different places, something which is impossible in the case of William VIII of Hesse-Cassel owing to the fact that his activity as a collector was concentrated within so brief a span of time.

In Brunswick in the middle of the eighteenth century Carl I, a great-grandson of Anton Ulrich, assisted in the enlargement of the gallery. The growing passion for the charms of uncorrupted rural life—one of the many reactions against the artificiality of the Rococo—led from 1740 onwards to a very high value being placed on the Dutch

190 From 1750 onwards the work of Dutch artists was greatly admired in northern and central Europe. The entry of the middle classes into the art markets was a factor in this development. Rembrandt's *Jacob's Blessing* (detail above) was bought by the Cassel Gallery in 1752

landscape painters. At that time four paintings by Jacob van Ruisdael, four by Wynants and one by Everdingen were added to the Brunswick collection. Rembrandt had already been well represented in the early eighteenth century. Pictures by him and his school continued to be acquired in large numbers. 'A Rembrandtesque manner in which the whole wild essence of being is unleashed is something that does not displease me'. These words were uttered about the middle of the century by an official of the Duke's; they enable us to see what it was that the period of 'Sturm und Drang' loved in Rembrandt.

191, 192 Paintings by Rembrandt were bought not only by north German princes but also by Catherine the Great and the King of France. The most successful purchases, however, were made by the Landgraves of Hesse-Cassel. *Nikolaes Bruyningh* (left) was bought in 1750 and *Landscape with Ruins* (below) in 1784

As a son of the Late Baroque, Johann Wilhelm of the
163 Palatinate had loved both the *Farnese Hercules* and
Rubens' pictures; he paid homage to the taste of
the eighteenth century by developing an affection
for the statuettes of Giovanni da Bologna and for
the works of small-scale painters like Netscher. After
the death of this great collector his successor,
Elector Carl Philipp, had a number of the latter
brought to Mannheim, which had now been chosen
as the residency. In the middle of the eighteenth
century it was almost exclusively Dutch paintings
that were bought, though there were also occasional
purchases of the Flemish. Small smoothly painted
pictures by Jan Bruegel, Dou, Mieris, Netscher and
Jan Huysum maintained their popularity: this also
accorded with the taste of the Paris collectors, the
effects of which were felt on the Rhine and in
northern Germany. As in Brunswick, however,
there became evident in Mannheim a pronounced
affection for Rembrandt and his school; purchases
included the *Holy Family* and the *Sacrifice of Isaac* by
Rembrandt, and the *Jewish Bride* by Aert de Gelder
(all now in the Munich Pinakothek). Pictures by
Aelbert Cuyp, Adriaen van de Velde and, from about
1740, other Dutch landscape painters of repute, were
also acquired in Mannheim.

In the petty principality of Zweibrücken on the
left bank of the Rhine, Duke Carl Augustus, who
was descended by a collateral line of the Palatine
House, assumed power in 1775. He had reason
to expect that all the Palatinate and Wittelsbach
lands would one day be taken over by his descendants and therefore did not hesitate to start a
picture gallery which within fifteen years had grown
to a thousand items. This collection is of particular
interest because it is such an excellent example of
collectors' tastes during the *Werther* period. Large
figure pictures by Rubens were no longer acquired
for the Zweibrücken collection; as against this,
small pictures by Brouwer and Teniers were
chosen. Among the Dutch grouped around Rembrandt were delicate, quiet pictures by Metsu and
Sweerts, and genre and peasant pictures by Adriaen
and Isack Ostade. Great interest was also shown by
the Duke and his advisers in the landscapes by
Jacob van Ruisdael and Wynants (all these pictures
are now in the Munich Pinakothek).

On the Upper Rhine, thanks to the collector's
zeal displayed by Caroline of Baden-Durlach in
the second half of the eighteenth century, there
developed a collection of paintings that became the
nucleus of the Kunsthalle in Karlsruhe. The
Princess, who was an active art-lover, championed the Parisian taste with an anxious narrow-
mindedness. A list of her requirements in 1761
began with Dou and Netscher, with Rembrandt's

193 In his still-lifes Chardin paid homage to the
Dutch painters of the seventeenth century. This *Still-life
with a Glass Bottle* was bought by Caroline, Margravine
of Baden, whose collection provided the basis for the
Kunsthalle in Karlsruhe

name only in tenth place. The Princess got rid of
her landscape by Rubens because the manner of
painting was not sufficiently smooth and delicate;
on the other hand, she boasted that in Netscher's
Cleopatra she had acquired the diamond of the
Vence collection in Paris. Caroline of Baden also
loved Chardin who had, as it were, composed a
French epilogue to Dutch painting in the spirit of
Vermeer.

In the Dresden Gallery the collecting of Flemish
and Dutch painters was also of great importance.
Figure pictures by Rubens, van Dyck and Rembrandt were first acquired, also works by the

194 In the years immediately preceding the French Revolution, the royal family no longer dominated Paris art circles. The professional classes provided an ever-increasing number of collectors and 'marchands-amateurs'. This engraving by Cochin comes from the catalogue of the Quentin de Lorangerie auction

notice, especially Berchem, 'the Theocritus of the Netherlands', and Poelenburg. Later on, those artists received particular attention who reproduced nature without pseudo-classical trimmings; about 1750 there were already a dozen or more works of Jacob van Ruisdael's in the collection, among them the *Jewish Cemetery*.

Of the sixteen important pictures by Rembrandt which belong to the Dresden collection, about a quarter came there as early as 1720, and the majority around the middle of the century. Lovers of Italian art took some exception to the forthright early works which often made fun of an idealized antiquity. 'Rembrandt chose a Ganymede whom Jupiter would never have chosen', they said. Nevertheless even Mengs, the Classicist, must have been greatly impressed by the Dresden pictures from Rembrandt's middle and later period. When he executed paintings for the King of Spain in the 1760s, he supported in Madrid the purchase of Rembrandt's *Saskia* and his *Artemisia* (now in the Prado).

When Frederick the Great, at the age of twenty-four, arranged his little Rococo palace of Rheinsberg, he and his friends were in the habit of pronouncing judgment on the starchy court of the 'Soldier-King' in his Baroque Berlin town palace. They called it something 'dans le goût de Rembrandt', while they regarded their own aestheticism as 'genre de Watteau'. When later a 'galerie toute nouvelle des grands maîtres' was created, paintings by the great Italians turned out to be for the most part so expensive and difficult to obtain that they had to fall back on Flemish and Dutch artists. Rembrandt's *Self-portrait with the velvet Biretta, Samson and his Father-in-Law* and *Moses breaking the Tables of the Law* (all now in the Berlin Museums) were already in the gallery building next to the palace of Sanssouci. In purchases of this kind Frederick the Great's personal interest was slight. He left the matter to his agents: 'I have already bought nearly a hundred paintings and I need fifty more; but I will not be subject to this passion for collecting for long, because as soon as I have enough, I'll stop buying', he wrote in 1755.

N 162

N 163

The somewhat summary manner in which Frederick the Great collected his paintings by the great masters within a short period was also true of the collections of Warsaw and St Petersburg. The last Polish king boasted in 1795 of a gallery with 2,289 items, in which Rembrandt was represented by original pictures, but which also contained numerous copies and works by pupils. When Russia incorporated Poland the collection was scattered all over the world.

B 188

painters of small pictures whom Augustus III of Saxony-Poland still continued to rate highly when he already possessed the masterpieces of the gallery of Modena. In vain did Winckelmann inveigh in 1755 against the 'wearisome industry of a Dou' and in vain did Hagedorn remark, in regard to a picture of Netscher's, 'that one would not mind seeing an Andromache instead of a lot of Dutch seamstresses'. At a very early stage an appreciation of landscape painting began to develop in Dresden. At first Italianizing Dutchmen attracted most

B 221

Peter the Great had already declared somewhat prematurely that 'in the great circulation of the arts it is now Russia's turn. If my instinct is right they are leaving the south and making their home with us'. Some decades later there were serious plans at the court of the Tsar for an 'Academy of the North' with a collection of paintings 'larger than any ever seen before'. Catherine II, shortly after ascending the throne in 1762, took up the idea. She had noted how quickly Augustus III of Saxony-Poland and Frederick the Great, whom she so much admired, had created collections, and as a sort of contrast with Sanssouci ('free of care') she called the annex to the Winter Palace, which contained her collection of pictures, the 'Hermitage', a name that continued to be used for the collection of the reigning dynasty when in the nineteenth century it was housed in its own mighty building.

Catherine described the nature of her acquisitions even more cynically than Frederick the Great. She spoke of them as prompted by greed rather than love of art. As early as 1767 people in Paris were complaining about the numerous and important purchases made at the Juliennne auction by Russian agents. 'How sad it is to see such lovely things going to the Scythians. In Russia there can hardly be ten people who will appreciate them, whereas, when they were here, the whole of Europe came to see them. Everyone can hope for the pleasure of seeing the Seine, but very few are curious enough to visit the frozen Neva'.

Catherine II acquired complete collections from Rome, Brussels and London. From Dresden the Brühl collection, containing four pictures by Rembrandt, five by van Ruisdael and several dozen by Wouwermann, was shipped to St Petersburg, and in Berlin the Tsarina was able, after the Seven Years War, to pay 180,000 thalers for a collection of 317 pictures which the art dealer Gotzkowski had got together by orders of Frederick the Great, but which the latter had not been in a position to purchase.

The French art-lover Fortia de Piles, who had been fascinated by Dresden, remarked in 1790, when speaking of Catherine's gallery, that it was 'without doubt the largest in Europe, but far from being the best-selected'. This was a severe judgment. Catherine II, by birth a German princess, was to some extent influenced by the taste of the time in her choice of pictures by southern masters, but later on, like so many others, she turned from Tiepolo to Murillo. Remarkable paintings by Flemish and Dutch painters came into the possession of the Tsars during Catherine's reign, for instance *Joseph accused by Potiphar's Wife* (now in the National Gallery, Washington) and some thirty other important paint-

195 In eighteenth-century Paris, small paintings, drawings and statues were in fashion. Many larger pictures were put up for auction and were bought by German and English collectors. In the Tallard auction in 1765 a Madonna by Giorgione found an English buyer. This engraving is taken from the title page of the auction catalogue

ings by Rembrandt. When making isolated purchases in her later years the Tsarina paid special regard to those Dutchmen, such as the landscape painters Jacob van Ruisdael and Wynants, who had been discovered during her lifetime, and so revealed a collector's taste which corresponded with that of the average princely court in Germany.

The great princely art collections of central and eastern Europe live on today in the form of museums which are known to every art-lover. In order to give a realistic account of what took place in Paris, one must also draw a picture of conditions which have now become past history and have left hardly any trace. In Paris about 1700 the quick change of collectors' tastes enabled foreign art-lovers to make worthwhile purchases. The vogue for Rubens had caused a number of paintings by Poussin to come on the market at a low price. The preference in eighteenth-century Paris for pictures of small size resulted in a number of large Flemish and Italian pictures leaving the country; the sudden turning away from Watteau enabled Frederick the Great to acquire half of all that this painter had ever produced. Some decades later Boucher too lost his reputation; important works of his reached Sweden (now in the N 166 Nationalmuseum, Stockholm).

The critical period of the Seven Years War led to the dispersal of most important Paris collections then in existence. The auctions of Tallard, Julienne and Mariette were reckoned to be the greatest of the eighteenth century, and works from these auctions reached Berlin, Dresden, Russia and a B 231 number of English private owners. Count Stroganoff, who lived in Paris from 1770, acquired important pictures from the collections of Randon de Boisset, Blondel de Gagny, Conti and de Choiseul. In Cassel and Dresden, in Berlin and St Petersburg the rulers were slaves of their passion for collecting. This was much less true of France. The last representatives of the Ancien Régime in Versailles never acquired a work by Watteau and only two pictures by Chardin. Purchases occasionally took place at the suggestion of competent authorities and this secured for the Crown many pictures which can now be admired in the Louvre. In the final analysis, however, these could only be accounted as unimportant additions to the stock of paintings handed down by previous generations.

Artistic life actually centred around interested and wealthy aristocrats, bankers, merchants, lawyers and the like, who filled the Paris salons. Nevertheless, around 1750 an observer remarked on 'the fickleness of taste' and 'love of profit' that marked the collectors. 'Art-lovers are all doing a bit of buying and selling. There is hardly a collector who doesn't either sell or exchange items from his collection.' Somewhat later Sedaine published some satirical conversations between an 'ancien amateur', an 'amateur philosophe', a 'curieux' and an 'amateur marié', a circle of friends that preferred to own a really important painting rather than a 'mistress who loses her beauty'. 'When I am old, this old friend will be sold, and the proceeds will support me, or else, by the time my beneficiaries get it, its value N 167 will have doubled', declared one of these characters.

The Paris collectors dissociated themselves remarkably early from the trends of Baroque taste and became receptive to the appeal of Dutch painting at about the same time as the creator of the Dresden Gallery. Around 1740 the elegant Wouwerman and Italianizing painters like Both and Berchem were held in high esteem in both Dresden and Paris. As in Germany, Jacob van Ruisdael was discovered; at about the same time the interest in Rembrandt grew stronger. For his *Return of the Prodigal Son* (now in the Hermitage) a certain M. d'Amezune paid 5,400 livres in Paris in 1765; *Christ at Emmaus* (now in the Louvre) was purchased for the French Crown in 1777 for the considerable price of 10,500 livres. N 16

Among the lovers of antiquity in eighteenth-century Paris, Count Caylus was the most distinctive figure. In an age of frivolity he outdid his contemporaries with his famous licentious supper parties. Pictures in the manner of Watteau he put in the same category as fans; antique statuettes especially interested him, among them not only Graeco-Roman but also Etruscan and Gallo-Roman work. In his house there was also an Egyptian statue (since recognized as a forgery). Of his bronze statuettes the Hellenistic *Negro Ephebe* was his favourite (now in the Bibliothèque Nationale in Paris). Count Caylus caused N 16 himself to be buried in a Roman-Egyptian sarcophagus of porphyry that rested on four sphinxes (the sarcophagus was transferred from the Church of Saint Germain l'Auxerrois to the Louvre at the time of the French Revolution). For the men of the Enlightenment the self-assured aristocrat was a thorn in the flesh. After Caylus' death in 1765 Diderot jeered at the rough antiquarian in his 'Etruscan jug'.

Compared with the France of the Ancien Régime, England strikes one as full of the promise of vigorous growth. The 'Glorious Revolution' had given the country a form of government which the

XV The cult of Raphael at the beginning of the neo-Classical era led to the rediscovery of Murillo in about 1750. Murillo's paintings soon found their way into all the major collections, including the Hermitage. During the Napoleonic Wars French generals serving in Spain did their utmost to acquire examples of his work. General Soult brought the *Immaculate Conception* back to Paris from Seville

majority of the population approved; for the progressively-minded on the Continent, England became more and more the supreme example to be followed. Increasing colonial possessions and industrialization brought the country riches which were widely distributed. The heyday of dilettantism had set in. Unfortunately, as in France, the paintings of this period have for the most part long left the walls on which they hung two hundred years ago, and those treasures of ancient sculpture, which were still admired in 1880, are regarded today as copies, often very indifferent ones, of Greek originals.

The company of art-lovers in England ranged from the bearers of great names and the heirs of great landed estates to politicians, merchants, lawyers and doctors. Besides the Dukes of Marlborough, Bedford, and Devonshire, the Earls of Pembroke and Radnor, there were untitled collectors such as Mead, Townley and Blundell. From 1700 onwards journeys to Italy became a veritable passion. South of the Alps the English gradually attained the first rank among purchasers of art. There was no lack of criticism from the Puritans. In 1737 the *London Magazine* declared that whole shiploads of pictures of the Dead Christ, Holy Families, Madonnas and 'other dismal dark subjects', were arriving from Italy in English ports. Hogarth, in his series *Marriage à la Mode*, showed Italian works with naked figures in his backgrounds. Such things, according to the Puritan view, accorded very well with the habits of a dissolute married couple. But hostility to southern art of the intensity that prevailed in Cromwell's day was no longer in evidence.

In contrast to the prevailing custom of the Late Baroque on the Continent, a rather loose arrangement of works of art became the custom at an early date in England—no doubt in line with the practices of Holland. Paintings were distributed over a number of rooms. It is thus natural that in 1770 an English lady should have found the dense juxta-position of paintings on the walls of the Venetian palaces very unusual. Whereas in Rome antique B 116 sculptures were arranged in rows, English collectors preferred to set them up singly in niches or to distribute them piece by piece, with only one piece to a room. This was also a habit of Frederick the Great, B 28 who in his later years was definitely 'anti-Baroque' in his attitude, being a Calvinist with considerable affection for England.

The influx of valuable paintings from the Continent to England is one of the most remarkable phenomena of the artistic life of that time. It is also noteworthy that the development of taste in England hardly varied from that demonstrated by the great princely galleries such as Dresden. Around 1700 certain Late Baroque trends were still in evidence. Lord Burlington, for instance, admired Italian contemporaries such as Pellegrini before he became an orthodox Palladian. It was consistent with what was happening on the Continent when, in the second half of the century, two pictures of 1719 by Watteau fetched only £ 42 and £ 52 respectively in England. N 171 At that time the more classically inclined masters among the southern schools, such as Dolci and Salvator Rosa, the Bolognese, and soon also Raphael himself, began to occupy positions of increasing prominence. When, in reference to some picture which they admired, people spoke in glowing terms of 'the head in the high Greek taste' and of 'the gracious contour', they were using almost exactly the same language heard in Dresden around 1750. In 1770 an English critic laid down the principle that 'only Raphael, Reni and Annibale Carracci have all the merits of a perfect master'. Even today England is still well furnished with pictures of Reni's late period. N 172

From about 1730 onwards works by Murillo were brought to England. Around 1745 the Duke of Bedford acquired the *Cherubs scattering Flowers* (still in the possession of the family in Woburn Abbey). The Frenchmen Poussin and Claude now began their triumphal entry into the collections of English art-lovers. N 173

England was already extremely rich in Flemish pictures. In addition to Rubens and van Dyck, their Dutch contemporaries were now being bought, as on the Continent. The particular partiality for painters such as Hobbema and Cuyp may be explained by the fact that the kind of landscapes reproduced in their work occur fairly frequently in England. Seascapes by Willem van de Velde and also works by Jacob van Ruisdael, Potter and Pieter de Hoogh were highly prized. Yet a delight in the art of Rembrandt as passionate as that displayed by William VIII of Hesse-Cassel hardly seems to have existed yet in England.

XVI The rejection of the artificiality of life in the eighteenth century and the 'return to nature' preached by Rousseau, resulted in renewed interest in the work of the Dutch landscape painters of Rembrandt's time. Cuyp was a particular favourite of English art-lovers, and his *Herdsman with Five Cows by a River* remains one of the most popular exhibits in the National Gallery in London

Shortly before 1780 George Nassau, the third Earl Cowper, had in his Florentine villa important paintings which reflected the new classicizing trend. In 1835 the Berlin curator Gustav Friedrich Waagen particularly admired these pictures, which at that time had already been removed to Cowper's country estate, Panshanger, among them two Raphael *Madonnas* (both now in the National Gallery, Washington, D. C., where they still bear the name of their former English owner) and also the *Head of a Sibyl* by Reni and a fine landscape by Salvator Rosa. (These two last-named pictures are now in the Mahon Collection in London.)

Around 1775 the collection of Robert Walpole in Houghton Hall was accounted one of the most important in England. Its pearl was the *Prodigal Son* by Salvator Rosa, but it also contained important pictures by Albani, Reni, Poussin and Claude as well as some by Rubens, van Dyck and Rembrandt.

196 After 1750 every new fashion in art found supporters, often from outside the ranks of the nobility. Joseph Smith owned this Vermeer, *The Music Lesson*, which George III bought from his collection in 1762

In 1778 Walpole's heirs sold this collection to Catherine the Great for £30,000, and so provided a considerable portion of the nucleus of the Hermitage. N 17

One of the most original figures of the English art world in the eighteenth century was the merchant Joseph Smith. Smith was resident in Venice and was for a time English Consul there as well as counsellor of travellers, agent and 'marchand-amateur'. He commissioned Tiepolo to paint *The Banquet of Cleopatra* which Algarotti was later to *183* bring to Dresden. About 1745 Smith commissioned paintings by Canaletto of Venetian buildings which corresponded with his Palladian taste. He also owned some Dutch pictures and was interested in drawings, gems, etc. In 1762 the greater part of his art treasures passed to the English Crown; among them was Vermeer's *Music Lesson* (shown in the Queen's Gallery, Buckingham Palace, in 1963). It was characteristic of conditions prevailing in England that King George III should have bought a commoner's collection in its entirety and regarded it as a very desirable piece of property. Aristocratic art-lovers on the Continent at that time took up a very critical attitude towards 'commoners' goods' and purchased only selections from them.

Continental connoisseurs watched with the greatest admiration, and often with resentment, the piling-up in London town-houses and in country estates of highly-prized works of classical art, above all busts, marble statues and vases, during the course of the eighteenth century. 'Before we know where we are', Winckelmann is supposed to have said in Rome, 'the British will take the whole of Trajan's Column to London'. It must be remembered that in the age of Winckelmann and Goethe antique sculptures were accounted among the highest of all earthly goods. The change from the taste of the early eighteenth century, among other things the decline in the popularity of imitation Chinese porcelain, was particularly marked in England. 'The smallness and ugliness of the Chinese, the dangerous enemies of the Muses', was the contemptuous judgment in London in the middle of the century. At that time there already existed 'The Society of Dilettanti', which immediately attained a European reputation when it came out with the first volume of its publication, Stuart and Revett's *Antiquities of Athens*, in 1762.

English travellers in Rome received advice there from two very active resident compatriots. Gavin Hamilton, originally himself a painter, acquired shortly after 1770 a magnificent marble vase from Hadrian's villa in Tivoli (since 1774 known as the *Warwick Vase* and still owned by the Earls of Warwick). From the Palazzo Barberini he acquired the piece that has become famous as the *Portland Vase* (now in the British Museum). An even more skilful man was Thomas Jenkins. Jenkins arranged for purchases from the collections of ancient Roman antiquities that belonged to the Altièri, Capponi and Mattei families; in Tivoli he reduced the stock of art treasures in the Villa d'Este and the Villa Montalto. Thanks to him a fine marble vase with Bacchic scenes came to England from the Villa Lante on the Janiculan Hill (this is the so-called *Lante Vase*, which is now in the possession of the Duke of

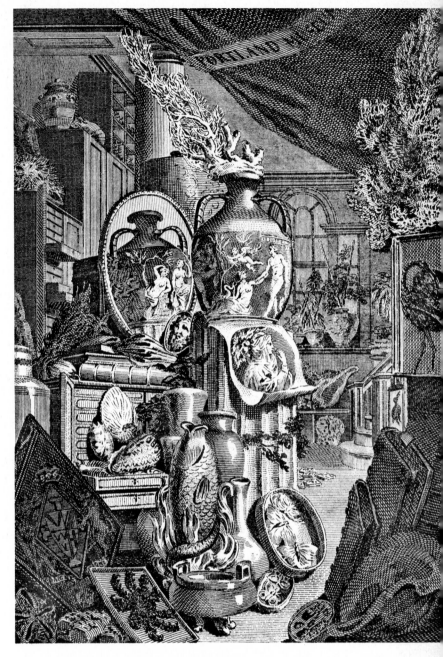

197 In 1786 the 'Portland Museum', belonging to the Duchess of Portland, came under the hammer. This copper engraving, taken from the auction catalogue, shows the famous *Portland Vase* which had been purchased from the Palazzo Barberini in Rome only a short while before

Bedford at Woburn Abbey). Together with Hamilton, Jenkins started in 1760 to organize excavations in the Roman Campagna, hoping thus to acquire the wares he needed.

As in the days of Arundel, Englishmen occasionally obtained antique works of art from the eastern

198 In English country-houses paintings and sculpture alike were freely arranged in the eighteenth century. Even today Wilton House gives a good impression of what an English collection must have looked like in that period

Mediterranean. Most of these pieces have preserved their reputation to the present day, for they are largely Greek originals. In 1744 a fragment of the Parthenon frieze was already in London, and shortly afterwards the *Sepulchral Relief of a Girl* came to N 179 London from Smyrna (now in the British Museum).

A rapid survey of typical English lovers of antiquity must necessarily begin with Thomas Herbert, eighth Earl of Pembroke. In 1715 he obtained a considerable part of the sculptures from B 327 the Mazarin collection. In 1720 he paid no less than

£270 for a bust belonging to the Valetta family. The most interesting object which is still at Wilton House today is a votive relief from Sparta dating back to the fifth century BC. In London Dr Richard N 18 Mead, the physician, was a collector of antiques; he was also a friend of Newton and was in touch with Joseph Smith in Venice. Mead possessed among other things the bronze head of Sophocles known as the *Arundel Homer* (now in the British Museum), *f* an excellent marble portrait of the Stoic philosopher Chrysippus (now in the Munich Glyptothek), as well as gems and coins. The auction of the 'Museum Meadianum' in 1755 was a major event in the London art market. N 18

Thomas Coke, later Earl of Leicester, started in the first half of the eighteenth century a choice little collection of antique sculptures. He succeeded in acquiring the bust of the Roman Praetor L. Cornelius which had been given a place of honour around 1700 in the Palazzo dei Senatori in Rome. In 1755 the Earl of Leicester built a noble sculpture gallery with niches in his country estate at Holkham Hall in Norfolk; for many generations this was one of the great sights of England. About 1750 the Earl of Egremont embellished his country house, Petworth, with a collection of antiquities which also maintained its reputation for a long time. One collection which was started in Italy in about 1770 has been preserved as a result of its coming intact into the possession of the British Museum. This was the very fine collection of vases belonging to Sir William Hamilton, British Ambassador in Naples.

About 1765 the rich merchant William Wedell acquired Newby Hall, near Ripon in Yorkshire. Wedell often stayed in Rome where, like German lovers of antiquity, he had himself painted by Batoni and made some cautious purchases; among other things Jenkins obtained for him a fine statue of Aphrodite from the Palazzo Barberini. In 1770 Wedell commissioned Robert Adam to build three small rooms for his antiquities, one of which was a circular hall with a cupola and top lighting in which there was also some furniture. The enjoyment of art thus had its place in the middle of the ordinary business of daily life. Until recently this characteristic ensemble of early Classicism was still kept very nearly in its original form. The Adam brothers also erected a noble room for the sculptures in Syon House.

Henry Blundell may well be considered the most successful English collector of antiquities in the eighteenth century. With Jenkins's help he finally assembled 553 pieces of sculpture, among them many items from the Roman collections of the Altieri, Lante, Mattei and Negroni. Blundell set up his collection in Ince Hall, Lancashire. Innumerable art-lovers in the nineteenth century made a pilgrimage there and stood in admiration before a statue of Zeus which had been the pride of the Villa d'Este in Tivoli.

In London itself Lansdowne House near Berkeley Square attained an almost legendary fame owing to its hall of antiquities, equipped at the narrower ends with two semi-circular exedrae. Between 1770 and 1780 William, Earl of Shelburne, created first Marquess of Lansdowne in 1784, acquired, largely thanks to Hamilton, a number of statues, portrait heads and statuettes. For the sculpture gallery Gavin Hamilton sent a sketch by Pannini from Rome, but the design was actually carried out by George Dance, and was completed by Robert Smirke. Here was housed the so-called *Lansdowne Hercules*, which had been excavated at Tivoli and was for a time greatly admired, as well as other statues of Greek gods and heroes. In 1920 this hall was still one of the most distinguished and tasteful creations of its kind to be maintained in its original

199 It was not only in its politics and trade that England was the model for the progressive elements in other European countries. The young Prince of Anhalt-Dessau (above) had his collection at Wörlitz displayed in the spacious English instead of the elaborate Baroque manner. Frederick the Great did the same at Sanssouci

form. Shortly afterwards the contents, including works of art and furniture, were dispersed at auctions.

The rationalism of the Enlightenment with its sense of system and completeness had called the Continent's attention to works of art dating back to the fifteenth century and earlier, though such attention may have done little more than inspire an abstract and somewhat cold contemplation. With English art-lovers, however, there was at first a genuine enjoyment of these older works. An English traveller in 1734 spoke in enthusiastic terms of the Memling altar in St Mary's Church in Danzig and praised its 'inestimable fineness'. German art-lovers about 1765 knew that panels from the age of Dürer

197

200 Many collectors in central and southern Germany continued to adhere to the Baroque style until as late as 1750. For example, small figurines by Ferdinand Dietz, based on Chinese originals, were still in fashion at that date

B 130

fetched higher prices in London than anywhere else. In Bamberg it was said in regard to two early German paintings that they would be valued at more than three hundred guineas in England. As early as 1777 Dr Richard Farmer of Cambridge acquired *The Trinity and Mystic Pietà* by Baldung (now in the National Gallery, London).

Horace Walpole, the son of Robert Walpole, was the creator of the neo-Gothic country house Strawberry Hill, which gained immediate fame. The eighteenth century's feeling for easy grace had a very strong influence on the interior decoration, and the resultant effect has been dubbed 'Rococo Gothic'. The most important part of the older works of art which Walpole had acquired on the Continent consisted of panes of painted glass from Switzerland. A prince of Anhalt-Dessau was so 199 impressed by his visit to Strawberry Hill that he equipped his typically English landscape park in Wörlitz with a 'Gotisches Haus'; he liked to live there himself and felt transported into a bygone world. N 18

Travelling Englishmen on the Continent not only promoted the rediscovery of early Netherlandish and German painters north of the Alps, but still more contributed to the revaluation of the early Italians in the south. In Florence, in 1767, the B 22 Englishman Hugford was already the owner not only of the *St Augustine* by Botticelli but also of the *Tobias* by Fra Angelico (both pictures now in the Uffizi Gallery); shortly before his death in 1778 Hugford acquired a *Death of the Virgin*, at that time attributed to Giotto (now classified as a work of the Angelico circle, in the Johnson Collection in Philadelphia).

Thomas Patch, who had lived in Florence since 1755, had engravings made of the frescos of Masaccio and the reliefs of Ghiberti which aroused the enthusiasm of Horace Walpole. In 1770 John Strange, the English Resident in Venice, acquired *St Jerome in a Landscape* by Cima da Conegliano XVI (now in the National Gallery, London) and paintings by Crivelli and Jacopo Bellini; he even had a panel dated 1412. Germans living in Italy around 1780 were in the habit of pointing to the English example when they concerned themselves with masters such as Masaccio. N 18

In the great mercantile cities of Frankfurt, Leipzig B 12 and Hamburg, the owners of gigantic fortunes considered themselves superior to the financially embarrassed petty princes and their hangers-on. A new phase of economic life had begun and the wealth of the bourgeoisie, which had been accumulated by trade, banking and manufacture, produced a number of important small collections. Furthermore, the bourgeois were beginning to flourish as a class, from which came a large number of assiduous modest collectors. Gathered around them was a band of art enthusiasts eager to cultivate their taste and knowledge.

In the princely collections there were many paintings and pieces of sculpture which, because of their very size, could never have found a home in an ordinary bourgeois house. Only the small pictures of the Dutch and Flemish schools were competed for simultaneously by both princely and bourgeois art-lovers, which was why, at Frankfurt auctions, the agents of princely collectors joined in the bidding. Many a picture offered for sale at the Leipzig fair reached Augustus III, while the art market of Hamburg played a large part in the founding of the galleries of Schwerin and Copenhagen.

Real 'commoners' goods', to use the expression of William VIII of Hesse, consisted for the most part of small-sized pictures by eighteenth-century German artists, who often made it their aim to adapt the art of famous Dutch masters to the taste of their own time. Their work fetched astonishingly good prices within and around their native cities. In Frankfurt in 1784 the *Portrait of a Boy* by Frans Hals (now in the Dessau Museum near Magdeburg) was auctioned for 16 guilders, while at the same time paintings by the elder Schütz, who worked for Goethe's father, fetched as much as 400 guilders. 'I would have been more confident of buying a head by Rembrandt for 50 guilders than of getting a head by Kupetzky for 100', Hagedorn noted down in Dresden shortly before this. According to the testimony of Wille, pictures by Dietrich were sold for as much as 4,000 francs in Paris. The popularity of Dou, the Dutch painter of small pictures, was the source of considerable profit to his Hamburg imitator Denner, who served in turn as the model for a Russian; yet certain St Petersburg art-lovers about 1750 were so well instructed that they recognized the complete style of the famous Denner in the work of Antropov who was then temporarily in vogue.

About 1770 there arose among German bourgeois, largely as the result of English influence, a general interest in early German and Netherlandish painting. While King Augustus III in Dresden still refused to include any panel by Cranach in his collection, a writer in Meusel's *Kunstzeitschrift* was complaining of the neglect of 'what has survived of the art of the elder Cranach'. As early as 1762 Hagedorn ventured to make some understanding remarks about the art of Jan van Eyck and his successors. Ten years later Herder and, under Herder's influence, Goethe made their voices heard from Strasbourg amid a slowly growing chorus. 'I can hardly say how I hate our berouged doll painters. Manly Albrecht Dürer, your wood-hewn figures are much more welcome to me.' It was thanks to the influence of Strasbourg that Friedrich Christian Lerse discovered Grünewald's *Isenheim Altarpiece* which he praised so highly, without knowing the identity of the painter.

The Frankfurt fairs were not only one of the reasons for the citizens' wealth in the old imperial city but also served as a place of sale for the Antwerp and Amsterdam art trade. Because of this, wealthy citizens began at a very early stage to engage in the collection of pictures. As early as 1660 an

201 The eighteenth century, which inclined towards tolerance in all things, upheld the same principle in art collecting. Around 1760 the Landgraves of Cassel placed an equally high value on a Greek statue of Apollo, a Rembrandt painting, and this Chinese porcelain statuette

auction took place in Frankfurt. The Dutch expression 'vergantung' was used here whereas in Vienna the Italian 'lizitation' was customary, as was the Spanish 'almoneda'. On the Rhine, on the other hand, the French expression 'vente', was occasionally used. The citizens of Frankfurt, 'for whom everything is merchandise', could not resist favourable offers, and agents of princely collectors who were well able to pay good prices found that this was an excellent place to acquire pictures, especially those of middling or small size belonging to the Flemish and Dutch schools.

From various references and above all from the catalogues of auctions one can trace some seventy collections in Frankfurt in the eighteenth century. Among the ten most important was presumably that of Goethe's father. In it young Wolfgang encountered numerous works of painters living in his native city. The story, 'The New Paris', which Goethe wrote at the age of ten was largely inspired by paintings by Seekatz and Trautmann. In later

202   In the second half of the eighteenth century, many ordinary citizens of the prosperous mercantile city of Frankfurt collected paintings—chiefly by Dutch artists. Their collections were arranged in the by then old-fashioned Baroque style, with no space between the pictures, as shown in this painting by Stöcklin

years Goethe began to realize that these men, who enjoyed a high reputation in Frankfurt, owed the best of their work to the Dutch. In *Dichtung und Wahrheit* there is mention of Schütz, 'who industriously continued the tradition of Saftleven'; of Juncker, 'who carried out neat paintings of flowers and fruit, still-lifes and people quietly working in the general manner of the Dutch'; and finally of Trautmann, 'who took Rembrandt as his model, with the result that he was once invited to paint a companion picture to one of Rembrandt's.'

As a student in Leipzig Goethe gained entry to the collections of local citizens and after his return made comparisons with those of his native town. 'The collections here', he wrote from Frankfurt on 24 November 1768 to Oeser in Leipzig, 'are indeed small compared to those of Leipzig but they are nevertheless numerous and choice. My greatest pleasure is to have a thorough look round them.' One of the most important Frankfurt collections was that of Johann Georg Bögner, a rich man who had the quaint habit of buying wildly and then, as the rooms of his house filled, of shutting them off one by one, forever. It was only in 1932 that a catalogue of Bögner's pictures auctioned in 1778 was discovered. According to this the total proceeds reached the sum of 27,000 guilders.

The collection of the banker Johann Friedrich Städel, which Goethe frequently visited, was raised in 1816 to the status of a public institution and still exists as such today. The greater part of its contents were gathered together between 1750 and 1790. Its creator, born in 1728, followed very conservative tastes. The Italian schools were represented by only a few Late Baroque pictures and Städel possessed only four German pictures of an earlier date than the seventeenth century. The great mass of his collection, which contained 495 items, came from the Flemish and Dutch schools. In this collection Goethe particularly admired the *Head of a Child* by Jacob Gerritsz Cuyp and the *Southern Landscape* by J.-F. Millet (both pictures now in the Städelsches Kunstinstitut).

One very precious object was associated with the new fashion of collecting early German paintings. It was a lock of Dürer's hair which was in the possession of Hüsgen, the friend of Goethe's youth. It came from the estate of Baldung and had long been kept in a Strasbourg 'Kunstkammer'; in the nineteenth century it reached Vienna.

Frankfurt's neighbour on the west, Mainz, had its own particular character in matters of art, being the seat of the most powerful of all the Catholic princes of the church. Whereas in Frankfurt one tended to look towards the north, the connections of Mainz were with Rome, Vienna and Venice.

In 1741 Hagedorn was staying in Mainz and had watched the Italian picture dealers at work, 'rogues in comparison with whom the worst Vienna huckster is a positive moralist'. They appeared at every ecclesiastical court of southern Germany and 'some change their name from one residency to another. Salozzi in Bamberg and Filiperti in Mainz are one and the same man'. In the Mainz collections, thanks to the activities of these Italian dealers, of whom no doubt Hagedorn had too unfavourable an impression, were some good pictures by the Venetians. When, around 1750, William VIII of Hesse began to interest himself in 'Italian pieces', he acquired from the estate of the Mainz counsellor of the exchequer Pfeiff the great historical picture *Antiochus and Stratonice* by the Venetian Baroque painter Antonio Bellucci. During his visits to the Cassel collection Goethe was very much attracted by this 'picture of a sick king's son' and there are

N 187 several references to it in *Wilhelm Meister*.

In the second half of the eighteenth century the principal of toleration, an ideal of the Enlightenment, began to establish itself in Mainz. While Lessing's *Nathan der Weise* proclaimed the ideal of toleration for those who held different beliefs, Catholic canons began to open their doors to Calvinist painters like Rembrandt. Count Eltz, the powerful nephew of the Archbishop of Mainz and one of the most successful private collectors of the eighteenth century, now began to add Dutch pictures to those of the Venetian school already well represented in his collection by paintings ranging from Tintoretto to Piazzetta and Tiepolo. At his death Count Eltz possessed 1,231 paintings, of which his heirs were permitted to select a hundred; they retained,

203 among others, Rembrandt's *Christ the Saviour*, a picture very non-Catholic in its conception (now in the Munich Pinakothek). According to the collector's final will, a catalogue of 1,131 pictures of second rank was to be sent to Russia, England and Amsterdam since pictures fetched the highest prices there.

At the court of the Elector and Archbishop of Cologne priests and high officials were particularly active as collectors in the eighteenth century. Of particular interest is the collection of Count Joseph von Truchsess-Zeil-Wurzach, who was born in 1748. Towards the end of the century this collection contained more than a thousand paintings, among them a large altarpiece by Hans Multscher of Ulm dated 1437 (now in the Berlin Museums), and an altarpiece by Hans Strigel (now in the Stuttgart Gallery). Up to the end of the century, but chiefly before 1790, 192 panel paintings by Aldegrever, Baldung, Bruyn, Cranach, Pencz, Schäuffelein, Schongauer, Wohlgemuth and other early German masters, were added.

203 The vogue for Rembrandt extended to the leaders of the Catholic Church in Mainz in 1770; up to then they had generally preferred paintings by Italian artists. Rembrandt's *Christ the Saviour* formed part of Count Eltz' collection

In Leipzig at the time of the fair the 'exhibition rooms' in Auerbach's inn were filled with merchandise. The most important collection in Leipzig and indeed the most valuable ever to be found in the eighteenth century in a German citizen's house, belonged to Gottfried Winckler. When he died in 1795 the collection contained 1,300 paintings, 8,000 drawings and 10,000 engravings. The overwhelming majority of the pictures came from the Dutch school. Winckler owned the *Head of an Aged Woman* (now in the National Gallery, Washington, D. C.), and nine other Rembrandt paintings. Murillo was represented by the *Flower Girl* (now in the gallery at Dulwich College, London).

most recently in the Rasch collection in Stockholm. The Berlin art trade had an active representative in the person of Gotzkowski, whose services were used by Hamburg and Danzig collectors. The Venetian 'marchand-amateur' Zanetti received from Gotzkowski a *Crowning of Christ* by Dietrich which was deservedly admired in 1760 at the exhibition in the Scuola San Rocco on the Saint's Day.

The dealer Triebel sold pictures from Berlin to the east and to the west; William VIII of Hesse bought from him the *Feast of the Three Kings* by Jordaens (now in the Cassel Gallery), and in Warsaw 'where paintings are twice as dear as they are in Germany, Italy or France' Triebel was offering an Italian primitive as early as 1778.

The artistic life of the flourishing mercantile city of Hamburg in the eighteenth century was on a level with that of Frankfurt. Both wealthy and modest collectors were active. Christian von Hagedorn was well aware of the peculiar quality of obstinacy which marked the great self-confident Hamburg collectors. Naturally, they paid well, and at the end of his life Hagedorn wanted to sell his collection there. About 90 per cent of the pictures in the houses of Hamburg were from the Dutch school; the rest was divided between Flemish, French, Italian and more recent German artists. It was only much later that early German portraits or altar panels, which appeared in Frankfurt and Cologne as early as 1780, attracted the interest of art-lovers in Hamburg.

In the eighteenth century the art market of Hamburg had a remarkable importance. Trade still used the waterways, and the Elbe connected Hamburg with the great cities of Saxony. There was as much traffic with St Petersburg and Stockholm as with the Dutch and English ports. A Dresden dealer sent paintings to Hamburg in 1770 so that 'rich Englishmen passing through might acquire them', and in 1786 an English collection of pictures which had been intended for Russia was auctioned in Hamburg. Works of art were exported chiefly to the north and the east. The distribution of German goldsmiths' work provides many indications of this. In 1911, 57.8 per cent of the older pieces of Hamburg goldsmiths' work were to be found in Russia, 8.5 per cent in the Scandinavian countries. In the Moscow Patriarch's treasure chamber in 1911, 67.2 per cent of the contents consisted of items from Hamburg.

In the course of a few decades St Petersburg had transformed itself from a settlement of huts into one of the most highly populated cities of Europe. Its building fever, its tremendous business activity and its trade in art were beginning to show all the typical symptoms of a boom. Travelling writers

204 While Frederick the Great bought antique sculpture and paintings by Watteau, and later Correggio, the prosperous citizens of his capital contented themselves with the work of Dutch artists. Chodowiecki, with a gentle irony, gives a contemporary view of Berlin collectors above

In the course of the eighteenth century in Berlin a number of collectors appeared from the ranks of both the aristocracy and the bourgeoisie in addition to the ruling House, and to these must be added a number of art dealers. Compared with Frankfurt, Leipzig and Dresden, activities in Berlin were rather provincial: Amsterdam collectors' taste set the tone. Count Kamecke owned Rembrandt's *Brother* (now in the Louvre), and the merchant Caesar his *Jeremias*, from the west kept entertaining their public, year after year, with descriptions of the spasmodic growth of the residence of the Tsars. 'One feels that one is close to Italy at one point and on the road to Siberia at another', was a typical pronouncement of the age when palaces decorated with pillars and peasants' wooden huts stood next to one another. Although it was easy to attract this or that architect from the Latin countries, the prevailing taste of the Court favoured Holland and northern Germany.

B 133

The economic superiority of Russia over the Europe of that day caused a steady inflow of works of art. If prices were twice as high in Poland as they were in western Germany, they were four times as high and more in St Petersburg. The fever of speculation was already infecting the artistic life of St Petersburg. 'In no country are there such passionate collectors as here; but this excessive zeal often impairs the permanence of the collection since its very costliness results in its being sacrificed sooner or later', remarked a German observer in 1780. St Petersburg's very active art trade, which was fed from central Europe and was mostly in German hands, flooded the market with merchandise. This often included works that did not correspond closely to the prevailing tastes of Europe.

It is illuminating to compare the collections of the high aristocracy in Vienna with those in St Petersburg in the second half of the eighteenth century. For their Late Baroque town palaces, the Viennese aristocracy appropriately preferred large or at least sizable pictures. Evidence of this is provided by such works as Rembrandt's *Blinding of Samson* which was in the town house of Count Schönborn (now in the Städelsches Kunstinstitut in Frankfurt); and the same could be said of many pictures of the Kaunitz and Czernin collections. In St Petersburg the great majority of pictures were small pieces, the works of such men as Dou, Dietrich and Denner. The Viennese collectors showed themselves receptive towards new trends; they were readily converted from the Late Baroque to the early classicizing style, and when purchasing Dutch pictures they quickly developed an affection for masters like Aelbert Cuyp and Wynants. In St Petersburg people were less particular. A picture brought in from the older Europe was in itself already an object of value, irrespective of the period to which it belonged or its provenance.

The economic weakness of Italy made it impossible to prevent numerous works of art from leaving for central and northern Europe. A kind of general sell-out began in Rome in 1725 and in Venice only a very little later. Nevertheless the Italian élite on the whole participated in the intellectual life of Europe to a much greater degree than is usually assumed. Muratori paid tribute in 1749 in his treatise *Della Pubblica Felicità* to the aims of the Enlightenment. When collections began to be formed, their general character, though not their extent, corresponded to those north of the Alps.

In Venice the Grassi, who had been ennobled only in 1699, acquired paintings by Titian and Veronese and also by Guercino and Reni. Count von der Schulenburg, a German general in the service of Venice, gave commissions to Pittoni and Piazzetta but also purchased Flemish genre pictures.

205 Whereas in England, France and Germany eighteenth-century private collections have, almost without exception, long since been broken up, in Rome several collections, as well as two papal museums, have remained virtually unchanged. But however impressive the overall effect of these various galleries, they do also contain fakes: for instance, the Herm of Bacchus (detail), based on a fifth-century BC Greek original, in the Galleria Borghese

Antonio Maria Zanetti, known as 'the Elder' to distinguish him from his cousin, visited Paris and Rotterdam. In London he acquired a drawing by

134

Parmigianino which had once belonged to Arundel (now in the Ashmolean Museum in Oxford) and in Vienna contrived to acquire pictures from the collection of Prince Eugen. In later years he combined a taste for mannerist and picturesque works in the neo-Classical Style by artists such as Ugo da Carpi

N 188

and Castiglione.

Filippo Farsetti, a descendant of a noble family, founded an outstanding collection of casts of antique sculpture, a collection which so impressed Canova that it very largely determined the path he

N 189

subsequently followed. In Verona, lovers of antiquity visited the collection of Marchese Scipione Maffei. It was here in 1786 that Goethe was moved to tears when for the first time in his life he saw

B 244

original Greek sculpture.

In Rome, in addition to the English art dealers mentioned earlier, numerous Italians were active as dealers, restorers and guides. The memory of the efficient Francesco de Ficoroni has been preserved by an Etruscan bronze, the famous *Cista Ficoroni* (now in the Villa Giulia in Rome).

Several times during his long life Cardinal Alessandro Albani, a nephew of Clement XI, assembled a considerable number of antique sculptures. Goethe admitted in his *Italienische Reise* that Albani had 'a degree of collector's luck that bordered on the miraculous'. In 1734 a great collection of antique busts which Albani had brought together came into the possession of the Popes and became the

B 219

basic stock of the Capitoline Museum; some thirty statues were sold by the Cardinal to the princely House of Wettin in Dresden. In later years another collection came into being—part of which still

N 190

exists—in the Villa Albani in the Via Salaria. Around 1780 the Borghese, too, were occasionally active as collectors of antique statuary.

A number of comments have been quoted from princely collectors of the Baroque age about earlier art; their tone was moderate and objective. Elector Maximilian of Bavaria or Archduke Leopold Wilhelm were as self-controlled before a painting as in the smoke of battle. This aristocratic attitude gradually disappeared during in the eighteenth century. The bourgeois of the age of *Werther* wore his heart upon his sleeve. In the early seventeenth century it was often said of a picture that it should not be looked at save with admiration. Three generations later, people were more emphatic and used such phrases as 'beautiful beyond measure'. It was with the incisive injunction 'to fall down and

N 191

worship' that Wilhelm Heinse in the age of 'Sturm und Drang' led visitors before his favourite pictures in the Düsseldorf Gallery. 'The fury of talking about the arts has especially seized Germany', remarked Herder in 1770.

In principle the viewing public of the age of the Enlightenment was all for toleration. 'You have no taste if you have only have one taste', declared Lessing. 'To be a contemporary of all ages' was Schiller's ambition. In 1797 Goethe attacked any kind of one-sidedness and did so in the persuasive manner for which he was famous. 'Who wants to be a complete purist?' he wrote in *Sammler und ihresgleichen*. More and more in the eighteenth century new classes of society began to claim some share in the ownership of the cultural assets until then reserved for the privileged. In the seventeenth century only travellers of distinction and learned men from foreign countries had ordinarily been allowed entry to the princely collections, which in those days were invariably housed in some place connected with the court and usually in the actual residential palace itself. After 1700 groups of travellers were led round the Vienna Imperial Gallery but had to pay the huge sum of 12 guilders to the custodian. The administrator of the princely galleries had only a very modest salary but he did have the right to the honoraria payable in the case of such conducted tours. It was from the custodians that violent protest began to be heard when there was talk of free entry among the public or at court.

Where the Catholic Church was concerned, especially in Rome but also in the big monasteries, social distinctions had always been more or less disregarded among visitors. Art-lovers who visited Rome in the eighteenth century had no difficulty whatever in seeing the *Apollo Belvedere* or the papal paintings in the Quirinal on certain days. Other conditions would have been considered intolerable in Rome. 'Those barbarians, the English, buy up everything and in their own country nobody sees it but themselves', protested Winckelmann in 1760. In London some years later a Member of Parliament rose in the House and praised Spain where everyone could see the royal art treasures. Presumably he was referring to the painting collection in the Escorial.

The pictures belonging to the French Crown that were distributed about the Palace of Versailles were inaccessible in the first half of the eighteenth century to the general public, while courtiers who enjoyed favour in the highest places could occasionally remove pictures on loan. In 1730 Raphael's *Portrait of Balthasar Castiglione* and Titian's *Pardo Venus*

103

hung in the Paris house of the Duke of Antin. From about 1740 onwards the authorities concerned began to be assailed with petitions such as: 'The priceless masterpieces of His Majesty's picture gallery are buried in small rooms in the Palace of Versailles and are unknown to strangers'. In order to escape further attacks, at least 110 pictures, among them works by Correggio, Leonardo, Raphael, Titian, Rubens, Rembrandt, Poussin, Claude and certain Flemish painters, were in 1750 provisionally hung in the Palais Luxembourg in Paris and shown to the public twice a week. But this solution did not last, and the Ancien Régime through its omissions incurred a reproach which might well have been avoided.

In Germany things developed more smoothly on the whole. The Dresden Gallery was easily accessible 180 from 1746 onwards, housed in a building outside the palace. In Salzdahlum near Brunswick, around 1770, conducted tours took place at specified times and lasted for two hours. In Vienna in the 1770's the collection of paintings was moved outside the Hofburg to the Upper Belvedere. Here the idealism of the enlightened Joseph II went so far as to introduce free admission, a step that aroused severe protests from artists. 'Waiters' helpers and the lowest type of women', it was alleged, disturbed the 'silent contemplation of the works of art'. In the English Parliament in 1777 there were attacks on the Crown when the Raphael cartoons were moved from Hampton Court to Buckingham Palace. The public did not want such masterpieces to be buried in that

N 192   inaccessible 'smoky house'.

Circles influenced by the philosophers of the Enlightenment and by the Encyclopedists intoxicated themselves with the idea of instructing and improving mankind by means of educational institutions. Just as older libraries in the principal cities and in the residencies were grouped together to form central libraries, and just as collections of natural curiosities were now no longer arranged according to the dictates of the eye but according to systems and rules, so people began to entertain the idea of ordered, comprehensive collections of works of art which were to 'give an account that stretched over three

N 193   millennia'.

In England where this trend was first in evidence the British Museum was created in 1759. This was a national institution founded with the authority of Parliament. It was justified in bearing the name which Greek culture in a comparable phase had given to the libraries and places of learning in the city of Alexandria. The most important element of the new foundation was the collection of the physician Dr Hans Sloane. It consisted predominantly of objects of natural history, but also contained 1,125 antiquities, 700 cut stones and 32,000 medals and coins. In his will Sloane had expressed the wish that

206 Cardinal Alessandro Albani, a nephew of Pope Clement XI, had a villa built for him by Marchionni (1743-46) on the via Salaria in the north of Rome. Its purpose was rather to house his antique sculpture than to provide him with an alternative home. The juxtaposition of reliefs and statues reveals the long survival of Baroque tastes in Rome

his property should be made accessible to the public, for 'the improvement of the Arts and Sciences and the benefit of mankind'. The collection was first housed in Montague House, formerly a nobleman's mansion.   N 194

The British Museum had a far-reaching influence and gave the Latin word 'Museum' a vivid reality it had lacked till then. In North America the London example was followed when in 1773 'the oldest museum in the territory of the present U. S.' emerged as a kind of overflow of the library in Charleston, South Carolina. Some years later Cassel obtained, through Frederick II of Hesse, its 'Museum Friderizianum'. The first storey was given over to a library while the ground floor contained newly-acquired antiquities, among them the *Cassel Apollo*, and elsewhere specimens of natural history. In 1785 the planning of the Prado Museum was begun by order of the Spanish King. Here, as in London, the emphasis was on exhibits illustrating natural history.

The idea of a systematic ordering, so typical of the Enlightenment, gradually began to be applied to many old and famous princely collections. In Madrid in 1775 Anton Raphael Mengs expressed his regret that all the King's paintings were not hung together in a single gallery, as art-lovers would then be able to have a survey which extended from the most ancient painters to those still living. Similar ideas were

207 As a result of the excavations of Pompeii and Herculaneum, and the transfer of the Farnese collection from Rome to Naples, the latter became a place of pilgrimage for all lovers of antiquity. Sculpture by Canova, who was greatly admired at that time, was displayed next to antique works. This also happened in the Vatican and, somewhat later, in the Munich Glyptothek. The head below is a copy by Canova of the *Rondanini Medusa* (see Ill. 42)

realized shortly afterwards in Florence by the reigning Habsburg Grand Duke Leopold II. In the Uffizi Gallery paintings from palaces and churches in Tuscany were grouped together. In Naples the royal House gathered together the whole of its art treasures, including the Farnese heirlooms, in one place. From Rome came the *Farnese Hercules* and other famous statues. The gallery in the old Farnese city of Parma was turned out; and by 1790 the Capodimonte Palace above Naples contained more than 2,000 items in paintings alone.

In Germany paintings usually remained separated from other exhibits, mainly because of the size of certain altarpieces (for instance, those by Rubens) but were nevertheless gradually given a new arrangement. Like the enlightened Habsburg who ruled in Florence, German princes were generally prepared to denude their private apartments and chapels of paintings so as to enrich the newly-planned central galleries. The public also demanded that as many altarpieces as possible should be removed from churches 'where they would be stolen from us by forgetfulness' and would, as it were, 'be in exile', since their 'deserved habitation' was a gallery. Religious works of art were often given profane titles which have remained with them ever since. A *Madonna* by Raphael in the Palace of Versailles was transformed into *La Belle Jardinière* (now in the Louvre) while in the museum at Cassel Rembrandt's *Madonna and Child with St Joseph* became *The Woodcutter's Family*.

The Enlightenment gained its greatest victory among Germans in the place one would least expect, namely the Habsburg capital. Certainly the reforms of Joseph II, which in many respects were somewhat premature, took the wind out of revolutionary sails. The imperial chancellor, Prince Kaunitz, in particular set himself the aim of putting the Habsburg states at the head of all others in art production as in everything else. Educational collections, among them the remodelled Vienna Gallery, were to serve these plans.

Joseph II found that the Late Baroque imperial 'Pinacoteca' in the Stallburg, a part of his Vienna Residenz, was ready to hand. There were also smaller pictures in the two treasuries as well as altarpieces in the chapels of many imperial palaces in the widespread Habsburg countries. There were also the picture 'Kabinette' in this or that secondary residency, as, for instance, in Graz and Innsbruck. When the Jesuit Order was dissolved in 1774 a number of large altarpieces by Rubens were acquired from the southern Netherlands (at that time under Habsburg rule) at the suggestion of Prince Kaunitz. All these items were now to be displayed to the public at a place outside the Hofburg in a systematic arrangement. Their new home became the Upper Belvedere, originally built by Prince Eugen. In 1781 Christian von Mechel, who had been summoned from Basle, completed the new presentation. At a time when not a single picture belonging to the French Crown could be seen by the public in Paris, the people of Vienna were admitted three times a week to the imperial gallery.

Mechel declared in the preface to his catalogue that he compared 'such a great collection to a well-stocked library, to give instruction rather than provide transitory enjoyment'. The Vienna catalogue was the first to indicate important paintings with asterisks; in another German catalogue the visitor was advised to look at a late picture of Rembrandt 'from a certain distance' so that 'he could admire the manner in which it was painted'. New sections of the public, who had no knowledge of these matters, were thus to receive instruction.

The general arrangement of the numerous rooms of the Belvedere Palace was thoroughly systematic. The pictures were chronologically arranged within the framework of the three schools of painting, those of Germany, the Netherlands and Italy. The art-historical conception which Winckelmann had been the first to apply to antique art was here transferred to the painting of Europe. Those who kept to the old method of hanging, which they considered more pleasing to the eye, spoke of the 'murder of the gallery', but the representatives of the enlightened bourgeoisie surpassed each other with their enthusiastic approval.

While in Vienna Joseph II in his wild optimism was admitting all ranks of society to view the gallery, other princes, who regarded themselves as fathers of their country, had misgivings. The naked goddesses and nymphs to be seen in so many pictures should not, they felt, be allowed to undermine the morals of the citizens.

On Sundays, when the working population would have had leisure to visit the place, only foreigners were admitted to the Hofgartengalerie in Munich. In Madrid the pictures with nude figures were gathered together into a few rooms, to which artists and foreign travellers were admitted. Whereas in the majority of rooms everything was 'decently draped', people found in the secret rooms only 'flesh colour and sensuality'. The bourgeois public was in the habit of putting its own interpretation on many older works of art in a touching manner and excluding the real meaning of the pictures. The visitors in the Vienna Gallery turned the courtesan 'Bella Gatta'—beautiful cat—who had been painted by Palma Vecchio, into 'Violanthe, the

208 Among the most admired Greek statues in Naples was this Psyche. The generation that was so moved by Goethe's *Werther* considered her modest gaze capable of touching every heart (detail)

Artist's Daughter', while Titian's portrait of a 'Donna lasciva' was now held to represent his highly moral daughter Lavinia, and suggestive Dutch brothel scenes were transformed into slightly sentimental 'fatherly admonitions'.

In the Late Baroque period, galleries on the Continent had been arranged according to a systematic and precise order, in which paintings were juxtaposed and luxurious frames, together with wall and ceiling decorations, all helped to form a single unity. These ideas began to change during the eighteenth century. In the so-called 'Green Gallery' of the Munich Residenz, created in 1733, the paintings with conspicuously light frames began to be moved away from each other. The damask-covered wall began once more to have its effect. In Vienna, Mechel, when called on to effect his rearrangement, would have nothing to do with the luxurious frames from the Stallburg gallery and

209 In about 1780 the sculpture collection belonging to the ruling House of Naples was kept in a castle-like building in the suburb of Portici. An unknown artist saw the proposed transfer of the collection to the present building in terms of the kind of triumphal procession familiar to Neapolitan opera audiences

N 197 succeeded in getting simple early classical frames made at a cost of 70,000 guilders. These isolated the individual pictures and made it easier to change the arrangement according to the art-historical views prevailing at any given time. Thus the conception of the Baroque gallery as a unified work of art was turned into its opposite at the very place where it had been realized in the most consistent manner. It was in fact turned into a 'speaking history of art'

which addressed itself entirely to the intellect of the beholder.

The admission of the public into galleries was one aspect of the ever-increasing interest in art; another, and equally important aspect, was the foundation of new galleries and museums and the extension of existing ones. From Dresden there came to Italy not only Mengs and Winckelmann but also a daughter of Augustus III of Saxony-Poland; as the wife of the 'King of the Two Sicilies' she acquired some influence in Naples in the matter of its museums. It was she who determined the arrangement of the museum in Portici (no longer extant), where the finds of Herculaneum and Pompeii were first housed. N 198

In Florence, as already mentioned, an enlightened Habsburg, later to become the Emperor Leopold II, rearranged the art treasures while he was still Grand Duke of Tuscany. In 1780 he built the

Galleria dell'Accademia as the home of an archae-ological collection designed for educational pur-poses, and increased the numbers of statues in the Loggia dei Lanzi. For the most precious antiquities, the *Niobids*, which had been brought from the Villa Medici in Rome, the Grand Duke had a room added to the west wing of the Uffizi Gallery which still serves its original purpose. The gay and courtly decoration in white and gold, Classicist in spirit, which was applied amongst other things

210

210 In about 1780 a room was added to the west gallery of the Uffizi to house the *Niobids* which had been in the Villa Medici in Rome. The unrestricted arrange-ment of these statues shows the influence of ideas prevalent in northern Germany, Holland and England

to the pediments of the statues, was inspired by the ideal of a discreet harmony between the works of art and the place where they were housed.

Under the influence of the ideas of the Enlightenment, the Papacy became a pedagogic force. The idea—which was having such explosive effects north of the Alps—that all should enjoy cultural goods, had in any case certain precedents in the tradition of the Catholic Church. In this age of tolerance the Curia's last misgivings in the matter of heathen religions disappeared. The Papacy approved of Graeco-Roman antiquity and raised no objection to the enthusiasm for Etruscan objects which began about 1740. About the middle of the century Benedict XIV officially gave permission for the Capitoline Museum to house Egyptian antiquities. The Borghese family no longer hesitated in arranging an Egyptian Room in their Casino on the Pincian Hill.

211 In 1740 the Pope opened the Museo Capitolino, the first public museum of antiquities. The relatively constricted arrangement of the various rooms, such as the one containing busts of the emperors, demonstrates the persistence of outmoded ideas in Rome

The first Roman foundation in the eighteenth century of a great collection of antiquities that has lasted to the present day was the Capitoline Museum, which assumed its final features in 1740. Late Baroque tendencies were still evident in it. The main room was dominated by two large statues of the two popes who had founded the museum and opened it to the public. Here Winckelmann wandered from morning till night after his arrival in Rome in 1755.

211

N 200

Soon afterwards, the last great collection of antiquities, that of Cardinal Albani, began to take shape in his villa, which had long been open to art-lovers. In its essentials it still exists today. The rooms were no longer named after their shape or colour, as was the Florentine Tribuna or the Green Gallery in Munich, but according to the systematically arranged works of art which they housed. While Mechel adopted a historical system in Vienna, Winckelmann arranged the collection in the Villa Albani by subjects, and placed goddesses, emperors and tragic reliefs together. Soon after, Prince Marcantonio Borghese had the new rooms of statues arranged by Asprucci on the ground floor of his villa on the Pinci. The splendid clarity of the rooms has been preserved, but the best statues went to the Louvre some time after 1800.

N 201

213

N 202

212 After 1800 some of the Borghese collection of antique sculpture was taken to the Louvre and never returned. Although it contains many copies, the Galleria Borghese still gives an excellent impression of how such collections were presented in about 1785. A detail of a wall of the entrance hall is shown above

213 A few decades after the opening of the Museo Capitolino, Romans also adopted the more spacious system of display. Particularly magnificent examples of the effect of this can be seen in the rooms designed by Asprucci after 1782 in the ground floor of Prince Marcantonio Borghese's casino (the present Galleria Borghese) in the Pincio Gardens

214 Perhaps the most perfect eighteenth-century museum is the Museo Pio-Clementino in the Vatican. Simonetti's design of a circular room top-lit by a dome freely alludes to the Pantheon. Though most of the original has remained unchanged, it was found necessary at a later date to add the balustrade in order to protect the antique mosaic floor ▶

The most magnificent collection created in the eighteenth century, indeed one of the most perfect museums in existence, was conceived by Pope Clement XIV in 1773 and was completed by his successor, Pius VI. The Museo Pio-Clementino in the Vatican developed as an extension of the Belvedere Court of Julius II. An octagonal portico was added to this, and its early Classicist style was considered 'elegantissimo' by contemporaries. The *Apollo Belvedere*, the *Laocoön* and their accompanying statues were placed in front of niches and thus isolated.

In the newly-constructed halls the leading Italian neo-Classical architect Simonetti partly made use of central planning. The statues placed on high pediments were set at an appreciably greater distance from the walls than in the Villa Albani. Their systematic distribution was now a matter of course, and statues of gods were gathered together in a round room designed after the Pantheon. A 'Sala dei Busti'

with portrait heads and busts of all kinds, and a 'Sala degli Animali', were also created.

The effect of the rooms of the Museo Pio-Clementino was originally freer and clearer than the one enjoyed today by the visitor to the Vatican. Too many additional statues were placed in the museum during the nineteenth century. Yet the fundamental mood of the whole, which was felt in 1800 to be 'vasta e maestosa', has not been lost. It is true that we see hardly a single Greek original

but instead mostly copies from the age of the Roman emperors; and that the architecture of the rooms is similarly derivative. Nevertheless, we share Jacob Burckhardt's admiration for 'those rooms which will always remain nobly classical and which gently, and yet with great power, move the beholder'.

215 The reverence with which Greek and Roman sculpture was treated in the neo-Classical age is indicated by the use of very high pedestals. Visitors to the museums were expected literally to look up to the poets, philosophers and heroes of antiquity. This pen-and-wash drawing of a room in the Museo Pio-Clementino is by Volpato

CHAPTER 5

The Nineteenth Century

The museum as temple | a French museum of medieval art | Napoleon's trophies in the Louvre | the British Museum and the Munich Glyptothek | discovery of the Italian primitives | the 'Sanctum Corpus' of the Boisserée brothers | the first American collectors | the cult of Tiepolo and the neo-Baroque | art and industry: museums of applied arts

IN PARIS, during the period when Emperor Joseph II was initiating the idea of a museum in Vienna for the public, neither French nor foreign art-lovers could see the paintings belonging to the royal family, though the administration was trying to prepare a great exhibition of masterpieces in the Grande Galerie of the Louvre. No doubt this project had the support of Marie Antoinette, Joseph II's sister, but here, as in other phases of the Ancien Régime in its last years, there was a lack, not of understanding, but of the will to act. The public was already counting on violent change and intoxicated itself with scenes of virtuous heroism from the days of the ancient Roman Republic. In the Academy Exhibition which took place in the Salon Carré of the Louvre in 1785, people crowded enthusiastically in front of the neo-Classical programme picture *The Oath of the Horatii* by David, and cursed the Queen, whose portrait by Mme Vigée-Lebrun happened to hang close by (both pictures now in the Louvre).

A few years later Louis XVI and Marie Antoinette were driven to the scaffold, while the artist David was freeing what had once been the royal palace from 'feudal art'. Rubens, the servant of princes, was viewed with disfavour, and 'monkish-fanatical' pictures were removed. The portrait of Charles VII

of France by Jean Fouquet, painted in 1450, was sold privately (after 1815 it was repurchased and is now in the Louvre). From such works as appeared suitable for the purpose, the Muséum de la République with its distinctly neo-Classical bent was built up in 1793, and this soon became the Muséum Central des Arts. The solemn Latin title 'Museum' implied a tribute to the British Museum in London and also to the people of ancient Rome, who at that time were much admired. It was only after 1800 that the French form 'Musée' finally asserted itself.

While in Vienna and other places the Crown itself had handed over all manner of art works to large central museums, and even religious pictures often found their way into galleries, the 'free people' of France deprived the ruling classes of their possessions. This circumstance gave to the Muséum Central des Arts the character of an exhibition of trophies acquired after a hard-won victory. In the Louvre in 1795 one could see next to the paintings from the palaces of the executed king and from profaned churches, precious works of art that had been the property of members of the aristocracy who had either fled or been condemned to death. The frames of pictures which are still in the Louvre today, were furnished with shields containing the hated names of the previous owners such as Richelieu, Penthièvre and Brissac, a circumstance which proved an added attraction for the visitors.

The system of ideas that marked the Enlightenment and from which the ideology of the revolutionaries was principally derived, underwent a significant change in 1790. 'The pomp of art must be the luxury and the religion of free people', proclaimed the revolutionary Chaussard. It will be remembered that in Germany in the time of Lessing, art collections were regarded, very much like large libraries, as educational institutes. Voices had already been raised against this dry rationalism shortly after the middle of the eighteenth century. When Winckelmann first saw the antique statues of Frederick the Great he spoke of 'the passionate, voluptuous delights' he had experienced. Heinse described his experience in the Düsseldorf Gallery in glowing words, while young Goethe in his 'Third Pilgrimage

N 204

N 205

N 206

216 The Napoleonic Wars resulted in the plunder of works of art on an unprecedented scale. From Antwerp, Cassel, Berlin, Munich and Vienna came paintings, and from Italy the most famous antique sculpture. In the centre of this contemporary engraving one can see the four bronze horses from St Mark's Basilica in Venice

to Erwin von Steinbach' of 1775 was already sounding religious notes. In 1787 the Vienna Gallery was called 'a temple of art'.

Through what was said and done in Paris these tendencies reached their culminating point. 'I compare the pleasure taken in noble works of art to prayer', wrote Wilhelm Wackenroder in 1797. In the gallery of Pommersfelden a picture attributed at that time to Raphael became for him an overpowering experience. 'The brush marks the halting speech of ecstatic vision': Wackenroder made this confession the basis of a German Idealist interpretation of the

saying that art is the religion of free people. Picture galleries, he declared, should not be 'fairs' but 'temples where in silent humility one may admire the great artists as the highest of earthly beings'. 'Art must become a religious love or a beloved religion' removed from the 'vulgar flux of life'. N 207

The masterpiece was to be transferred from palaces, private houses, churches and chapels and received into the great museum where 'a higher devotion prevails than in church', as the Hamburg painter Runge believed. The generation that lived around 1800 was tortured by doubts concerning Christianity and the ordering of the world that had been valid till then. The love of art replaced religious experience, the museum became an 'aesthetic church', a 'sanctuary' in which sculptures and N 208
paintings are 'set up for the holy purposes of art'. N 209

Intellectual Europe saw in the Paris Muséum Central a fulfilment of its dreams. Art-lovers of all countries, for whom the city was now the capital of the world, were prepared to make sacrifices for the new museum. Protests were seldom made when

French troops carried off art treasures from present-day Belgium to Paris. Spokesmen of the Revolution used weighty words in ascribing fine motives to this appropriation, and even gained support outside France.

The new name Muséum National now gained currency for the Palais du Louvre. The pictures by living artists were described as 'ouvrages appartenants à la nation'. The qualifying word 'national' had become widely used during the age of Enlightenment and signified at that time anything that was of concern to all, irrespective of their rank or racial origin. In Paris after 1795 the concept acquired an overtone of striking modernity. In the

B 201

nineteenth and twentieth centuries 'National Museums' and 'National Galleries' spread all over the globe.

The interminable French wars of conquest were used with rather excessive energy for the enrichment of that colossus of a museum in the Louvre. Some of its aura of idealism was lost when the antique sculptures, including the *Apollo Belvedere* and the *Laocoön*, which had long been freely accessible to all in Rome, were carted off to Paris. The entry of the heavily laden wagons into the French capital was arranged very much in the manner of an ancient Roman triumphal procession. A standard which was carried along with them bore the lapidary words: 'Greece ceded them, Rome lost them, their destiny has changed twice, but it will not change again'.

216

B 24

In 1803 the Palais du Louvre was rebaptized and received the name 'Musée Napoléon'. Napoleon's enemies, who lacked all understanding of art, mocked at the Louvre as a warehouse for the plunder of a usurper who engaged in the robbing of works of art without any qualm of conscience. With bitter irony a Princess of Brunswick wrote in 1806 that the world would rejoice now that all art treasures had come into 'such supremely legitimate hands'.

217

B 69

217 After Napoleon had gained power, the Louvre was renamed the Musée Napoléon. As this drawing by Benjamin Zix shows, the Emperor and his court sometimes visited the museum at night, and viewed the works of art by torchlight. In the centre of the picture is the *Laocoön* from Rome; on the left the *Medici Venus* from Florence

A room in the Louvre housed a colossal bust of the Emperor, above which hung the *Triumph of the* 219 *Victor* by Rubens from the gallery in Cassel, as well as flags and weapons captured in battle. When Napoleon, after the victorious campaign against Austria in 1810, entered into a second marriage with Marie-Louise, the daughter of the Habsburg Emperor, he had the Salon Carré decorated as a chapel for the wedding. The procession passed through the Grande Galerie where eight thousand illustrious guests had to pay him reverence. The paintings on the walls included Raphael's *Madonna della Sedia* from Florence, Correggio's *Leda and the Swan* from 130 Potsdam, and countless masterpieces from Cassel and Brunswick, Munich and Vienna, Milan and Rome, Brussels and Antwerp.

Descent from the Cross
FRANCIA

LEONARDO DA VINCI
La Belle Ferronnière

RUBENS
Last Communion of St Francis

RUBENS
Martyrdom of St John

ANDREA DEL SARTO
Holy Family

221 The cultured litterateur and art critic Vivant Denon, who had been appointed by Napoleon to the post of director of the art collection in the Louvre, tried to the best of his ability to remove from the building its character of a booty warehouse. He sought to make people forget that the pictures on exhibition had once come from the palaces and mansions of the nobility and from churches and galleries in conquered

218 When Napoleon married the Habsburg princess Marie-Louise on 2 April 1810, the Louvre, crammed as it was with plundered works of art, provided the most obvious evidence of his success. This detail of a drawing by Zix shows the marriage procession through the Grande Galerie and a few of the paintings which had been requisitioned from abroad

PERUGINO
Virgin and Saints

PERUGINO
Madonna and Saints

SOLARIO
Charles d'Amboise

RAPHAEL
St Cecilia

RAPHAEL
Transfiguration

RAPHAEL
Coronation of the Virgin

countries. Denon planned a chronological arrangement of paintings as had already existed in various places, such as Vienna, since the Enlightenment. He gradually built up the Louvre museum on the principle of completeness and of an equal proportion of space to the various schools, even though the centre of gravity remained with the great masters and above all with the Italians of the sixteenth century. The Grande Galerie was now top-lit, the side windows were closed, and accordingly more works could be housed. More than a thousand pictures by artists who were particularly well represented in the Louvre were systematically chosen by lot and sent to the twenty-two newly-founded French provincial museums or were sent away for purposes of exchange. Since that time the museum in Lyons has contained the *Adoration of the Magi* by Rubens from the Munich Pinakothek, and the museum in Mainz (at that time the capital of a French departe-

ment) *Jesus in the Temple* by Jordaens, from the Church of Furnes near Antwerp.

The classical sculpture which, like the paintings, had been assembled from all the countries of the Continent, was solemnly set up on high, smooth pedestals on the ground floor of the Louvre. Whereas the revolutionaries of around 1795 had looked upon the statue of a hero as a 'lesson in courage' the art historians' calmer way of looking at these things now began to prevail. The statues from the Vatican, which lost their plaster fig-leaves in Paris, the *Venus de Medici* from Florence, the *Praying Boy* (*Antinous*) from Sanssouci and other famous works, benefited, wherever this was needed, from a conscientious restoration.

The example of the huge art museum in the Louvre was imitated in many European capitals. Previous plans aiming at a central museum in each region were now realized. The dissolution of monasteries and the various other secularizing processes of the time immediately before and after 1800 furthered the purpose of State interference. In some places an attempt was made to counteract the effects of taking works of art to Paris by the creation of local central galleries and national museums. Finally, after the breakdown of Napoleon's empire and the dissolution of the museum that had been named after him, an excellent opportunity presented itself for

219 One room in the Louvre became a hall of fame devoted to the Emperor himself. Rubens' *Triumph of the Victor*, taken from Cassel, hung above a colossal bust of Napoleon

220 After 1805 Napoleon ordered top-lighting for the Grande Galerie of the Louvre. This improvement had been proposed by the artist Hubert Robert, but the architects Percier and Fontaine were not able to accept his proposals in detail. This painting shows the Grande Galerie as it would have looked had all Robert's ideas been adopted

221 In about 1813 Zix made this idealized drawing of Vivant Denon, the Director of the Musée Napoléon, sitting in one of the rooms in the Louvre surrounded by the art treasures of three millennia and three continents. In the foreground is a bust of Napoleon on the left and a statue of his wife on the right

using the returning works of art as the nucleus of new national or territorial museums in the various capitals concerned.

In London the idea of a national gallery first began to be discussed in 1792. The artist Benjamin West promoted the idea after a visit to Paris, but it was put into execution only in the early nineteenth century. In 1795 a small central museum came into being in Brussels, made up of confiscated works which had not been requisitioned for Paris. Around 1800 the House of Wittelsbach grouped the paintings that it had inherited, in particular the collections of Düsseldorf, Mannheim and Zweibrücken, as a central royal gallery in Munich; shortly after 1800 Darmstadt and Karlsruhe obtained central museums for themselves. In the Netherlands, which had been conquered by French troops, a national art gallery was arranged in the Hague in 1804 and transferred to Amsterdam in 1808; this was the origin of the Rijksmuseum in 1815.

In 1805 the French Viceroy opened a great central gallery in the Brera Palace in Milan which quickly increased through the addition of ecclesiastical property, confiscated private art treasures and also some purchases. Less important galleries in Bologna, Venice, and other cities of northern Italy were dependent on the Brera. A three-scale system operated here; works of the first order such as Raphael's *St Cecilia* from Bologna were exhibited in Paris; second choices in Milan; the rest for the most part were shown in the place where they belonged, usually in what had once been a monastery building.

In Naples in 1806 Murat arranged an enormous museum in the Palazzo degli Studi which today *209* houses the Museo Nazionale d'Arte Antica. In Spain, Napoleon's brother had been preparing since 1809 a central gallery for paintings which were not to go to Paris; this was a step on the way to the Prado Museum, which was opened after 1815. At about the same time the imperial Habsburg collections in Vienna were completed. Salzburg thus lost the antique *Ephebe of Helenenberg* discovered in Dürer's day. *89*

The Munich Zentral-Galerie was meanwhile greatly enriched through the addition of ecclesias-

222 After Waterloo nearly all the works of art in the Musée Napoléon were returned to their original owners, but the idea of large public museums was becoming more generally accepted. Even the Pope did not return the altarpieces to the churches from which they had been taken. Instead he included them in the Pinacoteca Vaticana on the third floor of the Cortile di Damasco. In this engraving the third painting from the right is Raphael's *Transfiguration* (see Ill. 218)

222

tical property, and as the result of the temporary incorporation of the Tyrol with Bavaria, received in 1812, from the old 'Kunstkammer' in Ambras, Boccaccino's *Christ*, and from a monastery south of the Brenner, Pacher's *Fathers of the Church* (both now in the Alte Pinakothek).

After the battle of Waterloo the Musée Napoléon was broken up. The Pope then decreed that the altarpieces from the churches in his state which had now been returned, should remain in the Pinacoteca Vaticana in Rome. Raphael's *Madonna of Foligno* was one of the pictures that returned, and the measure was justified as being of great utility to both artists and foreigners. Similar steps brought a considerable gain to the galleries of Florence, Parma, Venice, Antwerp and many other places.

Quite apart from the events mentioned so far, the French Revolution and the campaigns of Napoleon had sent all kinds of works of art on their travels. The greatest losses were those of Italy and Spain, but the private possessions of France suffered added depletion, since noble families with foresight had sent easily transportable works of art out of the country.

During the Napoleonic era England trebled its possessions in works of art. From 1793 onwards refugee collections of the French nobility, as well as some fresh war booty taken by French officers who wished to dispose of it, were sold in London; to these were added works which the art trade brought to England from the countries of the Continent that were shaken by economic crises. After the naval victory of Aboukir outstanding Greek and Egyptian sculptures were sent from their countries of origin to the British Isles.

B 35

Correggio's *Danaë*, already noted in Prague and Stockholm, was taken from the Orleans family to Hope House in London for 650 guineas (now in the Borghese Gallery in Rome). From Spain came Raphael's *Alba Madonna* (now in the National Gallery, Washington) and his *Madonna della Tenda* (now in the Munich Pinakothek), followed by Correggio's *Mercury instructing Cupid before Venus*, once the pearl of the collection of Charles I, and his *Madonna of the Basket* (both now in the National Gallery, London).

224

XIII

223, 224 As a consequence of the Napoleonic Wars, many works of art changed owners—quite apart from the official confiscations. For instance, two paintings that had once belonged to Charles I of England, Titian's *Jacopo Pesaro and Pope Alexander VI before St Peter* (above) and Correggio's *Mercury instructing Cupid before Venus* (right) were removed from Spain to Antwerp and London respectively

Major works that had been the property of the Borghese, Colonna, Corsini and Aldobrandini families came to England. Outstanding paintings by Italian masters of the sixteenth century were gathered together by such art-lovers as Viscount Fitzwilliam (in 1816 his works formed the nucleus of the Fitzwilliam Museum in Cambridge), the Duke of Bridgewater, Lord Carlisle, Angerstein and Sir George Beaumont.

N 211

Claude became the favourite of English art-lovers. His pictures were imported into England from Paris and Italy, and fetched prices never reached before or since. *The Marriage of Isaac and Rebekah* and *The Embarkation of the Queen of Sheba* changed hands in 1810 for £8,000 (both pictures now in the National Gallery, London). Another pair of landscapes actually fetched 12,000 guineas. In 1808 William Beckford spoke of the 'British rage for this kind of art'.

N 212
N 213

225 About 1800 the section of the British Museum devoted to ancient art was extended as a result of donations and purchases, mainly of Graeco-Roman sculpture. This engraving, made in 1812, shows part of a no longer existing Gallery of Antiquities

Meanwhile incredibly valuable stocks of Italian drawings were piling up in the hands of British collectors, among others Sir Thomas Lawrence.

The neo-Classical taste in art set a very high value on both Greek sculptures of the fifth and fourth centuries BC and ancient Egyptian works which gave, as G.F.Waagen said, 'the impression of exalted earnestness and religious solemnity' and were regarded as a kind of enhancement of the formal austerity of classical Greek art.

After the victory of Aboukir, Englishmen in the eastern Mediterranean were able to serve the interests of collectors and made purchases from which the British Museum sooner or later benefited. United States interests followed similar lines. More fruitful than any other activities were those of Lord Elgin, British Ambassador to Turkey. He used his influence and his private means with great energy and removed from the Acropolis in Athens the sculptures of Phidias which were subject to severe damage from the weather. Known as the 'Elgin Marbles', they reached London and from 1808 onwards were made accessible to the public. At first opinions differed. People had grown used to the elegant smoothness of the classicism of the age of Emperor Augustus. The painter Fuseli saw 'a god' in the *Apollo Belvedere* but 'only a man' in the recumbent so-called Dionysus of the Elgin Marbles.

B 28.

N 12
13

Among those who were immediately moved to great enthusiasm was Ludwig I of Bavaria, who visited London in 1814. Goethe saw the Elgin Marbles in plaster casts and exclaimed, 'Here alone the Law and the Gospels are together. One could well forget everything else'. At length, by an Act of Parliament, Lord Elgin received £35,000 for the sculptures (representing about half of the expenses he had incurred), and the institution which Sloane had called into life now became 'at one stroke the most distinguished museum of antiquities in the world, with a secure prospect of always remaining such'.

N 21

XVII The Gothic Revival, which began in England in the late eighteenth century and which was one of the main influences on the Romantic movement on the Continent, ensured that English collectors were among the first to discover painters who lived before Raphael. John Strange bought Cima da Conegliano's *St Jerome in a Landscape* in Venice probably as early as 1770; at the beginning of the nineteenth century this painting formed part of William Beckford's collection in the neo-Gothic Fonthill Abbey

When the French army surrendered in Alexandria in 1801 the booty taken by the English contained ancient statues and included some Greek items—for instance, a statue of the Emperor Marcus Aurelius—but especially Egyptian antiquities, among them the Rosetta Stone. Shortly after this, the English Consul-General Henry Salt sent from Alexandria the colossal head of Rameses II, the sight of which moved Shelley to write a famous sonnet. In the first years of the nineteenth century Charles Townley completed his valuable collection of antique sculpture which for the most part consisted only of Roman copies. It came to the British Museum, to which the Townley Gallery was added in 1808. At this time Lord Aberdeen acquired from Greece, which was still a Turkish possession, a fine head of the youthful Hercules; shortly afterwards Viscount Strangford secured the Apollo which has been named after him (both works now in the British Museum). In 1825 the frieze of the temple of Apollo in Phigalia-Bassae was acquired for the British Museum.

If England was able to vastly increase its possessions of works of art in the early nineteenth century, the other former enemies of Napoleon, above all Russia, did not go away empty-handed. In 1814 Tsar Alexander I acquired for 940,000 francs 48 particularly fine pictures which Napoleon's divorced wife Josephine had been able to gather together in her residence at Malmaison from French booty. Ludwig I of Bavaria also had his pick here. In Malmaison there were many pearls of the Cassel Gallery, among them works by Andrea del Sarto and Claude, which for a hundred and fifty years have been among the most admired of paintings in the Hermitage. Tsar Alexander I also bought Murillo's *Isaac* from the private collection of Denon.

In France a number of private collections outlasted the critical year 1815. The original of Holbein's *Burgomaster Meyer's Madonna* of which only a copy was known in Dresden—a copy that continued to be regarded as genuine—appeared again in Paris (now the property of the Prince of Hesse-Darmstadt). General Soult kept for a considerable time the collection of outstanding Spanish masters which he had

assembled in the Iberian Peninsula. Before 1800 a number of wealthy German art-lovers had been able to rescue very valuable paintings from revolutionary France—for instance, the Stuttgart collector Abel, from whom Goethe purchased a small landscape by Claude, a painter he valued quite as highly as did his English contemporaries (now in the Goethehaus at Weimar).

In the Napoleonic era and immediately afterwards an important phase of development took place in the museums of Munich and Berlin which should be examined in some detail. Canova's *Hebe* in Venice

226 In the early nineteenth century Egypt was a source of contention between France and England. At this time, too, collectors began to take an interest in ancient Egyptian art, and its solemn strength was regarded as an intensification of certain characteristics of Graeco-Roman art. This colossal head of Rameses II, which was brought to the British Museum in 1817, inspired Shelley's famous sonnet, *Ozymandias*

227 In about 1800 Charles Townley granted art-lovers free access to the collection of antiquities in his London house, one room of which was already top-lit, as shown in this painting by Zoffany. Townley's whole collection was later incorporated into the British Museum

became for Ludwig I of Bavaria, when he was eighteen years old, a decisive experience. Ludwig soon found his way from the neo-Classical sculpture of the time to the classic art of antiquity and conceived the idea of erecting a large museum of sculpture in Munich. A representative new edifice was to embellish that city, which was now the residence of a royal House and the centre of a greatly increased territory. The young Wittelsbach had been moulded by the idealism of his time and at an early age felt himself to be an educator in matters of art.

Immediately after the fall of Napoleon, Ludwig I laid the foundation stone of the 'Glyptothek', a Greek term that had been coined at the Crown Prince's wish by the court librarian and was intended to be analogous to the name 'Pinakothek'. Klenze, who was summoned to the task in 1815, was to erect a museum building in the form of a temple 'in Greek style'. As the former court architect of King Jérôme in Cassel, Klenze had an excellent knowledge of Parisian 'revolutionary architecture'. From this he took over the idea of limiting the façade of the

Glyptothek to a single storey and making it windowless, while in the interior he adopted stern semicircular forms. The buildings of Rome, from the halls of the Thermae of imperial times down to the Vatican's Museo Pio-Clementino of the late eighteenth century, also provided him with inspiration.

N 217 The Crown Prince and his architect endeavoured to avoid didactic features. There was to be no 'cynical simplicity' but a certain splendour 'which could communicate to the observer the concept of reverence' that 'should be paid to the masterpieces of antiquity'. Ludwig I opened the Glyptothek to the people, as he himself put it, without asking any admission fee. Nevertheless museum warders in their splendid liveries underlined the fact that the visitor was the guest of a prince. There were no seats for the visitors nor was there any description of the works on exhibition, though the iron guard-rails which had been customary in the galleries of the era of the Enlightenment and which were intended to make it more difficult for the curious to touch the works, were absent.

228 After 1800 museums were built throughout Europe in the dignified style of classical temples: the British Museum in London, the Fitzwilliam Museum in Cambridge, the Braccio Nuovo del Vaticano in Rome, the Altes Museum in Berlin, and the Glyptothek (below) in Munich

In the evenings the Glyptothek was occasionally opened for the privileged guests of the monarch. In such cases a back entrance was used which led to a banqueting hall in which there were no works of art; here drinks and refreshments were offered. After this there would be a tour by the light of wax torches round the rooms containing the statues. Thus Ludwig I brought to Munich certain customs which had been fashionable in Rome about 1800 and which had attained a new popularity in the residence of the Habsburgs during the Congress of Vienna. N 218

The first purchases for the planned museum of sculpture were arranged for by Ludwig I as far back as 1810. He clearly had the intention of competing with the Musée Napoléon at the time when it was at the height of its splendour. In Italy the pediment sculptures of the early classical temple of Aegina, which had been found in 1811, were purchased. The *Rondanini Medusa* was also acquired and in 1813, 42 at a price of 70,000 guilders, the *Barberini Faun*. Nine mules took fifty days to carry this heavy burden from Rome to Munich. A year later Ludwig I saw the Elgin Marbles in London, and toyed with the idea of acquiring them.

Shortly afterwards the dissolution of the Musée Napoléon provided some useful opportunities. Many noble Roman families could not afford the cost of transportation of the statues which had been taken from them, and were ready to sell. Important works

from the Albani collection came to Munich in this way.

In Vienna Ludwig I discovered in the home of a private enthusiast one of the principal items in the collection of Rudolph II, namely the *Ilioneus Son of* 123 *Niobe* which had thoughtlessly been given away by the Habsburgs. The price paid, which was 33,000 guilders, caused the young Wittelsbach to be discussed all over the imperial city. Ludwig I was also much impressed, as were art-lovers in England, by the severe forms of Egyptian art. In 1823 he acquired the sitting figure of Bek-en-Chon. According to the guide printed in 1830, works of art 'which can lead art back on the only right path, that of antiquity', were to be represented in a 'Room of Modern Artists' in the Glyptothek. In the interior and exterior of the

229 During the early nineteenth century many pieces of original Greek sculpture were acquired by museums throughout Europe, with the result that Roman copies, so much admired until then, were less sought after. By 1808 the *Elgin Marbles* were known in London, and a few years later Ludwig I of Bavaria acquired the sculpture from the Temple of Aegina for the Glyptothek in Munich—among them this head of a warrior

building the art-lover found himself reminded by portrait medallions or similar means of Niccolò Pisano, Ghiberti, Peter Vischer, Michelangelo and also of such contemporaries as Canova, Thorvaldsen, Rauch and Schwanthaler. Nevertheless only few contemporary works reached the Glyptothek, among them Canova's *Paris*, completed in 1812. Canova's statues had already been set up about 1800 in the Vatican and in the Museo Nazionale, Naples, close to works of antiquity.

While Ludwig I was creating his museum of sculpture he conceived the idea of extending the inherited treasure of paintings into the 'most glorious collection of pictures on earth'. At the begin- N 219 ning his purchases were entirely in line with the neo-Classical trend of taste. In 1808 the Crown Prince acquired for a very high price a self-portrait by Raphael from the Palazzo Altoviti in Florence, a painting which has recently been regarded as the portrait of young Bindo Altoviti by an unknown pupil of Raphael (now in the National Gallery, Washington). 230 Ludwig also bought in London Raphael's *Madonna della Tenda*, which until 1800 had remained in the Escorial. He liked to lay the foundation-stones of buildings for art on Raphael's birthday.

After the final defeat of Napoleon some items of booty which had been seized by French officers during the Spanish War went directly to Munich; Titian's *Seated Madonna* from the Escorial was handed over by General Sebastiani for 40,000 francs. The altarpiece of *St Thomas of Villanueva* which cost 20,000 francs was the sixth picture by Murillo to come into the possession of the Wittelsbachs.

The upheavals which had taken place around 1800 started new impulses in Berlin as in Munich. Even before 1806 King Frederick William III of Prussia had resolved to open his own collection of works of art to the public without charging for admission. In the 'Riga Memorandum' of the Prussian minister von Altenstein, the relationship between art and the State was newly interpreted in 1807 in the spirit of the then prevailing idealism. 'The fine arts are the expression of the highest condition of mankind': the State has the duty to give all men access to them. After the victory of Waterloo a new museum of considerable dimensions was also begun in Berlin. Wall-paintings to the right and left of the main entrance gave visible expressions to the theme of 'the development of world forces from chaos to light' and 'the formation of human culture and manners'.

Following the example of the Louvre, the building housed in the first main storey antique sculpture, and in the second one paintings. A huge circular room which followed the pattern of the Roman Pantheon and the Sala Rotonda of the Vatican Mus-

230 When they bought paintings, connoisseurs of antique sculpture preferred the work of Italian artists of the time of Raphael. In 1808 Ludwig I of Bavaria paid handsomely for this painting considered at that time to be a self-portrait of Raphael as a young man, and now identified as a portrait of Bindo Altiviti

231 In the early nineteenth century an artists' colony consisting mainly of English, German and Scandinavian painters, was formed in Rome. These painters worked in the early sixteenth-century Italian style. An early Raphael Madonna influenced this painting by Heinrich Hess of a young Italian girl

eum was intended for the most important antique statues. This 'sanctuary in which the most precious things were guarded' was to 'uplift' the visitors and to put them in 'a mood suitable to the enjoyment of what is housed in this building'. Karl Friedrich Schinkel was chosen to design the 'Royal Museum' in Berlin known today as the 'Old Museum'. He had travelled for a number of years in Italy, but for the façade of the museum he followed an 1803 design by the Frenchman Durand, and also the Paris Stock Exchange, which had been erected under Napoleon. When this new creation was complete, roughly at the same time as the Glyptothek, its solemn character made a great impression on the artistic world of northern Germany. Art-lovers spoke of a 'new National Museum', recalling the name given to the Louvre about 1795.

In Berlin, as in Munich, the ideas of the Enlightenment were attacked. A memorandum, drawn up by

the architect Schinkel and the art historian and curator Waagen, stated that a museum must first of all delight and then instruct. The King, himself admittedly a somewhat less colourful figure than Ludwig of Bavaria, announced that the new Institute was to bring about the 'honouring of the arts'. In 1800 Wackenroder had opposed the keeping of antique works of art 'in the everyday flux of life' and now, in Berlin, Rumohr demanded for the future an art expressly created for museums. Only such an art would provide 'tasks which, being less circumscribed than those imposed by the church or the home, could draw men towards the highest flights of the spirit' and could 'extend dimensions beyond the ordinary limits'.

N 220

In setting up the statues and presenting the paintings it was hoped to create a mood of sacred solemnity. In the great round hall, or 'rotunda', the antique statues, following the ideas of the Musée Napoléon,

232 Edward Solly, an Englishman living in Italy, built up an important collection of paintings, dating mainly from about 1500. This collection, which was bought by the King of Prussia in 1815, determined the character of the painting section of the Berlin Museums for some time and led to purchases of other paintings of the same period, such as Piero di Cosimo's *Venus and Mars*

were placed on very high pedestals; people were to look up to them. In 1826 Schinkel discovered in the picture galleries of the Palazzo Pitti the strong red ground of seventeenth-century silken wall coverings; he finally rejected the conventional 'grey half-tones which do injury to the depth of the paintings'. The picture galleries of the Berlin Museum were given a dark red wallpaper with a greyish-blue shaded pattern. There was a 'red Porphyry room' and a 'green Porphyry room', a 'red Aleppo room with light red pillars', and so on.

Red wallpapers also became popular with English art-lovers around 1830; Robert Peel had one in the N 221 picture gallery of his London house. Uniform frames, such as the late eighteenth century preferred, were not systematically introduced in Berlin. Important pictures were given particularly luxurious frames, though Schinkel had no objection to using fine old frames in special cases.

Whereas Alois Hirt, the man of the Enlightenment, insisted on the completeness of the different schools and epochs, this being necessary for educational purposes, Schinkel and Waagen championed N 222 the cause of classical art. From 1821 to 1829 three pictures by Raphael were acquired. The Prussian Crown Prince planned an entire Raphael room in

the museum; over his desk there hung a small copy of the *Sistine Madonna*. In 1832 Titian's *Lavinia* reached Berlin; this was followed by a large altarpiece by Andrea del Sarto and *St Anthony* by Murillo.

The Prado Museum in Madrid was at first, like the British Museum in London and the Friderizianum in Cassel, dedicated to collections of all kinds, and particularly to those concerned with natural history. N 223 In the complex of the Vatican building in Rome the Braccio Nuovo or new wing of the Museum of 234 Antiquities began to be built from 1817, according to earlier plans. Klenze had already been able to take its internal design as a model for the Munich Glyptothek. The sharply cut niches, the semi-circular colonnade and the barrel-vaulting with top-lighting make this edifice, which is rarely noticed and which has hardly changed at all since it was first built, one of the characteristic examples of the middle and severe phase of neo-Classicism, often called 'Empire'. The Raphael paintings that returned at this time from Paris were hung in a loggia of the Vatican's Damascus Court in a strict formal arrangement on 222 an exact horizontal central axis.

In London museums were built which up to our own day have been treated as models throughout the English-speaking world. In 1823 the new building of the British Museum was begun. Its main front and the great ground floor rooms for Egyptian art with their coffered ceilings preserve the spirit of the time of its origin in a very pure form. Then in the 1830's the main portion of the National Gallery was erected.

In St Petersburg, Klenze, the architect of the Munich Pinakothek, built a superb home for the artistic treasures of the Tsar's family in the neo-Classical style, later known as the New Hermitage, which

233, 234 The German architect Leo von Klenze designed both the Glyptothek and the Pinakothek in Munich for Ludwig I. The fame of these buildings reached the Tsar, and he commissioned Klenze to design the Hermitage in St Petersburg. On the ground floor Klenze proposed a series of rooms for the Tsar's collection of antique sculpture (above). The system of arrangement was to be similar to that adopted in the recently completed Braccio Nuovo del Vaticano (below)

still serves its original purpose. The affection of collectors for classical art was evident in nearly all the larger cities of Europe. Antique works of art also came now to Vienna, Copenhagen, Stockholm and St Petersburg. The strong preference for Egyptian art found expression in many places. In Florence and Turin relatively small Egyptian collections were created after 1820, while the Museo Gregoriano Egizio was opened in the Vatican. In America too an interest for Egyptian art was aroused around 1825.

235

N 224

In the epoch of neo-Classicism Raphael and the artists influenced by him were everywhere accounted the greatest painters of the past. This trend was to end in the 'New Renaissance'. In Rome about 1830 the Borghese family acquired for their collection new major pieces including for instance a Madonna by Bellini and Correggio's *Danaë* (now in the Galleria Borghese). The Tsar's family at this time paid £4,000 for Raphael's *Alba Madonna* (now in the National Gallery, Washington) and 29,600 guilders for the *Pietà* by Sebastiano del Piombo (still in the Hermitage).

In the Napoleonic era there appeared next to the main neo-Classical trend a secondary one, namely the romantic love of the art before Holbein and Raphael. In the eighteenth century this was already evident in the case of Strawberry Hill, and certain isolated collectors of early Italian and early German art. What happened around 1800 was to be judged some decades later in terms ironically exaggerated yet not wholly inapposite: 'When one had become weary in the arms of the antique Venus one turned to the muse of the Middle Ages, whom Winckelmann had so cruelly mocked, for help and forgiveness'.

N 225

In Paris the hatred of 'feudalistic' art, which was born at the time of the Revolution, soon gave place to the idea so popular during the Enlightenment of the safeguarding, collecting and display of works of art. While classical art reigned in the Louvre, a romantic historical museum was being founded on

235, 236 One of the first collections devoted solely to Egyptian art was founded in the Vatican in 1835 and it has largely retained its original character. The rooms containing the exhibits were decorated in the Egyptian style, and some of the walls were painted with landscapes of Egyptian temples and palm trees (above). The reclining lions (left), which until then had been out of doors in the Piazza Bernardo, were now brought into the new museum; they can be seen in the background of the print above the opposite side of the Seine in the former Monastère des Petits Augustins. Despite its short life it exercised a strong influence.

Soon after 1789 one could already hear thoughtful Jacobins saying: 'What superb museums could be established with the plunder from our suppressed churches and monasteries.' Of course, much was destroyed, above all bronzes and ecclesiastical objects of precious metals. Nevertheless a chalice *239* donated by Abbot Suger, which was among the treasures of the abbey church of Saint-Denis, was

237, 238, 239 By 1800 there were many less well-known art-lovers who collected antiquities of all kinds as well as medieval objets d'art. The vase (below), which contains elements of both Egyptian and Greek styles, was probably made about 1780 to fill the great demand. Strawberry Hill in England (right above) used to contain one of the most famous collections of objets d'art of all periods, but unfortunately this collection has long since been broken up. In the course of the French Revolution nearly all churches were stripped, and their treasures either entered state museums or passed into private hands, the latter being the fate of this gold chalice (right below) from the Abbey of St Denis near Paris, which was stolen from the Bibliothèque National in 1804, and appeared in an English collection in 1920. It is now in the National Gallery, Washington

to arrange the various works of art which were accumulating in his possession in a museum-like fashion, and as early as August 1793 people were allowed to view them.

The keynote of this new quasi-museum was primarily the desire for historical completeness of the kind that the spirit of the Enlightenment demanded. Nevertheless French patriotic pride had a great deal to do with the matter. In order to make clear the purpose of his 'Musée des Monuments Français' Lenoir commissioned amongst other things busts of 'Français célèbres', such as Rousseau. He managed to get hold of the mortal remains of Descartes, La Fontaine, Molière and Boileau and also the bones of General Turenne. Lenoir's preference in matters of art centred on the sixteenth century; he glorified Jean Goujon, who was well represented in his museum as 'the French Phidias', and acquired the *Diana d'Anet* (dated 1550) and *240* also, in 1794, the two famous *Slave* statues of Michelangelo which had been seized from the *241* Richelieu family (now in the Louvre).

240 One of the most popular sixteenth-century pieces of sculpture in Lenoir's Musée des Monuments Français, which survived only until 1815, was the *Diana* from the Château d'Anet

241 Percier made this engraving of Michelangelo's *Slaves* which, originally carved for the tomb of Julius II, were transferred from the Duc de Richelieu's palace to the Musée des Monuments Français

handed over to the Cabinet des Médailles of the Bibliothèque Nationale (now in the National Gallery, Washington). In the case of objects of stone and similar substances, which could not be converted into money, the general principle adopted was that of preservation.

Immediately after the outbreak of the Revolution, Alexandre Lenoir, only twenty-seven years old at the time, was in charge of a kind of collecting and disposal office, predominantly for sculpture, in the former Monastère des Petits Augustins (where the Ecole des Beaux-Arts stands today). Here he saved many bronzes and prevented them from being taken to be melted down by applying a grey varnish to make them look like stone. Soon he was inspired

242, 243   In about 1800 Hubert Robert painted pictures of both the garden (above) of the Musée des Monuments Français and some of its rooms (below). The *Diana d'Anet* (see Ill. 240) can be seen in the garden background

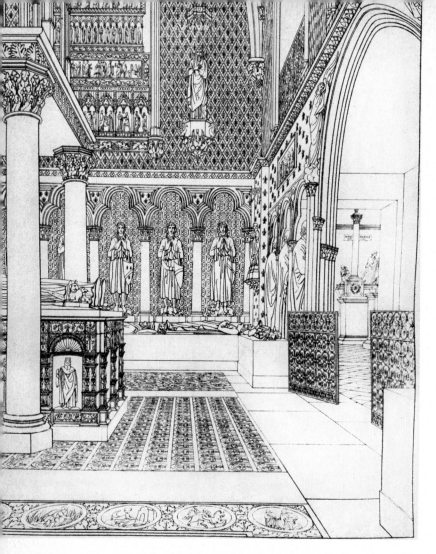

244 In the Musée des Monuments Français the initial emphasis was on sculpture of the sixteenth and seventeenth centuries, but between 1800 and 1815 medieval art became increasingly prominent. The fourteenth-century room was decorated with architectural fragments from the Sainte-Chapelle and the Abbey of St Denis

The main attraction for the public as a whole was the garden of the former Augustinian monastery which was now arranged in the manner of an English landscape park. In this 'Campo Santo 242 romantique', which Hubert Robert often painted, B 229 visitors liked to rest for a while 'in gentle melancholy', to quote Lenoir's words; before the mausoleums (the more or less artificial graves of great Frenchmen) shades seemed to wander in this place, to which Lenoir therefore gave the name 'Elysée'.

In the course of the years the number of medieval sculptures, stained-glass windows and architectural fragments grew ever greater. Both Lenoir himself and the visitors laid more and more stress on the period before 1500. From the church in Nogent-sur-Seine came parts of the grave of Abelard and

238

Héloise. Lenoir completed the recumbent figures of the popular twelfth-century Paris lovers and housed them in a small neo-Gothic building of the Elysée, before which sensitive souls could shed tears. Lenoir also had a bust of Joan of Arc made by the sculptor Beauvallet from an allegedly authentic old painting. Two draped twelfth-century Romanesque statues from the main porch of the Cathedral of Corbeil were made more acceptable to visitors by christening them King Clovis and Queen Clothilde and pre- 245 senting them as 'French sculpture of the sixth century' (now in the Louvre).

When Napoleon became Emperor, Lenoir's creation was given the title Musée Impérial des Monuments Français. The catalogue of the museum N 226 went through four editions during the period of the Republic; up to the end of the Empire there were eight more. Lenoir now called his museum 'une véritable histoire monumentale de la Monarchie Française' and dedicated his catalogues 'au Souverain illustre qui gouverne la France'. After Christian

245 Two Romanesque statues from the portal of the church at Corbeil held a place of honour in the Musée des Monuments Français. They were erroneously thought to have been carved in about 500

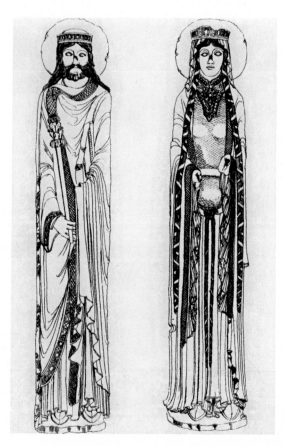

services had been reintroduced in France, Lenoir underlined more emphatically than ever the Christian character of the chronologically arranged rooms of his museum, and confessed that the fourteenth-century room had been built 'with the remains of the Sainte-Chapelle'. In this and the neighbouring rooms stained-glass windows, amongst others mid-thirteenth-century windows taken from the refectory of the Church of St-Germain-des-Prés (now in The Cloisters in New York) spread a dim light. 'The mysterious light reaches the soul and encourages meditation', said one of the official publications when speaking of this section of the museum. Lenoir had a great love for the developed Gothic style which he was also in the habit of referring to as 'Arabic' or 'Saracen'. In 1810 he eulogized Chartres Cathedral as 'the most imposing of Saracen monuments'.

Lenoir's museum rooms were highly regarded by foreign experts. Waagen, later to become the curator of the Berlin Museum and one of the best

246   This statue of an Old Testament king was taken by Jacobins from one of the doorways of the Abbey of St Denis in about 1790. It was later placed in the Musée des Monuments Français

247   This stained-glass window was transferred from the monastery of St Germain-des-Prés to the Musée des Monuments Français

instructed men of his time in matters of art and art collecting, praised the Musée des Monuments Français which, he declared, was 'as picturesque and tasteful as it was instructive'. Yet it was not to last. The shock of the Revolution and the results it produced in the course of its history had already provoked a powerful reaction in 1800. While in Germany, in the first decade of the nineteenth century, no qualms were felt about removing works of art from churches and keeping them together in storerooms in the capitals, the French poet Chateaubriand, in his outspoken confession *Le Génie du Christianisme*, restored the idea of the Cathedral. This development was disastrous for the museum which Lenoir had created in the former Augustinian monastery.

As early as 1796, when the free expression of opinion was no longer punished by the guillotine, architects and artists had presented a petition to the Directory opposing the removal of works of art from the places proper to them. This displacement caused 'préjudice à la science', according to the cautious wording. Of course the petition was primarily directed against the extension of the Louvre and, though in this respect it was totally ineffective, Lenoir felt that such ideas could be dangerous for his own creation. Together with the painters Gérard, Regnault and Isabey he drew up a counter-petition in which he asked for the further transference of works of art.

After 1800, Lenoir's opponents became more powerful. Their spokesman was the philosopher of art, Quatremère de Quincy, who now held a high government post. Quatremère's sympathies were with neo-Classicism and in his repeated attacks on the museum created by Lenoir his dislike of Gothic art may have played a part, although he remained objective in his arguments. Medieval sculptures in a museum, he declared, 'had no relation to the ideas that brought them into being'. In particular, sepulchres were not proper museum pieces but 'the visible form of faith'. When they were transferred to a museum 'the lack of taste' became 'impiety'. Obviously Quatremère represented views which enjoyed considerable support. Already the prefect of the département of Seine-Inférieure dared to refuse to have the sepulchre of Henri de Guise removed from the church in Eu to the museum. In 1806 Lenoir was able to obtain neither the sepulchre of Agnes Sorel from the church in Loches nor the Gothic altars from the Carmelite church in Metz. The return of the Bourbons spelt the end of the Musée des Monuments Français. Lenoir vainly suggested that the monarch should set up a Christian chapel in his museum where a mass for the dead whose mausoleums were there could be said daily.

248 In the Prince of Anhalt-Dessau's 'gotisches Haus', which had been modelled on Strawberry Hill, visitors around 1800 were able to study this *Portrait of a Lady* by Rogier van der Weyden

The return of all items to their churches and families was decreed and the decree was duly carried out.

Consideration of the Musée des Monuments Français, which had a considerable influence in its time, involves the attitude of art-lovers in the early nineteenth century towards early Netherlandish, early German and early Italian painting. The director of the Musée Napoléon, Denon, anxious as he was for complete representation of the various schools, placed great value on the period prior to 1500; he sometimes received advice from Lenoir. The *Ghent Altarpiece* by Jan van Eyck and the *Danzig Altar* by Memling had been on view in the Louvre since 1814. In Autun, van Eyck's *Madonna of the Chancellor Rolin* came into Lenoir's hands and thence into the

Louvre. From Vienna Altdorfer's *Nativity* was chosen, while from the Palace of Schleissheim near Munich the choice fell on the same artist's *The Battle of Alexander on the Issus River*. Works such as these were sometimes considered by French officers to be worth taking along as their personal war booty: for instance, van Eyck's Arnolfini wedding portrait, then in the Escorial near Madrid and the panel of *St Jerome in his Study* by Cranach, then in the Brunswick Gallery (now in the Ringling Museum at Sarasota, Florida).

95

Strangely enough, three Germans received impressions in Paris in 1803 which were to lead to the creation of an outstanding collection of old German masters. Immediately after the appearance of Chateaubriand's *Génie du Christianisme* and the revival of Christian services, there occurred that noteworthy encounter between the writer Friedrich Schlegel and the two young students Sulpiz and Melchior Boisserée from Cologne. We know that Altdorfer's *The Battle of Alexander on the Issus River* was, in Schlegel's words, regarded by the three friends as 'the highest adventure of ancient knighthood' and also that the Cathedral of Notre Dame made a profound impression on them. They must also have visited the Petits Augustins museum. After spending some months in Paris in 1803 and 1804 Schlegel finally went over to the Catholic Church to which the Boisserée brothers already belonged; from then on he was eloquent in his praise of the early German and particularly the Cologne painters of the fifteenth century, and set a higher value on Stefan Lochner's *Dombild* in Cologne Cathedral than on Raphael's *Sistine Madonna*, since 'the humble inclination of the gentle, radiant head is more faithful to the old idea'.

Around 1800, old Cologne, rich in churches, contrasted sharply with such princely seats as Munich, Berlin and Mannheim. In 1779 it had N 228 already been spoken of as a 'primeval magical city' and in 1811 the Romantic painter Zeller said that 'Cologne is Bethlehem; there is no other name and no other salvation to be found'. Even before 1800 N 229 in Cologne the remarkable collector Hüpsch had acquired a major work by Lochner, and his example had been followed by many collectors of early German art, among them Lyversberg and Wallraf. Soon, thanks to their systematic energy and their means, the Boisserée brothers were taking the lead. Schlegel's wealthy and shrewd young friends could acquire only five pictures directly from churches. They were already compelled to make use of the services of dealers like Nieuwenhuis in Brussels or to buy from other collectors. The little domestic altarpiece by Bouts known as the *Pearl of Brabant* cost 200 louis d'or in Brussels, Dürer's *Entombment* 1,500 guilders in Nuremberg. The collection rapidly

249 This portrait of Hans Schellenberger by Hans Burgkmair was bought by a Russian nobleman from an Augsburg collector. The painting has since returned to Germany

grew to two hundred items but included some forgeries attributed to Dürer and Cranach which 250 had been made between 1780 and 1810 on the upper Rhine and in Nuremberg.

When Schlegel had concluded his lectures in Cologne (then politically part of France) and moved to Heidelberg, the Boisserée brothers followed him. In 1810 their pictures were transported up the Rhine to the old town on the Neckar. When, after the victories of Jena and Wagram, it seemed that Napoleon would be able to realize his idea of a world empire, German youth gathered in Heidelberg, a fortress of patriotic Romanticism. Here the Boisserée collection became what Poensgen calls a 'Kultstätte' or place of worship. The two owners B 220

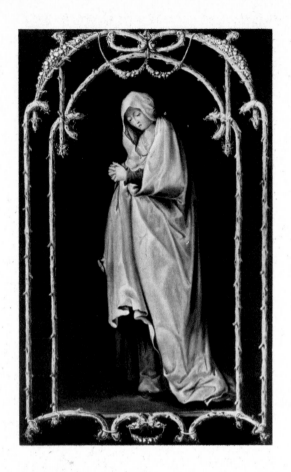

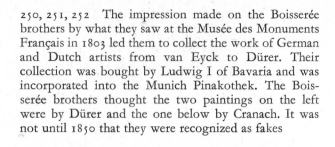

250, 251, 252 The impression made on the Boisserée brothers by what they saw at the Musée des Monuments Français in 1803 led them to collect the work of German and Dutch artists from van Eyck to Dürer. Their collection was bought by Ludwig I of Bavaria and was incorporated into the Munich Pinakothek. The Boisserée brothers thought the two paintings on the left were by Dürer and the one below by Cranach. It was not until 1850 that they were recognized as fakes

XIX The effect of the Gothic Revival and the consequent re-evaluation of artists working before the time of Raphael can be seen in the collections of medieval art in museums like the Germanisches Museum in Nuremberg, the Cluny Museum in Paris, and the Victoria and Albert Museum in London. One of the Victoria and Albert's most highly valued possessions is the *Syon Cope*, which once belonged to the nunnery of Syon in Middlesex

did not speak of a gallery or a 'Kabinett', but called the whole a 'Sanctum Corpus'. It was housed in a number of rooms of the Palace of Sickingen and shown to friends. In their comments the Boisserée brothers duly stressed the Christian character of the pictures.

In their presentation the brothers aimed at a maximum of effect, often changing the arrangement of the pictures. The most important items were side-lit after protective curtains had been solemnly removed. Important visitors such as Goethe were shown this or that panel by lamplight in the evening. In 1814 the superb *Adoration of the Magi* by Rogier van der Weyden (now in the Munich Pinakothek) is supposed to have caused the famous guest from Weimar to wonder 'whether Christianity won't yet N 230 get me into its power'. The poet Max von Schenkendorff expressed the wish that the Boisserée collection should travel around and that its effect might be such as to remove every heathen picture from every German wall.

In 1819 the Boisserée brothers moved with their collection to Stuttgart. The mood was no longer over-heated as in the Heidelberg days. Goethe, returned to Weimar and classical influences, declared that the paintings of a Lochner deserved 'great attention' but should not be raised 'to an exaggerated level or made unduly sweet by hymns'. The exhibition in the Stuttgart officers' pavilion was quieter than in Heidelberg, and the 'Sanctum Corpus' later went to Ludwig I of Bavaria for 240,000 guilders, finding its final home in the Munich Pinakothek, where the Boisserée paintings gained world fame.

Prince Ludwig von Oettingen-Wallerstein had been collecting in southern Germany since 1811 and was able to amass a total of 226 paintings, some of which passed to Ludwig I. From 1817 onwards the Catholic priest Johann Hirscher and the teacher of German philology, Baron von Lassberg were buying paintings of the fifteenth and sixteenth centuries.

When the Royal Bavarian Gallery took over the Boisserée and Wallerstein collections, prices began

253 Around 1810 the London collector, Douce, bought a number of drawings by Altdorfer as well as this drawing by Grünewald of Mary in prayer, which, though genial, corresponded in no other way to the sentimental taste of the early nineteenth century

to rise. In 1819 Baldung's *Christ as the Gardener* (now in the Darmstadt Landesmuseum) still cost only 18 Gulden in a private sale, but by 1830 the Städelsches Kunstinstitut in Frankfurt was already paying as much as 808 guilders for Rogier van der Weyden's *Madonna with Four Saints*. In 1835 Prince Pückler, a cultivated Prussian aristocrat, discovered in Aschaffenburg Grünewald's *SS. Erasmus and Maurice* (now in the Munich Pinakothek), noting down that 'it far surpasses anything in the Boisserée Collection'. N 231 This judgment demonstrated the taste for stronger colouring, which had recently begun to appear in the work of Delacroix and others.

In London in 1802 took place the important Truchsess-Wurzach auction. The early German panels in this collection, among them several by Multscher (now in the Berlin Museums), found buyers without much difficulty. Between 1803 and N 232 1810 Henry Blundell acquired a *Madonna* attributed to Jan van Eyck which, now in Australia, still bears 7 the name of his country seat, Ince Hall. In 1813 Douce, the expert in the graphic arts, acquired a

XX In the short-lived Rococo revival which took place in the 1860's there was a definite return to eighteenth-century painting. Sir Richard Wallace bought several paintings by French artists of the Watteau era. Boucher's *Diana after Bathing* was one of Renoir's favourite paintings

254 In 1845 an English collector bought an altarpiece painted by the Hamburg artist Bertram before 1400. This altarpiece was rediscovered in Horton Old Hall, Bradford, in 1929 (detail)

253 masterly drawing by Grünewald (now in the Ashmolean Museum, Oxford) and some drawings by Altdorfer. Some time afterwards Prince Albert (later Prince Consort) acquired from the Oettingen-Wallerstein family, to which he was related, early German pictures, some of which eventually reached the National Gallery. In 1845 an English collector bought an altarpiece of the Passion by the late 254 fourteenth-century Hamburg master Bertram (now in the Landesmuseum, Hanover).

Alongside the re-awakening of interest in early Netherlandish and German painting, a parallel interest developed for early Italian art. Affected by the Gothic revival and the Romantic movement, certain Englishmen and Germans had turned before 1800 towards the painters preceding Raphael. Italian art-lovers continued to show somewhat more reserve towards their own 'Primitives' and around 1825 Roman art dealers would say of paintings with a gold ground: 'Questa roba farebbe figura in Germania'—people like that kind of thing in Germany. Since it was principally non-Italians who paid attention to the early masters of Tuscany and Umbria, this inclination of collectors remained uninfluenced by any kind of patriotic feeling. It was merely a question of an interest, partly art-historical

and partly artistic, which the Christian revival of the early nineteenth century made propitious. B 47

When after 1800 a secularizing policy was put into force in Italy, an Englishman was immediately on the spot, Edward Solly the dealer, of whom we know very little, but who must often have stayed in Venice. His principal interest was in certain masters of the period between 1480 and 1510, though he also acquired a number of works of earlier periods. North of the Alps Solly further extended his collection and ultimately sold a number of the most important paintings for 500,000 thalers to the King of Prussia. Some rooms in the Berlin Museums still bear the stamp of Solly's very individual collector's taste. The art of the Vivarini brothers and that of Crivelli and Lotto was particularly well represented in his collection, but there were also Raphaels, Palma Vecchios and Titians. N 23

255 Edward Solly gave evidence of the individuality of his taste by liking Crivelli, an artist who was not highly regarded at that time. Among other works by Crivelli, Solly owned this *Annunciation, with St Emidius*, which had been in the Brera, Milan, from 1806 to 1811

OPVS CARO
LI CRIVELLI
VENETI

1486

LIBERTAS

ECCLESIASTICA

In England William Roscoe broadened his taste for Italian art so as to include works of the fourteenth and fifteenth centuries. In 1804 he acquired at an auction in London the panel of *The Finding of Christ in the Temple* painted by Simone Martini in 1342 (now in the Walker Art Gallery, Liverpool). He also had pictures that carried the names of 'Giotto' and 'Masaccio'. Around 1800 these were vague designations of certain phases of style, as were 'Cimabue' and 'Mantegna'. Another English collector of this period was William Young-Ottley. He possessed, among other things, paintings attributed to Duccio, Simone Martini and Giunto Pisano, but remarked in the presence of Continental visitors as late as 1832 that this part of his collection enjoyed little appreciation in England.

The first direct purchases of fourteenth-century Italian paintings for a great museum north of the Alps were made in 1805 through the agency of Dillis, the Catholic priest and artist who assisted in the enlargement of the Munich Central Gallery. Apart from a certain antiquarian inclination Dillis' main motive was a favourite idea of the Enlightenment, the complete representation of the various epochs and schools. Nevertheless the leading Munich curator, Mannlich, ensured that the early pictures were not shown in Munich itself, 'so that young disciples of art still under instruction should not become confused'. These pictures were hung in

the Palace of Schleissheim, which housed mainly second choices. The most important panel, which had been bought in 1805, was *The Last Supper* attributed to Giotto (now in the Munich Pinakothek); it once belonged, together with the *Christ on the Cross, Christ in Limbo* (in Munich), *The Presentation in the Temple* (in the Isabella Stewart Gardner Museum, Boston), the *Entombment* (in the Berenson Collection, Settignano), the *Pentecost* (National Gallery, London) and *The Adoration of the Magi* (Metropolitan Museum, New York), to the same altarpiece.

The personal taste of Ludwig I of Bavaria did not extend to works of the fourteenth and fifteenth centuries, but he did take the small step from the mature to the early Raphael. It will be remembered that in the seventeenth century King Philip IV of Spain obtained the late altarpieces of Raphael that pointed the way towards the early Baroque, while the Winckelmann epoch prized above all the balanced

256 Under the influence of German Romanticism, collectors in central and northern Europe liked to think of Dürer as a virile man and Raphael as an angelic-looking youth. In 1810 Franz Pforr drew them both kneeling before the throne of Art, basing his composition on Italian Renaissance altarpieces. The drawing is lost, but was reproduced in this etching by Georg Hoff

Sistine Madonna of the artist's middle period. About 1800, collectors and artists fancied the 'pre-Classical' Raphael. Ultimately in Germany he became a kind of idealized figure of the Romantic movement, thanks largely to his supposed but quite fictitious angelic youthful figure.

256

The 'stile grazile' of the Madonnas and Saints of the early Raphael and his contemporaries Perugino and Francia had quite a large circle of admirers around 1800. Already in 1790 Forster had paid B 222 tribute to the early Raphael in the Düsseldorf Gallery; he saw Raphael's *Canigiani Holy Family* there, a picture which formed part of the dowry of the second wife of the Elector Johann Wilhelm of the Palatinate (now in the Munich Pinakothek). Forster enthusiastically praised 'the sweetest unity which can be imagined to exist in such a family. The mother regards her child with a look of the most heavenly gentleness; virginal beauty sits enthroned upon her brow'. In 1799 the Grand Duke Ferdi- N 234 nand III of Tuscany acquired an early *Madonna* by Raphael which from then on he always took with him on his travels (this is the *Madonna del Granduca*, now in the Palazzo Pitti in Florence). The Brera Gallery in Milan purchased in 1806 Raphael's *Sposalizio*, and the *Tempi Madonna* (at first in the private rooms of Ludwig of Bavaria; now in the Pinakothek) went from Florence to Munich.

The Englishmen in Italy who were interested in early art were occasionally joined by Frenchmen. Jean-Baptiste Seroux-d'Agincourt, who had been living in Rome since 1782, acquired—around 1800—a number of pictures of the fourteenth century. François Casault, Napoleon's representative at the Curia, started a small collection between 1804 and 1805 which contained works by Sano di Pietro N 235 and Bernardo Daddi.

Since 1797 it had been possible to see a few early Italian panels in the Louvre. Works by Fra Angelico and Mantegna came to Paris at that time from Rome. While around 1810 Denon was transforming the Louvre into a chronologically arranged universal museum and at the same time, thanks to the political situation, was able to seize works in Tuscany, he *257* brought to Paris the *Madonna with Angels* by Cimabue, the *St Francis of Assisi* by Giotto and about two dozen other Italian paintings of the fourteenth and fifteenth centuries. In 1814 he exhibited them in Paris under the title 'Ecoles Primitives'. When a year later—after Waterloo—5,233 paintings in all were to leave Paris again, the representatives of the Grand Duke of Tuscany rather significantly proved to be so little interested in the confiscated works from the period before 1500, that they remained in the Louvre. The expression 'primitives', still common today, is derived from Denon's exhibition in 1814.

257 Towards the end of the Napoleonic era Denon, the Director of the Musée Napoléon, decided to set up an early Italian collection in the Louvre. He bought this altarpiece by Cimabue from a monastery in Pisa for five francs. When, after Waterloo, Italian officials took back the works of art which had been plundered from Italy, they did not think this altarpiece was worth the cost of transport, so it remained in the Louvre

Though it was above all the desire to give complete representations of schools and epochs that had led Dillis and Denon and their like to the early Italians, a deeper understanding of the painting before Raphael, and indeed before Fra Angelico, began to exist in 1815 among such German painters in Rome who were both Christians and Romantics. Around 1750 when Mengs had chosen the Raphael of the middle period and those artists of the Bologna school who strove to emulate him as the starting point for his own art, his enthusiastic contemporaries found a noble simplicity in these works. Around 1820 Mengs was held to be of little account among the young painters from Germany, Scandinavia and England in Rome; in their view he had not gone back far enough into the past. The Nazarenes, as this group called itself, not only rejected Guido Reni

N 236 as 'mean and unclean'—but already began to declare that there was in the middle and later works of Raphael a rebellion against the piety of the Middle Ages. Opinions of this kind prepared the ground for a few small collections of paintings with a 'Nazarene' colouring. Works from pious Siena or Umbria were usually preferred.

During their stay in Rome German painters at first acquired early panels. The largest number of these was collected by the Rhinelander, Ramboux,

N 237 from 1816. He possessed *Christ on the Cross* by a
258 follower of Giunta Pisano (now in the Wallraf Richartz Museum in Cologne) and the *Apostle James* by Simone Martini (now in the National Gallery, Washington). Johann Baese, who resided in Rome from 1821 to 1824, owned a graceful *Madonna* by Masolino (now in the Kunsthalle in Bremen). Peter von Cornelius obtained for the Düsseldorf Kunstakademie in the 1820's the *Madonna with Two Saints* by Cima da Conegliano.

German art-lovers who in 1820 had an affection for the early Italians caught on to this fashion in the

N 238 Café Greco in Rome. The Frankfurt historian Böhmer acquired eight pictures dating from before 1400 as well as suitable companion-pieces by his Nazarene artist friends. Count Raczynski, a Prussian nobleman and later diplomat, began his activities as a collector within the Nazarene circle. He ordered a picture from Overbeck and in 1824 acquired in Paris for 2,500
14 francs the Botticelli *Madonna* which is named after him (now in the Berlin Museums). Bernhard von Lindenau from Thuringia bought in Rome a very respectable number of early Italian pictures, among others by Guido da Siena and Pietro Lorenzetti, which he later presented to Altenburg.

Count Raczynski declared in his later years that the real passion for old pictures had affected Germany only from 1815 until 1825, and the Solly col-

N 239 lection was in fact acquired for Berlin in 1821, during

this brief period. When in 1830 Waagen, by then curator of the new museums of the Hohenzollerns, edited a catalogue, the neo-Renaissance movement was already knocking at the door as the legitimate offspring of neo-Classicism. In his introduction Waagen therefore only touched superficially on early days and ended by declaring to the visitors that Raphael represented 'the highest perfection'. In the principal rooms of the Berlin Museum at that time the most important Italian schools were represented 'from the time of the higher development of their characteristics until the beginning of their decline, that is, from the year 1450 to 1550'. While even later painters were given a proper amount of space, Waagen banished all the early pictures of the Solly collection into a number of secondary rooms and labelled them 'antiquities and art-historical curiosities'. Here there were panels by Cimabue and Giotto, and paintings by Spinello Aretino and Masaccio, Andrea del Castagno and Uccello, Gentile Bellini and Crivelli. In Berlin smoothly painted beauty was the quality chiefly favoured. If the mild Memling was preferred among the early Netherlanders it was Giovanni Bellini who headed the list of the Italians. Solly N 24(had a strong feeling for the precious formal language of the Vivarinis and Crivelli. From his collection two pictures by the latter had reached the Berlin Museum, while a third was later acquired by the National Gallery in London. In 1830 this preference was no longer 255 shared by the artistic world of Berlin. In his catalogue Waagen criticized the Vivarinis as exaggerated and harsh. Rumohr occasionally made remarks of a derogatory character about the art of Crivelli and spoke of it as an 'abnormality' and a 'sour morsel'.

It had been a fundamental principle of neo-Classicism that a work of art could make its effect wherever it was placed and that the truly beautiful was not dependent on any specific circumstance. This extreme view had already aroused some opposition before 1800, and ideas were being deployed against the bolder forms of rationalism which proclaimed the coming of historicism. In Germany Herder and Möser announced 'the connection with a specific locality of everything created by man'. Goethe said in 1815, 'It is so very pleasing and instructive if a Roman monument or altar is surrounded by a decoration which reminds us of the Appian Way'. Soon after 1830 these principles were realized in a particularly characteristic fashion in the new museum halls of the 235 Vatican. Egyptian sculptures were placed before painted landscapes of the Nile, and in 1837 Etruscan antiquities were similarly arranged.

The historical inclination of the decades after Waterloo was particularly in evidence among collections and exhibitions of early native art. It has been seen that Lenoir's Musée des Monuments Français had never wholly wiped out the stain which marked it in Christian and Royalist eyes as a result of its birth during Robespierre's Reign of Terror. Nevertheless its after-effects remained considerable and nowhere more so than among the former enemies of Revolutionary and Napoleonic France. In the period of restoration after 1815, 'throne and altar' were sympathetic to the trends which in England were designated as Gothic Revival and in Germany as Romantik.

The removal of medieval works of art from their place of origin and their housing in suitable surroundings became part of the movement of Romantic historicism. Members of the higher nobility—faithful legitimists—were present when churches were cleared of their contents; they were not scandalized at adding sepulchres to their collections. The revolutions of 1830 and 1848 compelled this upper social stratum, which now felt itself endangered, to start ingratiating itself with the masses. Subtle considerations about the purpose and meaning of graves, such as Quatremère de Quincy had expounded in Paris in 1800, were no longer considered apposite when it was a case of building impressive collections for public exhibition. In Paris Alexandre du Sommerard acquired what had once been the Paris residence of the Burgundian Cluniac monastery and filled the rooms with the product of medieval handicraft. In 1842 Sommerard, whom Balzac ridiculed as the 'prince du bric-à-brac', contrived to get the state to assume responsibility for what is today the Cluny Museum. In Germany Baron von Aufsess, a landed proprietor, started a small collection of a similar character which in the 1830's was housed in six rooms of the Scheurlsches Haus and later in what had once been the Carthusian monastery in Nuremberg. Aufsess was the editor of the *Anzeiger für die Kunde des deutschen Mittelalters*, a periodical devoted to German medieval subjects. He had little interest in the artistic value of individual pieces but regarded them chiefly as documents illustrating cultural history.

In Venice Teodoro Correr, offspring of an old family of the town, gathered together a collection of the same type, which has become the Museo Correr. In 1854 Pius IX founded the Museo Cristiano in the Lateran Palace.

Soon after 1840 the Bavarian Crown Prince Maximilian II visited Paris and was deeply impressed by Sommerard's ideas. In the Louvre he studied the newly-founded Muséum des Souverains which was intended to preserve the memory of great rulers and to make the public immune to Republican slogans. Returning to Munich, Maximilian II had preparations made for a Wittelsbach Museum which in his

258 The painter Ramboux, a native of Trèves who lived in Rome, began his collection of early Italian panel-paintings in 1816. It included this *Crucifixion* by a follower of Giunta Pisano

view 'would serve to revive piety and patriotism'. He himself bought for it a few Late Gothic sculptures. With a somewhat similar aim the Guelph Museum was founded in Hanover. This contained not only the famous ancient Guelph Treasure but also baptismal fonts, altars and other furnishings.

Many people among the ordinary bourgeois population were opposed to the trends of late neo-Classicism and the late Romantic movement. The incipient industrialization and the rising standard of living revived the ideas of the Enlightenment as the memories of 1789 died away and a new belief in progress emerged that centred wholly on this world. Those sections of society which had gained rather more than others from the economic advance turned against an idealism which they had outgrown, and wanted to realize plans of their own in the world of the arts as elsewhere.

259 The closing of the Musée des Monuments Français in 1815 was soon followed by the institution of similar collections throughout Europe, among them that of Baron Aufsess in Nuremberg. This collection, which later provided the basis of the Germanisches Nationalmuseum, included products of the applied arts as well as paintings and sculpture. This standing clock belonged to Philip the Good, Duke of Burgundy

Just as England with the British Museum had given a kind of cue to the epoch of the Enlightenment, so in 1824 the London National Gallery, founded without royal participation, may be regarded as the most typical new foundation of this period. The men of the French Revolution, following the London example, had chosen the word 'Muséum' for the various art treasures gathered together as a Muséum National in the Louvre. The qualifying word 'National' now moved northward across the Channel. The combination of 'National' and 'Gallery' had already occasionally been used around 1800 on the Continent, but the world-wide dissemination of this designation for a museum is due to the building in Trafalgar Square. In Italian cities, in Berlin, in Scandinavia and in all the English-speaking world, National Galleries came into being.

The ideas of bourgeois liberalism also led, in the middle of the nineteenth century, to numerous new National Museums on the Continent. In Munich in 1854 Maximilian II considered it wise to convert his Wittelsbach Museum into a Bavarian National Museum. In Florence, when the united Italian State was created, there was founded in 1859 in the Bargello Palace the Museo Nazionale, with sculpture and examples of handicraft.

East of the line Stockholm-Berlin-Athens, the ruling houses remained intransigent; in Graz a new museum was named after a Habsburg archduke, in St Petersburg after one of the Tsars. Up to the end of the century only anonymous gifts for the Hermitage were premitted.

The liberal-minded citizens in central Europe who were not yet wholly accustomed to the idea of acting independently, liked to join in various social groups. In Munich the Kunstverein, which had been founded in 1823, managed within two decades to assemble three thousand members; with its exhibitions of small realistic pictures it deliberately set its face against the large-scale idealistic art of Cornelius and his circle which had been encouraged by the House of Wittelsbach. From 1839 to 1848 the Cologne Kunstverein alone had a turnover of 342,000 marks. The amounts which the various Kunstvereine spent at this time on the purchase and distribution by lot of works of art were more than double that which the curators of princely museums had at their disposal for new purchases. In Düsseldorf a union of artists for mutual help and support was founded, and worked on public opinion by means of petitions and proclamations. At the same time an 'Altertumsverein' (Union of Friends of Antiquity), such as the one which in 1853 took over the 'patriotic collection' of Baron von Aufsess, was transformed into the Germanisches Nationalmuseum from which its founder himself soon withdrew.

260 The number of middle-class art-lovers increased with the new-found affluence of the nineteenth century. In London, for instance, the Royal Family played no part in the formation of the National Gallery. For the friends of the museum John Scarlett Davis painted interiors of famous Italian galleries, like this one at Parma. On the left of the painting can be seen Correggio's *Madonna with St Jerome*

Collectors among the nobility adjusted themselves to the bourgeois trend of taste. Count Raczynski asserted in 1835 that 'it is much more important to buy modern paintings than old ones which are often of less value than new pictures and are moreover likely to perish some three hundred years sooner'. When he purchased genre pictures of the new realistic Düsseldorf school, he was acting in the same way as the Berlin consul Wagener. In 1823 Wagener had purchased two romantic landscapes by Caspar David Friedrich but during the next decades he spent some 100,000 thalers on works of the new fashionable painters. The gift of this collection to the House of Hohenzollern led to the foundation of the Royal National Gallery in Berlin.

On the Continent art-lovers with a positivist and progressive point of view placed a particular value on the realistic art of their own day, and also on the Flemish and Dutch of the seventeenth century; in England things were much the same. Constable appeared to be far from edified by the founding of the National Gallery. He and others feared that the works of the great classical painters of the southern schools, from Raphael to Claude, would tend to prejudice the public against realistic art. These misgivings proved unfounded. In 1837 Constable himself entered the National Gallery with a picture which at that time was only eleven years old.

In the period of neo-Classicism and of the Romantic movement, the strong British feeling for Dutch and Flemish realistic art had continued as it were underground; now it gained fresh strength. The painting *Fisherman on the frozen Maas near Dordrecht*, by Aelbert Cuyp, traditionally the favourite of the English, was bought by the Duke of Bedford in 1807 for 1,200 guineas (still in the possession of this family at Woburn Abbey). George IV liked to acquire Dutch paintings of the seventeenth century. Rembrandt's magnificent picture *Christ as the Gardener*, which had been removed by the French from Cassel, became the property of the English Crown in 1816. In 1823 twenty thousand people saw Rubens' *Le Chapeau de Paille* at Mr Stanley's in Bond Street (now in the National Gallery, London); shortly after this the Marquess of Lansdowne paid 800 guineas for Rembrandt's *The Mill* (now in the National Gallery, Washington) and the same price was given by Peel for *The Avenue, Middelharnis* by Hobbema, who continued to be greatly appreciated in England (now in the National Gallery, London).

About 1850 people were speaking of museums in a matter-of-fact tone. The idealistic spirit of reverence which had prevailed in the early nineteenth century had disappeared. The preface to the Karlsruhe catalogue of 1852 describes the task of the collection in almost the same words as Mechel had done in 1780. 'It is to be looked at not only as a source of pleasure but much rather as a source of instruction.' The works shown were 'to promote the moral conduct of life'. The external aspect of the museum was levelled down to that of a library or a government office. The staircases and the size of the rooms were of more modest dimensions than in the first decades of the century.

In the second third of the nineteenth century critical voices began to be raised against such a one-sided and pedestrian conception. They bear witness to a connection between the idealistic trends of taste prevailing at the very beginning of the century and the epoch of Art Nouveau and fin de siècle. 'Democracy will give the death blow to the fine arts; the princes will buy no more pictures but invest their money in America so that in the event of their fall they will still be wealthy commoners; rich people who lack that finer culture essential to the appreciation of art will penetrate into the salons', Stendhal had said as early as 1829. The Goncourt brothers N 242

261 This picture of an exhibition held in the British Institution, Pall Mall, was painted by John Scarlett Davis in 1829. On the walls are paintings by Titian, van Dyck, Rembrandt, Cuyp and Murillo. The figures are based on portraits by Lawrence

262 About 1845 the Grande Galerie of the Louvre contained mainly contemporary works which, as a result of the Baroque revival, were hung close together, as they had been in the mid-eighteenth century

N 243

N 244

were repelled by the crowds that came to visit the museums on Sunday when 'the stupid glances of indifferent passers-by flitted over' works of art. The ailing poet Alfred de Musset used to have himself pushed in his wheelchair at night in solitude through the Grande Galerie of the Louvre, and Baudelaire mocked the bourgeois who could only understand carefully composed, realistic pictures.

In England William Dyce passed on the basic ideas of the Nazarene circle in Rome, such as those of Overbeck, to younger men. The Pre-Raphaelite Brotherhood delighted in the stylized art of the early Italians. John Ruskin set himself against 'prosaic', by which he meant realistic, art. Ruskin ad-

mired the early Italians as well as Tintoretto. Charles Eliot Norton acted as a kind of promoter of these views in the United States.

In Germany note should be taken of Count Schack, collector and litterateur, and an eager student of Ruskin. 'Giorgione, who can never be valued sufficiently highly', was represented by good copies in N 245 his private gallery in Munich. On the other hand, Count Schack despised 'art which imitates nature' and could see in Rembrandt only an artist of the second rank. Among living artists he gave his encouragement to Böcklin and Feuerbach. In the field of music he was one of the early enthusiasts for Wagner, whose *Tristan und Isolde* had its first performance in Munich at a time when Count Schack was making the decisive purchases for his collection.

The slightly 'aesthetic' trend was rapidly overwhelmed by the noisy ostentatiousness that marked the growth of big business after 1850. Self-assertive, self-made men surrounded themselves with works of art of a princely character for which they had paid a great deal of money. One of these was Chauchard, the Parisian manufacturer of underwear. American steel kings and the coal barons of the Ruhr needed conspicuous collections of art, not only because of some personal whim of their own but also for advertising purposes.

B 25

The industrialists, who considered themselves infallible, made a provision in advance when they donated their collections to the public, that no alterations could be made; for the most part they lacked the modesty and self-criticism which marked such patrons of Goethe's day as the Frankfurt banker Städel. Prices now rose rapidly to treble and even to five-fold their previous value. The country nobility and the upper bourgeoisie could no longer play any part in collecting; works of art that they had inherited slipped from their hands, having become the acceptable coin of a world currency.

N 246

The relationship between the artist and the new upper class became less and less happy. It is true that Michelangelo had had some differences with the obstinate popes whom he served, but the kind of estrangement that became almost normal after 1850 had not been known since the days of Rembrandt and his disputes with the wealthy Amsterdam merchants of his day. As an outsider the artist descended more and more into his own Bohemia; the founders of great fortunes, who were not used to being contradicted, avoided any contact with excitable artists. They bought at exhibitions or through dealers or preferred to concern themselves with earlier art.

In England, the homeland of free trade, industry and world exhibitions, the new class in 1857 gazed in wonder at the colossal Exhibition of Art Treasures in Manchester and saw what they lacked. Competition began, and around 1885 Sir Richard Wallace, the illegitimate son of the Marquess of Hertford, could boast that he possessed the most valuable private collection in the country, valued at that time at £ 3,500,000. Italian pictures from Titian to Tiepolo, and works by van Dyck, Murillo and Rembrandt, were arranged by Wallace on red-covered walls. He enlivened the rooms with superb eighteenth-century French furniture and marble tables on which were placed Renaissance statuettes. Even so, a number of rooms were devoted to the fashionable artists of the time. The Wallace Collection still retains its character as a magnificently equipped house of the mid-Victorian age.

Napoleon III, who became Emperor in 1852, had brought with him from London, his place of exile, a fine sense for the new possibilities confronting business. He wanted to reign as 'the Industrial Emperor' and he encouraged the formation of great fortunes. A few Paris collections that resemble the Wallace Collection in London are still in existence; for instance, that of the Jaquemart-André family (now a public institution). In Milan, Poldi-Pezzoli, the banker, started a similar collection which he presented to the city as a museum in 1871.

263 With unequalled verve and perspicacity Daumier recorded contemporary dealers and collectors. This painting of a dealer and his client is now in the Boymans-van Beuningen Museum in Rotterdam

Within the German-speaking areas the most cultivated new collections came into being where people
were in the habit of looking towards London and
Paris. In Munich, accounted the city of art *par ex-
cellence*, Lenbach, Kaulbach and Grützner were active
as artists in the midst of early paintings and other
early objects. There developed a kind of 'studio
style' in the matter of artists' collections, which had
its effect on the museums devoted to applied arts. In
the Glaspalast gigantic exhibitions of contemporary
art were put on but many thoughtful spirits looked
askance at these activities. 'The generation that
inhabits Germany today is only interested in the
most superficial things and is becoming more and
more the prey of speculators', wrote the old Count
Schack in 1881.

In Vienna, Makart set the fashion; the quiet
distinction of Schubert's day was disappearing.
Newcomers to the rapidly growing capital were
pushing to the front and having enjoyed a quick
success were forming a plutocracy devoted to pleasure. The imperial family gathered together their
inherited art treasures, without adding to them,
in the luxurious Kunsthistorisches Museum, a
veritable palace of art. Everything was exhibited
close together and the richness of the various forms
and categories of art, and of the material and artistic
values, was unsurpassed.

A certain parvenu style was still more marked in
Berlin, the capital of the newly-founded German
Empire. A great deal of work was done and a great
deal of money earned and enjoyed. The newly-rich
were particularly eager to ennoble themselves by
acquiring the veneer of age. In the house of Eduard
Simon there were paintings by Bellini and Titian
which had come from illustrious old collections. The
panelling of the study had decorated a Florentine
palazzo for three hundred years and even the doors
and the door-handles were antiques. Louis Ravené
opened his gallery on several days a week to his
customers in a warehouse not far from the Spittel-
markt. This example was followed by Rudolf Mosse
on the Leipziger Platz. Towards the end of the century wealthy people began to live in the Tiergarten
district. People out for walks would stop before the
villas of collectors and speak of the masterpieces inside and 'hear the prices rising'.

In the Berlin of the new Empire, Wilhelm Bode,
the 'strong man' of the museums, acquired a degree
of influence that was almost unbelievable. Art
enthusiasts called him a Renaissance condottiere,
who 'knows where every picture is, where it was
N 247 before and who is going to buy it'. The indefatigable
Bode caused art dealers and collections to become
'tributaries to the museums' by giving them advice
but in return pressing for gifts of works of art. That

264 By the middle of the nineteenth century an extensive market for works of art already existed in the United
States, and dealers found it worth their while to send
paintings by contemporary European artists across the
Atlantic. Genre paintings and landscapes were particularly popular. This engraving of 1857 shows part of
an exhibition of contemporary German paintings held in
New York. The statue in the foreground was the prize
in a lottery organized by the Cosmopolitan Art Asso-
ciation

the acceptance of such gifts put the State into the
humiliating position of a beggar was an idea Bode
rejected as outdated. In the Royal Prussian Museums
rooms were named after the art-lovers concerned;
there was for instance a 'Kabinett James Simon'
containing works of the Renaissance. N 248

From about 1870 onwards the United States participated in the general boom of economic activity. B 152
Around 1780, the Puritans who had settled in the
New World had already absorbed many of the ideas
of the Enlightenment and later of the Romantic

265 The transition from new-Classical simplicity to Baroque complexity, which took place in display techniques between 1830 and 1880, applied to sculpture as well as to painting. In direct contrast to the classical layout of the antique sculpture department of the British Museum in 1812, fifty years later, in the Belvedere Palace in Vienna (above), Egyptian, Greek and Roman works were crowded together indiscriminately

movement and of historicism. The entry into the States of many Catholics during the nineteenth century further helped to transform the Puritan outlook.

The first substantial collection was started by the railroad magnate William H. Vanderbilt. In accordance with the prevailing Anglo-Saxon views, nudes were not yet permitted; Vanderbilt favoured precise drawing and anecdotal themes. The principal apartments of his house were entered through a bronze portal which was a cast of Ghiberti's *Doors of Paradise* of the Florence Baptistery. Next came an atrium

B 33

in French Renaissance style with enamelled furniture and Persian faience vessels. The chief contents of the gallery itself were contemporary paintings hung one above the other in three rows. German genre paintings of that time were represented by Knaus, and there was no lack of pictures by fashionable French and English artists, such as Cabanel and Alma Tadema. A historical picture by Meissonier had cost Vanderbilt more money than any other. But works by Delacroix, Corot, Daubigny and Turner were also to be seen. The ordinary public was not admitted to this fairyland palace in Fifth Avenue and had to be content with turning the pages of the two-volume livre de luxe, *Mr Vanderbilt's House and Collections*. N 249

The beginning of Pierpont Morgan's activity as a collector also falls into this epoch. He was on the whole more sympathetic to Rome than to Paris. A visit to the Dresden Gallery in 1853 was probably the origin of his inclination towards Italian Renaissance art. Many decades later he acquired Raphael's B 303 *Madonna and Child Enthroned with Saints* (now in the Metropolitan Museum, New York).

266 The Baroque revival also influenced collectors' taste in antique works of art. Whereas Lord Elgin and Ludwig I of Bavaria had favoured classical Greek sculpture, art-lovers now turned their attention to the Hellenistic period. This head of Aphrodite was bought by the Boston Museum of Fine Arts

In the 1870's a new chapter was opened in the history of the museums of the United States. In 1870 the Metropolitan Museum was founded, and a year later William T. Walters in Baltimore opened the Walters Art Gallery to the public. In 1876 the Boston Museum of Fine Arts moved into a new building. In the halls of this and other museums devoted to art, the Americans created for themselves 'a past that was artificial but inspiring'.

In the presentation of works of art in private houses and museums the cool clarity of neo-Classicism was gradually lost during the course of the nineteenth century. It was replaced by plenitude and intoxicating riches. The uniform frame disappeared. The rooms of the museums—a clear indication of the influence of historicism—were sometimes modelled after the churches and living rooms of the past.

In the building of the Munich Pinakothek, Klenze had already broken away from the system of halls of equal size, and had arranged a series of low side-rooms on the northern side which resembled Dutch interiors of the seventeenth century. Bode went a step further in Berlin: he detested both abstract light from above and a north light that was consistently cool. Every museum room, he felt, should have its own size, height and shape, and also its own form of illumination. 'Every school of painting should have a wall specially coloured to suit it.' The symmetrical hanging of pictures was something which Bode would only agree to in quite exceptional cases. He criticized older galleries which had been arranged on these lines, such as the one in Dresden, as being 'too uniform'.

Bode had often carefully examined private collections of the same type as the Wallace Collection in London and Paris. In Vienna he was much impressed by Baron Nathaniel Rothschild—'as an architect and a decorator the most important of this art-loving family'. What mattered to Rothschild, wrote Bode in his memoirs, was less the work of art as such, but the general effect which it had as part of a greater whole. These words show one where to look for the models of Bode's famous 'mixed rooms'. 'Pictures and sculptures require a few good pieces of furniture, and occasionally some tapestries and decorative products of the applied arts in the character of that particular time. Thus every museum room, as a whole, will make an advantageous and distinguished impression and the effect of the pictures and statues

will be heightened.' The Berlin public was pleased that the unity of the artistic feeling of the past was thus brought before their eyes. Bode's 'historical interiors' were immediately imitated in America under the name 'period rooms'.

In 1800, when dealing with the sculpture of antiquity, people had regarded the classical works as the absolute peak of achievement. In the middle and late nineteenth century the Hellenism of 'Greek Baroque' was valued more highly, corresponding to the development of style in contemporary architecture. The *Venus de Milo* now became the most popularly admired statue of antiquity. Its place was no longer against a wall. It was moved to the centre of a seventeenth-century room in the Louvre where it could be looked at from all sides. A thoroughly Baroque enhancement of the total effect was accorded to the

267 In the course of the second half of the nineteenth century the *Venus de Milo* became one of the most popular works of art in the world (detail)

268   The Hellenistic *Nike of Samothrace (Winged Victory)*, a great favourite of Parisian art-lovers about 1875, occupies a commanding position half-way up a flight of stairs in the Louvre. This same method of isolating an object for display was used for group statues at Versailles around 1700

Winged Victory; as the *Triton and Silenus* group had once done in Versailles, for nearly a hundred years the *Winged Victory* has occupied a dominating position from a pedestal half-way up a flight of steps in the Louvre. In the British Museum a number of new aquisitions, above all the statue of Asclepius, fell in with the dictates of the new direction of taste. When realism became fashionable about the middle of the nineteenth century, the energetic bust-portraits of ancient Roman rulers, generals and merchants were looked on with favour.

268

269

269, 270, 271 The passion for 'Greek Baroque' was reflected in the British Museum's nineteenth-century purchases. The head of Asclepius (left) provides a particularly good example of this trend. But from about 1870 onwards antipathy began to be shown towards the intrinsic softness of the work of this period. Realistic portrait busts of energetic looking Romans (below) were bought by American industrialists who felt an affinity with them

The strong nineteenth-century taste for Egyptian art was enhanced by studies of social history and religion. Europeans also began to take note of Assyrian sculpture, so barbarically rich in its variety of forms, so sombre in its spirit. Shortly before this, Etruscan and archaic Greek works had widened the old, pure conception of Apollonian antiquity to one that was essentially Dionysian. The first Assyrian sculptures were acquired for the Berlin Museum in 1845. The excavations of Austen Henry Layard from 1845–1851 procured for the British Museum the unique Nimrud Gallery. Even before 1860 important ancient sculptures from Asia Minor had already reached America.

N 253

The Romantic preference for devoutly sweet Madonnas and pious saints of the early Italian schools never quite disappeared, least of all in the English-speaking countries. Thanks to the Prince Consort Albert, a cousin of the south German collector, Prince Oettingen-Wallerstein, a late Romantic preference for early Italian painting took root in London. In 1848 the National Gallery accepted the first early panels as a gift. Between 1855 and 1859 three paintings by Botticelli were acquired. In America a number of art-lovers shared these tastes. James Jackson Jarves obtained major works by Taddeo Gaddi, Sassetta, Gentile da Fabriano and Pollaiuolo; in 1871 his collection was acquired by Yale University in New Haven.

N 254

While the late Romantic trend was towards sweetness, an appreciation of the stricter painters of the Quattrocento was already evident here and there. Hans von Marées admired in the Munich Pinakothek the strong construction of early Italian painting. The National Gallery in London acquired between 1861 and 1882 three paintings by Piero della Francesca and two by Luca Signorelli. The Berlin Museum, which after the victory of Sedan immediately challenged London's predominating position in the Italian art market, contrived to secure in 1873 from the Marchese Stufa in Florence Signorelli's *Pan*, and J. P. Morgan acquired for a very high price the profile

272

portrait of Giovanna Tornabuoni by Ghirlandaio (now in the Thyssen Collection in Lugano).

Since about 1860 both the carved and painted portrait busts of energetic Florentine bankers and merchants, of their clever wives and self-assured daughters, had begun to migrate to the cities where

N 255

a kindred type had risen to power. Florence, the city of political and economic activity, began to take the place of 'pious' Siena, so beloved of the Romantics. The art market duly reflected this change. For 142 francs, the bust of Marietta Strozzi by Desiderio da Settignano (now in the Berlin Museums) was taken

272 As far as the work of the Old Masters was concerned, about 1880 collectors began to prefer the bold strength of linear as opposed to tonal paintings. Pierpont Morgan gave a place of honour in his house to Ghirlandaio's *Giovanna Tornabuoni* (see Ill. 70)

by Waagen in 1840, though he was not particularly interested in it. Its replica, which is not of the same quality as the original, cost Morgan a million gold francs. In this work Bode loved 'the spontaneous attitude', the 'illusion of youthful alertness' and 'the expression of gentle roguishness'.

N 256

With the decline of neo-Classicism, a different assessment was made of the masters of the sixteenth century. The hegemony of the central Italians was destroyed; the Venetians appeared once more upon the scene. This change took place at first in the traditional art centres of Paris, Munich and Vienna. Ingres had never tired of paying tribute to Raphael. Delacroix declared that 'if one could live a hundred years, one would prefer Titian to all others, but he is not a painter for young people'. In the second half of the nineteenth century Manet and Renoir set up their easels in the Louvre to copy paintings by Titian. In about 1850 the Hermitage alone acquired about a dozen of Titian's paintings, among them the mature masterpiece *Venus with a Mirror* (now in the National Gallery, Washington).

The attitude of a collector such as Count Schack to the painting of the sixteenth century was wholly in line with that of Archduke Leopold Wilhelm. Schack commissioned copies of the 'long-misunderstood' Venetians, from Giovanni Bellini to Tintoretto, since he could not pay for originals. Schack used to say that he would gladly meet Titian's *Young Englishman* (in the Palazzo Pitti) in another life. German art-lovers about 1880 preferred Titian's *Assumption* in Venice to Raphael's *Sistine Madonna*. In London, Wallace hung the mature works of Titian in the room of honour.

Of the great seventeenth-century painters who had been so highly esteemed in Goethe's day, those who were felt to be 'classicistic', like Guido Reni, were the first to forfeit their reputation. The high prices paid for Poussin and Claude began to fall. On the other hand, new aspects of Murillo were discovered. Through his softly-diffused, delicately differentiated colours he appealed to the contemporaries of Richard Wagner: the *Immaculate Conception* from the Soult collection fetched the highest price of the decade in the very years when *Tristan und Isolde* was being composed. It was purchased in 1852 for 615,000 francs for the Louvre (now in the Prado) while at that same time Rubens' *Henri de Vicq* only fetched 15,000 francs (now in the Louvre).

The cooler art of Zurbaran and, above all, Velazquez is today regarded as an element out of which Manet and his like developed their own individual manner. In these years, all Spaniards were looked on as relatives of Murillo. In England the public delighted in the sensual *Rokeby Venus* (exhibited in Manchester in 1857, now in the National Gallery, London) by Velazquez. In Boston in 1874 art-lovers streamed to an exhibition of Spanish painting from French private collections which contained works by Murillo, Zurbaran and Velazquez. It was this exhibition that was the starting-point of the passion of American collectors for the great century of Spanish painting.

At this time there began too the rediscovery of the painters of the eighteenth century. In the days of Hans Makart the residency of the Habsburgs, which had so often played a part as the herald of Venetian art, seized on the catchword 'Tiepolo'. About twenty of his pictures were in the hands of Viennese collectors and dealers as early as 1865. Many of these immediately continued their journey to St Petersburg. In 1870 Tiepolo's great *Virgin with the Three Magi* was brought from storage into the Munich

N 257

N 258

XV

18

N 259

273 The vogue among men of action for sober but energetic portrait sculpture resulted in a rise in the value of that produced in Florence in the second half of the fifteenth century. Many works of this kind went to buyers in New York and London, but this bust of an unknown Florentine merchant by Mino da Fiesole was purchased by the Berlin Museums

274 Apart from the re-evaluation of Greek Hellenistic sculpture, the Baroque revival also resulted in a widely-shared and lasting appreciation of seventeenth-century Spanish painting. This preference applied above all to the English-speaking world. Several major works by Velazquez, like this portrait of Mariana, Queen of Spain, went to the United States

275 Tiepolo, the last of the great Venetians, was rediscovered about 1870. High prices were paid for his work in Vienna, and in the Munich Pinakothek one of his paintings was brought out of store; it was later joined by two others from an affiliated gallery—one of them being his *Rinaldo and Armida* (above)

Pinakothek. In each of the years 1870, 1877, and 1881, the Louvre acquired one picture by Tiepolo. In 1873 and 1878 Berlin did the same. Cologne followed in 1883 and London in 1885.

The French of the eighteenth-century had the same festive palette and merry worldliness as Tiepolo. Boucher became the favourite painter of European bankers. The Wallace Collection alone acquired some three dozen of his pictures and Renoir was deeply XX impressed by Boucher's *Diana after Bathing*. Lancret and Fragonard also came back into favour and the more discreet art of Watteau found admirers. Louis La Caze, one of the most refined Parisian collectors, had acquired eight paintings by Watteau. For *Gilles* (now in the Louvre), a picture which Denon had

acquired against the advice of David for only 150 francs in a junk shop, La Caze paid 16,000 francs. He was said to have refused an English offer of 300,000 francs. N 260

When Tiepolo and Boucher were rediscovered, the English portrait painters of the late eighteenth century also began to be internationally appreciated. As early as 1835 Waagen had spoken enthusiastically of Gainsborough's *Blue Boy* because of its lively manner of painting and especially because of its 'most charming harmonics in the cool scale of colours', but it was not till 1876 that a work of this B 320 kind fetched a top price. In that year the portrait of *Georgina, Duchess of Devonshire* by Gainsborough N 261 changed hands for £ 10,500 in London. Wallace now placed a few English portraits in his collection. The Metropolitan Museum in New York received a portrait by Romney in 1888.

Concerning the early Netherlanders and Germans there were some changes of taste among collectors in the late nineteenth century, which corresponded to those just mentioned. While the Romantic movement loved the gothicizing Rogier van der Weyden, it was Jan van Eyck, more of this world and more realistic, who now came to the fore. Between 1840 and 1852 three of his major works were acquired for galleries in London, Frankfurt and St Petersburg respectively. In the case of the early Germans there was a shift from the mild Lochner to the forthright realists of the later fifteenth century. The shift from Siena to Florence had its counterpart north of the Alps in the transition from Cologne to Nuremberg, whose civic culture Wagner idealized in *Die Meistersinger*. Under the general influence of 'the German Renaissance' the mature Dürer, Baldung and the sculptors with whom they had an affinity began to be honoured. Admirers now crowded in front of Holbein's portraits of merchants. The bankers of 1880 saw in these their forerunners from the epoch of the Fuggers. Leibl studied Holbein's manner of painting, Degas his carefully considered composition.

N 262

The positivist mid-nineteenth century rediscovered the bourgeois art of the age of Rembrandt. While a Romantic such as Rumohr found Dutch still-life 'no more than indifferent', Wallace and others gladly included pictures by de Heem in their collections. Along with genre pictures by Knaus, Meissonier, Munkaczy and Menzel, works by Jan Steen, the Ostades, and Teniers were also acquired for the Metropolitan Museum, New York. It was in fact works of this kind that at first preponderated here. As the taste of the newly-rich grew more refined, particular attention began to be paid to the later work of Rembrandt and the discreet Terborch. Around 1890 one of the Paris Rothschilds paid a million gold francs for an *Interior with Figures* by Terborch. Along with Velazquez, Vermeer van Delft became the favourite of the painters. Frans Hals spoke to the art-lovers of the later nineteenth century through his daring realism and the illusion of the momentary. The National Gallery in London acquired two of his pictures in 1876 and 1888, and the Metropolitan Museum in New York four between 1871 and 1888. By the side of Murillo, Velazquez, Frans Hals and Rembrandt, Rubens also was given a place of honour. Personalities as different as Jakob Burckhardt, Sir Richard Wallace, Wilhelm Bode and Renoir were united in their affection for him.

N 263

276 The increasing application of iron in industry was matched, among the industrialists who benefited from this development, by a growing interest in the use of iron in previous ages. The effect of this, with its connotations of late Romantic historicism, can be seen in the cavalcade of knights in sixteenth-century armour which a Scotsman named Stibbert set up in his house in Florence

The increase of population in the industrial age and rising prosperity led about 1860 to a lively demand for old furniture, domestic objects and products of the applied arts. Whereas the Romantic movement

277 Elaborately wrought fifteenth- and sixteenth-century swords, such as this example from Germany, were especially favoured by industrialist collectors, and the previous generation's interest in Greek vases waned rapidly

N 264

had admired Gothic statuettes of Nazarene-like delicacy, the practice now became fashionable of using showy coats of armour, shields, axes, swords and the like for decoration in high, dark panelled rooms. This habit spread quickly to the United States and resulted in characteristic donations to museums.

At the dinner table people liked to use over-rich sixteenth-century silver. In Frankfurt in 1880 Baron Carl von Rothschild paid 600,000 marks to the Merkel family of Nuremberg for a silver centrepiece by Wenzel Jamnitzer. Furniture, glass and pottery of the sixteenth century, whether of German, Italian or French origin all began to fetch incredible prices. On the whole, secular pieces were preferred.

N 265

Since the original objects available were far from satisfying the demand, industry began machine reproduction of Renaissance handicraft. For this purpose, collections of models were necessary and this,

278

in its turn, brought a new type of museum into being. As an offshoot of the Great Exhibition of 1851, there was founded in London what is today the Victoria and Albert Museum and on the Continent the Vienna Museum für Kunst und Industrie. The various exhibits were arranged according to the material and the workmanship. Faithful copies of items which were to be found elsewhere filled the gaps.

The trend to support art-industry, as it was called in 1866, was also to be found in other places. Maximilian II of Bavaria, who often stayed in England, had his National Museum enlarged by the addition of art-industrial sections, and gave the institution the motto: 'Meinem Volk zu Ehr und Vorbild' (To my people as honour and model). In 1871 the coffins in the princely vaults of the church of Lauingen were opened and Late Renaissance garments taken from them for the costume section of the Munich National Museum, without any particular misgivings. Everywhere tombs were placed in the new applied art museums if the deceased were represented wearing dress or armour that might be interesting from the point of view of the history of costume.

When the fashion for the Renaissance began to fade away, the museums of the applied arts and collectors extended their horizon towards earlier or even later epochs; the search was for luxuriously ornamented objects, such as Rhenish reliquaries from about 1200, or for Baroque ivory carving, silverwork and pottery.

Bartholomeus Spranger around 1600, della Vecchia around 1650 and Mengs around 1750 were regarded as the equals of famous masters and fetched in their own times what were often exaggerated prices. The same kind of thing happened in the nineteenth century. J. L. David's *Leonidas before Thermopylae* was acquired by the French State in 1825 for 50,000 francs. The *Mocking of Christ* by Benjamin West, 'the American Raphael', fetched 3,000 guineas in 1820. Turner, regarded as a kind of executor of Claude's testament, was highly valued in England.

When neo-Classicism began to be less highly esteemed, Constable came into the foreground with the Dutch and Flemish, who were now once more greatly admired. Constable had begun by making copies of Rubens and van Ruisdael for purposes of study. The renewed interest in seventeenth-century pictures of morals and manners went parallel with the blossoming of bourgeois genre painting during this period. The *Reading of the Will* painted by Wilkie in 1820 was bought by Ludwig I of Bavaria and had a strong influence on the artists of Munich. Whereas Wilkie had concerned himself chiefly with Teniers,

278 The Great Exhibition of 1851 in London indicated the potential for the mass-production of furniture and other household effects, but the majority of designers were still influenced by late Romantic historicism. In this sideboard by William Burgess the decorative painting is partly classical Greek, partly medieval, in spirit

the Munich painter Wilhelm von Kobell turned his attention principally to Cuyp.

The Düsseldorf School achieved for a time a fame that was more than merely local by its genre pictures and its skilfully arranged landscapes. In 1830 the Düsseldorf painters had their first successful exhibition in Berlin. In 1835 the Frankfurt Städelsches Kunstinstitut acquired Achenbach's *Storm at Sea* for 1,500 guilders, while *The Madonna with Four Saints* by Rogier van der Weyden entered the same gallery for 808 guilders. In New York, under the patronage of the Prussian Consul, a Düsseldorf Gallery was opened as a permanent sales-room, and immediately

began to play an important part in the artistic life of America.

Genre painters like Meissonier were overpaid in France; this was true also of historical painters, amongst whom the Belgian Gallait was the first to achieve fame. In collections and museums, works by such painters as these, who enjoy little popularity today, mingled with earlier art. Wallace added no less than twelve works by Meissonier, including the much admired theatrical *Hired Assassins*, to his Dutch, Italian and Spanish seventeenth-century pictures. Indeed, even today in the Wallace Collection in London, large-scale paintings by Gallait and Delaroche

279 The concept of art in industry led to the formation in London, in 1852, of a Museum of Manufacturers, which was soon renamed Museum of Ornamental Art. It provided the basis for the Victoria and Albert Museum. This watercolour of 1856 shows a room in the Museum of Ornamental Art

occupy places of honour, whereas Delacroix and Corot are represented sparsely and by unimportant paintings. One would have seen in the homes of Boston art-lovers of the mid-nineteenth century pictures by Constable, Millet and Diaz. In New York at this time, August Belmont possessed works by Knaus, Meissonier, Delaroche, Rousseau and Dupré.

When prices rose in the boom period after 1870, the prestige of these artists was still so great that the boom benefited them as much as anybody else. The auction of the New York collector Seney's pictures in 1885 fetched the record sum of $214,000. Under the hammer came four pictures by Achenbach, fifteen by Diaz, nine by Dupré, five by Daubigny, as well as works by Schreyer, Munkacsy and Bouguereau. A few years later, Meissonier's picture *Perte de Jeu* fetched $26,300 at the James H. Stebbins auction in New York. Genre pictures by Knaus achieved equally high prices. The detailed and highly realistic historical picture *1807* by Meissonier went for $80,000 to the American tycoon, A. T. Stewart. Around 1880, the Louvre acquired the highly popular *Angelus* by Jean-François Millet, who had just died, for the exaggerated price of 800,000 francs.

The rediscovery of Baroque painting was reflected in the art of Makart. As far back as 1887 the Metropolitan Museum in New York acquired one of his pictures. *The Entry of Charles V into Antwerp* was viewed by no less than 40,000 people within five days in the Vienna Künstlerhaus and immediately afterwards was sold for a high price to the Hamburg Kunsthalle.

CHAPTER 6

From 'Fin de Siècle' to Modern Times

Art as miracle | Asian and Egyptian art: Nefertiti | the cult of El Greco | African art, the archaic and Romanesque | the Russian Revolution and purchases by Mellon | 'classicism' between the Wars | 'The Cloisters' | The Third Reich and 'degenerate' art | the ethnological object as a work of art | methods of presentation in modern museums | the present value of masterpieces

DESPITE THE GROWING TENSION caused by international rivalries, the twenty-five years before the start of the First World War were a period of great economic prosperity. Capitalism underwent further development. Its principal leaders and beneficiaries often had that unquestioned security and refinement that belongs to a second generation. Self-made men had little difficulty in adapting themselves when rising to eminence.

North America now began to play a leading part in the development of world affairs. From 1876 to 1901 the population of the United States rose from 38 to 91 million, and enormous fortunes accumulated in the hands of single individuals. 'In collecting, as in other matters, the Americans are developing the energy and toughness which is peculiar to themselves', wrote Bode in 1905. J. Pierpont Morgan, the start of whose collecting career has been mentioned, found himself in the later years of his life in the position to acquire a collection of works of art with a total value of $60,000,000. 'This man alone is a continent', exclaimed the curator of a European museum. A part of Morgan's collection became the property of various museums by way of gifts.

If Morgan's artistic tastes were catholic to the point of being wholly impersonal, posterity is in debt to Mrs Isabella Stewart Gardner of Boston for the creation of a collection which is highly characteristic of the whole 'fin de siècle' epoch. She had learned from Ruskin, among others, her enthusiasm for Venice. Fenway Court, where her works of art were housed, was a Venetian palace transferred stone by stone to Boston and there reconstructed.

In 1894 Mrs Gardner became acquainted with a young student named Bernard Berenson, whom she assisted and who in return educated her taste and obtained paintings for her. That same year she bought for $17,000 her first Botticelli, *The Tragedy of Lucrezia*, from the Earl of Ashburnham in London. But she could not make up her mind about the paintings by Watteau and Greco which Berenson put in her way. She would very much have liked Gainsborough's *Blue Boy*, but acquired instead what is considered the finest Titian in the US, *The Rape of Europa*, after Berenson assured her it was a far greater picture than the *Blue Boy*.

In New York the department store owner Benjamin Altman started collecting around 1885. Altman began with the Barbizon School and was occasionally interested in the applied art of the Renaissance. Not until later did he acquire important paintings of old masters, from Mantegna to Vermeer. His collection was eventually bequeathed to the Metropolitan Museum in New York.

Peter A. B. Widener, the traction and meat magnate, and later his son Joseph E. Widener, created a collection in Philadelphia from which mediocre works were consistently removed. The choicest pieces belong today to the National Gallery in Washington, among others the *David of the Casa Martelli* by Donatello and the *Small Cowper Madonna* by Raphael.

Around 1900 Henry O. Havemeyer was active as a collector in New York. Havemeyer was the owner of a sugar trust founded in 1887, which by 1900 had already brought him $150,000,000. In Baltimore Henry Walters, son of William, left at his death a valuable collection in which many items had not yet been removed from their cases. In 1900 William R. Hearst began to spend $4,000,000 annually on works

B 6
N 266
B 42
N 267
B 254
N 268

In Germany from 1890 onwards the public showed that it had a mind of its own. Kaiser William II vainly tried to press his personal ideas about modern art when the Berlin National Gallery made new acquisitions. The obstinate curator, Hugo von Tschudi, arranged for pictures which he could not buy as a Prussian royal official to be donated by friendly industrialists and bankers.

In Hamburg Alfred Lichtwark, curator of the Kunsthalle and a gifted publicist, outmanoeuvred the civic authorities, while in Mannheim Fritz Wichert looked to business men for support. When he wished to acquire Manet's *Execution of the Emperor Maximilian* and the budget of the Kunsthalle founded three years previously proved insufficient, Wichert collected the necessary sum from private individuals within half an hour by means of a few

280 Towards the end of the century more and more people became interested in Asian art: it ceased to be the province of the specialist. This eighteenth-century Japanese console was designed to carry a statue of Buddha

281, 282 Collectors who valued the harmony of line so apparent in Art Nouveau recognized this same quality in Oriental works of art, such as this fourteenth-century Chinese vase (below) and the eleventh-century Japanese wood-carving of a deity (right)

of art of one kind and another, such as tapestries, faience, and old silver. In California, the railroad magnate Henry E. Huntington created a valuable collection. The unusual collection of medieval sculpture formed over many years by George Guy Barnard, himself a sculptor, became, with the generous financial assistance of John D. Rockefeller, Jr., the basis of The Cloisters, which has been, since 1926, an administrative part of the Metropolitan Museum, New York.

In the U.S. the initiative for art collecting and for the enrichment of museums at the turn of the century definitely lay with certain private individuals, while at the same time the influence of reigning princes and of state authorities in Europe was diminishing.

telephone calls. In manufacturing towns of the Ruhr district such as Elberfeld, Barmen and Essen, active collectors attracted some attention. Karl Ernst Osthaus, the industrialist, founded his Folkwang-Museum in Essen in order, as he himself declared, 'to annoy Berlin'. Many cities which were the residencies of princes began to stagnate; Darmstadt was an exception, for here the Grand Duke stepped forward as the patron of the avant-garde of the early twentieth century.

In line with the interest of big business in promoting the arts and helping museums was the growth of a world art market. Those who had been chiefly concerned with such matters in the past, namely the nobility and the leading bourgeois of the cities of Europe, now had dealings with that market only in so far as they were obliged to part with property they had inherited. It is true that around 1900 museums in Berlin and London were still making purchases on a grand scale, but even so they could not check the emigration of many important works of art from the Old World to the New. Italian art of the sixteenth and seventeenth centuries was bought chiefly from English country seats; early Italian panels and Spanish works of art were often acquired for American collectors in their place of origin.

283, 284 British art-lovers were the first to give attention to Indian art, and the former India Museum in London contained the earliest public collection of such work in Europe. But it was not until about 1900 that collectors as a whole showed an interest in works of art like the sensual figure of a tree spirit (above) and the graceful dancing Shiva (below)

285 Manet, Whistler and other artists were among the early discoverers of the delicate charm of Oriental coloured woodcuts. By 1900 collectors throughout Europe and the United States were following their lead. This sixteenth-century Chinese painting on silk of a legendary queen was bought by the British Museum

The American art trade concentrated at first on famous works by recognized masters, which constituted a sort of 'brand merchandise'. The ending of the American import duty on works of art in 1909 caused a sudden rise in prices. In 1911 Widener paid £95,000 for Rembrandt's *The Mill* from the collection of the Marquess of Lansdowne in London (now in the National Gallery, Washington). At about the same time a group picture by B 13 Frans Hals fetched $400,000, and the etching of *Jan Six* by Rembrandt $18,000. In 1913 Benjamin Altman paid 600,000 gold marks for Dürer's *Virgin and Child with St Anne* (now in the Metropolitan Museum, New York) which had been sold in 1858 by the officials of the Munich Pinakothek for 65 guilders as a supposedly worthless third-class picture. The art-lovers of the New World were often concerned that a first general impression should be very good indeed. A New York dealer once admitted in court that it was usual to 'Americanize' pictures, in order to make them 'pretty and saleable'.

The First World War resulted in a loss of economic strength in western Europe which was never made good. In Germany and Austria it brought about the fall of the dynasties. A great many works of art became available because impoverished museums could not afford to keep them. From the possessions of the former royal House of Hanover, parts of the Guelph treasure went to the Cleveland Museum of Art and Holbein's *Edward VI as a Child* eventually to the National Gallery in Washington. Of the paintings privately owned by the 322 Hohenzollerns, the *La Camargo Dancing* by Lancret also left Europe. The last Grand Duke of Sachsen-Weimar parted with his Filippino Lippi *Madonna and Child* and the House of Anhalt-Dessau sold a 248 *Portrait of a Lady* by Rogier van der Weyden (these three pictures are now in the National Gallery, Washington).

In Austria after 1919 there was a veritable sell-out. Among other paintings, the Vienna Kunsthistorisches Museum handed over to a dealer 135 Veronese's *Rebecca at the Well*, a picture which in 1655 had been the pride of the Archduke Leopold Wilhelm (now in the National Gallery, Washington). The Counts Harrach sold sixteenth-century pictures from their collection to Holland and America. Even England's proud private collections began to N 269 break up. The *Ince Hall Madonna*, attributed to 7 Jan van Eyck, went for £100,000 to the National Gallery of Victoria, Melbourne. In 1922 Gainsborough's *Blue Boy* entered the collection of Henry E. Huntington in San Marino, California, for $825,000.

As a result of the Russian Revolution about one-third of the more easily movable works of art in private ownership, left the country. Prince Youssoup- B 52 off, the executioner of Rasputin, brought Rembrandt portraits out of Russia; these were bought by Joseph Widener and are now in the National Gallery in Washington. The Soviet Government, after its victory over the White Russian Army and its own assumption of power, confiscated all the works of art in churches, country seats or town houses, so that the contents of the museums were temporarily increased by some 40 per cent. B 137

In accordance with the new ideology, works of art were used for didactic purposes. The pictures of Rubens illustrated the fact that the great Antwerp merchants had plenty to eat, while Gauguin bore testimony to 'late bourgeois decadence'. The idea of N 270 the intrinsic artistic value of any individual painting or piece of sculpture was completely lost. About 1930 innumerable works of art, which could not be used as ideological object lessons or could be replaced as such, were handed over to the European and American art trade. Germany at that time received Burgkmair's *Portrait of Schellenberger* (now in the Wallraf Richartz Museum 249 in Cologne); a *Madonna* by Rubens (now in the Landesmuseum, Hanover), and Platzer's *Concert* (now in the Germanisches Museum, Nuremberg). The Historisches Museum in Basle bought back monstrances of the fourteenth and fifteenth century which had been given away by the Swiss in the early nineteenth century. The Museum of Fine Arts in Antwerp and the Mauritshuis in The Hague bought paintings by Mor, Rembrandt, de Keyser and Jan van der Heide.

Masterpieces of a quality that had not been seen on the market for more than a century now found their way into the galleries and collections of America and Australia. For $150,000 the Metropolitan Museum in New York acquired Watteau's *Mezzetin;* XII and for about the same price the Museum of Art in Philadelphia obtained Poussin's *Triumph of Neptune and Amphitrite*, a masterpiece which the artist had sent to the Duc de Richelieu in 1639. Andrew

XXI One of the effects of the rise of Impressionism was that collectors looked for impressionist characteristics in the work of earlier artists—be it in the use of broad brush-strokes, free grouping of figures, or general spontaneity of expression. While Manet, Monet and Renoir were painting their most important pictures, museums in Europe and the United States bought the work of artists like Frans Hals, whose *Yonker Ramp and his Sweetheart* is shown opposite

Mellon, who at this time was the leading American collector in Washington, became at one stroke the owner of a selection of the most celebrated paintings from the Hermitage, among them Jan van Eyck's *Annunciation*, Raphael's *St George and the Dragon* and his *Alba Madonna*, Titian's *Venus with a Mirror* and Rembrandt's *Joseph accused by Potiphar's Wife* (all now in the National Gallery in Washington). Certain of these paintings are said to have cost well over $500,000. Tiepolo's *The Banquet of Cleopatra*, which had once belonged to Catherine II of Russia, went to the National Gallery of Victoria in Melbourne.

From 1933 related events began to take place within Hitler's sphere of power. The government of the Third Reich allowed many sacred buildings, such as the cathedrals of Quedlingburg and Brunswick, to be profaned and transformed into 'national memorial halls'; and, following the Russian example, the removal of works of art from churches began. The confiscation of all privately-owned works of art—as in Russia in 1917—applied to people who politically or in other ways were disliked by the new powers. Hitler himself did not hesitate to demand works from the German museums quite arbitrarily. The curator of the Kunsthalle in Karlsruhe was able to save Feuerbach's *Feast of Plato* for his museum only by pointing out the homosexual inclination of Alcibiades, one of the chief figures in the picture. Shortly beforehand, Hitler had had the SA leader Röhm executed as a homosexual and could not allow himself to have a painting with this sort of subject.

Hitler had a plan to set up in Linz a 'Führer-Museum' of such importance that the railway line was to be moved some three miles away in order to accommodate it. Three hundred pictures were held in readiness by 1941, and a special organization, the 'Sonderauftrag Linz', procured various works including masterpieces by Rembrandt, Rubens and Vermeer.

XXII Renoir, who admired the light colours and gracefulness of eighteenth-century art, painted a portrait of the Parisian dealer and collector Ambroise Vollard in which the latter is shown with a collection of eighteenth-century objets d'art

The main object was to glorify nineteenth-century German art by excluding any works by non-German artists after 1800. The museum never came into being, but over 5,000 paintings and a huge collection of other objets d'art were rescued at the end of the war from a salt-mine at Alt Aussee where they had been stored. Göring laid the foundation of a great collection partly from the contents of the Prussian museums which were under his authority. From the Wallraf Richartz Museum in Cologne he chose a Cranach *Madonna*.

Goebbels dedicated himself to the battle against post-van Gogh art. He had a number of confiscated 'degenerate' works of art brought one by one into his own home by persons commissioned for this purpose, though in other cases he allowed such works to be sold at rock bottom prices abroad; for this reason they have fortunately been preserved. The curator of the Kunsthalle in Basle paid 4,000 Swiss francs to the Reichspropagandaministerium for Kokoschka's *The Tempest* from the Hamburg Kunsthalle; 8,000 francs for Corinth's *Ecce Homo* from the Berlin National Gallery, 6,000 francs for Franz Marc's *Animal Fates* from the Halle Museum and 1,600 francs for Chagall's *Rabbi* from the Mannheim Kunsthalle. Shortly afterwards the same museum had to pay 22,000 francs on the open market for Chagall's *Cattle Dealer*.

The nationalist slogans of the Hitler period led many a German museum to undertake rash exchanges with the international art trade. The Munich Pinakothek got rid of Raphael's *Bindo Altoviti* (now in the National Gallery in Washington) together with pictures by Canaletto and Renoir. The Kaiser Friedrich Museum in Berlin parted with early Italian paintings, for instance the *Nativity with the Prophets Isaiah and Ezekiel* from Duccio's high altar in Siena Cathedral (now in the National Gallery in Washington) as well as a French fourteenth-century statue of the Virgin Mary (now in The Cloisters in New York). In such cases, paintings of inferior value by German masters reached Munich and Berlin. The Third Reich fortunately did not succeed in carrying out further measures in the sphere of the arts.

A number of important art dealers were of service to the collectors of the United States in the 1920's and 30's. M. Knoedler and Co. was concerned with bringing over individual works from the Hermitage to Washington. Joseph Duveen, who was eventually given a title in England, once sold 42 pictures en bloc for $21,000,000 to Andrew Mellon, Secretary of the Treasury and later Ambassador to the Court of St James, the most successful of American collectors of our time, who originated the plan to create a great

masters of the fifteenth to the nineteenth century, this collection has a somewhat American character. The dealers and museum experts who were Thyssen's advisers were instructed to obtain famous pictures from old and famous collections. The N 275 Thyssen Gallery, which reached its peak in 1940, has since then been broken up: Fragonard's *Education*, for example, is now to be found in the new Museu de Arte of São Paulo in Brazil.

After the end of the Second World War, the Soviet sphere of power in Europe was considerably extended. Many people fled before the advancing East, and with them went movable goods, including works of art. A silver reliquary of Saint George by the late

286 The sensitivity and subtlety of taste of connoisseurs at the turn of the century made them incline towards Amarna sculpture, which represented one of the more refined phases of Egyptian art. Several of these pieces, like this head of an unknown princess, were excavated by German archaeologists for the Berlin Museums

287 Viennese art-lovers attached particular importance to this torso of a goddess dating from the seventh century BC, which formed part of the small Egyptian section in the Kunsthistorisches Museum

B 13 picture gallery in the United States. Mellon made over 115 of his finest pictures to the new National Gallery in Washington and subsidized its building. To this nucleus were added a selection of the B 309 Widener collection, the highly varied Kress collection and a selection of the notable pictures owned by Chester Dale. The National Gallery, thanks to N 274 donations, is continually being enlarged.

Another remarkable European collection made by an industrialist of the second generation on neutral soil was that of Heinrich Thyssen, born in 1875 in the Ruhr and died at Lugano in 1947. In its rather impersonal and museum-like selection of recognized

Gothic master of Lübeck, Bernt Notke, owned by an Elbing merchant guild, went to the Museum für Kunst und Gewerbe in Hamburg. A similar item from Riga is today in the Lüneburg Museum. The House of Wettin, the former royal Saxon dynasty, gave the Louvre a crown reliquary which Saint Louis, King of France, had once presented to the Dominicans of Liège. They also gave the Museum of Art in Cleveland a hunting scene by Cranach. The Dukes of Gotha sold their celebrated early medieval Echternach Gospels to the Nuremberg Museum and Rembrandt's *Self-Portrait as a Young Man* to the Munich Pinakothek.

In Germany itself, some of the items from the Berlin museums took part in the general migration of works of art from east to west. The famous Roman Hildesheim Silver Hoard is today housed in the Municipal Museum of the town in whose immediate neighbourhood it came to light. The Guelph treasure, which has been somewhat diminished by sales abroad, is now shown in the fortress of Dankwarderode in Brunswick.

Since 1945 similar things have been happening in Austria. In 1951 Count Czernin of Vienna sold Dürer's *Portrait of a Clergyman* for $200,000 to a New York dealer for the Kress Collection (now in the National Gallery, Washington) and handed over the still very considerable remaining portion of the collection on loan to the Salzburg Residenz-Galerie. This example was followed by Count Schönborn-Buchheim. Prince Liechtenstein took his fine family collection from Vienna to Vaduz, and for some time art dealers have been dipping into this great reservoir. Important pictures from this collection, which until 1939 was one of the greatest sights of central 144 Europe, have already travelled across the Atlantic, to the National Galleries in Washington and Ottawa 276 among other places.

Since about 1950 a new industrialization has brought to most countries of the western world an unexpected rise in business activity. This has led to an important increase in the stock of art treasures owned by museums at the expense of their previous possessors, who were either the hereditary nobility or private individuals of bourgeois status. The Greek *Chatsworth Head* was acquired from its owner, the Duke of Devonshire, by the British Museum. The Earl of Radnor sold the *Israelites Crossing the Red Sea* by Poussin to the National Gallery of Victoria in Melbourne.

German curators were particularly concerned to close the gap which had been created during the Third Reich through the confiscation of 'degenerate' art. The works by Munch, van Gogh, Gauguin, Marc and Kokoschka, which at that time had been

288 In the beginning of the twentieth century the head of Nefertiti came to be accepted as the artistic ideal of female beauty, thereby eclipsing the Greek goddesses and Raphael Madonnas of former times. Nefertiti's glory has scarcely diminished to this day, and she remains the prize possession of the Berlin Museums

virtually thrown away, could not be recovered, but in a number of other cases arrangements could be made for an exchange. The Bremen Kunsthalle again owns Corinth's *Portrait of the Painter Grönvold*, and the Mannheim Kunsthalle Beckmann's *Pierrot and Columbine*. N 277

Many purchases could not be effected by official action alone. Industrial firms now took the place of the discreetly helpful bourgeois art-lover. Most of

289　The beginning of this century saw a fantastic increase in the popularity of the Greek artist Theotocopoulos (El Greco). In 1910 his *Annunciation* (left) was still in Budapest; it is now in São Paulo, Brazil

290　In 1895 the National Gallery in London received El Greco's *Christ Driving the Traders from the Temple* (above) as a gift from Sir J. C. Robinson. Today the Gallery owns three works by the master

them, however, were not prepared to agree to anonymity. In respected German galleries there are pictures hung today with labels such as 'A gift from [such and such a company]'. Nevertheless there are encouraging exceptions. The industrialists of Milan, who gave to the Museo del Castello Sforzesco in their native town Michelangelo's *Rondanini Pietà*, refrained from asking that an advertisement of their firms be placed directly in front of the sculpture.

12

278

At the present, prices in the world art market are rising still further. Particularly in the eastern Mediterranean, in Latin America and Japan, collectors have begun to appear with adequate resources at their disposal. But the boom is limited mainly to paintings of acknowledged masters, which it will always be easy to sell. In 1962 the New York Metropolitan Museum acquired Rembrandt's *Aristotle Contemplating the Bust of Homer* for $2,300,000.

B 236

155

291 Since his rediscovery, El Greco's popularity has not waned, and in the past decade fortunes have been paid for his paintings by museums in Berlin, New York and Washington. His *Christ on the Cross with Landscape* now belongs to the Cleveland Museum of Art

Rubens' *Adoration of the Magi*, which was once destined for a convent in Louvain, Belgium, fetched £275,000 at the 1959 auction of the Duke of Westminster's collection in London. The Stuttgart Staatsgalerie managed to obtain an early picture by Picasso for DM 1,200,000. Corot's *Italian Woman*, which changed hands in 1936 for $25,000, fetched $275,000 when sold to the Greek shipowner, Stavros Niarchos.

366

The general intellectual climate between 1890 and 1950 had a strong influence on collecting and the policy followed by museums. Around 1890 the younger generation often felt the need to break away from the 'unspiritual' tendencies of the capitalist movement. A thoughtless worship of progress and materialism was considered dangerous. Refinement

became the main objective. The new feeling about life found expression in both a major and a minor key. Optimists felt like the Berlin art critic Meier-Graefe, who liked to behave partly as a Prussian officer and partly as a Bohemian from Montmartre. 'We seem very decadent to ourselves, but are really ready to jump to the ceiling from sheer joie de vivre.' 'Art as celebration of life' was in those days an often repeated catch-word. The collection of the Austrian coal magnate Marcel von Nemes, which was shown publicly for the first time in Budapest in 1910 and contained early Netherlandish panels and paintings by El Greco, Rubens, Goya, Manet and Cézanne, was called by G. von Terey, at that time director of the Budapest Museum, 'a jubilant dance, joyous in its colours'.

This tendency had a melancholy and rather precious counterpart in the mysteriousness of Gustave Moreau's paintings. Art for everyone was something that displeased the aesthetes, who 'sought to make a face out of the grimace of the time'. Meier-Graefe asked that 'the mob' N 280 should be shut out of the museums. 'We experience so much so hastily and with so little reverence or clarity,' complained the young Hugo von Hof- N 281 mannsthal in 1892.

The aestheticizing tendencies, in whose stylistic expression the influence of Asia was perceptible, gradually developed as early as 1900 into a general N 282 criticism of culture and a weariness of Europe. 'To become a savage again and create a new world', was an often quoted saying of Strindberg's. 'The important thing today is not to have good pictures', wrote Meier-Graefe, 'first let us have good walls'. In the Futurist Manifesto, which preached a love for the machine and the straight line, a new phenomenon was already visible (though before the First World War the indications were still slight): a desire for the sobriety and elegant precision of technology. The nineteenth century was being attacked from many sides.

Lichtwark, curator of the Hamburg Kunsthalle, opposed the practice of hanging pictures in several rows one next to the other in over-filled galleries. An 'artistic spirit' should give a new shape to such 'storerooms'. In 1908 the German periodical N 283 *Museumskunde* called upon curators to 'cleanse', according to the principles of the modern style, where once over-abundance had confused.

In museums devoted to antiquities, reliefs were no longer to be fixed into the walls but were to stand free. The practice of setting up busts in a symmetrical arrangement or even arranging them according to size was now frowned on. Bode's principle of uniting paintings, sculptures and a few isolated pieces of old furniture in a single room was rejected from all sides. In historicizing period rooms, masterpieces were lowered to the level of 'decorative marginal notes'. At a meeting in 1903 of the German Workers' Welfare Society, devoted to the theme of 'Museums as places of popular education', a young museum curator laid it down that 'great works of art are not a means of decoration. They should be placed on an altar, not over a sofa.'

In the Far East, as we know, pictures painted on material that can be rolled up are displayed only one at a time. In the United States this idea had combined around 1880 with the Pre-Raphaelite dream of an aesthetic chapel, and soon this was taken up in London. In vain Bode warned people against the 'Japanese principle of isolating works of art up to the point of scattering them far

292 Before El Greco's sudden popularity, Wilhelm von Bode, the Director of the Berlin Museums, received this *Mater Dolorosa* by El Greco as a makeweight in a purchase of Dutch paintings. He regarded the painting as unimportant and transferred it to the Strasbourg Museum

apart'. The authorities of the National Gallery in London decided shortly before 1900 to hang every picture at a considerable distance from its neighbour and only to have one row of pictures on each wall. In 1906 the Berlin National Gallery followed this example and two years later—at first only in the Rembrandt Room—the Louvre.

The question of the colour of the walls was also dragged into the argument. A mood of solemnity, of holiness should be communicated to visitors by means of the wall covering. At a time when all living-rooms were kept dark, bright violet or radiant white were best designed to fulfil this task. In Germany old masters, for instance panel pictures from the time of Dürer, were hung against a white background for the first time in the Munich Pinakothek in 1910. Of the frames in natural wood with Jugendstil designs, which were produced at this period, one surrounding a picture by Refinger

293 Though Magnasco became popular at much the same time as El Greco, the prices paid for his work remained relatively low. *The Shipwreck* (above) is in the Phillips Collection in Washington, D. C.

294 Goya's demoniac fantasies were not really known or greatly valued until the beginning of the twentieth century. This scene from 'El hechizado por fuerza' has been in the National Gallery, London, since 1896 ▶

in the Staatsgalerie in Augsburg and one belonging to a painting of Schäuffelein in the Stuttgart Gallery have remained well preserved. In the British Museum Asiatic Saloon, and in many other museums of the English-speaking world, walls also received fresh colour.

The revolt against the historical and didactic tendency of the outmoded 'museum of learning' resulted about 1910 in the revival of the old idea of single rooms for the most powerful paintings. Algarotti had just such a room in mind in Dresden in 1742. In Vienna in 1780, Mechel with his art-historical arrangement had prepared the way for

several later generations. But in 1910 Wilhelm Worringer attacked the museums which were 'mere dead herbaria illustrating a process of development' and which 'only recorded history instead of making it'. In Munich, Tschudi held an exhibition of the Nemes collection in 1911 and showed paintings of the fifteenth and nineteenth centuries next to one another. When Tschudi died shortly before the outbreak of the First World War he had just begun to throw out all works of mediocre value in the Pinakothek and to fill two rooms with the major works of recent and even contemporary German and French painters.

N 284

The new ideas found supporters in the United States just as quickly as they did in Europe. In the new Boston Museum of Fine Arts, which was completed in 1907, the main storey contained works N 285 of the first order. It was explained to American art-lovers that a museum was not only a 'kind of scientific or social instrument' but that it 'should serve essentially to give the highest type of pleasure to those able to experience it'.

The tendencies described above were in line with an idea discussed in Germany—that of an 'Elite Museum'. In it, if possible, the ancient Egyptian sculptures of Berlin, the Romanesque tapestries of the Quedlinburg churches, and the Darmstadt Holbein *Madonna* could be united. Hellenistic and Roman sculpture, minor Dutch painters and the like were to be excluded and those epochs were to be stressed 'whose works are particularly close to

our own feelings'. A master of architecture was to N 28 erect this new all-German central museum upon a height not far from some small centrally located town. N 28

Although such Utopian ideas were expressed, there was no lack of advocates of views which had been generally held till then. In particular Bode never wearied of defending the liberal point of view. 'If the visitor has to look around, as he does now, and decide for himself what appears good to him, he will be much more likely to find his way to pleasure and understanding than if people dictate to him what he is to see and admire'.

In the collections and museums that were predominantly concerned with modern art, the new tendencies exercized here and there a greater influence. 'The organic art of space' was to make the museum a total work of art. To arrange his Folkwang-Museum in Hagen, Osthaus summoned one of the fathers of the Jugendstil, the Belgian van de Velde. Paintings from Daumier's era and relatively recent pieces of sculpture were joined by 'truly noble objects from the earliest up to the most recent time'; N 28 there where also natural products, insects, fossils and minerals. Here the pantheistically-inclined 'fin de

295 The rejection of nineteenth-century realism also brought about a change in collectors' tastes with regard to Dutch painting. Momper, a contemporary of El Greco, found acclaim among connoisseurs with his fantasticated precipitous mountain landscapes

296 After 1900 enthusiasm for the positive, temporal style of sixteenth-century Venetian artists such as Palma Vecchio and Paolo Veronese diminished. They were replaced by Tintoretto, the predecessor of El Greco. Tintoretto's *Moses striking Water from the Rock* is now in Frankfurt

siècle' came strangely near to the old idea of the 'Kunstkammer' as a 'Theatrum Mundi'.

For Osthaus and men like him the prime purpose of a collection of works of art was to awaken reverence and devotion. Museums were to be temples, and those who directed them were addressed as though they were the keepers of sanctuaries, the priests of a temple. Art was assigned the function of replacing religion. Altarpieces in churches 'point towards God', wrote Meier-Graefe, but the mystery of art was something higher than anything pertaining to religion. In this age deserted by all the gods, the museum must become our sole rescuing anchor.

The 'education for art through art', now no longer tied to any minimum of actual knowledge, was to be the right of men and women of whatever degree of education. In Great Britain ideas of this sort had already been expressed soon after the middle of the nineteenth century. They now became more widely diffused. The Museum of Art in Toledo, Ohio, wooed the public in 1935 with the slogan: 'a hospital gives health to the sick; a museum does more: it turns the healthy into better men.'

London was probably the first place in the world where—around 1910—museums were opened in the evening, so that the population could visit them even on working days. Shortly before this Lichtwark in Hamburg had declared that it was necessary to bring art out of the museum on to the street. Lichtwark was enthusiastic about 'People's Centres' in the suburbs, where a hall for music, a place for sport, a collection of natural objects and a small art museum should all be joined together. He appealed to the great old-established museums by saying that we did not want a museum that simply stands and waits, but an institution that seeks to play an active part in the people's education.

The voices which, since the days of Nietzsche and Strindberg, van Gogh and Toulouse Lautrec, had been expressing their hatred of the cultural tradition and urging a Utopian desire for renewal, intensified

297 From about 1890 onwards, people's awareness of the fact that they were living in a quickly changing world resulted in the early recognition of contemporary artists. Soon after 1900 Gauguin's paintings could be seen in collections throughout the world. His *Nevermore* (above) is in the Courtauld Institute Galleries in London

298 The receptiveness of individual Americans to the latest trends in art became noticeable around the turn of the century. The collector Arthur Jerome Eddy bought Franz Marc's *The Bewitched Mill* (right) almost as soon as the artist had completed it, and it is now in the Chicago Institute of Art

in the epoch of the First World War. In France the artists in the van of this movement were called 'les Fauves'—the beasts. In Germany the formula 'Expressionism' was invented. The spokesmen of the new radical ideas mocked at painters like Gauguin and called them 'perfumed romantics'. The 'art for art's sake' view of the 'fin de siècle' had merely given expression to a narrow self-centered mind and was a retreat into an ivory tower. The artist had to turn towards life again. 'If the museum diminished art would grow'. When, as occasionally happened, artists sold their pictures to museums, they did so unwillingly. They preferred to 'work for life' and were glad to receive commissions from churches, school authorities, industry and private individuals, all of which the previous generation had thought to be fetters of the artist's creative freedom.

In these years public collections of Old Masters again showed an astonishing readiness to hand over major works to their places of origin. The panels of Tommaso da Modena in the Vienna Gallery

were returned to the Chapel of Burg Karlstein; the Church of San Zeno in Verona had its Mantegna altar set up again in 1918; the Uffizi in Florence handed over its panels by Fra Angelico to the monastery of San Marco; Titian's *Assumption* returned to its place in the choir of the Frari Church in Venice. N 289

Pictures, it was said in 1913, should not induce comfort, nor be a delight to the eye. Rather they should impart an electric shock and add an extra dimension to the spirit. Art as the craft of masters was an outmoded conception; art as a miracle spoke to all. Meier-Graefe sought 'freedom from the materialistic splendour of the Venetians' in El N 290 Greco. 'In the desecrated north, let his Madonnas, behind whose Grecian foreheads lurks the maidenly lust of a Judith' for murder, arouse 'the storm that will carry us forward.'

Picasso, after his El Greco period and the Blue Period pictures, gave a fresh cue to the Art Nouveau phase of 1907 by introducing two masks from the Congo in his *Demoiselles d'Avignon*. At the same time Kirchner and other German artists of the Brücke circle discovered in the Dresden Ethnological

Museum the African world of forms. Art as a miracle was represented for the Europeans by a Negro idol or a primitive object of folk art. The deliberate shock-effect of such works was crassly realized about 1920 in German collections and museums. Dance masks from the South Seas took the place of Lenbach portraits, enormous worm-eaten and fragmentarily preserved medieval wooden crucifixes mingled in the salons of bankers with Expressionist works, which conservative art-lovers condemned as 'crude sailors' art'. In the museums of the Rhineland the most up-to-date art was shown together with ancestor-figures of primitive peoples.

In the English-speaking world similar trends and tastes were in evidence. The American, Albert C. Barnes set his extraordinary collection of modern paintings next to works by the French primitives and Negro sculptures in his private gallery at Merrion, Pennsylvania. The effect of such juxtapositions can best be seen nowadays in the Courtauld Institute in

299 The development that led from Gauguin to the Fauves in France and the Expressionists in Germany was accompanied by the discovery of primitive art around 1910. Objects that had previously interested only anthropologists now became expressive works of art. This war-god originates from Hawaii

300 Many collectors juxtaposed the most modern works of art and crude Negro or medieval peasant sculpture. The German banker Eduard von der Heydt was one of the most important of these innovators about the time of the First World War. These Sudanese ancestor figures were formerly in his collection

London. Paintings by Rouault and Seurat, peasant pottery, a mask from the Congo and an 'ancestor guardian figure' from Equatorial Africa are all placed together in one of the rooms.

The refined colours of the 'fin de siècle' now appeared sickly to the younger generation. In the Hanover museum, Gothic statues were placed in front of deep coloured walls. The stairway of this great museum building, constructed about 1900, was painted red, green and blue in abstract fashion so as 'to make a contribution to the miracle of life.' In the Städelsches Kunstinstitut in Frankfurt dark blue was chosen as the background for the small early fifteenth-century panels; in Oldenburg a dark violet was decided upon.

In the mid-1920's the trends just described were followed by a reaction which took several forms. Many painters and sculptors became once again 'of this world'. The German search for new objectivity ('Neue Sachlichkeit'), the Italian group 'Valori Plastici' and similar movements in France and the Anglo-Saxon countries attracted public notice.

The new phase might sometimes have neo-Classical overtones as in many of Picasso's pictures, or it might strike a geometric and technological note, as did Léger and others. The same tendencies were to be seen in the realm of museums. Museum buildings which owe much to the High Renaissance or neo-Classical styles were erected almost everywhere between 1930 and 1940. In Rome there was the Pinacoteca Vaticana, in Paris the Musée de l'Art Moderne, in London the additional rooms donated by Lord Duveen to the British Museum and National Gallery; in America the new National Gallery in Washington.

327
332
324

At the same time, the style of Le Corbusier, which had spread over several continents and was related to the Bauhaus in Germany, gave rise to a new, soberly technological ideal for a museum first consistently realized by Morris and O'Connor in Hartford, Connecticut. White walls, regarded in 1900 as providing a solemn and festive contrast to pictures by Böcklin and Gauguin, now seemed to speak—in the post-Expressionist years—with the voice of a healthy and prosaic objectivity. Whether the exterior of the buildings had pillars or gave a factory-like effect, the brightness of the interior was in each case the same. Meier-Graefe now grew enthusiastic about rooms where, 'with all the devices of the modern age, visibility is enhanced —sober as in an operating theatre'.

292

While the neo-Classical type of public collection clung to the conventional framework and hung pictures slightly above eye-level, galleries and

301 Particular value was attached to African Benin art, in which one can see an element of European influence introduced by the Portuguese in the sixteenth century. In this ivory mask the hair-decoration consists of a row of tiny heads representing Portuguese killed

museums in the style of Le Corbusier everywhere stressed their character as a storehouse and place of study. The frames were painted white or made from light metal, and in some cases dispensed with altogether, since they were mistakenly thought of as 'ornaments' rather than a neutral zone. In museums of this kind all the paintings and sculpture were shown at low wall level. There was no intention of presenting 'works of art', but only of displaying 'documents'.

After the end of the Second World War the public, which all over the world had been cut off for years from the great masterpieces, crowded into exhibitions both large and small. Sections of the population which had hitherto held aloof, and the new generation which had only just grown up, joined the rest. The large numbers involved had an intoxicating effect: 60,000 people saw the principal works of the Munich museums in Berne, and even more saw the works on loan from the London museums in Hamburg. Two hundred pictures from the Berlin museums travelled 20,000 miles in America. Millions of visitors crowded in front of them in fourteen different cities. The 'flight of the museums to the exhibitions' became the norm.

When the material reasons for these travelling exhibitions ceased to exist, a number of museums continued the practice to which they had grown accustomed. The São Paulo Museu de Arte showed an original painting by Rembrandt for days in the window of a department store. Even Samuel Kress, a man of great delicacy of feeling, exhibited a painting by Giorgione for a time in one of his New N 293 York shops. On occasion fashion-displays took place amongst paintings by Tintoretto. Sometimes works were taken from museums to popular resorts. Around 1950 the idea was being entertained of having a branch of the Munich Pinakothek set up at the winter sports centre of Garmisch-Partenkirchen.

The fact that works of art were continually travelling was not without detrimental effect on their preservation. What was perhaps more important, the more thoughtful part of the art-loving public insisted on seeing a suitable number of works in their usual place. In some museums the authorities were anxious to find a thoroughly startling solution to this problem. When the contents of the museums began to be divided up into 'exhibition collections' and 'storage', the ideas expressed by Tschudi around 1910 found new defenders who held that museums of bygone art only have a right to exist in so far as N 294 they reflect the artistic situation of today. Under the influence of such arguments the curator of one of the Rhineland museums dared to show his antique works of art only when, by way of legitimizing his action, he placed between them a number of lithographs by Picasso with Graeco-Roman mythological subjects. Countless Dutch and Flemish pictures of the seventeenth century and German works of art of the later nineteenth century remained in the cellars. Some museum directors endeavoured to make the public better acquainted with what they considered to be important works by putting them next to others, related by style or motif, from epochs which at that moment happened to be in fashion. Such daring juxtapositions could degenerate into a questionable habit.

In relation to content as well as to form, certain developments of the first third of the century were

once more taken up in 1945. After the Second World War a neo-Classical note was struck by many museums in Latin and Anglo-Saxon countries. In the Brera Gallery in Milan, a Mantegna Room was given the character of a shrine through the introduction of antique marble pillars. The walls of the Grande Galerie of the Louvre were furnished with niches surrounded by pillars with gilt capitals, containing antique statues of only decorative importance.

As had happened twenty years before, the technological movement was opposed to such tendencies. In 1948 its champions requested, though unsuccessfully, that the ruins of the Munich Pinakothek should be cleared away and replaced by a group of modern pavilions. The idea of the 'objective' museum, which had first triumphed in Hartford in 1934, was accepted in Germany in 1950, when the Essen Museum was newly built and the Germanisches Museum in Nuremberg extended.

In the exhibition rooms of the Palazzo Bianco in Genoa in 1952 the technological conception *341* found its extreme expression. Unframed paintings suspended from iron stanchions hanging freely in space, together with fragments of Gothic sepulchral sculptures mounted on hydraulic ramps, were surrounded by showcases made of glass and light metal, with neon tubes that served as interior lighting. If Le Corbusier had once spoken of the house as a machine to be lived in, the museum was now to become a machine for presenting works of art. The example of Genoa was followed in many other places. In the Venice Accademia Giorgione's *La Tempesta* was taken out of its frame, and in the Kunsthistorisches Museum in Vienna early German panels were hung free in space and sometimes exhibited without their frames, or hung on white free-standing screens which were carried by thin metal supports. This mode of presentation changed the well-known works so remarkably that they might be compared to a Beethoven Symphony in an atonal transposition.

XXIII Towards the end of the nineteenth century connoisseurs began to collect Asian works of art in earnest. This painting from the manuscript of the Persian book of Kings (Shahnama) by Firdausi is in the Metropolitan Museum in New York

The first protests against the aberrations of the technological movement came from Paris. Museums of art must not be 'abstract, like a laboratory or clinic', nor must they be inspired by the ideal of a 'neutral, stripped, stark arrangement'. Glass cases should not remind one of a dentist's instrument cupboard; every picture with perspective, from the fifteenth to the twentieth centuries, demanded an enclosing frame, whereas abstract compositions, which often were not a formal unity at all, could remain unframed. Free-standing screens were no doubt of value in a department store, but many other devices of the technological movement came, all too obviously, from the arsenal of modern window-dressing. In contrast with the over-bright sobriety of the 'musée laboratoire', a new formula was devised in Paris: the creation of a lively environment that could develop into the 'spectacle suggestif'. The Expressionist heritage did good service in the realization of these aims.

The cold white gave place to warm tones. The *Mona Lisa* was given a wine-red velvet background, the Rubens cycle a deep burgundy red; in the Musée de l'Art Moderne the walls behind the pictures were coloured lemon yellow, brick red and Prussian blue. The thirst for colour, so long suppressed, was celebrated in an orgy that reached its peak in the London Council of Europe Exhibition, 'The Romantic Movement', in the summer of 1959. In some ten rooms of the Tate Gallery the walls were covered with glaringly coloured cloth and a valerium hung up above; in the French Room a poison green mingled with a blood red, punctuated by thin black lance-like staffs with gilded points.

Among the means by which sobriety was to be avoided the principal one was artificial light used in permanently darkened rooms. Small medieval objets d'art were to be grouped together in 'treasure chambers'. When these rooms were open in the evenings, there were to be not only spotlights, but even music from loudspeakers. If the museum had been ranged next to the library in periods of enlightenment, it was now to go beyond mere theatre and draw near to the modern world of the film.

Today, in place of the extremes resulting from a misunderstood conception of a 'living' or 'liberated' museum, one can observe quieter solutions showing a better sense of proportion. Instead of the fashionable high-level art exhibitions which 'uproot culture', the museum should offer what it has to show at the place where it belongs, and 'be attractive when people feel like turning to it, but not shrilly to solicit attention from those who are busy with affairs of their own'. B 214

For old and new art-lovers a museum must become 'a region for self-examination and a continuous dialogue'. Violence should not be done to B 154 the creation of the artist; otherwise 'an over-ingenious apparatus of illumination could falsify the work'. The true place of the museum lies midway between the library and the stage, and not far from that of the concert hall.

In recent years, there have been instances of colour applied to gallery walls in a manner that discreetly harmonizes with the general effect of the pictures—a dull brown for the Dürer Room in the Prado Museum in Madrid, olive green for the Holbein portraits in the Louvre, violet as a background for the deep-coloured pictures of the Pre-Raphaelites in the Tate Gallery in London. In the British Museum the walls above the yellowish antique reliefs have been painted light blue or turquoise, as a result of which the marble gains in warmth. In Paris the authorities are anxious to replace the ceiling light wherever possible with natural side-light. The windows of the Grande Galerie of the Louvre, which look onto the Seine and were closed more than a hundred years ago, have now been partly re-opened.

The practice of hanging pictures systematically in rows with one base-line had spread early in the century all over Europe from the National Gallery in London, which was also the first to depart from the practice. The arrangement at Trafalgar Square has become freely rhythmical, though symmetry has not been rigidly avoided. To display smaller pictures in two rows, one on top of the other, or to hang large still-lifes of the Rubens period high up, is no longer reckoned as sacrilegious in either London, Paris or Munich, and the fact that showcases tend once again to be much more densely packed, as in the exhibition 'L'Occident Romain' in the Louvre in 1963, is another sign of our changing attitudes in such matters. After

XXIV At the beginning of the twentieth century early medieval works of art, which until then had been collected primarily with a view to their historical significance, began to be valued on aesthetic grounds. American collectors took an active part in this shift of emphasis. This Byzantine reliquary for a fragment of the Cross was brought back from the East by a crusader

302 Picasso incorporated African masks in his *Les Demoiselles d'Avignon*. A few years later several of the German Expressionists, like Nolde in this *Still-life*, did the same

the re-organization of the Musée de l'Impressionnisme in Paris in 1959, it was observed that all the pictures were hung perceptibly higher on the walls than before.

In Paris René Huyghe recognized the dangers of the technological movement particularly early: around 1937 he was already asking for richer and more traditional environments for old paintings. In the Louvre there are now many beautiful early gold frames from the seventeenth and eighteenth centuries which have been acquired since the end of the Second World War. The Medici series of Rubens have been given new black and gold frames, faithfully recalling the Antwerp type of frame of the early seventeenth century. Old gold frames can also be extremely effective with pictures by Gauguin and Cézanne. As for showcases containing highly valuable objets d'art of gold, silver or ivory, there has been a return to organic materials. The glass is held not by light metals but by wood, the base inside the case being covered with textiles.

368

The period rooms, which have so often encountered sharp criticism and which in the final analysis must be viewed as an expression of romantic historicism, have once more found their defenders. In the United States it is pointed out that in a modern, technically stylized museum atmosphere, pictures such as those by Kandinsky would be very much at home, whereas medieval objets d'art would be somewhat estranged from the beholder. A slight indication of the 'actual use of the genuine objects' should be permitted. A period room must not, of course, be turned into a 'stage set'.

N 29

It was the mature creations of Greek sculpture that had appealed to art-lovers of the mid-nineteenth century; the change of taste around 1890 caused people to lay more emphasis on the early phases of Greek art. Rilke, when in the Louvre, no longer paused before the *Venus de Milo*. His most profound experience of ancient art was the torso of an Apollo of about 520 BC from the theatre of Miletus.

The most important central European acquisitions of Greek sculpture immediately before the First World War belonged to the period of transition between the archaic and the classical epochs. Such are the enthroned goddess from Taranto, for which the Berlin Museums paid a million gold marks, and the excellent replica of Myron's *Athena*, which was donated to the newly-founded municipal museum of sculpture, Liebighaus, in Frankfurt. In 1925 the department of antiquities of the Berlin Museums concentrated their means on the purchase of a strictly archaic *Standing Goddess*. At that time the classical red-figure vases enjoyed less regard than the earlier black-figure ones. A secondary branch of archaic art, that of the Etruscans, now became a much sought-after field for collectors. Museum directors and collectors of both the New World and the Old paid tribute to this fashion and were occasionally fobbed off with forgeries.

From about 1910 attention was also paid to post-classical portraits which were thought to express a certain spirituality. The Expressionists were *310* particularly fond of the spiritualized, large-eyed heads of late antiquity, such as that of Constantine the Great in the Uffizi, which had been rejected by Montesquieu as 'totally Gothic', or the so-called *Eutropios* in the Vienna Kunsthistorisches Museum. The sculptures of Palmyra and the mummy portraits from Fayum were accorded places of honour in many museums. Since this period the British Museum has been systematically increasing its stock of late antique art, and has recently acquired N 296 the *Lycurgus Cup* from the fourth century AD.

Devotees of Surrealism were particularly delighted when they saw, in the Uffizi and the Louvre, third-class statues that had been patched together in about 1600 from pieces of varying origin. For Picasso, and other artists and art-lovers who considered themselves avant-garde, the great classical period, along with Ingres and Raphael, became important again at the beginning of the 1920's.

Around 1900 the heritage of ancient Egypt moved out of the quiet world of learned research into the very centre of artistic life. The archaic and at the same time often refined style of Egyptian art harmonized with the taste of Art Nouveau. Painters like Hodler, Gauguin and Maurice Denis took over principles of composition from ancient Egyptian reliefs. At the house of Behrens in the artists' colony in Darmstadt everyone admired the music-room, which had been conceived as a temple of Isis. American collectors and museum directors acquired Egyptian works of art in large numbers. Turning their backs on everything that was loose and picturesque, they preferred hard

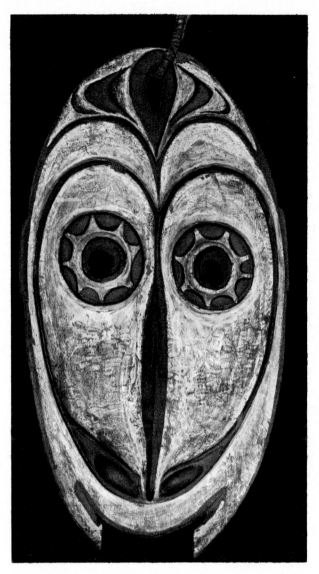

303 In addition to primitive African art, the western world also became interested in carvings from the islands of the South Pacific, such as this mask from New Guinea. The idea of a return to primitivism was common among poets and artists in both Paris and Munich

materials, sculptures of basalt and objets d'art N 297 made from precious stones.

About 1910 those works which combined naturalism and the somewhat Pre-Raphaelite line of a Beardsley were held in particular esteem by the public in both America and Europe. This was the case in works of Amarna art. Overnight, *286-7* Queen Nefertiti became the most beautiful wom- *288* an's head ever produced. Her headdress corresponded to the coiffures of the ladies whom

304 Neo-Classicism had favoured the classical period of Greek art and the Baroque revival its Hellenistic development, but it was not until about 1900 that archaic Greek art really came into its own. This relief from the tomb of Aristion in Athens dates from the sixth century BC (detail)

Klimt, in Vienna before the outbreak of the First World War, painted in profile and with a strong suggestion of Egyptian frontality. From time to time nine different types of reproductions of Nefertiti were sold in the Berlin Museums ranging from postcards to full-size coloured plaster casts. The world fame of Nefertiti outlasted the Second World War. Thousands of American soldiers paid tribute to the Egyptian Queen at the 'art collecting point' of Wiesbaden and disregarded every other work exhibited there. Though we have long since recognized the art of Amarna as 'perfected mannerism with all the charms and weaknesses of such', our age is still subject to its fascination.

A little later than the art of Egypt, that of Asia Minor began to come to the attention of collectors. Around 1925 people began to concern themselves with its earliest epoch. The British Museum at that time received its unique Babylonian Room with the statuette of a goat from the royal cemetery at Ur. Its companion-piece found a home in the University Museum in Philadelphia.

Since about 1890, not only archaic Greek and ancient Egyptian art, but also painting, sculpture and the applied arts of the Middle Ages have moved into the foreground of taste. The Late Renaissance, admired so much in 1870, was now at a discount; the prices of Nuremberg silver and Rhineland earthenware of the late sixteenth century began to fall. Weapon-collectors turned away from the over-engraved and etched armour of the period of Charles V and Philip II to the simpler and more severe products of an earlier age. People took a dislike to the stiff bourgeois characteristics *343*

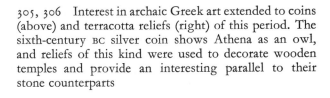

305, 306 Interest in archaic Greek art extended to coins (above) and terracotta reliefs (right) of this period. The sixth-century BC silver coin shows Athena as an owl, and reliefs of this kind were used to decorate wooden temples and provide an interesting parallel to their stone counterparts

of the average early German painter and had misgivings about the flat realism of Florentine sculptors from the circle of Verrocchio.

The 'fin de siècle' rediscovered Grünewald. Huysman's celebrated hymn in honour of one of his Crucifixions shows us how 'the disquieting decadence of this epoch blossoms with an almost perverse joy' in Grünewald's pictures. During the First World War the *Isenheim Altarpiece* was shown in the Munich Pinakothek and there exercised the very greatest influence; it has since gained world fame. Whereas in 1900 the Kunsthalle in Karlsruhe had paid 40,000 marks for two altarpieces, in the middle of the century the National Gallery in Washington had to pay about twenty times as much for *The Small Crucifixion* from the Koenigs Collection in Haarlem.

Art Nouveau and Expressionism brought even less important 'anti-classical' masters of the age of Dürer to positions of honour. Both the early expressive and the later Cranach, who embraced a gothicizing mannerism, began to receive attention. A typical work in Cranach's latter style came to the Philadelphia Museum of Art. In 1949 at the Paris exhibition of the 200 finest pictures in the Berlin Museums, Cranach's *Lucrezia* scored a triumph. Dürer's paintings have been held in esteem since about 1900, particularly those early portraits that are perceptibly Late Gothic.

Since about 1920 the painters of the 'Danube School', especially Altdorfer, have been the subject of much admiration. Kokoschka has repeatedly expressed homage to *The Battle of Alexander on the Issus River* in the Munich Pinakothek. Altdorfer is today

B 192

XXVI

336

N 299

307, 308 Before the beginning of this century collectors
had recognized the value only of pure Greek art, placing
special emphasis on the work of the Athenian masters.
But from 1900 onwards their interest extended to works
of art in which the basic Greek form was influenced by
other cultures. Instances of this change are the Graeco-
Phoenician sculpture (above) and the Graeco-Etruscan
clay tile (right). The latter came from a wooden temple
in Veii

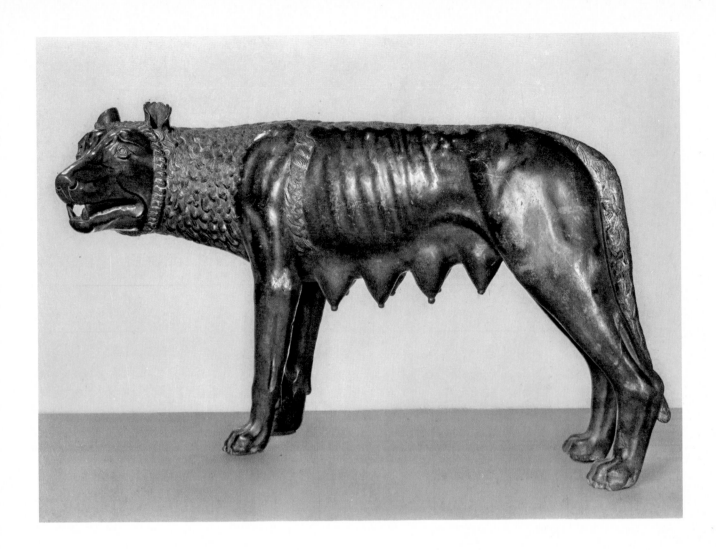

309 The revived interest in archaic Greek art meant that the Capitoline *She-Wolf*, which until then had been venerated as a historical symbol, was now valued as a work of art. Small fifteenth-century copies of the statue soon found buyers. This particular one, formerly in the Castiglione collection in Vienna, is now in the National Gallery in Washington

represented in numerous American museums and, since 1961, in the National Gallery in London.

The 'fin de siècle' rediscovered the star of Hieronymus Bosch. Rilke, during his Paris period, delighted not only in the Romanesque statues of Chartres and the precious series of tapestries of *The Lady and the Unicorn*, but also in the pictures of Bosch. Through the abnormal features of his art the last of the Dutch Gothics became, after the First World War, the patriarch of Surrealism.

Even a conventional collector like Thyssen acquired two pictures by Bosch for his gallery in 1930. Bosch also entered the new museum in São Paulo as one of the representative masters of Europe, with an *Annunciation* which had once been in a monastery in Seville. Original works, copies and imitations of Bosch were brought out from the store-rooms of the older museums and put in places of honour.

Meanwhile fifteenth-century works of the Netherlands emerged as one of the great phases of bygone art. As early as 1913 the Louvre had to give 800,000 francs for a triptych by Rogier van der Weyden, while the Berlin Museums paid the sum of 1,180,000 francs for the centre panel of an altar by Hugo van der Goes which had been discovered in Spain. Mellon was compelled to pay as much for the van Eyck panels from the Hermitage (now in the National Gallery in Washington) as for the paintings of great Italians. The *Belles Heures* of Duc Jean de

Berry, a sort of incunabula of early Netherland painting, went from the Paris mansion of Baron Maurice de Rothschild to The Cloisters in New York.

Next in value were early German paintings from before the time of Dürer, though few major works of this kind came upon the market. Around 1900 numerous early panels, which had found their way into village churches in the seventeenth century, came into the museums of northern Germany. The Hamburg Kunsthalle now regards its Master Bertram altars as its most precious possessions. A Bertram altar which had been hidden in an English country house suddenly turned up in 1930 and was acquired by the Landesmuseum in Hanover for about 300,000 marks. The Metropolitan Museum in New York acquired a Westphalian panel from about 1420 which came from the Marienkirche in Bielefeld, while Gulbenkian included a *Presentation in the Temple* by Lochner in his exquisite collection. 254 N 301

An interest even more lively than that felt for painted panels was aroused both in Germany and abroad by late medieval sculpture. In 1913 the Berlin Museums already had to pay 52,000 marks for a figure of the Virgin Mary from Dangolsheim, while a wooden group from Gnadenzell of Christ and St John, which had been unsuccessfully offered to the Stuttgart Museum some years before for 600 marks, was purchased by the Museum of Art in Cleveland in 1928 for 150,000 marks. The Lübeck Museum failed to acquire the *Reval Altar* by Bernt Notke, but in 1922 was happy to obtain at least a faithful cast of the Stockholm *St George* group by this great artist. In recent years the number of sculptures by Riemenschneider in the United States has risen to ten. 319 317 321

The change in collectors' tastes over the past seventy-five years is particularly evident in the assessment that is made of early Italian panel paintings. The epoch of Gauguin turned from the harmony of the High Renaissance to what was often the hard colour of the Quattrocento. In this context, traditions which led from the Nazarenes to Ruskin were of some importance in the English-speaking countries. Around 1880 Ruskin's views had influenced the elder Walters in Baltimore and some fifteen years later caused Mrs Gardner in Boston to acquire paintings by Filippino Lippi and Botticelli. It is significant that she purchased at the same time pictures by the Pre-Raphaelite Dante Gabriel Rossetti, one of the forerunners of English Art Nouveau. In England and America the somewhat precious Crivelli, who had already been highly praised in London around 1820, again enjoyed particularly high esteem. Mrs Gardner purchased an important picture by him. Already in 1900 the National Gallery in London had seven of N 302

310, 311 About 1910 the art of late antiquity came into fashion, thereby reversing the judgment of the lovers of classical antiquity, who had scorned these staring, stylized portraits as degenerate. This Hellenistic mummy portrait from Fayum (above) and the sculpture from Ephesus (opposite) were regarded as important acquisitions

312 This painting by Rouault, *The Holy Shroud* (1937–38), was based on the stylized, full-face portraits of Christ to be seen in mosaics in churches in Ravenna, Rome and Monreale

his works. Bode, as so often, followed the English taste and added to the two Crivelli pictures already in the possession of the Berlin Museums three others, among them the large *Sacra Conversazione* from the Earl of Dudley's collection in London. The New York collector Philip Lehman acquired a *Madonna* by Crivelli in 1912.

As the severe compositions of Cézanne's paintings drew art-lovers increasingly under their spell, people felt that Botticelli, Crivelli and their like were too near to Art Nouveau. The more austere and formal masters of the fifteenth century, such as Piero della Francesca, Luca Signorelli, Uccello and occasionally even Mantegna, now came to be respected.

Around 1910 Henri Rousseau (le Douanier) copied paintings by Pisanello in the Louvre.

It was not long before the step was taken from the fourteenth century back to the thirteenth. In Berlin in 1905 Meier-Graefe placed Giotto at the side of Gauguin, while in Frankfurt Georg Swarzenski attacked the realism of Verrocchio and praised the painting of the Trecento. Avant-garde collectors in New York in 1910 valued Giotto and Sassetta as much as Raphael and Titian. Many painted panels by B 33 fourteenth-century Italians went straight to America from their countries of origin during the period of the First World War. The early Sienese school enjoyed particular regard during the Expressionist period. N 303

313 Byzantine art which had, on the whole, been regarded as relatively unimportant was re-evaluated in the twentieth century in terms of its affinity with Christian art of late antiquity. This Russian painting dates from the twelfth century

Mellon reckoned the *Nativity with the Prophets Isaiah and Ezekiel* by Duccio (National Gallery, Washington) among his most valuable possessions, but in the last few decades the pendulum has swung once more to the Florentines of the Giotto School.

N 304

'Art as a miracle' was what works from the tenth to the twelfth centuries became for the world of collectors. At least as soon as in Europe, taste in the United States went back in time from the Gothic 'art of the cathedrals' to the monumental sculpture of the Romanesque epoch. When the 'style-phase 1' of the statues of Chartres reached its greatest fame Mrs Gardner already possessed three Romanesque capitals, and the New York collector Michael Dreicer a statue of a prophet. Whole monastery cloisters, with richly ornamented capitals and numerous sepulchral sculptures from southern France and Spain, particularly from Catalonia of the Romanesque epoch, went over to the New World.

N 305

N 306

The most important example of this trend in taste was The Cloisters in New York. There had been some anticipation of this in Europe from the Musée des Monuments Français in Paris to the Bavarian National Museum in Munich. The Cloisters was rightly accounted by American art-lovers as the most considerable attempt yet made in their country to recreate the whole effect of arts in the past. Twenty years ago an enthusiast remarked that only on this spot in the New World could one obtain an idea of the greatest art that the Christian era has produced.

In the complex of buildings known as The Cloisters there are a number of parts of Romanesque churches and monasteries, transferred stone by stone from Europe to the United States, among them the apse of the Church of Fuentedueña in Spain. There are adjoining buildings with museum halls and a garden that was planted according to a list that has been preserved of the flowers and other plants in a garden of Charlemagne. Wall graves of Spanish noblemen, the statue of a saintly king from the Abbey Church of St-Denis and a Blessed Virgin from Strasbourg Cathedral are the chief examples of monumental stone sculpture.

B 246

320

318
N 307

While the New York Cloisters was rapidly growing in the 1920's, tribute was also paid to this trend in other American cities. Today we find the cloisters

314 For centuries illuminated manuscripts of the early Middle Ages had remained unnoticed in sacristies and monastery libraries. In 1951 the Echternach Gospels (*c.* 1020) was bought by the Germanisches Museum in Nuremberg from the Sachsen-Coburg family for DM 1.100.000

from Saint-Denis-des-Fontaines in the Philadelphia Museum of Art, and the collection of Oberlin College, Ohio, contains two Romanesque statues of bishops from the façade of the Abbey Church at Moreaux-en-Poitou. Collections of similar objects may also be found in Toledo, Ohio, and elsewhere.

In European museums a similar shift from the age of Dürer and the Gothic to the early Middle Ages was also in progress, though in a less conspicuous

manner. Thus the Bavarian National Museum acquired in 1898 an Italian *Madonna* dated approximately 1200; similar items found their way into the Berlin Kaiser Friedrich Museum and into the newly-founded Liebighaus in Frankfurt.

During the Expressionist period the collecting of medieval sculpture and carving became, though only for a while, a widespread fashion. Around 1925 the banker Eduard von der Heydt placed a large medieval crucifix next to modern paintings and a Buddha in the hotel which he built on Monte Verità near Locarno. On the Rhine all that had once been designated as 'early German' (i. e. about 1460–1520) now disappeared from the houses of art-lovers. In its stead early and late medieval sculpture and carvings were bought which were enjoyed even as fragments. It was not unusual to see Romanesque carving and statues of the twelfth century next to paintings by Nolde or Rouault.

There was a similar change in the matter of ecclesiastical objets d'art and the products of the applied arts in general. Whereas around 1870 in Paris the lover of medieval bric-à-brac was liable to incur ridicule in the auction rooms of Drouot, in 1925 Rhenish enamel of about 1200 was a favourite decoration for tables and sideboards. There was a special liking for the Ottonian period. Anecdotes were told of an American collector who was in the habit of rejecting any product of the applied arts from the thirteenth century as 'too late'. The Cleveland Museum of Art persistently chose quite early pieces from the saleable stock of the Guelph treasure. For some thirty years it has owned a portable altar and two crosses from that collection.

The passion of the public for the eleventh and twelfth centuries diminished somewhat before the Second World War, but the best examples of the early and late Middle Ages still retained value for the trade. About 650 small works of art, mostly dating back to between the tenth and thirteenth centuries, have been acquired for The Cloisters since 1945.

When after the Second World War connoisseurs of modern art admired the sculpture of Brancusi and Moore, special values of expression were discovered in the markedly stylized iron helmets of the *343* Middle Ages. In 1951 Picasso equipped warriors in his painting *Massacre in Korea* with helmets of the age *344* of chivalry, and the art historian Walter Pach discovered a formal relationship between this branch of the medieval applied arts and the sculpture *Mademoiselle Pogany* by Brancusi in the Philadelphia Museum of Art.   B 214

Around 1910 art critics began their first attacks on Raphael. His portraits were declared to be 'bourgeois', his altar pictures not 'religious' at all. Even at very

315 At the beginning of the twentieth century the word Romanesque became almost a term of praise. A fragment of the famous ivory altar which Emperor Otto the Great had donated to Magdeburg Cathedral is now in the Liverpool Museum

N 308

XV

low prices the art trade could scarcely get rid of any majolica with decorations in the style of Raphael or of Italian Renaissance chests, while in the galleries second- and third-rate pictures by artists of the period around 1520 were removed from exhibition and put into storage. If the reputation of the painter of the *Sistine Madonna* tumbled, that of Murillo, the 'Raphael of Seville', dropped almost to zero. In 1940 the Louvre handed over to the Prado Museum *The Immaculate Conception* which it had acquired around 1860 for a fantastically high sum, and received in exchange a quite unimportant portrait by Velazquez. Not a whisper of objection was heard in Paris. In America an expert on the art market declared that a picture by Murillo could not be sold for 'a tenth of the price it had fetched a hundred years ago'.

Tiepolo, whose reputation had risen in the Vienna of Makart's time, was able to preserve his name rather more easily. Since the luxuriant richness of his art had recommended him in the boom period when French Impressionism established its world fame, people were inclined to appreciate the bright quality of his palette. Tschudi praised in his pictures 'the absence of the deep gallery tone', and the painter Slevogt liked to look at the frescoes in the Bishop's Palace at Würzburg.

N 309

A new discovery of the epoch that began in 1890 was Guardi. His colours, usually bright, made possible an Impressionistic interpretation of his art, while the nervous quality of his brushwork was, after 1910, considered an Expressionistic characteristic. From about 1890 to 1920 Guardi thus contrived for one reason or another to enter nearly all the collections and museums. Four of his pictures entered the Kaiser Friedrich Museum between 1899 and 1918; seven of them between 1898 and 1931 entered the

Städelsches Kunstinstitut in Frankfurt, the Dresden Gallery, the Munich Pinakothek, the Kunsthistorisches Museum in Vienna and the Kunsthalle in Hamburg respectively; and fifteen were acquired by the National Gallery in London between 1895 and 1920. In 1956 £10,500 was paid at Christie's auction house in London for a small Guardi, and his popularity shows no signs of decreasing.

Along with Guardi, the masters of the French eighteenth century came once more into the foreground. They benefited by the morbid elegance and non-bourgeois and unrealistic style of art which marked the 'fin de siècle'. In 1895 Oscar Wilde gave the following stage directions for the first act of *An Ideal Husband:* 'Over the wall of the staircase hangs a great chandelier which illumines a large

316 German Expressionists like Nolde and Beckmann recognized an affinity with Grünewald and German sculptors of the late Gothic period whose style resembled Grünewald's. This contorted carving of St Sebastian was made in Germany about 1500

tapestry from a design by Boucher. Two very pretty women are seated together on a Louis XVI sofa. Their affectation of manner has a delicate charm; Watteau would have loved to paint them'.

The National Gallery in London acquired three pictures by Watteau between 1912 and 1925. The New York Metropolitan Museum chose from the pictures of the Hermitage, which were for sale in Leningrad, the painter's *Mezzetin*, once the pearl of the collection of Count Brühl in Dresden. In Berlin a higher value began to be placed on the fine stock of Watteau pictures from the time of Frederick the Great. Because of his 'Impressionist' manner of painting Fragonard was held in higher esteem, but, because of the proverbial frivolity of their themes, his paintings were not greatly sought after by American collectors. H. C. Frick was an early exception when he bought several Fragonard panels originally painted for (and rejected by) Mme du Barry. These are now the feature of a room especially designed for them in the Italianate palace which Frick, with the advice of Duveen, had built on Fifth Avenue, and which is now one of New York's most interesting and intimate museums.

Around 1900 Venetian painting of the sixteenth century received particular attention again. It was no longer relatively classical painters such as Palma Vecchio and his contemporaries that were appreciated but rather the late Titian and Tintoretto, Jacopo Bassano and the fascinating heir of their art, El Greco. In the Louvre in 1899 the young Nolde was copying the richly coloured allegory of the Marchese d'Avalos by Titian. In the Munich Pinakothek the *Crowning with Thorns* became the centre of interest, as did the late picture *Nymph and Shepherd* in the Vienna Gallery. Next to the classical *Sacred and Profane Love* attention was now paid in the Borghese Gallery at Rome to the *Education of Amor* painted fifty years later.

From about 1900 Tintoretto, the great rival of the aged Titian, also came to the fore. Though still rejected by Burckhardt in 1855, he found friends in Ruskin and his circle as far back as 1870. The cultured Paris collector Chéramy paid homage around 1880 to three stars of the first magnitude which he grouped together in a manner that was characteristic of that time: Renoir, Richard Wagner and Tintoretto. But it was only the 'fin de siècle' and Expressionism that did justice to Tintoretto. In 1910 Tschudi took the Gonzaga cycle from the Gallery in Schleissheim to the Pinakothek. Soon afterwards there began Kokoschka's Tintoretto period, of which the finest result is *The Tempest*. In 1914 the Frankfurt Städelsches Kunstinstitut purchased Tintoretto's *Moses striking Water from the Rock*, and in 1917 the Munich Pinakothek acquired his *Mars and Venus*.

XII

296

317 In Stockholm, Reval (Tallinn), and along the whole Baltic coast, Expressionism focussed interest on sculpture by north German artists which had been exported from Lübeck around 1500. In about 1920 the Swedes gave the town of Lübeck a copy of Bernt Notke's *St George* in the Church of St Nicholas in Stockholm

Between 1900 and 1950, 19 paintings in all by Tintoretto were acquired by museums in Berlin, London, Munich, New York, Stockholm, Stuttgart and Vienna; the total was increased to 22 through the acquisition in Vienna of the *Scourging of Christ* in 1923, while the number of Tintorettos in Munich rose to 13 with the *Portrait of a Young Man*, which was added in 1938. In 1949 the public, at the exhibition of 'Masterpieces of the Vienna Museum' in Washington, gave the highest number of votes to Tintoretto's *Susanna and the Elders*, while a portrait of *The Infanta Margarita Teresa* by Velazquez and Titian's *Diana and Callisto* had to be content with the second and third places respectively.

Shortly before 1900 the most sensational discovery of the last hundred years was made. Domenicos Theotocopoulos, the Greek who had been born in the colonial territory of Venice, learned his art in the Venice of Tintoretto and developed his later anti-classical and anti-realist style in Toledo, where he was called 'El Greco'. This most unusual artist was never quite forgotten in Spain, the home of his choice. In 1827 the Prado Museum in Madrid acquired *The Holy Trinity* for the considerable price of 15,000 reals from a sculptor who owned it at the time. El Greco was represented in the 'Spanish Gallery' of the House of Orleans, which created something of a stir in the Paris of 1850. The painter Jean-François Millet was the possessor of El Greco's *St Ildefonso* (now in the National Gallery, Washington), while on the other hand Wilhelm von Bode, in a purchase of Dutch paintings made in 1880, was given a *Mater Dolorosa* by El Greco as a free addition to his purchases. Being fundamentally uninterested in this 292 kind of art, Bode casually handed it over to the Strasbourg Museum which he had arranged.

The deeper features of El Greco's character have only been grasped since about 1890. Tschudi was a witness of this change and declared that people had learnt to understand El Greco through Cézanne. On one occasion in a German exhibition a *Holy Family* by El Greco was hung next to a ballet scene by Degas (who incidentally owned an El Greco himself). Today it strikes us as strange that even before the actual beginning of the Expressionist period, pictures by El Greco were being passionately collected and seemed to go very well, in the eyes of the art-lovers of the day, with works by Rubens and Hals, Constable and Manet, Cézanne and Degas.

The recent argument as to whether it was France or America that rediscovered El Greco is in itself a symptom of a cult which continues as strong as ever. Professor Charles E. Norton of Harvard University had actually acquired before 1900, together with two pictures by Tintoretto, a *Marriage at Cana* by El Greco, obviously an early and still very Venetian picture. At that time, however, Chéramy already possessed *The Disrobing of Christ* (now in the Munich Pinakothek), while the French collector Maurice Kahn owned the *Portrait of the Grand Inquisitor Guevara* (now in the Reinhart Collection in Winterthur). The first three El Greco pictures entered the Louvre in 1893, 1903 and 1908. For the second of these purchases, namely *St Louis*, 70,000 francs were paid. It was in front of this picture that Rilke appears to have had his first experience of El Greco. In 1895 the London National Gallery had been bequeathed El Greco's *Christ Driving the Traders from* 290 *the Temple* which Sir J. C. Robinson had acquired at Christie's in 1877. It is well known that Picasso began to paint pictures in the El Greco manner before 1900, and later destroyed them as being too close to the model and thus valueless. In 1910 the fame of the painter of Toledo had already reached its peak. At that time Meier-Graefe declared El Greco to be 'the sum of all great Frenchmen' and to have 'risen during the course of his life to ever bolder forms, to ever more pure abstractions'.

N 311

On the art market El Greco was quickly recognized as a magnitude which could not be diminished. America, on this occasion, was anxious not to be too late and many of his paintings went from the churches and sacristies of Spain to New York. In 1906 two altarpieces of the Chapel of San José in Toledo were sold to Joseph Widener for a very high sum (now in the National Gallery in Washington). In 1910 prices of up to $100,000 were already being paid for pictures by El Greco. At that time Tschudi exhibited the Nemes Collection including 12 El Grecos in Munich, while Bode, as before,

persistently refused to acquire for Berlin a picture of this painter who had now attained world fame. N 312 The Munich Pinakothek received its first El Greco in 1909, the St Petersburg Hermitage its first (a gift) in 1911.

After the Expressionist phase El Greco's fame momentarily weakened. The Paris El Greco Exhibition in the year of the World Exposition, 1937, was not conspicuously successful. With the second Expressionist wave after 1945, El Greco's star rose again. Whereas in 1895 Wilde had conceived his stage figures 'à la Watteau', Tennessee Williams wanted to have the scenery for his play *The Glass Menagerie* designed partly in the manner of the compositions of El Greco. In 1955 the National Gallery in London purchased the *Adoration of the Name of Jesus*, a smaller version of the picture in the Escorial, while the new art museum in São Paulo at this time bought the *Annunciation*. In 1959 a picture from 289 the well-known *Apostles* series by El Greco fetched £72,000 in London and the famous *Opening of the Fifth Seal* (part of the estate of the artist Zuloaga) is said to have been acquired lately by the Metropolitan Museum for over $500,000. In 1964, an El Greco picture at last entered the Berlin Museums.

Around 1750 the fame of Raphael was helpful to many minor painters who were felt to be faintly Raphaelesque, and similarly the admiration for El Greco since 1900 has proved profitable to many Baroque painters. Born four generations after El Greco, the Genoese Magnasco, though he had only a small scale of themes, appealed very strongly to art-lovers of the twentieth century with his nervous brush work, the flickering movement of his compositions and the strangely dark character of his pictorial subjects. Since the prices for

XXV The passing of realism led to the rediscovery of El Greco. His *The Agony in the Garden of Gethsemane* is in the National Gallery in London (see Ill. 290)

his pictures never attained more than a fairly moderate level, the Berlin collectors gave Magnasco the rather spiteful nickname of 'The Poor Man's El Greco'. In Magnasco's case too, the first wave of real appreciation lasted from 1900 to 1920 and a second began again in 1945.

The 'fin de siècle' further discovered the somewhat affected Giuseppe Bazzani, the Late Baroque painter who worked in Mantua. His *Annunciation* (now in the Vienna Gallery) hung in the home of Hugo von Hofmannsthal when he was writing the text of *Der Rosenkavalier*. Thanks to his witty style of painting Bazzani still has admirers today and recently some of his pictures entered the Kunsthalle in Bremen and the National Museum in Stockholm. In the English-speaking world people began to turn again to Italian artists of the type of Magnasco or Bazzani only in the 1920's. The London Magnasco Society was active from 1924 to 1930. The study of the Baroque and the turning to sophistication occurred rather earlier in America than in England. At present this Baroque trend of taste is in evidence all over the world.

As far back as 1906 the name of Poussin began to be mentioned among the artists of the Café du Dôme on the Boulevard Montparnasse. Henry O. Havemeyer and his wife, frequent visitors to Paris, where the American painter Mary Cassatt was their confidante and adviser, brought to their Fifth Avenue mansion Poussin's *Orpheus and Eurydice* (now in the Metropolitan Museum, New York) together with pictures by Cézanne and Degas. Many museums, particularly in the period between the two World Wars, began to acquire paintings by Poussin.

XXVI El Greco's sudden popularity was matched by that of Mathis Grünewald who, from being one of a mass of painters active around the time of Dürer, has come to be regarded as undoubtedly the greatest German painter ever. The *Small Crucifixion* was found in the attic of a house in Essen in 1922. After it had been proved that the painting had belonged to the Elector of Bavaria in Munich, it was sold to the National Gallery in Washington for an enormous sum of money

A slow resurrection of Claude followed soon after. In America the landscape painting of the Barbizon School was pushed into the background in the leading museums and collections, thanks to the influence of the great classical school headed by Claude. At present all important landscapes by Claude, for which English private owners are still the principal source, command very respectable prices.

When the 'Valori Plastici' movement emerged in Italy Caravaggio was discovered, and among his successors the Spaniard Zurbarán, who was for a while in the 1920's a particular favourite of painters and art-lovers. In the case of Baroque and Late Baroque paintings, the balanced type of painter now came to be respected once more. After the ebbing of the first Expressionist wave, Max Friedländer declared that in Guardi, Ricci, Magnasco and their like the bravura of brushwork had been admired too much. In the period of the 'new objectivity' Canaletto was set against Guardi, Chardin against Boucher, Hubert Robert against Fragonard. It was at this time that Duveen succeeded in forcing up the price for busts by Houdon to nearly $150,000. After 1945 most of the quieter seventeenth- and eighteenth-century Latin masters, with their considerable strictness of form, contrived to hold their own. In 1957 the Munich Pinakothek acquired its first two pictures by Hubert Robert. At the same time Prince Liechtenstein sold for a very high price Chardin's *The Attentive Nurse* to a New York art dealer (now in the National Gallery in Washington).

The perceptible renewal of interest about 1920 in the age of Phidias was advantageous to the masters of Florence and Rome who, in the sixteenth century, had considered the classical heritage as the starting point of their own art. In 1920 an observer who watched developments with great delicacy of perception was already attacking those museum curators who seemed to be positively ashamed of their pictures of the Tuscan High Renaissance and were even ready to 'exchange them for any inferior El Greco or Magnasco'. In 1925 Derain called Raphael 'the greatest of the misunderstood'. The few paintings of the first order by Raphael and his central Italian contemporaries which have changed hands in the last three decades fetched the very highest prices.

A characteristic new discovery of the twentieth century is the art of the so-called Mannerists in central Italy. The painters who between about 1520 and 1580, especially in Florence, worked in the classical forms of the High Renaissance and subjected them to a process of disintegration, or even 'quoted' them with a certain irony, were bound to please the epoch that produced Surrealism. Painters like Franciabigio, Rosso and their like were suddenly

respected by the visitors to museums and collectors: Dan Fellows Platt in Englewood, New Jersey, acquired a picture by Beccafumi, and Frank L. Babbot in New York one by Pontormo (now in the Brooklyn Museum). Samuel Kress, one of the most cultivated independent collectors of the twentieth century, the bulk of whose acquisitions are now in the National Gallery in Washington, began, in 1919, to turn away from the Venetians towards those painters once active between Florence and Rome. He acquired a picture by Franciabigio and also Dosso Dossi's principal work *Circe and her Lovers in a Landscape* (now in the National Gallery, *337* Washington).

In the galleries of Europe the despised central Italian pictures of the decades immediately following Raphael's death were now exhumed. Around 1920 lovers of sculpture discovered preferences similar to those of Emperor Rudolph II: the small bronze group *Hercules and Antaeus* by Giovanni da Bologna fetched 63,000 marks at the auction of the Eduard Simon Collection in Berlin in 1929.

The artists just named have maintained their reputations virtually intact up to the present. In 1952 the Munich National Museum acquired a small version of the *Rape of the Sabine Woman* by Giovanni *105* da Bologna, while in Florence the exhibition 'Pontormo e il manierismo fiorentino' was a great success in 1956.

Since 1890 the northern schools, from approximately the death of Holbein to about 1800, have tended to lag behind the southern painters in popularity. 'The large number of Dutch minor masters must disappear from our galleries', declared the art historian, William Reinhold Valentiner after 1900. Great collectors like Widener in Philadelphia would recognize only the following six Dutch painters apart from Rembrandt: Hals, Vermeer, Hobbema, Cuyp, Terborch and Steen. Since the eighteenth century Cuyp and Hobbema had been special favourites of English collectors. North of the Channel and later in the New

318, 319 The European vogue for medieval art was at once adopted by the United States and found its fullest expression in The Cloisters in New York. The thirteenth-century Madonna (left) from the former choir screen of Strasbourg Cathedral is now in The Cloisters, and the wood carving of Christ and St John (right), originally made for a monastery in Württemberg, is now in the Cleveland Museum of Art

World, their manner of presenting landscapes was felt to be attuned to the Anglo-Saxon character. That discreet painter Terborch and the highly inventive Steen maintained their popularity, while van Ostade and other representatives of the noisy peasant genre began to be regarded as intolerable. A high value was placed on Vermeer's fine craftsmanship and his bright colours.

XXI Frans Hals, who comes second in the above list, had first attracted some attention around 1860 as a coarse, aggressive realist. Because of his manner of painting, leaving the individual brush strokes visible, he enjoyed a special market, though one of strictly limited duration, when French Impressionism began to acquire world fame. In the preparation for the Hudson Fulton Exhibition in New York in 1909 it was evident that there were about thirty portraits by Frans Hals in the United States. Four were made available by Morgan, three by Huntington. Otto H. Kahn at that time had just paid about $400,000 for *The Artist with his Family*, a picture that has recently entered the Thyssen Collection in Lugano for a much lower price.

A fairly short interval of time saw both the steep ascent and the rapid decline of English painting of the late eighteenth century. The worthy landed nobility of that time, their lovely wives and their well-groomed and often slightly coquettish children, painted by Gainsborough or Reynolds and their friends, were for the rich people of the boom years in London the indispensable means of covering their walls and so hiding the absence of a gallery of ancestors. When Oscar Wilde wrote his society comedies and London formed the model of upper-class life from Moscow to the Pacific, English portraits of the eighteenth century became fashionable all over the world. Their unconstrained elegance was in harmony with the ideal of the 'fin de siècle'. Pictorial delicacy and the apparently indolent manner of applying colours that were often bright gave painters like Gainsborough, quite undeservedly, the reputation of insufficiently appreciated masters.

320, 321 The transfer of medieval works of art from Europe to the United States continued in the 1930's. The monastery church of Bellpuig de las Avellanas near Lerida provided The Cloisters with the tomb of the Count of Urgel (left). The Cleveland Museum of Art purchased Riemenschneider's *St Lawrence* (right), the tenth work by that sculptor to reach America

From 1880 to 1910 the prices of English portraits multiplied tenfold. The great galleries on the Continent in St Petersburg and Berlin, Budapest and Vienna, Munich and Stuttgart, paid huge prices between 1900 and 1914 for works by Gainsborough, Reynolds, Romney, Raeburn and Hoppner. Morgan, Frick and other American collectors outbid each other in the sums which they spent on female portraits by Gainsborough. In this process Huntington sounded a loud, final, concluding chord when he bought *The Blue Boy* from the Duke of Westminster's collection for $ 825,000.

Immediately after this, people turned to Expressionism, tectonics and the like. The elderly Bode declared that even van Dyck's portraits had always cost too much and that this applied even more to his London imitators of 1780. The more pretentious type of American art-lover complained about the large number of fashionable English portraits which were being brought to the U. S. for very high prices; works by Hogarth or Blake would have represented

322 The political upheavals in Russia, Austria and Germany, which followed the First World War, resulted in the sale—mainly to Americans—of numerous works of art from the private collections of ruling-class families. Lancret's *La Camargo dancing* (above), once a favourite painting of Frederick the Great, was sold by the Hohenzollerns and now hangs in the National Gallery in Washington

323 Prince Youssoupoff, who was involved in the murder of Rasputin, managed to save Rembrandt's *Lady with an Ostrich-feather Fan* from his palace in Petrograd in 1917. The painting was eventually bought by Joseph Widener, and is now in the collection of the National Gallery in Washington

324, 325 After the First World War, architects adopted a strong, purist style that alluded to both Greece and the Renaissance. The National Gallery in Washington provides a good example of this development in museum design

326 The monumental dignity of the exterior of the National Gallery in Washington indicates the continuation of the nineteenth-century tradition of museum architecture as reflected in buildings like the Munich Glyptothek

English painting more aptly. The art market drastically reflected the change in taste. *The Tambourine Girl*, a pleasant, smooth picture by Hoppner, had been purchased in New York in 1914 for $350,000. The picture returned recently to the market and fetched only $10,000. If we take into account the devaluation of the dollar which took place a generation ago, this makes the present price only 2 per cent of that paid in 1914.

When Magnasco and other painters of the Italian Baroque were discovered, a glance was also cast at their German contemporaries. Shortly after the First World War a Baroque Museum came into being in Vienna; paintings by Maulpertsch, Kremser-Schmidt, Troger and other painters strongly indebted to the art of the south were placed in a palace-like building dating back to the days of the Turkish Wars. The Germanisches Museum in Nuremberg authorized the arrangement of a section devoted to German Baroque painting. Baroque statuettes, previously only 'a useful object for picturesquely decorative effects almost in the taste of Makart', became a passion with serious collectors from 1910 onwards in Germany and after that in Scandinavia and the Anglo-Saxon countries; the appropriate sections of many museums, in London, Oxford, Frankfurt and Munich among others, were filled with new acquisitions.

B 298

The general trend of taste at the time of the First World War coincided very largely, as mentioned above, with that of Emperor Rudolph II. When Tintoretto, Giovanni da Bologna and gothicizing early Germans once more came into favour, Pieter Bruegel could not long remain unnoticed. Toulouse-Lautrec was one of the first to study his pictures afresh, while the art-historian Ernst Heidrich declared in 1910 that after Jan van Eyck, Bruegel was the greatest representative of Netherlandish painting in the centuries before Rubens. A picture from the collection of Rudolph II, the *Land of Cockayne*, had turned up again before 1900 and changed hands for less than 100 francs. In 1917 it was acquired by the Munich Pinakothek for 220,000 marks. Ten years previously pictures by this artist had reached America and entered the Museum of Art in Philadelphia among other places.

327, 328, 329 In many European cities around 1935 ornamental elements were eliminated from the neo-Classical style of museum architecture to such an extent that it began to approach the ideal represented by Le Corbusier in architecture and Mondrian in painting. These photographs are of the interior of the Museum of Modern Art in Paris, completed in 1937

330 The Hellenistic Altar of Zeus from Pergamum was reconstructed in Berlin in 1930; many of the original fragments were used. The contrast of the mobility of the relief with the classical calm of the pillars proved very popular among museum visitors, who regarded Baroque expressiveness and classical dignity as equally worthwhile ideals

In the period of Expressionism people were strongly aware of the medieval side of Bruegel's art, for instance his neglect of conventional perspective representation. After 1920, and thanks to the catchword 'magical realism', he became one of the greatest masters of the past. Crowds gathered round his pictures in the Bruegel Room of the Vienna Gallery. Reproductions of his pictures of the Months went all over the world in incredibly large editions. From a Vienna collection the London National Gallery acquired in the 1920's for a very high price Bruegel's *Adoration of the Kings* dated 1584. At the same time his *Harvesters*, which had been appropriated in 1805 from the Habsburgs by a French officer, reached the Metropolitan Museum in New York.

Along with Bruegel, other Netherlandish painters of the late sixteenth century gained in reputation. Bode in the last years of his life was already showing a liking for the highly fantastic landscapes of Momper and his contemporaries; after 1945 this trend of taste expressed itself in many new acquisitions by museums and collectors.

Many aspects of Rembrandt's work were attractive to the epoch that began in 1890. The bourgeois portraits of his middle Amsterdam years received less attention. The early Baroque Rembrandt was now discovered. In the Berlin Kaiser Friedrich Museum, *The Rape of Proserpine*, that vehement work of his youth, received new honour. The House of Orange had sent it in 1720 as an heirloom to the Hohenzollerns. In 1905 Ludwig Justi, the curator of the Städelsches Kunstinstitut in Frankfurt, made a great unconventional masterpiece the centre of the Dutch section which till then had had an all too bourgeois character: this was Rembrandt's violent *Blinding of Samson*, acquired from the old Baroque gallery of Count Schönborn in Vienna. The price of 336,000 gold marks cannot be considered excessive when compared with the sums being paid N 317 at that time for English portraits.

It was the later Rembrandt especially that spoke to the twentieth century in strong terms. Kandinsky underwent an experience which was decisive for his own development when viewing works of the master's last years that Catherine II had once 190 acquired for the Hermitage. In Cassel *Jacob's Blessing* became the chief attraction for lovers of modern art, while in Brunswick the *Family Group* was the centre of attention. The Cologne Museum acquired with the Carstanjen Collection Rembrandt's last self-portrait, expressing a combination of worried gaze and helpless laughter, which was given an Expressionist and a Surrealist interpretation together.

The relatively peaceful and optimistic mood of the Twenties allowed Vermeer van Delft and the

331 One of the characteristics of the work of Le Corbusier and painters like Mondrian and Nicholson was their preference for light flat surfaces. This same trend appears in the Hodler room in the Berne Museum where the paintings are fairly widely spaced and all at the same height from the floor

'quiet' Dutch masters to gain fresh esteem under the catchword of the 'New Objectivity'. This change of taste corresponded exactly with that which caused people to turn from Guardi to Canaletto. Vermeer, having supplanted Frans Hals, now took second place immediately after Rembrandt, and the prices of his pictures rose. The most talented forger of this time, van Meegeren, specialized in Vermeer. In the National Gallery in Washington, Vermeer's *Woman Weighing Gold* from the Widener Collection immediately moved into the company of the most important works. In the early nineteenth century this painting had been in the possession of the Wittelsbachs in Munich, but its value being at the time unrecognized, it was given away in 1850. Vermeer's *The Painter in His Studio*, which Count Czernin sold in 1940 for the proposed Gallery of the Führer in Linz, is regarded today in Vienna as the most important acquisition which the museum has made for a long time.

The period of Expressionism had set a high value on the 'romantic' pictures of the Netherlanders, for instance van Ruisdael's *Jewish Cemetery*, already greatly admired in the 'Sturm und Drang' age. After 1920 the calmer Jan van Goyen came to the fore. Among painters of architecture Emmanuel de Witte and above all Saenredam, who up till then had been 335 regarded as somewhat dry, came to be respected, and there was a similar change of taste in the assessment of still-lifes.

After 1945 the trends just described become somewhat blurred. Despite this a moderate-sized landscape by van Goyen fetched a high price in 1959. The

332 The *Elgin Marbles*, the greatest expression of Greek art outside Greece, were housed in a new building of the British Museum specifically designed for them in 1930. The essential clarity of the arrangement suited the spirit of the Parthenon frieze

principal works of Rembrandt are accorded a very high value among art dealers and the same would of course apply if a picture by Vermeer were to turn up. The great mass of second- and third-rate Dutch genre, animal and still-life painters have not however recovered from their fall about 1900.

The summary rejection by the 'fin de siècle' of straightforward realism, which was admired by the majority of art-lovers around 1870, was particularly fatal to the genre painting of the mid-nineteenth century. The Düsseldorf school, which had at one time enjoyed world fame, has never recovered since. A picture by Knaus, purchased in 1887 by an

American collector for the sum of $27,500, was recently auctioned in New York for a mere $500 (which in terms of purchasing power means that it fetched between 3 and 4 per cent of its original value). Troyon's landscapes and many others by his French and German contemporaries, which in 1880 had still fetched good prices, also lost their internationally recognized place.

The high esteem of Parisian Impressionism often had as its consequence the discovery of 'early Impressionists'. Many an artist who had had to retire from the scene as a realist became cherished again thanks to his more or less 'Impressionist' early works. While in 1903 in the Berlin National Gallery, the uninstructed gathered in front of Menzel's *Rolling Mill* painted in 1875, the avant-garde of art-lovers and collectors admired his *Balcony Room*, painted in 1845, which had just been purchased. The artist, at that time eighty-eight years old, was still able to witness this situation.

Many parallels to this story could be given. In England Constable attained new fame, in France the 'Corot d'Italie' was discovered, but even Courbet was

333, 334 The period between the wars saw a temporary revival of neo-Classicism, not only in architecture but also in the fine arts. Many galleries, like the Liebighaus in Frankfurt, acquired classical Greek sculpture while contemporary artists, including Picasso, reflected the timeless Greek ideal of human beauty in their work. Features of the fifth-century BC head of Aphrodite (left) appear in Picasso's *Head of a Young Girl* (below), engraved about 1925

335 Before the Second World War there was a vogue for Saenredam, until then a little-known artist who lived at the time of Rembrandt. His predilection for clearly defined, fresh-looking rooms with light-coloured rectangular wall-surfaces matched the preferences of a generation that admired Le Corbusier. This interior of a church at Assendelft is in the Rijksmuseum, Amsterdam

N 318

able to maintain his position with a number of middle-sized and smaller pictures. In Munich Spitzweg was rediscovered, in Vienna the early Waldmüller, in Dresden Rayski. In Hamburg, Lichtwark bluntly declared that Runge had created about 1810 the first example of European 'plein-air' painting.

The trend just described became related in Germany to the rediscovery of the Romantic movement and of Biedermeier. Caspar David Friedrich enjoyed fresh esteem alongside Runge, while Wilhelm von Kobell was preferred to Spitzweg. It is significant that Franz Marc, when he turned away from realism in 1912 and began to paint blue cows and red deer, declared that

in addition to Cézanne and Gauguin, Caspar David Friedrich and Kobell had become painters of importance for him. The Hamburg Kunsthalle alone N 319 acquired twelve pictures by Friedrich and eight by Kobell between 1904 and 1914. Samuel Kress represented a similar development of taste. Immediately before the First World War his interest was partly centred on drawings by the English and German romantics.

The laborious rise of the Impressionists (among whom Degas, Toulouse-Lautrec, Cézanne, van Gogh and Gauguin were often included) has been frequently described. It was only around 1890 that an increasing number of art-lovers began to approve the colourful palette of the typical Impressionists.

The French art dealer, Durand-Ruel, helped the Impressionists to gain recognition by mounting special exhibitions outside Paris. Around 1890, American collectors such as George N. Tyner, Alfred A. Pope, Harris Whittemore and Mrs Potter Palmer were already taking note of Monet and Sisley. From 1889 Mrs Palmer owned a painting by Degas, and Widener bought Manet's *The Dead Torero* in 1894. Widener and his friends now turned against the Barbizon School.

Starting in 1892 Durand-Ruel showed small collections of the Impressionists in the Hotel Kaiserhof in Berlin. In 1896 the first important picture by Manet was donated to the Berlin National Gallery. The Paris art dealer Vollard later wrote in his memoirs that 'around 1900 Paul Cassirer's gallery in Berlin seemed to be a continuation of the Rue Lafitte'. At the auctions in the Hôtel Drouot, Berlin collectors and German curators of museums who were particularly active pushed up the prices of the modern school. Cassirer himself said in about 1910 that French Impressionist pictures were imported into Germany every year to a total value of 500,000 gold marks. The most important collectors were Eduard Arnhold, Mendelsohn, Gerstenberger, Rothermundt, Oskar Schmitz and Behrens. Nearly all of them lived east of the Elbe in Hamburg, Berlin, Dresden and Breslau.

In the first decade of the new century the prices of Impressionist pictures rose steeply. In Bonner's auction rooms in New York in 1900 three pictures by Monet were sold for a total of $3,000; in 1902 Osthaus paid 16,000 marks for Renoir's *Lise* (now in the Folkwang Museum in Essen); in 1910 the *Execution of the Emperor Maximilian* by Manet entered the Mannheim Kunsthalle for 100,000 marks. In the same year the Russian collector Morosoff paid 80,000 francs for Renoir's *The Actress Samary* which he acquired through Durand-Ruel and which had fetched 1,500 francs in 1875 (now in the Museum of Fine Arts in Moscow). By 1907 the National Gallery in Berlin already possessed four pictures by Monet. In 1914, within a period of scarcely twenty years, the paintings of the Impressionists had largely left the houses of the French bourgeoisie and had found homes all over the world, including Japan. For the art centre of Munich it was a question of prestige to counter-balance the group of French artists who had so rapidly achieved a reputation. Munich was concerned to ensure that the prices for Leibl's early works should reach at least the height which Manet's pictures had attained: in 1913 Leibl's *Frau Gedon* was acquired for 154,000 gold marks by the governing body of the Munich museums.

In German-speaking countries it was the art of Böcklin which came very close to the general direction of taste that marked the 'fin de siècle'. It is this art that has been called the decisive experience of Tschudi, and it has already been seen how this man, with his great delicacy of feeling, learnt from Böcklin to love El Greco, Goya and Toulouse-Lautrec. Hofmannsthal stood deeply moved in 1890 in front of the 'dream-like pictures of Böcklin' which appeared to him to be 'pagan as the hymns of Orpheus and uncanny as the tale of the juniper tree'. On the occasion of the memorial service held in honour of Böcklin in Vienna Hofmannsthal wrote *The Death*

of *Titian;* at the same time he showed himself deeply impressed by the paintings of van Gogh. Later Titian, Böcklin and van Gogh were for him three related masters of the 'art of style'.

In the long run, and despite the rather nationalistic good will of many German curators and critics, Böcklin was unable to play the part of a German Gauguin which had been allotted him. Meier-Graefe made one of those attacks which artists so greatly feared. Böcklin, born twenty-one years before Gauguin but only fourteen years after Richard Wagner, was often regarded from about 1910 like Wagner as a 'controversial case'. When, after a phase of passionate rejection, people later began to recognize in the works of Wagner the origin of a tonality which was free from major and minor, so around 1925 more favourable assessments of Böcklin began to be heard.

Germans were among the first to develop an affection for the Post-Impressionists outside their own country. Already before 1900, Cézanne's *Card Players* was hanging in the Berlin house of Julius Elias, the friend of Knut Hamsun and Munch. In 1897 Hugo von Tschudi arranged for a twenty-year-old landscape by Cézanne and Degas' recent *Conversation* to be donated to the Berlin National Gallery. A few years later Osthaus acquired for his Folkwang Museum that astonishing series of masterpieces by Gauguin, Cézanne and van Gogh which were confiscated almost without exception on Hitler's order in 1937. For all these pictures taken together—and with the addition of a major work by Daumier—he had to pay less than he had had to give for his great Feuerbach, *Orpheus and Eurydice*. But Osthaus had soon seen enough of this and sold it to the Vienna museums.

At this time the Americans began to take a hand in the game, and prices of Post-Impressionists continued to rise. In New York Havemeyer added 16 pictures by Manet and Monet, no less than 36 works by Degas and 5 by Cézanne to his collection, while also procuring pictures by El Greco and

XXVII Surrealism, a movement in modern art, gained ground after the First World War and attention was drawn to Surrealist elements in the work of earlier artists from Bosch to Goya. Many of the paintings of the German Romantic artist Caspar David Friedrich, for example his *Wreck of the 'Hope'*, were regarded as having Surrealist significance

N 320

Poussin. Degas and El Greco were often regarded as artists related in style, while Cézanne and Poussin had an architectonic quality in common.

In Dresden in 1909 Oskar Schmitz had four pictures by van Gogh, Gauguin and Cézanne for which he had paid a considerable price. Eduard Arnhold, who had found his way from Menzel to Manet and Renoir, now also secured pictures by Cézanne. In 1911 one major work of van Gogh entered the Bremen Kunsthalle, the Wallraf Richartz Museum in Cologne, and the Städelsches Kunstinstitut in Frankfurt respectively. All these works were fortunate enough to survive the Hitler era, except for the *Portrait of Doctor Gachet* by van Gogh in Frankfurt which was sent out of the country as 'degenerate' (now in the Kramarski Collection in New York).

Just before the First World War, two memorable events finally established the fame of the Post-Impressionists: the 'Sonderbund-Ausstellung' in Cologne and the Armory Show in New York. In Cologne in 1912 Cézanne, Gauguin and van Gogh and their immediate successors were for the first time grouped together as initiators of a movement which was already called 'Expressionism', and were decisively separated from Monet, Renoir and the Impressionists. At that time there were in Germany, chiefly in private hands, about 25 paintings by van Gogh, 20 by Gauguin and 20 by Cézanne. At the Armory Show the Metropolitan Museum paid $6,700 for its first Cézanne. In 1915 the first work by Degas entered the Tate Gallery in London and in 1917 the first Gauguin. German and English collectors were equally bold, but the curators of the German museums had more scope for initiative than their colleagues in Britain and America.

N 321

The Tate Gallery in London, which opened in its Millbank building in 1897 through the pressure and support of the sugar millionaire, Henry Tate, was originally created to house British works of art and was administered by the National Gallery.

XXVIII European avant-garde painters, among them Picasso and Matisse in Paris and Nolde and Kirchner in Dresden, discovered African carvings, masks and idols between 1907 and 1910, and used their exaggerated expressiveness in their own work. The effect of this new phase in modern art can be seen in Picasso's *Woman with a Fan* in the Hermitage, Leningrad

It became independent of the older institution twenty years later and, though it was still officially considered a gallery devoted primarily to British art, and contained a large number of outstanding Turners, its trustees were soon able to acquire important works by modern foreign artists and Manet, Cézanne, Rouault, Seurat, Braque, Picasso, among other modern masters, were represented in its expanding collection.

A few western European artists, from the period around 1800 and the epoch following it (who had long remained unrecognized), were held to have something relevant to say as the star of the Post-Impressionists began to rise. Goya had already attracted the lovers of Impressionism. At the turn of the century, people felt a sense of kinship with his spirituality. Toulouse-Lautrec admired him above anyone else. Already in 1894, a Goya entered the National Gallery in London. Mrs Havemeyer in New York bought twelve of Goya's paintings in the first years of the twentieth century. Prices rose, forgeries went into circulation, and one of them deceived even leading officials of the Munich Pinakothek.

N 322

For half a century now Goya has held an undisputed place as one of the great painters of Europe. Minor pictures of his have entered respected galleries in Germany, Sweden and England. Goya was one of the first to enter the Museu de Arte in São Paulo, where he is magnificently represented by the portrait of Don Juan Llorente from the Arnhold Collection. Recently a Goya portrait of the Duke of Wellington fetched £140,000 at an auction in London.

365

N 323

At about the same time as Goya, from about 1910 on, Delacroix, Géricault and Daumier came to the fore. As the enthusiasm for bright colours and 'pleinairisme' waned, people admired Delacroix because his works 'had moved away from the hard chalk tone of Tiepolo'. The themes and style of Delacroix had inspired van Gogh, and the works of these two painters were often hung close to one another, as for instance in Oskar Reinhart's collection at Winterthur. In 1921 the Louvre paid 800,000 francs for a large picture by Delacroix.

In 1900 Chéramy was buying pictures by Géricault. At the same time in Paris that Swiss eccentric and 'marchand-amateur' Otto Ackermann was devoting himself to Géricault's rediscovery. 'He was in the habit of picking up a picture on the Left Bank of the Seine in the morning and selling it on the Right Bank in the afternoon'. Great museums and collectors in the years immediately before the First World War were eager to obtain paintings by Daumier. He was represented in Nemes' collection and in 1906 Tschudi introduced him into the Berlin National Gallery and soon afterwards into the Munich museums.

336, 337 The inter-wars period which saw the birth of modern Surrealism also, and not surprisingly, witnessed the rediscovery of sixteenth-century Mannerism. The Surrealists venerated Hieronymus Bosch, but they also admired paintings by Cranach, such as this portrait of Margrave Georg von Brandenburg Ansbach (left), with its Manneristic treatment of the hands. Italian artists like Pontormo and Dosso Dossi, whose work included Mannerist elements, also suddenly became fashionable. Dosso Dossi's *Circe and her Lovers in a Landscape* (above) was bought by the American collector, Samuel H. Kress, and is now in the National Gallery in Washington

Of the German nineteenth-century artists who were rediscovered the most important was Hans von Marées. He had long been overshadowed by Feuerbach. It is true that the devotees of French Impressionism made fun of Marées' paintings which allegedly were as feeble as hot-house blooms,

but they could not prevent the rise of this artist who was born at almost the same time as Cézanne. It was only about 1900 that people understood Marées' 'language of artistic form which went far beyond Feuerbach's sympathetic longing and penetrated into a realm of shadows, being released from every earthly tie'.

Of the artists who only developed their particular genius in the twentieth century, a few who were accepted by the public show the way things were tending. Pablo Picasso, born in 1881, aroused the greatest enthusiasm in men like Rilke with the melancholy pictures of his Blue Period which were related to the work of Toulouse-Lautrec. By 1910 Alfred Flechtheim had already brought a N 325 number of works by Picasso to Germany. He had to pay between three and four hundred marks each for them, whereas pictures by van Gogh were already fetching 8,000 marks. Flechtheim used to point out that the Academy Professor, Eduard von

338, 339 Surrealism gave new validity to the work of many earlier artists. Géricault's strange *Portrait of an unknown Painter* (left) received greater attention, and the *Scene from Milton's 'Paradise Lost'* (above) by Fuseli, who had been regarded until then as an eccentric, was bought by the Munich Neue Pinakothek

340 After the Second World War modern techniques were used in the display of works of art. In the exhibition entitled 'La Vierge dans l'Art', held in Paris in 1951, only the sculpture was spotlit, while the rest of the rooms remained in darkness

Gebhardt, was in the habit of asking and receiving 30,000 marks for his scrupulously naturalistic paintings.

The first picture from which Picasso himself made as much as 1,000 francs was a composition with several figures, *Les Saltimbanques*. This work already changed hands in 1914 for ten times that amount. Shortly before the First World War Rilke admired *Les Saltimbanques* in the collection of Herta von Koenig in Munich. In 1931 this picture fetched 1,000,000 francs. It has found a permanent home in the National Gallery in Washington as part of the Chester Dale Collection.

The rise of prices in the case of pictures by Degas and van Gogh caused art dealers and collectors to become adventurous regarding contemporary young artists. In Paris the Fauves and in Germany the first Expressionist paintings gained esteem fairly quickly. The spokesmen of the Expressionist group Die Brücke attacked the Hamburg curator Lichtwark, who was still alleged to have some sympathy for 'the valet's art' of the Biedermeier artists. The collector Ida Bienert sold her Böcklin paintings in 1910 at a low price and turned towards Nolde, while in 1913 the Mannheim Kunsthalle acquired Kokoschka's *Portrait of Doctor Forel* almost before the paint was dry. Many German collectors were happy to be able to confront the French with artists from their own nation, but excessive expectations were often aroused in regard to many representatives of the new line. In Berlin a collector with speculative intentions acquired some forty pictures by Pechstein. The painters of the 'Blaue Reiter' in Munich rapidly achieved international success. Franz Marc was made intelligible when interpreted in terms of the Cubism of Paris and the Futurism of Milan. In Chicago

298

341, 342 The use of modern technical aids and the fear of excessive formality in galleries sometimes resulted in making them look like workshops. An experimental exhibition using unusual display techniques was held in the Museo del Palazzo Bianco in Genoa in 1955. In this exhibition a fragment of a thirteenth-century tomb-sculpture was mounted on a hydraulic jack (right) and Baroque paintings were hung without their frames from free-standing metal stanchions (below)

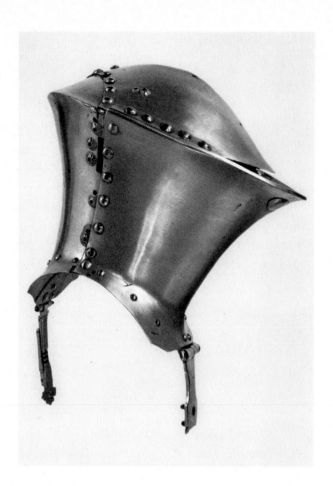

Arthur Eddy acquired a picture by Marc before the First World War (now in the Art Institute of Chicago). N 32●

After the first great wave of anti-naturalism had begun to die down around 1925, the attitude of art-lovers and collectors changed towards the painters and sculptors of the period after 1800. When Raphael was newly discovered by artists in Paris and when, in the ever-changing Bienert Collection, pictures by Schlemmer began to displace the works of van Gogh, the art of neo-Classicism was revived. Around 1920 three paintings by Ingres entered the museums of Stockholm and New York, while drawings were acquired for the Havemeyer Collection. In all, six pictures by David, Prud'hon and Mme Vigée-Lebrun were purchased between 1921 and 1928 by the galleries of Stockholm, London and New York. William Randolph Hearst was also among those who turned their attention towards the Parisian 'Empire' style. He acquired a large painting by Gros.

343, 344 The quest for elegance in technical design and the preference for the stylized simplification of the human form, characteristic of our age, led to the recognition of simple medieval helmets of the fourteenth and fifteenth centuries (as opposed to later heavily ornamented versions) as genuine works of art rather than mere historical curiosities. The fifth-century helmet shown here (left) belonged to Archduke Sigmund of the Tyrol. In his painting *Massacre in Korea* (detail below), Picasso makes symbolic use of such helmets

345, 346 After the Second World War heavily stylized yet extremely compelling animal heads, the artistic expression of primitive peoples, gained the attention of the artists and collectors of a second generation of Expressionists. There is a clear affinity between the Benin leopard mask (below) and Picasso's *Minotaur* (right)

During this same period, works by Carstens and Wilhelm Schadow were bought by German museums, in Hanover for instance. A typical new discovery resulting from this trend was Feuerbach. Around 1925 seven of his pictures were acquired by museums in Basle and Hamburg, and also by the collectors Reinhart and Thyssen.

A certain neo-Classical rigidity was characteristic of the pictures which were grouped after the First World War in Germany under the concept of 'magical realism'. The more incisive term Surrealism, which has become known all over the world, has caused the

347, 348   After the Second World War, as a result of the tendency towards abstraction in sculpture, artists took a new interest in prehistoric grave goods. Those who admired modern art also admired prehistoric Cycladic art (left) and animal figures from central Europe (below)

349 Interest in primitive art led artists and collectors from Benin art, in which European influences were still discernible, to that of the Yoruba. This bronze hunter was made in the seventeenth century

older formula to lapse into oblivion. When the early de Chirico and the most recent paintings by artists like Xaver Fuhr began to be noticed shortly after 1920, the public discovered new aspects in the work of many artists of the first half of the nineteenth century. Caspar David Friedrich was now felt to be a 'magical realist', even a Surrealist. René Huyghe, at that time Curator of the Louvre, was fond of showing photographs in lectures of the Berlin pictures of Friedrich, for instance the *Monastery Ruin in the Snow*, and wrote that he was wrongly ignored. His sharp realism had a 'singular connection with the most modern tendencies of certain Surrealists'. Privately owned paintings by Friedrich began to be hunted. In 1921 *The Cross in the Mountains* came to the

Düsseldorf Museum. Oskar Reinhart acquired five pictures by Friedrich for his collection in Winterthur. Strikingly surrealist features were thought to be shown by Friedrich's contemporaries, Blake and Fuseli. In Grenville Winthrop's collection in New York early Sienese panels, an important painting by El Greco and drawings by David, Prud'hon, Ingres and Chassériau were joined about 1920 by a small collection of the works of William Blake. The Neue Pinakothek in Munich acquired in the 1920's the *Scene from Milton's Paradise Lost* by Fuseli while the Basle Museum and Reinhart endeavoured to secure works of this artist, who till then had often been overlooked. Surrealist elements were also discovered in Goya's œuvre.

XXVII

N 327

339

From Surrealism and Magical Realism, artists and art-lovers of the early 1920's found their way to the realistic reproduction of the visible world. This was called at the time the New Objectivity ('Die Neue Sachlichkeit'). This trend led to the higher esteem of certain painters of about 1830. A large Munich publisher of picture-postcards declared in 1926 that the sale of van Gogh's *Sunflowers* had fallen very heavily and that the *Rider By the Tegernsee* by Wilhelm von Kobell was now the most popular subject. In those years ten pictures by Kobell entered the museums of Berlin, Düsseldorf, Elberfeld, Hanover and Stuttgart and also the Reinhart collection in Winterthur.

Where French painting was concerned, the mood of 1925 showed a preference for particularly objective masters and paintings. People were now less excited about Delacroix. The early Corot and Impressionists such as Sisley found new favour with the collectors, as did Monet, especially his early pictures. The really new discovery was Utrillo, who had a distinct kinship with Sisley. Utrillo liked to borrow the theme and composition of his paintings from cheap postcards and thus appeared 'objective'. Around 1910, when he painted his best pictures, he had not been recognized. In 1925 he was discovered and immediately overvalued. In the years 1925 to 1927 pictures by Utrillo entered the museums of Bremen, Cologne, Mannheim, London, Stockholm and Paris. The first Utrillo to enter the Palais du Luxembourg in Paris (in 1926) was a gift from a New York art dealer who had an interest in ensuring that when his clients went to Europe, they should find the master whom he was boosting in America in a museum in Paris.

About twenty years later, the Second World War produced another phase of Expressionism which could be distinctly seen in literature, in films and in stage sets. Under this influence the painters of Die Brücke in Germany were reaccorded new esteem; and thus the honour was saved of those artists who had been defamed in the Third Reich, some of whom were still alive.

350, 351 Between 1951 and 1960 modern artists were influenced by primitive art objects such as the Australian wood carving of the sea god Tangaroa (left) and above all by the Pre-Columbian art of Mexico, represented here by a terracotta funeral urn (right)

352 The art of the Dark Ages, particularly when it contained an element of primitive striving after form, was the object of special interest for artists and dealers around 1950. This decoration, from a purse found in the ship burial of Sutton Hoo, shows birds of prey attacking ducks (detail)

The special demand for German Expressionist painting was evident in the market prices. Nolde's *Christ and the Woman Taken in Adultery*, a picture painted in 1912 that had been acquired by Justi for the Berlin National Gallery and had been sold abroad by Goebbels for a ridiculously low figure, was returned to Germany for 112,000 Swiss francs. Paintings by Kirchner are at present valued about 50 per cent higher in the German Federal Republic than they are abroad.

Under the influence of the second wave of abstract art, which began about 1945, special attention was given to such early abstract compositions as could be found from the years 1912–1914. In the period of the First World War and the years that followed, these pieces rarely left the homes of the artists themselves or of their friends. Even the most daring German curators took no notice of abstract works when they first appeared. When Hitler's commissioners in 1937 rummaged through the German museums, the seizure of abstract or mainly abstract art amounted only to about 3 per cent of the total of the allegedly 'degenerate' works. They encountered, in all, four compositions by Kandinsky in the museums of Berlin, Halle and Hanover, to which must be added one picture each by Mondrian, Baumeister and Lissitzky, and a still-life by Braque.

B 225

During the Second World War, earlier abstract works first attracted marked attention in New York. The Museum of Modern Art, which had been founded in 1929 and handsomely sustained through bequests and donations, especially by the Rockefeller family, acquired Cubist paintings and sculptures by Braque, Marcel Duchamp, Duchamp-Villon and Gris during the 1940's. After 1950 the prices of Cubist paintings, especially by Braque and Picasso, began to rise. In New York in April 1960 a *Still-Life With Violin* by Braque, painted in 1912, fetched

$ 145,000. In the case of abstract paintings or paintings inclining towards abstraction by other artists active during the First World War, there was never any real international boom despite the interest of dealers. In 1960 a picture by Kandinsky was sold in Stuttgart for 118,000 marks, but in New York a similar composition fetched only $ 7,200. The largest single collection of Kandinskys anywhere in the world was formed by the Solomon R. Guggenheim Foundation, founded in 1937. The Guggenheim Museum in New York, designed by Frank Lloyd Wright and a matter of aesthetic controversy from the day it opened in 1959, is devoted to all phases of modern art from Impressionism to the contemporary American movements.

The Art Nouveau of the 'fin de siècle' was rediscovered, after decades of depreciation, about 1950. The Viennese painter Klimt was admired at exhibitions. Picasso's early works achieved unexpectedly high prices. The Stuttgart Staatsgalerie in 1959 paid 1,200,000 marks for *The Artistes*, painted in 1905.

Just as had happened in 1920, a trend set in after the Second World War which was concerned with the visible world. It was now called 'neo-Realism'. Painters such as Bernard Buffet in Paris helped to win back appreciation for the older masters, from Constable to Utrillo, who thirty years previously had been held in high esteem. A collector in New York who specialized in 'realism' paid $ 19,000 for a landscape by Courbet. Denys Sutton recently observed a slight rise in the price of works by the Barbizon painters. A picture by the Berlin painter Menzel recently entered the Munich museums for the first time.

The affection for neo-Classical art which made itself felt after 1920 has returned in recent years. This became evident on the art market and in the new arrangement of museums. The arrangement completed in 1959 in the Haus der Kunst in Munich of the paintings of the Neue Pinakothek, destroyed in the war and abandoned in 1946, is typical of the taste now prevailing. Here, after their long exile in dark storehouses, late neo-Classical paintings such as the *Spinning Women of Fondi* by the Belgian, Navez, and neo-Classical sculptures are once more on exhibition, and Feuerbach too is effectively displayed.

353, 354 There was a short-lived vogue for Celtic coins with their stylizations of the designs of Greek coins. Artists like Braque were influenced by them, and they attracted the attention of collectors

Little has been said so far of non-European art. The relative frequency with which we come across Far Eastern pottery in European collections formed between the Renaissance and Baroque or between late Baroque and neo-Classicism, is an interesting phenomenon. These are not the real flowering periods of European art but intermediary phases in which alien products achieve an enhanced importance. Thus it is not surprising that the epoch of transition which began about 1890 and which has still not yet reached its conclusion should have felt a certain affinity with the art of non-European peoples. In intellectual life a parallel is provided by the marked influx since 1890 of Buddhist ideas into Europe and the United States.

From the very beginning of the 'fin de siècle', the products of the greater non-European cultures began to attract attention—in particular the graphic and minor arts of Japan and China, the sculpture of India and the applied arts of Islam from Asia Minor and Spain. As far back as 1880 Edmond de Goncourt found his way from the light and delicate creations of his beloved eighteenth century to Japanese coloured woodcuts. The Impressionists also studied Japanese prints and occasionally represented them on the walls that form the background of their portraits. The *Nocturnes* of Whistler were called 'sisters' of the prints of Utamaro. What Toulouse-Lautrec owes to the Far Eastern calligraphic style of line is well known. The creators of Art Nouveau in the applied arts profited by the lessons they learned from the great masters in China and Japan. Around 1900 the Paris financier Isaac de Camondo, a well-known admirer of the late Monet, was also accounted the most discriminating expert and collector of Chinese and Japanese works. In London such interests were becoming widespread.

355, 356 Small figurines from the fringe areas of highly developed early cultures have become increasingly popular in recent years. Their naive, often grotesquely simplified versions of the art-forms of their more sophisticated neighbours are appreciated by the same sort of people who appreciate child art and the paintings of Grandma Moses. The talisman (above) comes from Luristan, the votive figurine (below) from the Danube region

XXIX From the beginning of the present century Egyptian art has been regarded as one of the greatest artistic manifestations of all time. Painters like Gauguin, Maurice Denis and Hodler gleaned many of their principles of composition from Egyptian art. This detail is taken from an eighteenth dynasty wall-painting now in the British Museum.

The collecting of Far Eastern art started very early in the United States. Boston shipowners had already come to know the Far East in the early nineteenth century. The pioneer and explorer instinct which marks the Americans combined in the period which followed with a strong love of collecting strange and exotic things. John La Farge, since 1863 the possessor of Japanese prints, embarked in 1886 on a special journey to the East with a view to completing his collection. The activities of Morse, Fenellosa, Freer and Ross were of particular importance for the spread of Far Eastern art in the United States. Havemeyer and Altman in New York showed that they, as well, were under the influence of the new collecting fashion.

The great collectors soon paid less attention to the late and over-ornate items and quickly turned to the simpler forms of archaic Chinese work. Small smooth bowls and jugs, and ornamental plates made of nephrite and jadeite, generally referred to by the over-all term 'jade', as well as statuettes of onyx and chalcedony, were widely sought in the very years when ancient Egyptian art established itself and when a preference was everywhere given to early works. The firm, indestructible material and the former magic ritual significance of such items gave them value to the restless white man in his great cities. Art as the everlasting thing in a godless world, as an amulet in the restless struggle for existence—these were the motives that no doubt moved men unconsciously in the collecting of such works.

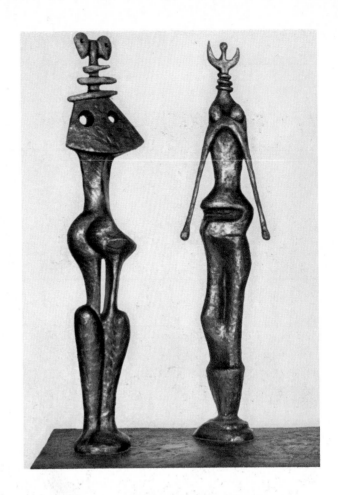

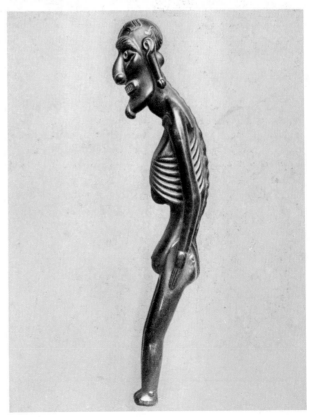

357, 358 Small figures by Henry Moore, like the *King and Queen* (above), often appealed to the same type of collector as did the nineteenth-century ancestor figure from Easter Island (right)

XXX After 1900 the interest of connoisseurs gradually extended towards previously unappreciated works of art in which external influences from other cultures are apparent. In this Phoenician ivory of a lion guarding a sacred tree, the lion wears the headdress and breastplate of the Egyptian goddess Hathor

359, 360 In the 1950's, judging by the prices paid at auctions and the interest shown by museums, important paintings dating from the turn of the century were valued as highly as the work of the Old Masters. This applied not only to paintings by Gauguin, Toulouse-Lautrec and van Gogh whose *Cornfield and Cypress Trees* of 1889 (in the National Gallery, London) is shown above, but also to the early work of Picasso, Kandinsky and Chagall, who painted *The Rabbi* (right) in about 1917 (now in the Kunstmuseum, Basle)

361, 362   After the Second World War, just as after the
First, works of art from private collections came onto
the market. Count Czartoryski rescued Simon Marmion's
Madonna and Child (above) from his palace in Cracow
and sold it to the National Gallery of Victoria in Melbourne; Count Czernin sold Titian's *Doge Andrea Gritti*
(right), once in the collection of Charles I, to the National
Gallery, Washington

363, 364 Economic necessity forced members of the aristocracy to sell works of art which, in many cases, their families had owned for centuries. The Earl of Derby recently sold an early work by Rembrandt, *Belshazzar's Feast* (above), which had belonged to his family since 1736. It is now in the National Gallery in London. The Prince of Liechtenstein sold several of his most important paintings to the National Gallery, Ottawa, including Chardin's *Cook returning from the Market* (right)

Charles L. Freer, the Detroit tycoon, donated his collection in 1906 to the city of Washington, where it is still located as the Freer Gallery of Art. Denman W. Ross presented the Far Eastern section of the Boston Museum of Fine Arts with 11,000 items, among which were more than 400 screens and some 4,000 paintings. In the richness of their contents, the 'Buddhist Room', arranged after the manner adopted by Bode in the Kaiser Friedrich Museum, and the 'Japanese courtyard' of the Boston Museum, were surpassed by nothing comparable in the museums of Europe in 1909. After the revolution of 1911 in China, the art treasures that emigrants were able to get away were brought for sale to the United States. The important collection of the former Prince Kung was auctioned in New York. Before the First World War museums in New York, Chicago and Philadelphia also acquired sections of Far Eastern art. In

Europe the best opportunities for studying this art were offered in the museums of London, Paris and Berlin.

Long before 1900, British officials had little difficulty in becoming acquainted with Indian art in its place of origin. Indian art received a home in London in the India Museum. The most important items of this collection, no longer in existence, are N 330 now housed in the Victoria and Albert Museum. In Paris the Musée Guimet acquired early a rich section of Indian statuary. In the United States the Boston Museum of Fine Arts began to make the public familiar with Indian art soon after 1900. Not only a few sculptures of the Ghandara style, which had been influenced by Greece, were exhibited, but also the large collection of Ananda Coomaraswamy which also took into account earlier periods.

The 'fin de siècle' also concerned itself with Islamic art. At first the most value was placed on relatively late and richly ornamented items. The stylistic qualities and delicacies of colour and the fine patina of bronze objects had a strong attraction for the followers of Art Nouveau. Around 1890 the Marchesa Arconati-Visconti, members of the Rothschild family and Octave Homberg specialized in this kind of collecting. In 1893 the Turkish art dealer Kelekian had great success with a special exhibition in Chicago. Mrs Gardner and Widener were amongst those who bought from him on that occasion.

After 1900 German expeditions brought early work, especially the pottery of Rhagès and Sultanabad, before the public. There was a strong demand for Sassanid and early Caucasian bronzes, and among carpets, particular value was set on the oldest ones. The extension of the Islamic section of the Berlin Museums as a result of the gift made in 1904 by Sultan Abdul Hamid to Kaiser Wilhelm II, together with the finds of the Samarra expedition and above all the great Munich Mohammedan Exhibition of 1910, gave Islamic art considerable influence. Matisse came expressly to Munich and admired the play of colour in Persian tiles and the abstract ornamentation of other pottery work, while Franz Marc passionately absorbed the pure red and blue of Persian miniatures. These impressions were reflected in the creative work of both artists. All museums and private collectors recognized the ornamental as a complete work of art. This development occurred at a time when the first abstract pictures were being painted in Europe.

From 1910 onwards, American collectors and museums displayed great energy in acquiring important works of Islamic art. The Medallion carpet from the Paris palace 'La Bagatelle', already famous in the eighteenth century, entered the Yerkes Collection N 331 in New York. Everett Macy in Chicago pur-

chased a superb velvet cover which, after the liberation of Vienna in 1683, had been found in a Turkish tent; and the Boston Museum of Fine Arts acquired in 1914 the important collection of Persian miniatures formed by Victor Golubieff.

The transition that took place just after 1900 from Gothic to Romanesque art, from Phidias to the archaic art of Greece, from Japanese woodcuts to the applied arts of the early age of China, has already been mentioned. It was in line with this transition that the showcases of ethnological museums should overnight form the basis of a new exciting art world, which revealed itself here for the first time.

The first objects to attract attention in this new manner were the strange by-products from the hands of semi-primitive peoples in the marginal territories of the great cultures. Where such objects were concerned, people enjoyed the simplification or expressive exaggeration of the borrowed and imperfectly understood forms. The hybrid style of Benin 345 produced by sixteenth-century Negro craftsmen, stimulated by Portuguese art, have been fascinating European artists and art-lovers since about 1900. The Lombard reliefs in Cividale, the provincial Roman art of antiquity and the derivatives from the art of Egypt, spoke a language that was suddenly understood. European folk-art also became of interest, in particular the cruder items.

The primitive people of distant continents had even spicier fare to offer the tired European palate. While the bourgeois Degas was still making fun of Parisian painters who believed that they could learn something 'from people with flowers in their hair and a ring in their nose', Matisse discovered in the possession of Père Sauvage in the Rue de Rennes a number of Negro masks from the Congo. Matisse showed them to Picasso, who shortly afterwards reproduced some of them in his paintings of 1907.

XXXI The rooms devoted to the art of Asia Minor have always been popular in museums in Paris, Berlin and London. The British Museum has on permanent loan from the Louvre part of a wall of coloured glass bricks, showing archers of the royal guard, from the palace of Darius in Susa

At exactly the same time the German painters of Die Brücke discovered the Dresden Ethnological 302 Museum. Nolde and Pechstein occasionally painted still-lifes with Negro idols.

The French devotees of modern art turned with amazing speed towards African art and the art of the South Seas. Thoughtful curators of museums like Georg Swarzenski at Frankfurt expressed their misgivings about a situation in which contemporary creations and the work of primitive people were looked upon by collectors as having more or less interchangeable value. Eckart von Sydow, the most passionate prophet of 'exotic art' in the second decade of this century, also had something to say about these problems. The extent to which people profited by the inspiration of Africa and the South Seas could hardly be over-estimated—least of all in the case of Picasso. Schmidt-Rottluff 'had found a quite astonishing formulation of feeling' in exotic art which made his *Maria* appear to be 'at least of equal value with the greatest achievements of Dürer'. Nevertheless, wherever German Expressionist works and those of primitive peoples were placed next to each other, it was all too evident 'to what extent the N 332 art of the South Seas outshines its European rival'. As against this, spokesmen of 'Art Nègre' even found in 1925 in the work from Benin a 'regrettable residue of cultivated sophistication'.

Von Sydow and others like him hoped that the art of primitive peoples would produce a regeneration of European man: 'The only museums which have any real significance today are collections of the works of art of primitive and exotic peoples.' All other museums show us 'the yawning gap between the individual man and his culture'. 'Is not the cry for unity, the search for community, to be heard everywhere among us? How perfectly it seems to be realized in

those exotic collections. If we wander among such primitive things with our senses alert, does not the subconscious in us once more come to light, the contemplation of being, wholeness, unity?'

Such appeals did not die away unheard. At the beginning of the 1920's, people flocked to special exhibitions of the art of primitive peoples. In 1923 the Mannheim Kunsthalle had a conspicuous success with an exhibition that bore the title 'A View of the Primitive World of Forms'. Works by Nolde or the Parisian Fauves were shown, and masks from the Congo or the South Seas came soon after. In the British Museum a colossal stone figure from Easter Island, which had been kept in a quite inconspicuous place since 1869, was set in the position of honour on the landing halfway up the main staircase, and since then has become the first artistic impression received by a visitor to the Museum. In the United States in 1913, the Armory Show of works by the Fauves caused attention to be drawn not only to masks and idols from South Africa and Tahiti, but raised the relics of ancient American cultures and the more recent products of Indian craftsmen to the rank of works of art. Pre-Columbian textiles from Peru, ancient Mexican pottery and Indian popular jewellery held the attention of collectors like Henry G. Marquand and Pratt. The public of the N 333 early 1900's viewed from a new angle the rich contents of the New York Museum of the American Indian, of the Fields Museum in Chicago, of the University Museum in Philadelphia and of the Peabody Museum of Harvard University. The important collection of Maya sculptures at Harvard was significantly transferred to the Fogg Art Museum about 1920.

Interest in the art of non-European peoples naturally weakened in the age of 'new objectivity', but revived after the Second World War, this time without the accompaniment of ecstatic outcries. Along with Nolde, Kirchner and the Fauves of 1907, Negro sculpture again entered important collections. Henry Moore, and other representatives of abstract 357 art who enjoyed labyrinths of form, delighted in the ancient American sculptures, though no questions were asked concerning the significance of the strongly stylized symbols which always surrounded the heads. Important pieces of ancient Mexican sculpture are today sold for prices which go as high as $ 80,000. An American critic recently quoted the admiring words of Dürer, which he uttered when seeing examples of this art in the collection of Margaret of Habsburg, regent of the Netherlands, at Malines. 'We have been slow in catching up with Dürer', the critic went on, 'but this result has now been attained.' The great achievement of the art of early America is no longer doubted by anyone.

XXXII Ever since the turn of the century Pre-Columbian works of art have been bought by museums throughout the Old World. But there also exist rare items, like this Aztec mask from Mexico, which were brought back to Europe either in Columbus' own lifetime or at most a few years after his death

The mighty patrimony of works of art which has been handed down to us has had to be divided up into isolated particles in this book and connected with events in some cases long past and in others relatively recent. We have seen artists and enthusiasts in company with one another and learned something of the initiative supplied by the art trade, of the passions of collectors, of the activity of forgers and of danger from fire, shipwreck and war. The actual number of details which the art-lover who reads this book retains in his memory is of little consequence, but the reading of the text and the sight of the illustrations will, it is hoped, open up to him ways which he has hitherto overlooked and by which he can more easily approach works in the great collections and museums. To take a certain amount of trouble in this matter is something from which nobody should shrink. When thirty years ago Paul Valéry composed an inscription for a French museum that was just about to be built, he had similar thoughts:

It depends on those who pass by
whether I be tomb or treasure,
whether I speak or am silent
depends entirely on you, friend,
do not enter without desire.

365, 366 In recent times the work of Old Masters and that of the great painters of our own century seem to be equally valued. The São Paulo Museu de Arte recently bought Goya's *Don Juan Llorente* (left) and the Staatsgalerie in Stuttgart acquired Picasso's *Mother and Child* (right)

362

367 The presentation of works of art in museums today is characterized by a rejection of all extremism. In the Munich Pinakothek the paintings are hung in two rows, one above the other, on coloured walls, as shown at left

368 The walls of the great Rubens room in the Louvre (right) have for some years now been covered with dark red velvet. The paintings have been given the type of frame common in Antwerp in Rubens' lifetime

369 In the Carpaccio room in the Accademia in Venice (left), the paintings were fitted with narrow gold frames and hung close together to give the impression of a frieze

370 Since 1965 the presentation of the Elgin Marbles in the British Museum (above) has been changed to give the viewer a clearer impression of them as they are believed to have appeared in their original site (Compare Ill. 332)

371 In the recently altered Renaissance sculpture room in the Victoria and Albert Museum in London (below), a successful compromise has been arrived at between the display of individual items, on the one hand, and the overall effect of a collection, on the other

372, 373 In Italy and Germany many museum-directors still prefer light-coloured walls. They also like screens, as in the Brera Gallery in Milan (left).

In New York City, the most distinguished American architect, Frank Lloyd Wright, designed an extremely controversial building for the Solomon R. Guggenheim Museum. The interior circular ramp is shown below

Author's Acknowledgments

THIS BOOK is the result of more than thirty-five years devoted to the study of all aspects of art collecting throughout the ages. For planting the seed of the idea I am indebted to the former general director of the Frankfurt museums, Georg Swarzenski, who suggested in 1929 that I might engage in research into the problems of art collecting in eighteenth-century Frankfurt. During the following years my interest in the subject extended, of course, far beyond the confines of Frankfurt, and it became my ultimate aim to write a comprehensive history of the factors and personalities that have governed the collecting of works of art in all parts of the Western world. A first sketch of this book was published in German under the title *Künstler, Sammler, Publikum* in 1960. The present book, which represents a rewriting and expansion of my earlier work, offers notes, index and bibliography, which should be of particular assistance to those who wish to take up further study of the subject.

My findings are to a great extent the outcome of visits to private collections in many different countries; a series of such visits in London in 1932 were particularly valuable. But even more important have been my enquiries into earlier collections by means of old catalogues, auction papers, travel books, and the like.

Special research I undertook in London in 1963 owes much to the kind assistance of the officials of the British Museum Reading Room, the Warburg Institute and Thames and Hudson. I am also grateful to Denis Mahon, Lady Radnor and Count Seilern for the information they gave me.

Notes on the Text

THE THEME

1 Goncourt, E. de *La Maison d'un artiste*, Paris 1881.

2 M. J. Friedländer's preface to the auction catalogue of the Marcel von Nemes collection, Munich 1931.

3 Dürer's *Thyssen Madonna* is now in the National Gallery, Washington, D.C. Another example is the *Cista Ficoroni*, an Etruscan bronze vessel decorated with scenes from the legend of the Argonauts, which bears the name of its first owner in modern times, Francesco Ficoroni, a learned contemporary of Winckelmann. It is now in the Villa Giulia museum in Rome. The splendid *Lucca Madonna* by Jan van Eyck, now in the Städelsches Kunstinstitut in Frankfurt, belonged, until 1847, to Charles Louis of Bourbon, Duke of Lucca. Giorgione's *Allendale Adoration*, now in the National Gallery, Washington, takes its name from Lord Allendale, a Victorian collector.

CHAPTER 1

4 The earliest signed vessel still in existence is probably a bowl by Aristonothos (seventh century BC) now in the Museo Capitolino in Rome. The vase by Euthymides with a derogatory reference to Euphronius depicts scenes from the Trojan War.

5 These tributes to beautiful youths are not usually thought of as homoerotic, but the archaeologist E. Buschor has nevertheless pointed out, in *Von griechischer Kunst*, Munich 1956, that in representations of non-religious games, dating from the sixth century and later, 'lustful elderly male spectators' are to be seen. There is a bowl from Athens with the inscription *philos Nicola* ('dear Nicola'). Feminine names do not appear very often, but a vessel dating from about 550 celebrated the beautiful Kalisanthe. Both these vases are in Munich.

6 Lysippus made a *Hercules* for Alexander the Great to serve as a table-decoration. No. 136683 in the Museo Nazionale in Naples is probably a copy.

7 See under 'Herondas' in Pauly's *Realenzyklopädie der klassischen Altertumwissenschaft*, vol. 8, Stuttgart 1912.

8 The temple of Hera on Samos, together with its immediate surroundings, has been described as à kind of museum of sculpture.
In 1904 a Danish team working in the temple of Athene at Lindos on the island of Rhodes found remains of votive offerings dating from the Trojan War period (these were probably forgeries), from the sixth to fourth centuries, and from the Hellenistic period.

9 See under 'Sikyon' in the *Wörterbuch der Antike*, 5th ed., Stuttgart 1958.

10 These princely collections might now be described as 'museums'. But the word *mouseion* itself, probably coined by Aristotle, means a literary academy.

11 Tarquinia boasts an exceptionally large collection of Greek vases, as well as an Egyptian porcelain vase (now in the Museum of Tarquinia) that was already about a hundred years old when it was brought to Etruria in the seventh century BC. After the defeat of the Etruscans at Cumae in 474 BC, fewer Greek works of art were imported into Etruria.

12 The Porticus of Octavia now forms the vestibule of the church of Sant'Angelo in Pescheria, near the Theatre of Marcellus.

13 The price paid by Caesar for a work by Timomachus painted about fifty years earlier suggests a comparison with the prices now offered for a Gauguin.

14 A number of the works of Hellenistic art now in Roman museums must have been brought to Rome while still new. Examples are the statue of a young girl from Antium (Anzio), and the *Ephebe* from Subiaco.
The *Laocoön* group, which was already in Rome, clearly influenced the description of the death of Laocoön during the capture of Troy.

15 A statue of Augustus found near Prima Porta reproduces the attitude of the much-admired classical Greek *Doryphorus*: another Augustan work is the frieze found under the Cancelleria in 1937. Both are now in the Vatican Museums.

16 The return to favour of pre-Phidian art probably accounts for the place of honour occupied by the *Ludovisi Throne* on the terrace of Sallust's garden. This is the most important piece of ancient Greek sculpture in Italy (Ills 6, 30); there is a well-known companion-piece in the Museum of Fine Arts in Boston.
The relief of Leucothea with the child Dionysus (Villa Albani, no. 980) is considered to be a genuine archaic work. There are also archaic Greek tomb reliefs in Rome, including one of a young man and a boy (which has been in the Vatican since 1903; Ill. 29) and another of a man and a dog (now in the Museo Nazionale, Naples, no. 6556, but formerly in the Borgia collection formed in and near Rome c. 1800).
It is impossible to list all the imitations and forgeries of archaic art. There are especially rich collections of these in Rome and Naples. A charming example is the statuette of a girl with a daintily lifted skirt, in the British Museum (Ill. 32).

17 The pyramid of Cestius in Rome, as well as numerous imported obelisks, bear witness to the enthusiasm for things Egyptian that prevailed in Rome in the reign of Augustus. The oriental convention of symmetrical composition probably also reached Rome from Egypt, and led to the carving of numbers of laterally inverted copies of statues.

18 Nearly everything that has been recovered from Pompeii is now in the Museo Nazionale, Naples. Among the paintings is a copy of an *Iphigenia in Tauris* by the same Timomachus whose work Caesar valued so highly (see N 13).

19 This bronze head of a centaur, now in the Historisches Museum in Speyer, is illustrated in B 140, p. 19.

20 The decoration inside this bowl, which is now in the

Landesmuseum in Stuttgart, is illustrated in B 140, p. 23.

21 Hamann, R. *Geschichte der Kunst von der Vorgeschichte bis zur Spätantike*, Munich 1952.

22 The Emperor Hadrian had taken lessons in sculpture and painting and still painted occasionally even after he became Emperor. He restored the supposed tomb of Ajax near Troy after it had been worn away by the sea. In 1954 copies of the caryatids on the Erechtheion in Athens were discovered in his villa near Tivoli. He also had a taste for sculpture in the archaic style: relief no. 991 in the Villa Albani museum in Rome is from Hadrian's collection.

23 The sculptures in the temple of Isis near the Pantheon in Rome were probably added to or restored in Hadrian's time. Two figures of recumbent lions, found on this site at the close of the Middle Ages, were carved by order of Pharaoh Nectanebo *c.* 370 BC. They are now in the Vatican. With them was a *Reclining Nile-God* (also now in the Vatican) which is thought to be a copy, made in the reign of Hadrian, of a Hellenistic work from Alexandria.

24 In one private house in Messina travellers could admire works by Praxiteles and Polycletus. Art-lovers made the journey to Cnidus for the sole purpose of seeing the *Aphrodite* of Praxiteles. In the second century AD Apuleius gives us, in his *Florida*, a detailed description of an archaic statue of a youth in the temple precinct on Samos, with its soft Ionic contours and its ancient Samian costume. There were complaints from Roman tourists irritated by the superficial commentaries given by the guides in Greek temples such as the one at Ephesus.

25 In the remoter parts of the civilized world, a more or less classical style of Graeco-Roman art remained popular for a very long time. This is illustrated by the *Corbridge Lanx*, the Mildenhall Treasure (Ill. 43) and the plate with a classical head of a woman from the Sutton Hoo burial, which dates from as late as AD 660: all three are in the British Museum.

26 Meyer, P. *Europäische Kunstgeschichte*, Zürich 1947.

27 Weigert, H. *Geschichte der Europäischen Kunst*, Stuttgart 1951.

28 This explains why the Capitol in Rome, once the seat of the highest of the gods, was later regarded by the Christians as the dwelling of a 'Beast'.

29 In about 1870 several statues were found carefully buried in deep pits in the Roman theatres at Arles and Vaison and perfectly preserved. The *Apollo of Tenea*, now in Munich, the *Laocoön* in the Vatican and many of the well-preserved statues in the Farnese collection in Naples, were carefully buried by the last pagans.

30 Benedict, a monk from the monastery on Mount Soracte, mentions the Capitoline *She-wolf* in his chronicle.
The hand and head of a colossal statue of the Emperor Constantine, found on the Lateran, were thought to be fragments of a statue of Samson. They are now in the Palazzo dei Conservatori in Rome.

31 Another important example is the tomb of Cardinal Fieschi in San Lorenzo fuori le Mura, Rome, which incorporates an ancient sarcophagus. See also Curtius, E. R. *Europäische Literatur und lateinisches Mittelalter*, 4th ed., Berne 1963, p. 407.

32 The *Brunswick Chalice* was regarded in Italy, where it remained until 1630, as a part of the treasure of Solomon's Temple. An onyx vessel made *c.* AD 35 has been in the abbey of St Maurice d'Agaune in Switzerland since the fourth century. Late antique ivory reliefs frequently underwent modification in the interests of a Christian interpretation; there are examples of this in the Monza Cathedral treasure and in the Kestnermuseum in Hanover. Inscriptions were sometimes added. The allegorical representations of the cities of Rome and Constantinople, now in Vienna, bear the names of two Christian virtues, *Temperantia* and *Caritas*. The forms of the letters show that the inscriptions were added around AD 800 (Ill. 50).

33 Many thirteenth-century statues have such a look of antiquity that their true date of origin has only recently been established. The marble bust of Frederick II in Acerenza, for instance, was long thought to be that of some despot of antiquity. Other examples are the head of a woman in the Palazzo di Venezia in Rome, now ascribed to Niccolo Pisano, and the so-called *Berta* on the exterior of the church of Santa Maria Maggiore in Florence.

34 Henry of Blois, Bishop of Winchester and brother of King Stephen, visited Rome in 1151. He took his acquisitions back to Winchester and later to the abbey of Cluny.

35 Just as the Greek term *staurotheke* has survived to this day in Limburg, the reliquaries in Brescia and Nonantola in northern Italy are known by the name of *lipsanoteca* (Greek *leipsana*, relics). Valuable relics reached the west from Constantinople after 1204, including, for instance in 1239, the Crown of Thorns to which the Sainte-Chapelle in Paris owes its special sanctity.

36 The coronation robe, made in 1133, is ornamented mainly with Oriental motifs, and only the Norman bronze ship-standards give an indication of the identity of those who commissioned the work. The robe is now in the Schatzkammer of the Hofburg in Vienna. In 1255 the English court possessed quantities of Islamic tapestries.

37 This piece was certainly used for a time as a chalice. The *Lacock Cup*, now in the British Museum, a fine example of the work of English goldsmiths around 1400, was also a secular cup used as a chalice.

38 A sapphire cameo of St George and an old gold crown with sixty-five cameo gems, both from the Habsburg treasure, were given to Elizabeth I of England in 1578 as guarantee for a loan. Nothing is known of the subsequent whereabouts of these objects (see B 175).

CHAPTER 2

39 As it developed, religious art freed itself from its rigidly ecclesiastical setting. Careful examination of Botticelli's *Adoration of the Kings* in the National Gallery, London (Ill. 71) reveals that the vanishing-point is above the centre of the picture. This work was therefore probably painted with a specific location in mind, low down on the wall of a private house.

40 Florentine artists studied ancient works of art very closely from an early date. The chancel of Santa Maria Novella, which was designed in 1443, incorporates motifs from Trajan's Column, while Bernardo Rosselino adorned the tomb of Leonardo Bruni in Santa Croce with the eagles of Zeus. The same artist patterned his decorations in the Chapel of the Cardinal of Portugal in San Miniato in Florence on an ancient porphyry sarcophagus which, since 1737, has formed part of the tomb of Pope Clement XII in San Giovanni Laterano, Rome. Around 1480 the pagan influence of antique sarcophagi found its fullest expression in the Sassetti tombs in Santa Trinità (see Kaufmann, G. *Florenz*, Stuttgart 1962, p. 313).

41 Lorenzo de' Medici possessed many small bronze statuettes, although his father appears to have taken no

interest in works of this kind. The copy of the *Spinario* now in the National Gallery, Washington, was probably made in Florence in about 1485. Another former Medici possession that has left Italy is the series of representations of the Months by Luca della Robbia now in the Victoria and Albert Museum.

42 Few works from Lorenzo de' Medici's collection remain in Florence. There is a large ancient horse's head in the Museo Archeologico, and in the Bargello are a relief of a battle by Bertoldo, and Pollaiuolo's bronze group *Hercules and Antaeus*.

43 On the Capitol, the *Spinario* was brought under cover in 1471, but the *She-wolf* stood in the open air overlooking the arcades of the old Palazzo dei Conservatori, until Michelangelo's new palace was built in 1544. Mabuse's drawing of the *Spinario* finally found its way into the Welcker collection in Amsterdam (*Gazette des Beaux-Arts*, 1953, p. 167, fig. 16).

44 The *Standing Hercules* pictured in the *Codex Escurialensis* is now in the Galleria Borghese. The *Three Graces* group in Siena Cathedral is not the only example of the use of pagan art in a church. Giuliano Cardinal Cesarini, Deacon of San Sergio (died 1510), used a Roman *cippus* as the base of a tabernacle in a church. It later passed from the Ludovisi collection to the Museo delle Terme. This fine first-century marble bears reliefs depicting cock-fighting; on the corners are goats' heads with eagles under them, so there was no possibility of a Christian interpretation. The inscription (added *c.* 1500–10) has not received the attention it deserves. It reads as follows: EVCHARISTIAE : IVL : CAR : SAXVM : EX : VRBICA : RVINA : RELICTVM : OB : ELEGANTIAM : EREXIT (because of its beauty, Cardinal Julian set up this stone from the ruins of Rome in honour of the Eucharist). Cesarini clearly sought to gratify his taste for antique art even in church. He also placed an ancient statue of an eagle in the vestibule of the church of Santi Apostoli, again with an inscription bearing his own name as donor.

45 This picture was originally part of a triptych painted *c.* 1440–5. Queen Isabella acquired it some fifty years later. It was for many years in the collection of the Dukes of Osuña in Madrid.

46 The earliest pictorial representation of the *Apollo Belvedere* is to be found in the *Codex Escurialensis*, which was drawn by a pupil of Ghirlandaio between 1490 and 1494. The caption reveals that the statue was then still in San Pietro in Vincoli.
Such was the fame of the *Laocoön* that the epitaph of its discoverer Fredi in Santa Maria in Aracoeli describes him as having deserved immortality. Pico della Mirandola, in 1512, was not the only unfriendly critic (B 97). The pious Pope Hadrian VI said in 1523: 'They are idols of the ancients.' Pope Clement VII was not of the same opinion and added the seated Hercules, known as the *Belvedere Torso*, to the other works of art in 1530. A beautiful little clay 'Belvedere Torso', which has been in the Ashmolean Museum in Oxford since 1961, was probably made at about the same time.

47 The *Boy with a Goose* is depicted in Mabuse's altarpiece *The Virgin with St John* (in the Prague State Museum). The Galli collection included the front of a sarcophagus depicting Persephone (now in the Louvre). It is very probable that the staff of the Casa Galli collection described Michelangelo's *Bacchus* to Francisco de Hollanda, when he saw it in 1538, as an antique work.
The *Aphrodite Kallipyge* (Museo Nazionale, Naples), probably a statue of a dancer dating from the first century BC, was another work excavated at this time.

48 There is a small bronze *Dionysus* by an artist from the circle of Francesco da Sant'Agata in the Kestnermuseum in Hanover. In the Ashmolean Museum, Oxford, are an *Inkwell with the Spinario*, and a copy of one of the four horses on the façade of St Mark's. The Louvre has a number of small bronzes of antique appearance that are now regarded as forgeries (B 164).
In Venice in the early sixteenth century, Simone Bianco produced pastiches of ancient art to which he added inscriptions in Greek.
From 1495 onwards, antique-looking statuettes appear in the interior settings of Carpaccio's pictures. An example is the *Sleep of St Ursula*.

49 Above the head of Andrea Odoni's bed hung a picture of a reclining female nude.
In about 1525 Giorgione's *Sleeping Venus* belonged to Geronimo Marcello (it is now in the Dresden Gallery), and the same artist's *La Tempesta*, now in the Accademia in Venice, was owned by Gabriele Vendramin.

50 Differences in taste between Italy and the countries north of the Alps may have been exaggerated. Works that were easy to transport reached the north from Mediterranean countries in large numbers in the fifteenth century. Jan van Eyck copied an Islamic tapestry in his *Guistiniani Altarpiece* (now in Dresden); Memling copied no fewer than six.

51 In Augsburg in the early days of the Reformation a picture was painted of the early Christians destroying pagan idols (Germanisches Museum, Nuremberg, no. 909). Scenes like this must have had a special topical relevance for the followers of Luther, and might be interpreted as an injunction to cast down images of saints in the same way.
There was a recurrence of iconoclasm in a Swiss village church as late as 1957; murals showing Catholic saints were accidentally uncovered and the villagers destroyed them.

52 In some towns there were people with the presence of mind to keep the churches locked during the short period of a riot. A fraternity in Riga which had presented a costly reliquary of St George to the church was able to rescue it (see Holst, N.von *Riga und Reval*, Hamlin 1952).
Other outbreaks of iconoclastic fury occurred in Scandinavia and later in John Knox's Scotland (1552).

53 In his woodcut *Medusa*, Dürer draws inspiration from an archaic Greek coin—another illustration of the breadth of his artistic horizon.

54 Margaret of Austria was Regent of the Netherlands from 1507 to 1530. Van Eyck's *The Marriage of Giovanni Arnolfini and Giovanna Cenami* (Ill. 95) passed to her successor, Maria of Hungary, and was taken to Spain in 1555.

55 American works of art sent by Cortez were seen by Dürer in Mecheln. Surviving examples are Montezuma's feather head-dress (now in the Völkerkundemuseum in Vienna; Ill. 120) and the turquoise mosaic mask of the god Tlaloc, later presented by Charles V to a member of the Medici family (now in the British Museum; Col. Pl. XXXII).

56 A reliquary found in one of the altars of the Stiftskirche in Aschaffenburg in 1954 once belonged to Cardinal Albert. It was basically a gaming-board, made in Venice *c.* 1300, similar to the one in the Guelph treasure, and apparently contained the bones of St Rupert. It is not known whether it was placed inside the altar by order of Cardinal Albert or one of his successors. It is now in the museum at Aschaffenburg (see Huseler, K. 'Das

Aschaffenburger Schachbrett', *Aschaffenburger Jahrbuch*, 1957). A fuller account of Cardinal Albert's collection of paintings is to be found in Holst, N. von 'Die ersten deutschen Kunstsammler', *Weltkunst*, 1953.

57 The *Portrait of Duke Rupert of Mecklenburg*, painted in Berlin in 1507, is mentioned in 1685 in the inventory of Heidelberg Castle; it is highly probable that this portrait (now in the Mauritshuis in The Hague) also belonged to Ottheinrich. This would suggest a particular interest in Jacopo de' Barbari on Ottheinrich's part. (*Catalogue des tableaux*, Mauritshuis, The Hague 1955, p. 7)

58 In 1402 the Duc de Berry acquired a gold version of the *Medal of Constantine*. (The reverse of this medal is shown in Ill. 7.) But in the course of the siege of Bourges in 1412 many of the valuable items in the Duke's collection were melted down. In the museum in Bourges there is a bowl with sixteen embossments which the Duke presented to the cathedral. The carved stones of its cameo cross are in the Louvre. Part of the Duke's collection apparently passed on to the German Habsburgs by way of Charles the Bold and the Emperor Maximilian, his son-in-law. It is also thought that an antique sculpture, the *Aix Persian*, was the model for Adam in one of the Books of Hours belonging to the Duke.
In 1965 an exhibition entitled 'Mécènes et Amateurs d'Art Berrichons du Moyen Age et de la Renaissance' was held in Bourges. Examples from the Duke's books of miniatures are now to be seen in the Musée Condé in Chantilly and in The Cloisters in New York.

59 It is probable that the *Rubens Vase* which had belonged around 1380 to Louis of France, Duke of Anjou, and which formed part of Francis I's collection in Fontainebleau, was in the same place at the same time as the *Gemma Augustea*. It is quite likely therefore that both items were taken from Fontainebleau by the Huguenots in 1591.

60 In 1515 Francis I asked the Pope in vain for the *Laocoön* group. Baccio Bandinelli subsequently made him a full-size copy in marble, but it never left Italy (now in the Uffizi).

61 Justi, C. 'Philipp II als Kunstfreund', *Zeitschrift für bildende Kunst*, 1881.

62 In the age of Mannerism the prices paid for works of art from previous generations rose considerably. For instance in 1587 the Farnese family paid 500 scudi for the Cavalieri collection of drawings by Michelangelo. Bartolomeo Passarotti (1529-92) faked Michelangelo drawings.

63 Paolo Lomazzo was a painter and art theorist; he wrote *Idea del Tempio della Pittura*, which was published in Milan in 1590.

64 Tietze, H. *Tintoretto*, London 1948.

65 The statues in the Valle collection were sold to the Medici towards the end of the sixteenth century, among them several female figures and the *Thusnelda* (now in the Loggia dei Lanzi in Florence), as well as the *Marsyas* (Uffizi, no. 155). The *Venus de Medici* probably came from the Valle collection too.
In the cortile shown in Ill. 106 Francisco de Hollanda saw inscriptions which claimed that these works of art were not put there 'ad voluptatem' (for mere pleasure), but to delight the artistic sense of 'friend and fellow citizens'.

66 It has been suggested that collectors actually liked the fragmentary nature of certain sculptures. This applied even to relatively recent works like the *David of the Casa Martelli* by Donatello. But the passion for restoration would appear to contradict this theory.

Lucius Verus in the Uffizi (*Catalogue of Sculptures*, 1960, vol. 2, no. 190) and *Ganymede and the Eagle* (formerly in Newby Hall, present whereabouts unknown) are two fakes of antique sculptures typical of the second half of the sixteenth century.

67 Vincenzo Scamozzi was a well-informed architectural theorist. His *Idea dell'Architettura*, published in Venice in 1615, was widely read.

68 For older views of the Tribuna and the galleries in the Uffizi see B 140 and *Antiquità Viva*, 3 May 1964. The gallery in the Gonzaga palace appears not to have been finished before 1611. Its superb restoration in 1934 was due to the generosity of the famous American collector Samuel Kress (see Kümmel, S. *Die Galerie als architektonische Raumform*, Heidelberg 1947.)

69 This quotation is taken from a letter, dated 29 February 1568, written by the Italian art dealer Stoppio, which was discovered by H. Zimmermann and published in the *Mitteilungen des Instituts für Österreichische Geschichtsforschung*, in 1901.

70 One of the models for the hall of the 'Antiquarium' in Munich must have been the gallery which Giovanni Grimani, the Patriarch of Aquileia, had built to house his collection of about 100 pieces of antique sculpture in his palace in Venice. We also know that in the Palazzo Grimani antique heads and busts formed an integral part of the architecture of the gallery (B 171).

71 In his *Dialogo degli errori dei pittori* in 1564 Gilio lamented the fact that artists demonstrated only their technical ability.

72 Lassels, J. R. *Voyage of Italy*, London 1670.

73 The manuscipts are now in the Staatsbibliothek in Munich.

74 Doering, O. *Des Augsburger Patriziers Philipp Hainhofer's Beziehungen zu Herzog Philipp II von Pommern*, Vienna 1894.

75 The small bronze copy of the statue of Marcus Aurelius was made by Filarete; it was given in 1585 by Guiliano Gonzaga to Duke August, the ruler of Dresden. In those times princely collectors kept in close touch with each other irrespective of differences of creed or nationality. The works mentioned here are in Dresden.

76 For an illustration of the copy of the *Bed of Polycletus* in the Palazzo Mattei see Goldscheider, L. *The Drawings of Michelangelo*, no. 143.

77 Just as Philip II had works of art brought from the Netherlands to protect them from the iconoclasts, so too in 1580 Rudolph II ordered Mabuse's altarpiece *The Virgin with St Luke* (painted in 1515) to be transferred from the Church of St Romuald in Malines to Prague Cathedral. It is now in the State Museum in Prague.

78 Karel van Mander wrote about artists and described his travels in *Schilderboek*, Alkmaar 1604.

CHAPTER 3

79 Reber, F. von *Maximilian I als Gemäldesammler*, Munich 1892. Weiss, J. 'Kurfürst Maximilian und seine Galerie', *Historisch-Politische Blätter für das katholische Deutschland*, 1908.

80 In the sixteenth century the reliquary containing St Elisabeth's skull was still in the possession of the Teutonic Knights in Marburg. From there it was probably taken to Mergentheim, where the Knights had another settlement, and from here removed to Würzburg.
Mention must also be made of the Iron Throne, an interesting example of German craftsmanship of the

sixteenth century, which had been given to Rudolph II by the city of Augsburg, and which was later taken from Prague by the Swedes. It is now owned by Lord Radnor of Longford Castle, near Salisbury.

81 For an illustration, see Granberg, O. *Inventaire Général des Peintures en Suède*, Stockholm 1912, vol. 2, p. 33.

82 Among paintings by Arcimboldo which reached Sweden was the *Rudolph as the God Vertumnus*, which had been celebrated in a poem by G. Comanini some twenty years after its completion. It is now in the possession of Baron Essen in Skokloster, Sweden.

83 The gift of the Dürers to Madrid indicates that the Queen's letters to Prince Orsini were sometimes merely designed to flatter an Italian. Christina also took works by German and Netherlandish masters with her to Rome. There one can find numerous mementoes of the Queen's stay. On the wall by the *Ariadne* (*Cleopatra*) in the Vatican Museum is a Latin poem addressed to 'Regina Suecorum, Goteorum, Vandalorum'. In Rome Christina owned Veronese's charming *Mars and Venus united by Love* which doubtless came from Prague as well (now in the Metropolitan Museum, New York).

84 In 1539 the French ambassador Marillac wrote that Henry VIII delighted in painting — which, in the context, referred to contemporary painting. The most important picture owned by Henry VIII still in England is Mabuse's *Adam and Eve* (in Hampton Court).

85 The *Self-portrait* (in the Prado) and *The Painter's Father* (in the National Gallery, London). Arundel also acquired two portraits by Dürer of a young girl (a member of the Furleger family). One of these is in the Städelsches Kunstinstitut in Frankfurt, and the other was known to be in a private collection in Paris in 1950.

86 Hervey, M. F. S. *The Life, Correspondence and Collections of Thomas Howard, Earl of Arundel*, Cambridge 1921.

87 It is now accepted that Holbein's *Sir Henry Wyatt*, *Nikolaus Kratzer* and *Bishop Warham* in the Louvre were once in the Arundel collection.

88 In 1637-38 Arundel apparently paid £10,000 for a large collection of drawings previously owned by Nys, the art dealer. He also purchased a portfolio of drawings, which had been assembled by Pompeo Leoni, and which after 1608 had belonged to Don Juan de Espina. Apart from the Leonardo drawing mentioned in the text, Arundel also owned his *Neptune* and his *Study for the Sforza Monument* (both now in the Royal Collection). F. Grossmann proved that Arundel must have owned the painting by Antonello now in the Dresden Gallery (*The Burlington Magazine*, 1944).

89 These additions appear in the second edition of 1634.

90 There is a portrait of Buckingham by Rubens in the Palazzo Pitti in Florence. The *Catalogue of the Curious Collection of Pictures of George Villiers, Duke of Buckingham*, London 1758, includes only a fraction of the paintings which remained in England throughout the Commonwealth and which were passed on to Buckingham's son. The most valuable of them were sold on the Continent.

91 Collectors of classical works of art influenced by Arundel included Lord Roos, Sir Michael Dormer and Philip Herbert, Earl of Montgomery (later the fourth Earl of Pembroke), and, after 1628, Charles I himself.

92 Cammel, C. R. *The Great Duke of Buckingham*, London 1939.

93 Mentioned by Carducho in his *Dialogues*.

94 From a letter sent by Rubens in 1625. Philipps, C. *The Picture Gallery of Charles I*, London 1896; Hoff, U. *Charles I*, London 1942.

95 Charles I's seal is still on the back of Holbein's *Erasmus* (in the Louvre) as well as Cranach's *Cuspinian* (in the Reinhart Collection in Winterthur; Ill. 140). In 1637 the complete collection of a certain Fröschl reached the King from Germany. On the subject of Bartolomeo della Nave's 224 paintings see Waterhouse, E. K. 'Paintings from Venice for 17th Century England', *Italian Studies*, 1952.

96 The painting by van Dyck showing Charles I's head from three different angles—considered to be one of his finest portraits—was painted in 1636 with the intention of giving Bernini in Rome something on which to base a portrait bust of the King. Much later the picture returned to England, and is now in the Royal Collection.

97 The dealer de Critz apparently played a part in the sale. Of the King's collection there remained in England the *Wilton Diptych* of 1400 (now in the National Gallery), Dürer's *Young Man* and Holbein's *Derich Born* (both in the Royal Collection).
A parallel to the rejection of Italian Renaissance paintings by the Puritans of Cromwell's time can be seen in the behaviour of the Bohemians thirty years earlier. There the Protestants wanted to dispose of the paintings that had been bought by Rudolph II on account of their 'shameless representation of the naked human body'.

98 The collector Jabach who lived in Paris seems to have been able to acquire paintings from Charles's collection without undue delay. He bought Giorgione's *Concert Champêtre*, which soon became the property of Louis XIV, and also van Eyck's little *Giustiniani Altarpiece*, which Charles had been told was a Dürer. The Dutch connoisseur Reynst purchased a few of King Charles's paintings, but almost all of these returned to the House of Stuart a few decades later. The Mauritshuis in The Hague, however, retains a beautiful portrait of a woman by Holbein.

99 Fetti's *Parable of the Sower and the Tares* (now owned by Count Seilern in London) was mentioned in Prague in 1718, 1737 and 1763, so it must have been taken there almost immediately.

100 When it came to small objects, their scruples were not so apparent. Archduke Albert owned two small replicas of the *Dawn* and *Night* figures by Michelangelo from the Medici tomb in Florence. In 1617 Jan Bruegel the Younger reproduced these statuettes in a painting which is now in the Prado.

101 Rubens might have seen Titian's *Woman in a Fur* (Ill. 138) either as a young man in Spain or in England in 1629 when he was knighted by Charles I and given an honorary doctorate at Cambridge.

102 Rubens' house in Antwerp has been skilfully restored and it now gives us a clear picture of how the artist displayed his own collection. He had a special circular room for his statues.

103 Letter from Rubens to Carleton. Saunders-Magurn, R. *The Letters of Peter Paul Rubens*, Cambridge (Mass.) 1955.

104 See also Mayer, A. L. *Pantheon*, 1931, vol. 7, p. 114.

105 Joachim Sandrart mentions this in his invaluable *Akademie der Bau- und Malereikünste*, 1675.

106 *The Triumph of Charles V*, a delightful small relief carved by Daucher in 1522 (now in the Metropolitan Museum, New York) was certainly among the works of art belonging to the Emperor.

107 Boschini, M. *Carta del Navegar pittoresco*, Venice 1660.

108 Sandrart also stated that in 1650 King Charles X of Sweden bought a painting which he was led to believe was by Giorgione, but which was in fact by Pietro della Vecchia.
Leopold Wilhelm's collection included Titian's *Flora*

(now in the Uffizi) and a portrait of the Doge Gritti (Ill. 362).

109 Archduke Leopold Wilhelm owned Veronese's *Rebecca at the Well* (Ill. 135). Among the paintings by Fetti, a Mantuan artist of the early seventeenth century, whose work is now highly prized, was the *Return of the Prodigal Son* (now in Count Seilern's collection in London). The Archduke also bought from Charles I's collection the small replicas of famous Roman statues (Ill. 85) made by the Mantuan artist Alari Bonacolsi, known as Antico, and he owned one of the best Rubenses in the Berlin Museums, *Neptune and Amphitryon*. This painting was unfortunately destroyed in 1945.

110 Geertgen's *Lamentation* came from Charles I's collection. The Bruegel paintings reached the governor's palace in Brussels in 1594.

111 By the end of 1651 Leopold Wilhelm had already sent Steen's *Peasant Wedding* and Terborch's *Woman Peeling an Apple* to Vienna.

112 See B 140, p. 97. Painting no. 1813 in the Prado, by David Teniers the Younger, is a picture of this kind; its presence in Spain as early as 1666 has been authenticated. In it one can see paintings by Raphael, Titian, Mabuse, van Dyck, Ribera, etc. Van Haecht's *The Atelier of Apelles* (1635) shows several famous paintings which, contrary to previous opinion, were certainly not all owned by the collector Cornelius van der Geest. This painting is now in the Mauritshuis in The Hague. The Kansas Museum of Art has recently acquired a similar work by Gilles van Tilborgh. (See also S. Speth-Holterhoff in the *Register of the Museum of Art of the University of Kansas*, 1955, and in the *Bulletin des Musées Royaux*, Brussels 1960.)

113 Leopold Wilhelm also introduced the idea of standardized frames.

114 The word 'pinacotheca' may well have been first revived in Mantua in about 1600. The word appears from time to time in Munich about ten years later.

115 These evolutions refer to a Haarlem collection that was up for sale in 1674. Today paintings by Lastmann can hardly find a buyer. Vermeer's *The Lacemaker* fetched 150 guilders in 1778, 9 in 1815, 260 in 1851, and 7,270 francs in 1870. These prices were, of course, influenced to some extent by political and economic conditions.

116 This famous picture, painted by Holbein for a Catholic in Catholic terms, reached Holland in about 1610. The fake was probably commissioned from Sarburgh by the art dealer Le Blond. Until about 1900 it was accepted by the Dresden Gallery as a genuine Holbein.

117 See *Ostasiatische Zeitschrift*, 1932, Pl. 19.

118 Illustrated in B 140, p. 107. For the head of a youth (now thought to be a Roman copy of a Greek original) see *Katalog der Skulpturen der Antikenableitung der Berliner Museen*, 1931, vol. 4, K 141.

119 A Madonna from Pilsen in Bohemia, which contributed to the defeat of the Winter King (brother-in-law of Charles I of England), was brought to Rome and placed in the Church of San Paolo—thereafter known as Santa Maria della Vittoria. In 1656 a miraculous statue of the Madonna (probably an Italian copy of a thirteenth-century French original) was incorporated in the high altar of Santa Maria in Campitello in Rome.
Around 1640 the Habsburg treasure was divided into the sacred and the profane. (It is only recently that the two have been re-combined). During the period of the Thirty Years War, Catholics found the juxtaposition of holy relics and objets d'art, such as the *Gemma Augustea*, intolerable. Several altarpieces which had belonged to Charles I of England were reconsecrated by the King of Spain; they included Raphael's *La Perla* and Titian's *Jacopo Pesaro and Pope Alexander VI before St Peter* (Ill. 223).
And finally, when an Italian art-lover was shown Leonardo's *St John the Baptist* in 1625, he said it was not pious enough (B 116).

120 For the Merian family collection of drawings see *Berliner Museen, Berichte aus den preussischen Kunstsammlungen*, 1940, p. 58. The Great Elector had learned, as a young man in Holland, to value both classical sculpture and eastern art (*cf*. N 118).

121 The Saraceni altarpiece was in the Orleans collection in the eighteenth century; the collection was sold to three English collectors during the Revolution. In 1890 the 9th Earl of Carlisle donated it to the Benedictine monastery at Ampleforth—where it remains today, virtually forgotten (see Holst, N. von 'Elisabeth Charlotte von der Pfalz als Kunstsammlerin', *Rhein-Neckar-Zeitung*, 25 May 1952).

122 Rubens' *St Christopher and a Hermit* is in the Munich Pinakothek.

123 Wittkower, R. *Gian Lorenzo Bernini*, London 1954.

124 This famous Greek statue, dating from *c*. 200 BC, was most probably bought by the Medici as part of the Valle collection of antiquities, but it did not leave Rome for Florence till 1677.
The manner in which sculpture was displayed in Rome followed the Valle pattern of using a courtyard. In this respect the Palazzo Mattei was rather old-fashioned. Asdrubale Mattei lined the walls, as an inscription confirms, with 'signa veterum' and 'spolia ex antiquitate'. But here too, in the upper loggia, one can see a *Fredericus* (*c*. 1625?), probably Frederick Barbarossa. Perhaps Mattei had intended to have a series of great rulers.
Most of the antique statues and busts in Cardinal Scipione Borghese's collection were used to decorate the façade of the 'Palazzetto' or 'Casino' on the Pincian, the upper storey of which today contains the famous Borghese collection of paintings. In 1807 these sculptures went to the Louvre, and the only indication we have of their previous arrangement is a picture painted before 1640 by Guglielmo Baur (B 116, Pl. 6).

125 When she married an Austrian archduke, Claudia de' Medici's dowry included a Renaissance work—Rossellino's relief of the Virgin Mary (now in the Kunsthistorisches Museum in Vienna).

126 Barri, G. *Viaggio pittoresco*, Venice 1671. Barri himself was a minor painter.

127 In 1668 Donatello's organ loft in Florence Cathedral was repositioned in the choir so that it could be more easily admired.

128 The small Flemish landscapes in the Pinacoteca Ambrosiana were purchased by its founder Cardinal Federico Borromeo. The Roman patron and collector Vincenzo Giustiniani spent four months travelling in the Netherlands and after that occasionally granted free board and lodging to artists who came from there. In 1687 Cosimo de' Medici bought two large paintings by Rubens from the abbey of Saint Sépulchre near Cambrai (they are now in the Uffizi).

129 The most important paintings from the Borghese collection remained in Rome, but many of the classical sculptures—43 statues, 70 busts and 144 reliefs—went to Paris in 1807. The *Borghese Fencer* and the *Borghese Hermaphrodite* are still in the Louvre. The *Borghese Hera* (Ill. 4) was sold to Ny Carlsberg Glyptothek, Copenhagen, in 1890.

Ludovico Ludovisi, the nephew of Pope Gregory XV, started a collection of antique sculpture which grew to be perhaps the most valuable in all Rome during the seventeenth century. (It included the remains of the Cesarini collection.) Ludovisi also owned an extensive collection of paintings.

The third largest collector of ancient sculpture, after the Borghese and the Ludovisi, was the Marchese Vincenzo Giustiniani. The *Giustiniani Pallas*, the statue of a Roman preparing a sacrifice (both in the Vatican) and the *Giustiniani Apollo* (in the British Museum) remind us of the one-time glory of this collection. His picture gallery contained no less than thirteen Caravaggios.

Though of lesser importance, Camillo Massimo and Cassiano del Pozzo must also be mentioned as owners of sizable collections.

130 The paintings in the Palazzo Pitti were housed in a series of rectangular rooms rather than in a long 'galleria'; for that reason the collection there is usually called a 'quadreria' (collection of paintings). The decorated ceilings were completed c. 1665 and have since been little altered.

131 The d'Este in Modena were already beginning to sell works of art at the end of the seventeenth century. Several bronze statuettes were bought by Louis XIV through the intermediary of Le Notre, the architect and landscape gardner.

Part of the Farnese picture collection was brought from Rome to the Palazzo del Giardino in Parma in 1662; about a century later it was transferred to Naples. A selection of paintings from the collection can be seen in the Museo di Capodimonte.

132 Boschini, M. *Carta del Navegar pittoresco*, Venice 1660. Also Fagiolo-dell'Arco, M. *Domenichino*, Rome 1963.

133 Rose, H. *Tagebuch des Herrn von Chantelou über die Reise von Bernini nach Frankreich*, Munich 1919.

134 Part of Jabach's collection reached Cologne, where he was born. Some items also went to Austria via his nephews Franz and Bernhard von Imstenradt (B 12, B 15).

135 Mazarin owned paintings by Correggio and Titian, including the *Pardo Venus*, which he bought when Charles I's collection was broken up. Surprisingly, he also purchased the work of an old German master: the painted table-top by H. S. Beham (now in the Louvre), which had once belonged to Cardinal Albert of Brandenburg. (See also the catalogue of the Mazarin exhibition organized by the Bibliothèque Nationale, Paris, in 1961.)

136 The first painting by Tintoretto known to have reached Paris was *Susanna and the Elders* (now in the Louvre), which was bought by the Marquis Hauterive in 1684.

137 Other paintings by Rubens in his collection included *Andromeda* (Detroit Institute of Arts), *The Judgment of Paris* (Dresden Gallery) and six landscapes (two in the Berlin Museums, two in the Palazzo Pitti, one in the Hermitage and one in the British Royal Collection).

138 In this collection there were about 400 drawings by Parmigianino, 125 by van Dyck, 103 by Titian, about 50 by Giorgione but also 154 by Caravaggio.

139 Madame de Verrue had married in 1683 when she was 13 years old. Much later she became the mistress of a member of the House of Savoy. After her death, as her possessions were being auctioned, the prospective buyers were heard to repeat the epitaph she herself had jokingly composed.

> Ci-gît dans une paix profonde
> Cette dame de volupté
> Qui, pour plus grande sureté
> Fit son paradis de ce monde.

140 Italian collectors such as Ferdinando de' Medici and Marchese Ruffo commissioned paintings to match their most important pieces in size and composition so that the walls could be symmetrically decorated. Guercino had to provide the Marchese with a painting to match Rembrandt's *Aristotle contemplating the Bust of Homer* (Ill. 155).

141 The Munich Residenz provides an example of the use of the display cabinet. These china cabinets were only used where valuable porcelain from the Far East, which often came via Holland, was readily available. The Hohenzollerns around 1700 had porcelain cabinets in their castles of Oranienburg, Charlottenburg, and Monbijou.

142 When in 1657 Leopoldo de' Medici wanted a painting by Tintoretto, his agent could not find one in Venice. He did, however, manage to purchase a portrait of an admiral in Vienna (no. 921 in the Uffizi).

143 In Turin, among the pictures from Prince Eugen's collection, are Rembrandt's *Portrait of the Artist's Father* and some van Dyck portraits. See Bludau, H. *Kunst und Wissenschaft im Leben des Prinzen Eugen*, Berlin 1942.

144 Levin, T. 'Beiträge zur Geschichte der Kunstbestrebungen in dem Hause Pfalz-Neuburg', I-III, *Jahrbuch des Düsseldorfer Geschichtsvereins*, vols 19, 20, 23, Düsseldorf 1905, 1906, 1909.

145 In 1660 the Dutch government presented Charles II of England with a collection of works of art thought to have included 24 paintings and 12 antique statues (chiefly works of art from Charles I's collection which were sold to Holland after the King's execution). Among them was Lotto's portrait of Andrea Odoni, the collector (Ill. 88). This picture is now in Hampton Court. William III of Orange brought some of these paintings back to Holland. This is certainly true of the *Young Mother* painted by Dou in 1658 and Holbein's *Jane Seymour* (both in the Mauritshuis in The Hague).

CHAPTER 4

146 This statement was made by Winckelmann; see B 221.

147 Fortia de Piles made his observations on collections in central and eastern Europe in the years 1788–90. See also B 134.

148 Carl Justi also deals with the founding of the Dresden Gallery in *Winckelmann in Deutschland*, Leipzig 1866.

149 This saying was quoted by Algarotti in a letter in 1749. But it is significant that though Algarotti supported contemporary Italian painting, the Watteaus in Berlin held even him temporarily in their sway.

150 Jonathan Richardson (1665–1745) and his son, also Jonathan, were both collectors and dealers. They published *An essay in the theory of painting*, London 1715; *The Connoisseur*, London 1719; and *An account of the Statues, Bas-reliefs, Drawings and Pictures in Italy*, London 1722, all of which had an enormous influence on collectors.

151 Even as a young man Algarotti seems to have recognized the value of Domenichino and Annibale Carracci in Rome and of Fra Bartolommeo in Florence (B 116). Later, in England, Algarotti became very interested in buildings which showed the influence of Palladio.

152 Winckelmann, J. J. *Gedanken über die Nachahmung der griechischen Werke*, Dresden 1755.

153 Carl Heinrich Heinecken, born in Lübeck in 1706, was an agent who assisted in the choice of pictures for the Dresden Gallery. His *Nachrichten von Künstlern* was published in 1768.

154 Baumecker, R. *Winckelmann in seinen Dresdner Schriften*, Berlin 1933.

155 The prices paid are listed only in the Amsterdam version of the catalogue (B 136). In Spain Tiepolo's work suffered a similar setback. In 1770 the altarpieces he had just painted for Aranjuez were replaced with paintings by Mengs.

156 This work, much admired by Burckhardt, was in 1760 still thought to be by Giorgione.

157 A. von Drach's 'Zur Geschichte der Kasseler Gemälde-galerie', in the 1888 edition of the gallery catalogue.

158 The idea that one should not have too many paintings by any one artist, but rather an example of the work of as many of them as possible is typical of the rationalism of the Enlightenment. When Leopold II ruled Florence, two of Uccello's three battle paintings were given away (now in the Louvre and the National Gallery, London).

159 Catherine II owned Watteau's *Mezzetin* (Metropolitan Museum, New York), but she also remained loyal to the great sixteenth-century Venetians and bought Titian's *Woman in a Fur* which had previously been in Crozat's collection in Paris.

160 They included Raphael's *St George and the Dragon* (Ill. 78), Poussin's *Triumph of Galatea* (sold to the Philadelphia Museum of Art in 1936) and Murillo's *Rest on the Flight into Egypt*.

161 Lessing, G. E. *Brief antiquarischen Inhalts*, 1768.

162 Seidel, P. 'Friedrich der Grosse als Sammler', *Jahrbuch der Preussischen Kunstsammlungen*, 1892.

163 The King wrote this letter to his sister in Bayreuth; see also B 125.

164 They included Rembrandt's magnificent *Joseph accused by Potiphar's Wife* (now in the National Gallery, Washington).

165 Fortia de Piles, A. *Voyage . . . en Allemagne, Russie etc.*, *1790–1792*, Paris 1796.

166 Count Tessin, the Swedish ambassador in France, took Mme Boucher as his mistress, and so acquired some of her husband's best paintings. In Venice the Count bought Tiepolo's *Danae* (now in the National Museum in Stockholm).

167 These remarks are recorded by A. Bonnafé in *Les collectionneurs de l'ancienne France*, Paris 1873, p. 67. Sedaine's conversations were published anonymously in 1778, and later repeated in the *Revue Universelle*, 1861.

168 Rembrandt's *Christ at Emmaus* went for only 170 guilders at the Six sale in Amsterdam in 1734. But in 1743, when the painter Rigaud died, the Rembrandts in his collection were already considered to be worth more.

169 Babelon, J. *Choix de Bronzes de la Collection Caylus*, Paris 1928, Pl. 23.

170 'In hanging pictures, opposition makes harmony. Histories should be mixed with landscapes or heads.' (Horace Walpole; see B 324.)

171 These pictures had been painted for Dr Mead, and in 1755 they were auctioned as part of his estate.

172 The first remark was by Hogarth, the second by Horace Walpole (B 324).
Many excellent examples of Reni's work can be seen in the gallery of Dulwich College and also in the Fitzwilliam Museum in Cambridge. The Fitzwilliam also owns Salvator Rosa's *Umana Fragilità*, an important work.

173 Around 1770 Robert Walpole owned three Murillos; in 1787 Gainsborough bought *John the Baptist in the Wilderness*, either by Murillo or a follower, which has been in the National Gallery in London since 1924. The 2nd Duke of Devonshire owned the *Liber Veritatis* by Claude (now in the British Museum).

174 Among 198 paintings sent direct to St Petersburg were Poussin's *Rest on the Flight into Egypt*, Claude's *Evening* and *Bay of Bajae*, Rubens' *Bacchanal* and several van Dyck portraits, including those of Charles I, the Archbishop of Canterbury and Inigo Jones.

175 Joseph Smith's main importance lies in his dealings with the artists of his day. George III of England received 53 Canalettos from him, and later, from his widow, 7 paintings by Piazzetta, 4 by Longhi, and 38 by Rosalba Carriera.

176 Lord John Somers (1630–1714) bought Father Sebastiano Resta's famous collection. Later many of these drawings reached William Cavendish, the 2nd Duke of Devonshire (1665–1729).

177 John Zoffany painted a picture showing hordes of Englishmen looking at the antique sculptures in the Tribuna of the Uffizi. This painting became part of the Royal Collection probably soon after 1781 (now in Windsor Castle).
Greek red-figure vases were so popular that Wedgwood made copies of them.

178 Jenkins once declared that it was difficult to get English collectors to buy 'statues without heads'—and, without a single pang of conscience, he proceeded to add the missing parts where he deemed them necessary. In order to sell tomb-sculptures from the Villa Mattei more easily, Jenkins had inscriptions carved on them, and for a long time these inscriptions were thought to be genuine.

179 The fragment of the Parthenon frieze belonged to the 'Society of Dilettanti'. In 1725 a Greek relief reached London, in 1779 a statue of Hercules was discovered in Syria (see *Ancient Marbles in the British Museum*, vol. 2, Pl. 41 and vol. 3, Pl. 2 respectively).

180 He had also inherited quite an important collection. His purchases were later restricted by the increase in the price of antique sculpture brought about by neo-Classicism.
In 1830 the archaeologist Westmacott rearranged the sculpture in Wilton House. Since then many items from the collection have been sold.

181 The *Arundel Homer* reached 130 guineas at Dr Mead's auction. The portrait head of the philosopher Chrysippus is now considered to be a copy of a lost original by Eubulides of Athens.

182 Batoni's portrait of William Wedell (1736–92) was painted in 1766. The walls behind the sculpture were painted red.

183 Like Wedell, Blundell had a circular room with top-lighting constructed to house the most important sculptures in his collection. He also collected paintings and owned the *Ince Hall Madonna* by Jan van Eyck (Ill. 7).

184 The *Lansdowne Hercules* was excavated in Hadrian's Villa in 1791.
Other important collectors of the period before 1800 include Margaret, the Duchess of Portland and Charles Townley. In 1785 the Duchess of Portland acquired what came to be known as the *Portland Vase*. One year later, when the 'Portland Museum' was being auctioned, a bid of £1029 was made for the vase. The *Portland Vase* has belonged to the British Museum since 1945.
Charles Townley was among the most active English collectors in Rome around 1770. His collection was incorporated in the British Museum.

185 Horace Walpole bought Strawberry Hill in 1747. The first period of 'Gothicization' took place between 1750 and 1753. In 1760–61 several rooms were designed with Late Gothic fan-vaulting probably based on Henry VII's

Chapel in Westminster Abbey. Extensive use was made of gilding and mirrors.

As a collector, Walpole's interests were widespread. In addition to the Swiss glass panels he bought after 1740, his purchases included, in 1745, an antique eagle and a small Egyptian basalt head of Serapis. The last two items were included in 1842 in a sale of objets d'art from Strawberry Hill. French furniture from Strawberry Hill was auctioned at Christie's on 26 June 1895.

The 'Gotisches Haus' in Wörlitz near Dessau, which was designed after 1775, retained much of its original decor until the Second World War. The name 'Gotisches Haus' seems to have been first used in 1789.

186 Hugford died in 1778, Patch in 1782. Richardson also owned drawings by Gozzoli, Lippi and Pollaiuolo. John Strange, who lived in Venice till 1788, bought a painting by Crivelli (now in the National Gallery, London), and Frederic Hervey, who died in Italy in 1803, was interested in the work of Cimabue and Giotto.

Another English collector in Venice was Peter Edwards. From 1778 onwards he owned a 'Gabinetto di restauro'. When the Galleria dell'Accademia was founded in 1810, Edwards used his influence to see that some early masters were included (Andrea del Murano, for instance.)

187 See Holst, N. von 'Ein Lieblingsbild Goethes', *Mainzer Zeitschrift*, 1949–50.

188 Piazzetta's *Simple, noble country Life* (c. 1740), once part of the Schulenburg collection, is now in the Wallraf-Richartz-Museum in Cologne. Its companion piece is in the Art Institute of Chicago. Mention should also be made of another Venetian art-lover, Sagredo, whose collection included Piazzetta's *Angelo Custode*. Piazzetta had hoped to sell this painting to a church, but finding no buyer, he offered it for sale at an exhibition held to commemorate the Feast of San Rocco.

In the eighteenth century it was no longer thought strange that a religious work of art should immediately find its way into a private collection.

189 Farsetti also had casts of works by Michelangelo and Cellini in his collection. Canova stayed in the Palazzo Farsetti in 1768.

Another Venetian collector, Angelo Querini (born 1721), was interested in Egyptian as well as Greek and Roman sculpture.

190 From 1758 onwards Winckelmann acted as Albani's adviser. About this time the head of the philosopher Chrysippus, which had previously been owned by Dr Mead in London, returned to Rome, where it was bought by Albani. This is perhaps the only instance in the eighteenth century of a classical work of art being taken from north to south and not vice versa.

Though Englishmen living in Italy were the first to appreciate the work of fourteenth and fifteenth-century artists, their example was followed to some extent by the linguist Angelo Maria Bandini whose gallery, founded in Fiesole near Florence in 1795, has survived to the present day.

Interest in local history was the chief reason for the abbot Carlo Lodoli (1690–1761) in Venice and the historian Jacopo Facciolati (1682–1769) in Padua concerning themselves with the painting of the late Middle Ages. Facciolati apparently already owned a number of Byzantine panel-paintings.

191 Heinse was a writer influenced by the ideas of 'Sturm und Drang'. His *Briefe aus der Düsseldorfer Gemälde-galerie*, which was republished in 1914, reflects the movement's attitude to art.

192 The Raphael cartoons were in Buckingham Palace from 1766 till 1804, when they were taken back to Hampton Court. (They are now in the Victoria and Albert Museum.)

John Wilkes, in a speech he made in Parliament in 1777, called the cartoons 'the pride of our island' and described Buckingham Palace as a smoky house. He said that England was at last becoming an art centre and he wanted a public picture gallery to be added to the British Museum.

It was difficult for art-lovers to gain admittance to the Palazzo Pitti; the attitude of the Uffizi was more liberal. In 1739, when the Medici family died out, its collection was bequeathed to the state 'ad utilità pubblica'.

Around 1765 the Uffizi was opened to the public, and soon afterwards, for the first time, the paintings were provided with small plates bearing the artists' name.

193 Goethe, J. W. von *Kunst und Altertum am Rhein*.

194 Hans Sloane (1660–1753), physician and botanist, succeeded Newton as president of the Royal Society for Improving Natural Knowledge. For him the word 'museum' had much the same meaning as it did for the zoologist Linné, who in 1754 wrote that 'the world is a museum filled with the works of the Great Creator.'

In Hans Sloane's collection of antiquities there were relatively few works of any real value. Most of the 1,125 items were rarities of one kind or another. Dr Sloane had stipulated that if his collection was not turned into a public museum in London, it should be offered in turn to St Petersburg, Berlin, Paris and Madrid. This list of cities reveals the high regard in which he held the intellectual life of Russia and Prussia. Vienna and Rome are not even mentioned. But English collectors of the time would not have agreed with him.

195 By 1780 the Uffizi already contained paintings by earlier artists, among them Starnina's *Thebais*.

196 It is difficult to date the first use of the plaster fig leaf. It was probably sometime between 1760 and 1780, when middle-class parents, accompanied by their daughters, began to visit the museums.

197 The same happened in Dresden. Few elaborate frames from Saxony survived.

198 The Portici museum was founded in 1743. In 1822 its contents were transferred to the Museo Nazionale in Naples.

199 The long galleries of the Uffizi contained the sculpture acquired by the Medici family up to 1737. They included items as famous as the *Etruscan Chimaera* (Ill. 104) and Michelangelo's *Bacchus* (Ill. 87).

200 Looking down on the Capitol from the staircase of the Palazzo Senatorio, one can see two identical façades: on the left, the Palazzo dei Conservatori, which was begun by Michelangelo, and on the right, the Palazzo Nuovo, transformed into the Museo Capitolino by Pope Clement XII, who died in 1740, and his successor Benedict XIV. (The new name was used soon after 1740.)

An inscription in the courtyard of the museum states that the collection was created 'ad bonarum artium incrementum'. Rooms II and V in particular give an impression of what the museum looked like in 1740.

Pope Benedict XIV also founded the picture-gallery in the Palazzo dei Conservatori and he was responsible for the nucleus of the Pinacoteca Vaticana.

201 A number of antique statues were brought from the Villa Albani to Paris in Napoleonic times. After the defeat of Napoleon the cost of returning them was considered too great and they were sold in Paris. The

Wittelsbachs bought many of these statues (now in the Munich Glyptothek).

202 This rearrangement of the Casino Borghese was in full swing in 1782. Rooms I and III are particularly representative of that period. Asprucci (1723–1808) also designed Room VII 'in gusto egizio' (in the Egyptian taste).

203 Burckhardt, J. *Cicerone*, 1855.

CHAPTER 5

204 The idea of a museum in the Louvre was first proposed by Lafont de Saint-Yenne in 1746. By 1765 vol. 9 of Diderot's Encyclopaedia contained a detailed plan of the project, and by 1789 work on the Grande Galerie was already in progress.

205 Rubens' *Henry IV and his Wife* (then known as 'The Tyrant Henry IV and his Wife') was among the paintings condemned. A Jacobin critized (in the *Décade philosophique* of 20 brumaire, III) the 'hideous crucifixions' still in the Louvre, which he claimed were not suitable for the gaze of 'a people delivered from Catholic superstition'. Pictures thus rejected were burned. In the year II of the new calendar, 180 'feudal portraits' were burned in the garden of the former abbey of St-Germain-des-Prés (B 232). See also Gould, C. *Trophy of Conquest*, London 1965.

206 Winckelmann said this at Sanssouci; the statues in question are now in Berlin. See also Justi, C. *Winckelmann in Deutschland*, Leipzig 1866.

207 Wackenroder, writing towards the end of the eighteenth century, was one of the first people to express typically Romantic views about art. See Waetzoldt, W. 'Wilhelm Wackenroder', *Deutsche Kunsthistoriker*, Leipzig 1924.

208 H. Schrade mentions this phrase of Hölderlin's in *Das deutsche Nationaldenkmal*, Munich 1934.

209 Goethe said this in 1810, when his autobiography was in the course of being published. He was recalling his first visit to the Dresden Gallery when he was a student at Leipzig.

210 The *Venus de Medici* was brought to France in 1802. Arms had been added to a figure of a youth to transform it into a *Praying Boy* (now in the Berlin Museums).

211 According to Kenyon (B 155), the real 'period of accumulation' of paintings in England was between 1795 and 1870. The Calonne collection, auctioned in 1795, was the first important collection from France to be sold in England. It was soon followed by the superb Orléans collection which was purchased *in toto* by a consortium comprising the Duke of Bridgewater, Lord Carlisle and the Marquess of Stafford. In 1798 they sold off the items they themselves did not want. The Orléans collection included Correggio's *Danaë* (now in the Borghese Gallery in Rome), *The Circumcision* from the studio of Giovanni Bellini and Sebastiano del Piombo's *The Raising of Lazarus* (both in the National Gallery, London), Holbein's *Gisze* (now in the Berlin Museums) and Rembrandt's *The Mill* (in the National Gallery, Washington).
In 1801 William Young Ottley, the art dealer, had a catalogue printed of the *Pictures from the Colonna, Borghese and Corsini Palaces etc., purchased in Rome in the years 1799 and 1800.*
In 1806 Titian's *Bacchus and Ariadne*, which had been in the Aldobrandini collection, reached England. It is in the National Gallery in London.

212 To put these prices in their true perspective it must be remembered that Raphael's *Madonna della Tenda* was sold to Ludwig I of Bavaria for £5,000 and that Correggio's *Danaë* changed hands for £300. Holbein's *Gisze* made 200 guineas in 1810.

213 A letter from the English connoisseur William Beckford to his agent Franchi, 8 June 1808. See Boyd, A. *Life at Fonthill*, London 1957.

214 Buschor, E. *Von griechischer Kunst*, Munich 1956.

215 This statement was made by the German archaeologist Michaelis in about 1880 (B 198).
The Venetian admiral, Morosini, had tried to lower the central figures of the west pediment of the Parthenon, but the tackle collapsed. Though in *Childe Harold's Pilgrimage* (1812) Byron spoke of the Parthenon as 'defaced by British hands', the majority of art-lovers at the time regarded Lord Elgin's activities as a rescue operation.

216 In May 1800 Christie's sold works of art which the French had only a short while before looted from the Pope's private apartments in the Vatican. Blundell bought ten pieces of antique sculpture, including a relief which he had himself presented to the Pope some years previously.
The Townley collection was sold to the British Museum for £28,000—a high price.

217 Klenze, L. von *Beschreibung der Glyptothek*, Munich 1830.

218 This custom continued in Paris and Berlin as late as 1870–80. For an illustration of such a scene see *Le Monde Illustré*, 26 July 1873.

219 Rave, P. O. *Karl Friedrich Schinkel*, Munich 1953.

220 Carl Friedrich Rumohr was an influential Berlin art historian in the early nineteenth century. See Waetzoldt, W. 'Rumohr', *Deutsche Kunsthistoriker*, Leipzig 1924.

221 The colour of the walls in a gallery was not of prime importance until about 1740 because it was only then that works of art began to be given a certain amount of space.
In Munich in the middle of the eighteenth century the Green Gallery was so called after its green damask-covered walls. Red walls were popular around 1790–1800, but a little later pale colours came into fashion. The niches in the Museo Pio-Clementino in Rome, which had been red, were now painted pale grey. In 1810 the Louvre had pale yellow walls. With the rise of Romanticism the walls became dark again. In Lansdowne House in London in 1835 Waagen noted purple drapery behind the statues. Soon afterwards the Louvre also changed to red.

222 See also Kühn-Busse, L. 'Der erste Entwurf für einen Berliner Museumbau', *Jahrbuch der Preussischen Kunstsammlungen*, vol. 59, 1938.

223 One must bear in mind that a very large part of the British Museum was occupied by a natural history collection which was not transferred to South Kensington until 1881–83. In 1847 two enormous stuffed giraffes held a place of honour in the entrance hall!

224 Cardinal Stefano Borgia (1731–1804), whose various collections were incorporated in the Naples Museum, owned a number of Egyptian works of art.
Near Eastern art also began to interest collectors. In 1811 an Englishman, C. B. Rich, brought from Babylon a stele showing a king in front of symbols of divinity (now in the British Museum). A little later Henry B. Haskell shipped five large statues from Babylon to America (now in the Bowdoin College Museum of Fine Arts, Brunswick, Maine).

225 This was said by the German critic Eduard Koloff who lived in France. See also Waetzoldt, W. 'Koloff', *Deutsche Kunsthistoriker*, Leipzig 1924.

226 The name 'Musée des Monuments Français' was used from 1795 onwards. The new museum soon became influential. In 1803, for instance, an English edition of Lenoir's book about the museum was published under the title, *The Museum of French Monuments*.

227 About 100 pieces of sculpture, which could not be returned because either the collections they came from had ceased to exist or the families that had owned them had died out, were taken to the Louvre where they became the nucleus of the department devoted to the sculpture of the Middle Ages and the Renaissance. Among these were the statues from Corbeil and Michelangelo's *Slaves*.

228 The Frankfurt painter Christian Georg Schütz said this with reference to the 'Sturm und Drang' movement (B 130). He should not be confused with a relative of the same name.

229 Jean Hüpsch was a Belgian living in Cologne. Little is known about him except that he was one of the first collectors of medieval art. In 1805 he bequeathed his collection to the Landgrave of Hesse-Darmstadt. It now forms an important part of the Landesmuseum in Darmstadt (B 75).

230 Goethe was reported as saying this: he was far more reticent in writing (B 220).

231 Pückler, H. von *Briefe eines Verstorbenen*, 1832.

232 The date of the discovery of oil painting was a controversial topic before 1800. The catalogue of the Truchsess collection, printed in London, claimed that the Multscher panels were painted in 1436, 'which is nearly the period when oil painting was first introduced, and renders them particularly valuable.'

233 Sometime before 1820 Solly bought two altar panels painted *c.* 1440 by the Master of the Darmstadt Passion (now in the Berlin Museums).

234 Johann Georg Forster expressed in his *Ansichten vom Niederrhein*, Düsseldorf 1791, opinions on art that were typical of his time. See also Waetzoldt, W. *Deutsche Kunsthistoriker*, Leipzig 1924.

235 A French general brought Agostino di Duccio's *Madonna and Angels* relief back with him to France (now in the Louvre) and between 1820 and 1824 Ingres' purchases included paintings by Masolino and Butinone (now in the museum at Montauban; see B 47).

236 Attributed to the painter Peter Cornelius.

237 Johann Anton Ramboux, a Rhinelander of French origin, is now recognized as an important Romantic painter. He was equally noteworthy as a collector (B 75).

238 In the Via Condotti in Rome.

239 Raczynski, Count A. *Histoire de l'art moderne en Allemagne*, Paris 1836–1841.

240 Francia and Perugino were popular, and so were Botticelli and Piero di Cosimo, whose *Venus and Mars* (Ill. 232) was bought for the Berlin Museums in 1829.

241 In England too at this time there were collectors who specialized in medieval objets d'art. The jeweller Joseph Mayer of Liverpool bought medieval ivory reliefs, including a fragment of the altarpiece (Ill. 315) donated by Otto the Great to Magdeburg Cathedral.
An early thirteenth-century Limoges relief of St John the Evangelist was presented to the British Museum in 1850.

242 From Stendhal's diary.

243 From Edmond de Goncourt's diary.

244 In 1853 Dyce encouraged the National Gallery to purchase Karl Wilhelm Krüger's small collection of old German paintings. Rossetti and Hunt preferred Gozzoli to Raphael. Ruskin bought Carpaccio's *Scene from Ovid's*

'*Metamorphoses*' (now in the Philadelphia Museum of Art).

245 Schack, A. F. von *Ein halbes Jahrhundert. Erinnerungen*, Munich 1881.

246 In 1860 it was still true to say 'England is to works of art what the grave is to the dead—her gates do not open again to let them out.' But ten years later the exodus began—chiefly to the United States.

247 This remark has been attributed to the painter Max Liebermann.

248 James Simon was an extremely cultured Berlin collector who was helped and advised by Bode. His small but perfect collection remained unaltered in the Kaiser-Friedrich Museum for several decades.

249 The earliest collection of any note in New York was arranged by John Taylor Johnston in 1860 in his Fifth Avenue house. Visitors were allowed on Thursdays; to be admitted, they were required to show a card, but these cards were easily obtained. Turner's *Slave Ship* (now in the Boston Museum of Fine Arts) belonged to Johnston. His collection, which was dispersed in 1877, contained excellent examples of the work of American and French painters of his time. See also Brown, H. C. *Fifth Avenue Old and New*, New York 1924.

250 John Taylor Johnston took part in the formation of the Metropolitan Museum, and became its first president.

251 The James Jackson Jarves collection was offered to the city authorities in Boston as early as 1859—'as a nucleus for a public museum'—but the offer was rejected. The Museum of Fine Arts was not founded till 1870; to start with, it used rooms in the Boston Athenaeum (see *Illustrated Handbook of the Museum of Fine Arts*, Boston 1937). In 1876 the first stage of the building was opened to the public, to be followed by additional wings in the 1880s. Legacies have made the museum one of the richest and most comprehensive in all America.

252 One of Bode's most original ideas was the 'Kirchenraum' on the ground floor of the Kaiser-Friedrich Museum. He considered it the appropriate place for large altarpieces.

253 Among Prince Albert's acquisitions were excellent paintings by Duccio, Gentile da Fabriano and Gozzoli. (Most of these paintings are now in the Royal Collection at Hampton Court.)

254 James Jackson Jarves represented enlightened American taste. His 145 early Italian paintings were put on public display in the Institute of Fine Arts, New York, in 1860–1861. His most important book was *Art Studies: The 'Old Masters' of Italy*, New York 1861.

255 Of 19 portraits painted in Florence between 1425 and 1460 more than half are now in the United States.

256 Bode, W. *Die italienische Plastik*, Berlin 1902.

257 Delacroix's Journal.

258 Count Schack, who studied the artistic climate of the nineteenth century in depth, said this with reference to the rise in popularity, under the influence of Classicism, of Tuscan painting at the expense of Giorgione and Titian.

259 Pierpont Morgan's collection, which has long since been scattered throughout the world, contained several paintings by Velazquez.

260 *Notice des tableaux, légués au Musée du Louvre par Louis la Caze*, Paris 1870.

261 Probably the version now in the National Gallery, Washington.

262 The National Gallery, London, acquired *The Marriage of Giovanni Arnolfini and Giovanna Cenami*. In 1850 the Städelsches Kunstinstitut in Frankfurt paid 3,000 guilders for the *Madonna* formerly owned by the Duke

of Lucca. The *Annunciation* which went to St Petersburg is now in the National Gallery in Washington.

263 At this time there was a marked increase in the prices paid for paintings by Rubens. At the Marlborough auction in 1885 Alfons de Rothschild paid £55,000 for two of them.

264 The Wallace Collection in London has one room devoted to armour. Among the exhibits is the suit of armour made in 1532 for Ottheinrich of the Palatinate, which the French brought with them from Munich in 1800. One of the first collectors of arms and armour in America was J. S. Ellis of Westchester, N. Y. Several items from his collection are now in the Metropolitan Museum in New York.

265 In 1892 a French enamelled hunting-horn dating from around 1535, which had at one time been in Strawberry Hill, changed hands at Christie's in London for £6,615. The increase in the price of small Renaissance bronzes dated from the Piot auction in Paris in 1864. But, in contrast, there was a slump in the market for the small classical pieces, which had been so highly valued at the beginning of the century.

CHAPTER 6

266 Bode valued Morgan's purchases in the years 1902–4 alone at $15,000,000. In 1900 he paid $500,000 for a Raphael altarpiece (now in the Metropolitan Museum, New York). But Morgan did not restrict his liberality to large works of art. When a Syrian glass jug of the third century AD was offered to him in London in 1908, he immediately bought it for $65,000. This same item changed hands at Sothebys in 1950 for $1,180. The Metropolitan Museum in New York contains many important works of art from Morgan's collection, among them Sebastiano del Piombo's portrait of Columbus (Ill. 99).

267 On 31 December 1902 Mrs Gardner, then 62 years old, for the first time allowed an exclusive party of guests to see her complete collection. But New York reporters managed to get in by dressing themselves as waiters and musicians.

268 Of the 300 pictures in the Widener collection in 1908 only 47 found a permanent home in the National Gallery in Washington. Of the paintings purchased after 1908, 53 were incorporated into the museum.

269 Duveen was particularly talented at tracking down masterpieces in old noblemen's houses. When American collectors came to London, he provided them with 'theatre tickets and sons-in-law as well as paintings'.

270 Rado, A. *Kunst in Sowjetrussland*, Berlin 1922.

271 See Lauts, J. *Meisterwerke der Staatlichen Kunsthalle Karlsruhe*, Honnef 1958, p. 36.

272 An exhibition of 'degenerate art' confiscated from German museums was held in Munich in 1937. Its purpose was to reject all works of art created after about 1890. It contained, among other paintings, five Klees, three Kandinskys and a Mondrian. By devious ways even some of these were spirited out of Germany.

273 Michel Knoedler came to America in 1846 as the representative of a Paris firm. In the twentieth century Michel Knoedler & Co. was ably managed by a descendant. Among the paintings acquired by the firm for Gulbenkian was Boucher's *Cupid and the Graces*, now in the National Gallery, Washington.

274 Andrew Mellon (1855–1937) bought his most expensive pictures, those from the Hermitage, when he was 75 years old. In 1930 he paid $747,500 for Raphael's *St George and the Dragon* (Ill. 78); shortly before this he had paid $1,000,000 for Raphael's large *Cowper Madonna* —and these prices were before the devaluation of the dollar in 1936.

Mellon shared the prejudices of nineteenth-century American collectors. He disliked dark paintings and those that depicted unpleasant or harrowing scenes. He also would not allow any paintings of nudes to be hung in his house, and so, until the National Gallery in Washington was founded, he kept Titian's *Venus with a Mirror* in his cellar.

275 Thyssen purchased Mabuse's *Adam and Eve* which had been in the 'Gotisches Haus' in Wörlitz, and he brought back to Europe one of Morgan's favourite pictures, Ghirlandaio's *Giovanna Tornabuoni* (Ill. 272).

276 The Liechtenstein collection provided the National Gallery, Washington, with Gentileschi's *Woman playing a Lute* and Chardin's *The Attentive Nurse* and the National Gallery, Ottawa with paintings by Rubens, Rembrandt and Chardin.

277 After 1945, a whole mass of works of art, appropriated in 1937 in what is now East Germany, were offered by dealers to the new museum directors, only to be rejected because they did not meet the demand for 'social realism'. Kokoschka's *Woman in Blue*, once owned by the Dresden Gallery, was recently bought by the Staatsgalerie in Stuttgart.

278 The price was not very high because the Italian government imposed an export ban on the sculpture. The family of the Duke of Sanseverino received the equivalent of about $100,000.

279 Scheffler, K. *Die fetten und die mageren Jahre*, Munich 1946.

280 Meier-Graefe, J. *Entwicklungsgeschichte der modernen Kunst*, Munich 1923.

281 From the first prose volume of the 1956 Frankfurt edition of the collected works of H. von Hofmannsthal.

282 In 1902 Klee wrote in his diary: 'I want to be born anew knowing nothing of Europe or of paintings.'

283 Schur, E. 'Die Museen als Gesamtkunstwerk', *Museumskunde*, 1908.

284 Wilhelm Worringer was an art historian and critic whose ideas were regarded as very avant-garde in the Germany of 1910. He was also the author of the widely-read *Abstraktion und Einfühlung* (B 323).

285 The idea of a single room containing all the most important works persisted up to 1914 in the Salon Carré of the Louvre.

286 The art periodicals in Germany in those years were full of the pros and cons of such a plan. No full report of the controversy has yet been published. (See B 323 and Knapp, K. 'Randbemerkungen zur Valentinerschen Museumsschrift', *Museumskunde*, 1920.)

287 Paul Otelet's utopian idea of a world museum, a 'Mondaneum', was discussed in the late 'thirties.

288 Osthaus used this phrase in the pamphlets he wrote about the museum he founded in Hagen in Westphalia. The most important paintings in this museum later came into the possession of the Essen authorities, and they now form the basis of the Folkwang Museum (B 323).

289 In 1918, the panel of the *Ghent Altarpiece* which had been in the Berlin Museums since 1821 was restored to the altarpiece.

290 Meier-Graefe, J. *Spanische Reise*, Munich 1910.

291 Even as talented an observer as Georg Swarzenski of Frankfurt commented in 1920 that as far as the unthinking mass of modern art-lovers were concerned, African idols and modern works of art were interchangeable.

292 Meier-Graefe, J. *Entwicklungsgeschichte der modernen Kunst* Munich 1923.

293 Giorgione's *Adoration of the Shepherds* (now in the National Gallery, Washington) was purchased for $750,000.

294 Fabri, a Cologne art critic, defended this thesis in articles in newspapers and periodicals.

295 The Cloisters succeeds in its aim of arranging objects in appropriate surroundings. In Europe, museums in old buildings, like the Cluny Museum in Paris, the Germanisches Museum in Nuremberg and the Bargello Museum in Florence, are once again in favour.

296 Montesquieu was right in saying that the art of late antiquity was the basis of medieval art. The word 'gothic' was used in the sense of 'barbarian'. But since then it has come to be used purely objectively, to describe a certain style.

297 An Egyptian Society had already been formed in Boston in 1880. Soon after this the Boston Museum of Fine Arts bought a small Egyptian collection belonging to an Englishman, Robert Way.

298 Hamann, R. *Geschichte der Kunst von der Vorgeschichte bis zur Spätantike*, Munich 1952.

299 Cranach's *George the Pious of Brandenburg*, 1529 (Ill. 336).

300 Rilke makes a number of interesting observations on art in his *Malte Laurids Brigge*.

301 *The Crucifixion*, painted in about 1420, had belonged to Krüger in Minden in 1840.

302 But the public at large had different tastes. The excellent early Italian paintings which went to Yale University with the Jarves collection were almost completely ignored (B 254).

303 The Berenson collection, though small, contains a large proportion of paintings dating from between 1300 and 1450. Berenson bequeathed his collection to Harvard University, but the Italian authorities forbade this and insisted that it remain in his villa at Settignano.

304 Duccio's *Nativity with the Prophets Isaiah and Ezekiel* was in the Berlin Museums until 1936. It is now in the National Gallery in Washington, and has been joined by a second fragment from the same altarpiece (originally painted for Siena Cathedral), entitled *The Calling of the Apostles Peter and Andrew*.

305 'Chartres I' refers to the statues carved around 1250–80 for the 'Portail Royal'; they mark the transition from Romanesque to Gothic.

306 A famous late nineteenth-century New York jeweller and art collector, he bequeathed the best items from his collection to the Metropolitan Museum in New York. See H. W. B. 'The Michael Dreicer Collection', *Bulletin of the Metropolitan Museum*, 1922.

307 In the 1920s, John D. Rockefeller acted the Maecenas to The Cloisters scheme. In 1926 the collection became an offshoot of the Metropolitan Museum.

308 Relatively, collectors today pay for Italian Renaissance *cassoni* a fifth of what was paid in Morgan's time.

309 Hugo von Tschudi was first the director of the National-galerie in Berlin, and then the director of the Munich Pinakothek. From about 1900 onwards, he devoted his attention to bringing recently rediscovered artists like El Greco, Tiepolo and Goya into the forefront of public taste.

310 In England Wallace indicated his love of Guardi's work. The exhibition of eighteenth-century Venetian painting held in the Burlington Fine Arts Club in 1911 increased the number of the artist's admirers.

311 Meier-Graefe, J. *Spanische Reise*, Munich 1910. Such hypotheses were characteristic of the time, and did not always represent an art historian's considered opinion.

312 Lehmbruck's sculptures clearly show El Greco's influence.

313 This description was attributed to Max Friedländer, the art historian and wit.

314 In America Martin A. Ryerson apparently appreciated Magnasco. A Magnasco from his collection is now in the Art Institute of Chicago.

315 The Hamburg Kunsthalle paid 850,000 DM for a Claude landscape in 1962.

316 Around 1905 Morgan and Frick willingly paid $250,000 -$300,000 for paintings by Gainsborough. *The Blue Boy*, painted in 1770, is a portrait of Jonathan Buttel, the son of a rich iron merchant.

317 When the Hudson-Fulton exhibition of 1909 was being prepared, there were about 70 paintings by Rembrandt in the United States. Nearly all of these were portraits; only four dealt with religious themes. When, by 1919, American collectors had outgrown their traditional prejudices, they bought unusual pictures like the *Return of the Prodigal Son* (now in the National Gallery, Washington).

318 Zeromski, A. von *Alfred Lichtwark*, Hamburg 1924.

319 *Im Kampf um die Kunst*, an anonymously compiled pamphlet, was published in Munich in 1912. It contained articles by museum directors and artists, including Marc.

320 Pauli, G. *Erinnerungen*, Tübingen 1936.

321 When, in 1917, the Tate Gallery became independent of the National Gallery, its directors made full use of their greater freedom.
The Museum of Modern Art in New York, which was founded in 1929, immediately embarked on an extensive exhibition programme, and primarily as a result of the Mrs John D. Rockefeller, Jr Purchase Fund, it was able to buy important works of art by modern artists.

322 See B 140, p. 226.

323 The buyer was an American, Charles B. Wrightsman.

324 Meier-Graefe, J. *Entwicklungsgeschichte der modernen Kunst*, Munich 1923.

325 Alfred Flechtheim, originally a corn merchant in Düsseldorf, was one of the most active art dealers in Berlin between 1905 and 1925; he threw in his lot with the still controversial young artists much earlier than the majority. He was also the author of numerous witticisms on the subject of the contemporary art scene.

326 Eddy also owned paintings by Kandinsky, Derain and Vlaminck.

327 Huyghe, R. *Discovery of Art*, London 1959.

328 *Les Toits*, painted in 1907, now belongs to the Musée de l'Art Moderne in Paris.

329 See Holst, N. von *Moderne Kunst und Sichtbare Welt*, Heidelberg 1957.

330 Part of the third-century *Stupa of Amaranti* reliefs were saved by Colonel Mackenzie in 1816. They are now in the entrance hall of the British Museum. The Indian Museum was closed in 1880.

331 In 1903 a 4-yards-long Persian wool carpet was auctioned in the United States for more than $30,000 (see Erdmann, K. *Europa und der Orientteppich*, Mainz 1962).

332 See Sydow, E. von *Exotische Kunst*, Leipzig 1921.

333 See Means, *Peruvian Textiles*, New York 1930.

334 These lines, written in 1935, decorate the Musée des Monuments Français in Paris which was built on the site of the 1937 World's Fair.

Bibliography

The following bibliography is alphabetically arranged and covers various countries and periods. Publications concerning individual museums and collections (e.g. catalogues) are included only where they are of particular relevance to the history of a collection. Titles of journals have been abbreviated only in the case of the *Burlington Magazine (Burl. Mag.)* and the *Gazette des Beaux-Arts (GBA)*. A selection of subsidiary publications may be found in the 'Notes on the Text'.

1 ADHÉMAR, J. 'The Collection of Paintings of Francis I', *GBA*, 1946

2 ADLER, B. 'Das Museumswesen in Russland während der Revolution', *Museumskunde*, 1924

3 ALBERTS, E. *Die ehemalige Düsseldorfer Gemäldegalerie*, Düsseldorf 1961

4 ALLAN, D. A. 'The Crusade for Museums', *Museums Journal*, 1953

5 ALLEN, B. S. *Tides in English Taste*, Cambridge (Mass.) 1937

6 ALLEN, F. L. *The Great Pierpont Morgan*, New York 1949

7 AMELUNG, W. *Führer durch die Antiken in Florenz*, Leipzig 1897

8 ARNAU, F. *3000 Years of Deception in Art and Antiques*, London 1961

9 AULANIER, C. *Histoire du Palais et du Musée du Louvre*, 5 vols, Paris 1948–55

10 BAKER, C. *Catalogue of Pictures at Hampton Court*, London 1929

11 BARBIER DE MONTAULT, H. *Les Musées et Galeries de Rome*, Rome 1870

12 BAZIN, G. *The Louvre*, London 1962

13 BEHRMAN, S. N. *Duveen*, New York 1951

14 BENCIVENNI, G. *Saggio storico della Real Galleria di Firenze*, 2 vols, Florence 1779

15 BENESCH, O. *Die fürstbischofliche Gemäldegalerie in Kremsier*, Vienna 1928

16 BENOIST, P. 'Muséologie', *Que sais-je?* No. 904, Paris 1960

17 BENOIT, F. *L'art français dans la Révolution*, Paris 1897

18 BERINGER, A. VON 'Goethe und der Mannheimer Antikensaal', *Goethejahrbuch*, 1907

19 BERLINER, R. 'Zur älteren Geschichte der allgemeinen Museumslehre', *Münchner Jahrbuch für bildende Kunst*, 1928

20 BIALOSTOCKI, J. 'Kunstsammlungen im alten Polen', *Europäische Malerei in polnischen Sammlungen*, Warsaw 1957

21 BIET, J. E. AND BRES, J. P. *Souvenirs du Musée des Monuments Français*, Paris 1821

22 BILDT, C. DI 'Cristina di Suezia e Paolo Giordano II, duca di Bracciano', *Archivio della Società Romana di Storia Patria*, 1906

23 BILLE, C. *De Tempel der Konst of Het Kabinet van den Heer Braankamp*, 2 vols, Amsterdam 1961

24 BLUMER, M. L. 'Catalogue des peintures transportées d'Italie en France de 1796 à 1814', *Bulletin de la Société d'Histoire de l'Art Français*, 1936

25 BODE, W. 'Der Kunstsammler', *Spemanns Buch der Kunst*, Berlin 1901

26 'Die amerikanische Konkurrenz im Kunsthandel', *Kunst und Künstler*, 1903

27 *Mein Leben*, 2 vols, Berlin 1930

28 BOLTON, A. *The Architecture of Robert and James Adam*, 2 vols, London 1922

29 BONNAFFE, E. *Les collectionneurs de l'ancienne France*, Paris 1873

30 *Dictionnaire des amateurs français au XVIII siècle*, Paris 1884

31 BORENIUS, T. *The Picture Gallery of Andrea Vendramin*, London 1923

32 BRIGGS, M. S. *Men of Taste, from Pharaoh to Ruskin*, London 1947

33 BRIMO, R. *L'Evolution du Goût aux Etats-Unis d'après l'histoire des collections*, Paris 1938

34 BRUYN, J. 'The Dutch Gift to the Royal Collection', *Burl. Mag.*, 1962

35 BUCHANAN, W. *Memoirs . . . of the importation of pictures*, 2 vols, London 1824

36 BUCHNER, E. *The Munich Pinakothek*, London 1957

37 BURCKHARDT, J. 'Die Sammler', *Nachgelassene Beiträge zur Kunstgeschichte*, Basle 1898

38 BURDEN, G. 'Sir Thomas Isham, an English collector in Rome in 1677', *Italian Studies*, 1960

39 BURN-MURDOCH, W. G. *The Royal Stuarts in their connection with Arts and Letters*, Edinburgh 1908

40 CAGIANO, M. *Il gusto nel restauro delle opere d'arte antiche*, Rome 1949

41 CAMPORI, G. *Raccolta di cataloghi . . . dal secolo XV al secolo XIX*, Modena 1870

42 CARTER, M. *Isabella Stewart Gardner and Fenway Court*, 2nd ed., Boston 1940

43 CECI, G. 'Un mercante mecenate del secolo XVII, Gaspare Roomer', *Napoli Nobilissima*, 1920

44 CHAMPEAUX, A. DE *Les travaux d'art exécutés pour Jean de France, Duc de Berry*, Paris 1894

45 CHAMPIER, V. *Le Palais Royal*, Paris 1900

46 CHASTEL, A. 'L'école du jardin de Saint Marc', *Studi Vasariani*, Florence 1952

47 'Le goût des Préraphaelites en France', *Catalogue de l'exposition 'De Giotto à Bellini'*, Paris 1956

48 CLARK, K. *The Gothic Revival*, 2nd ed., London 1950

49 COLEMAN, L. V. *The Museum in America*, Washington 1939

50 COLSON, P. *A Story of Christie's*, London 1950

51 CONSTABLE, W. G. *Art Collecting in the United States of America*, London 1964

52 CONWAY, M. *Art Treasures in Soviet Russia*, London 1925

53 CORNETTE, A. H. *Florent van Ertborn, een Antwerpsch Maeceen*, Antwerp 1938

54 COURAJOD, L. *Alexandre Lenoir*, 3 vols, Paris 1878–87

55 CUST, L. *History of the Society of Dilettanti*, London 1914

56 DAVIS, F. *Victorian Patrons of the Arts*, London 1963

57 DELEN, A. J. J. *Het huis van P. P. Rubens*, Antwerp 1940

58 DENUCÉ, J. *Art-Export in the 17th century in Antwerp. The firm Forchoudt*, Antwerp 1931

59 *The Antwerp Art-Galleries. Inventories of the art-collections in Antwerp in the 16th and 17th centuries*, Antwerp 1932

60 DESCARGUES, P. *The Hermitage*, London 1961

61 DESCHAMPS, P. 'Madame de Verrue', *GBA*, 1864

62 DEUCHLER, F. *Die Burgunderbeute. Inventare der Beute-stücke aus den Schlachten von Grandson, Murten und Nancy 1476, 1477*, Berne 1963

63 DREIER, F. A. 'Zur Geschichte der Kasseler Kunst-kammer', *Zeitschrift des Vereins für hessische Geschichte und Landeskunde*, 1961

64 DUFFUS, R. L. *The Arts in American Life*, New York 1933

65 DUVEEN, J. H. *The Rise of the House of Duveen*, London 1957

66 EHLICH, W. *Bild und Rahmen im Altertum*, Leipzig 1954

67 EINEM, H. VON *Karl V und Tizian*, Cologne 1960

68 FAGE, A. *Le collectionneur des peintures modernes*, Paris 1930

69 FINK, A. *Geschichte des Herzog-Anton-Ulrich-Museums in Braunschweig*, Brunswick 1954

70 FISCHER, H. 'Kurfürst Lothar von Schönborn und seine Gemäldegalerie', *Berichte des Historischen Vereins Bamberg*, 1928

71 FIRMENICH-RICHARTZ, E. *Sulpiz und Melchior Boisserée als Kunstsammler*, Jena 1916

72 FLEISCHER, V. *Fürst Karl Eusebius von Liechtenstein als Bauherr und Kunstsammler*, Vienna 1916

73 FLÖRKE, H. *Studien zur niederländischen Kunst- und Kultur-geschichte*, Munich 1905

74 FOCILLON, H. 'La conception moderne des Musées', *Actes du Congrès d'Histoire de l'Art de Paris*, 1921

75 FÖRSTER, O. H. *Kölner Kunstsammler vom Mittelalter bis zum Ende des bürgerlichen Zeitalters*, Berlin 1932

76 FORD, B. 'A Portrait Group by Gavin Hamilton', *Burl. Mag.*, 1955

77 FRÄNKEL, M. 'Gemäldesammlungen in Pergamon', *Jahrbuch des Kaiserlich deutschen Archäologischen Instituts*, 1891

78 FRANCISCIS, A. DE 'Per la storia del Museo Nazionale di Napoli', *Archivio storico per le provincie Napoletane*, 1944–46

79 FREEDEN, M. H. VON 'Probleme des Mainfränkischen Museums in Würzburg', *Deutsche Kunst und Denk-malpflege*, 1958

80 FRIEDLÄNDER, M. J. *On Art and Connoisseurship*, London 1943

81 FRIMMEL, T. VON *Gemalte Galerien*, 2nd ed., Berlin 1896

82 *Geschichte der Wiener Gemäldesammlungen*, Munich 1913

83 *Handbuch der Gemäldekunde*, 3rd ed., Leipzig 1920

84 FRISCH, E. VON *Wolf Dietrich von Raitenau, Erzbischof von Salzburg, im Lichte seiner Kunstsammlung*, Salzburg 1949

85 FURCY-RAYMOND, M. *Les Tableaux … saisis chez les Emigrés*, Paris 1913

86 FURTWÄNGLER, A. *Über Kunstsammlungen in alter und neuer Zeit*, Munich 1899

87 GAUTHERET, G. *Le vandalisme jacobin*, Paris 1914

88 GAYA, J. A. N. *Historia de los Museos in España*, Madrid 1955

89 *La pintura española fuera de España*, Madrid 1958

90 GERHARD, E. *Neapels antike Bildwerke*, Stuttgart 1828

91 GERSON, H. *Ausbreitung und Nachwirkung der holländi-schen Malerei des 17. Jahrhunderts*, Haarlem 1942

92 GIBBS-SMITH, C. H. *The History of the Victoria and Albert Museum*, London 1952

93 GLASER, C. 'Kunst als Ware', *Kunst und Künstler*, 1929–30

94 GLÜCK, G. 'Fälschungen auf Dürers Namen', *Jahrbuch der Kunsthistorischen Sammlungen des Allerhöchsten Kaiserhauses Wien*, 1909–10

95 GNOLI, P. 'Il Giardino e l'Antiquario del Cardinal Cesi', *Mitteilungen des Kaiserlich deutschen Archäologischen Instituts, Römische Abteilung*, 1905

96 GOLDSCHNEIDER, L. *Michelangelo's Bozzetti for Statues in the Medici Chapel*, London 1957

97 GOMBRICH, E. H. 'The Belvedere Garden as a Grove of Venus', *Journal of the Warburg and Courtauld Institutes*, 1951

98 GOMEZ-MORENO, M. E. *Anuario-Guia de los Museos de España*, Madrid 1955

99 GRANBERG, O. *Kejsar Rudolf II's Konstkammare*, Stockholm 1902

100 *Svensk Konstsamlingar*, 3 vols, Stockholm 1929–31

101 GRIGSON, G. *Art Treasures of the British Museum*, London 1957

102 GRONAU, G. 'Venezianische Kunstsammlungen des 16. Jahrhunderts', *Jahrbuch für Kunstsammler*, 1924–1925

103 GROSSMAN, F. 'Notes on the Arundel and Imstenraedt Collections', *Burl. Mag.*, 1944

104 'A Painting by Georges de la Tour in the Collection of Archduke Leopold Wilhelm', *Burl. Mag.*, 1958 and 1959

105 GRUNCY, C. R. 'American Collectors', *The Connoisseur*, 1926

106 GUIFFREY, J. *Inventaires de Jean, Duc de Berry*, 2 vols, Paris 1894 and 1896

107 HAAK, B. 'The History of the Rijksmuseum', *Catalogue of Paintings*, Amsterdam 1960

108 HÄNDLER, G. *Fürstliche Mäzene und Sammler in Deutsch-land von 1500–1620*, Strassburg 1933

109 HALM, P. 'Zur Geschichte der Staatlichen Graphischen Sammlung in München', *Bayerische Kulturpflege, Festschrift für Kronprinz Rupprecht*, Munich 1958

110 'Eine Altdorfer-Sammlung des 17. Jahrhunderts', *Münchner Jahrbuch der bildenden Kunst*, 1960

111 HAMANN-MACLEAN, R. H. 'Antikenstudium in der Kunst des Mittelalters', *Marburger Jahrbuch für Kunstwissenschaft*, 1949–50

112 HARRIS, E. *The Prado*, London 1940

113 'La mission de Velasquez in Italia', *Archivo Español de Arte*, 1960

114 HARTIG, O. 'Die Kunsttätigkeit in München unter Wil-helm IV und Albrecht V', *Münchner Jahrbuch der bildenden Kunst*, 1933

115 HASKELL, F. 'Art exhibitions in seventeenth-century Rome', *Studi Secenteschi*, 1960

116 *Patrons and Painters*, London 1963

117 HAUSER, A. *The Social History of Art*, 2 vols, London 1951

118 HAUTTMANN, M. 'Dürer und der Augsburger Antiken-besitz', *Jahrbuch der Preussischen Kunstsammlungen*, 1921–22

119 HEIKAMP, D. 'Zur Geschichte der Uffizien-Tribuna', *Zeitschrift für Kunstgeschichte*, 1963

120 HEINSE, W. *Briefe aus der Düsseldorfer Gemäldegalerie*, Leipzig 1914

121 HEINZ, G. 'Die Entstehung der Galerie der Grafen Harrach in Wien', *Katalog der Galerie Harrach*, Vienna 1960

122 HELD, J. 'C. van der Geest, an Antwerp Art Patron', *GBA*, 1957

123 HENDY, P. *The National Gallery, London*, London 1955

124 HENRAUX, A. S. 'Muséographie', *Guide Illustré de la sec-tion 'Musées' de l'Exposition Internationale*, Paris 1937

125 HENSCHEL-SIMON, E. *Die Bildergalerie Friedrichs des Grossen*, Berlin 1930

126 HOLMES, C. *The Making of the National Gallery*, London 1924

127 HOLST, N. VON 'Die Frankfurter Kunstkabinette des 18. Jahrhunderts', *Alt-Frankfurt*, 1930

128 'Kunstkammern des 18. Jahrhunderts', *Repertorium für Kunstwissenschaft*, 1931

129 'Danziger Kunstsammlungen des 16.–19. Jahrhunderts', *Mitteilungen des Westpreussischen Geschichtsvereins*, 1934

130 'Nachahmungen und Fälschungen altdeutscher Kunst im Zeitalter der Romantik', *Zeitschrift für Kunstgeschichte*, 1934

131 'Deutsche Barockmalerei in Osteuropa', *Mitteilungen aus dem Brukenthalischen Museum zu Hermannstadt*, 1938

132 'Beiträge zur Geschichte des Sammlertums und des Kunsthandels in Hamburg', *Zeitschrift des Vereins für Hamburgische Geschichte*, 1939

133 'Russische Kunstsammlungen des 18. und frühen 19. Jahrhunderts', *Baltische Monatshefte*, 1939

134 'Sammlertum und Kunstgutwanderung in Ostdeutschland und den benachbarten Ländern bis 1800', *Jahrbuch der Preussischen Kunstsammlungen*, 1939

135 'Alte Kunstsammlungen in Riga, Reval und den Baltischen Landen', *Wallraf-Richartz-Jahrbuch, Westdeutsches Jahrbuch für Kunstgeschichte*, 1942–43

136 'La Pittura veneziana tra il Reno e la Neva', *Arte Veneta*, 1951–52

137 'Russlands Besitz an deutscher Kunst des 15. bis frühen 19. Jahrhunderts', *Weltkunst*, 1952

138 'Italiens Museen auf neuen Wegen', *Weltkunst*, 1954

139 'Bilderhängen – einst und jetzt', *Die Kunst und das schöne Heim*, 1954

140 *Künstler – Sammler – Publikum, ein Buch für Kunst- und Museumsfreunde*, Darmstadt 1960

141 'Tizian in Ungnade: – der Gemäldetausch Wien–Florenz 1792 und verwandte Vorgänge', *Weltkunst*, 1960

142 'Kunsthandel im Spiegel der Malerei, von Tizian bis Daumier', *Speculum Artis*, 1962

143 'Zur Geschichte der Münchner Pinakothek', *Speculum Artis*, 1964

144 HUBBARD, R. H. *European paintings in Canadian collections. With an essay on picture collecting in Canada*, Toronto 1956

145 HÜBNER, P. G. *Le Statue di Roma*, Leipzig 1912

146 HÜLSEN, C. 'Römische Antikengärten des 16. Jahrhunderts' *Abhandlungen der Heidelberger Akademie, Phil.-Hist. Klasse*, 1917

147 HUTH, H. 'Museum and Gallery', *Beiträge für Georg Swarzenski*, Berlin 1951

148 ILG, A. *Wiener Galerien*, Vienna 1893

149 JACOB, E. F. 'Some aspects of classical influence in Mediaeval England', *Vorträge der Bibliothek Warburg*, 1930–31

150 JACOBS, E. 'Das Museo Vendramin und die Sammlung Rheynst', *Repertorium für Kunstwissenschaft*, 1925

151 JARVES, J. J. *Art Thoughts*, New York 1869

152 'Museums of Arts and Amateurs in America', *Galaxy*, 1870

153 JUCKER, H. *Vom Verhältnis der Römer zur bildenden Kunst der Griechen*, Frankfurt 1950

154 KAUFFMANN, H. *Lebendiges Museum*, Cologne 1952

155 KENYON, F. C. *Museums and National Life*, Oxford 1927

156 KIRCHER, G. *Karoline Luise von Baden als Kunstsammlerin*, Karlsruhe 1933

157 KITSON, M. 'The Altieri Claudes and Virgil', *Burl. Mag.*, 1960

158 KLEINER, G. *Die Begegnungen Michelangelos mit der Antike*, Berlin 1950

159 KOCH, G. 'Kunstausstellungen in der Antike', *Wissenschaftliche Zeitschrift der Universität Rostock*, 1953–54

160 KORDT, W. 'Die Düsseldorfer Galerie des Kurfürsten Johann Wilhelm von der Pfalz', *Das Tor*, 1958

161 KUHN, C. L. *A Catalogue of German Paintings in American Collections*, Cambridge (Mass.) 1936

162 LACROIX, P. 'Physionomie des ventes de tableaux au XVIIIe siècle', *Revue universelle des Arts*, 1861

163 LADENDORF, H. *Antikenstudium und Antikenkopie*, Berlin 1953

164 LANDAIS, H. *Les Bronzes italiens de la Renaissance*, Paris 1958

165 LEHOUX, F. 'Le Duc de Berry, les Juifs et les Lombards', *Revue historique*, 1956

166 LELIÈVRE, P. *Vivant Denon, directeur des Beaux Arts de Napoléon*, Angers 1942

167 'La Formation du Museum au Palais du Louvre', *Urbanisme et Architecture. Etudes écrites en l'honneur de P. Lavedan*, Paris 1954

168 LESSING, W. 'Die Erwerbung der Madonna della Tenda Raffaels', *Münchner Jahrbuch der bildenden Kunst*, 1938–39

169 LEVEY, M. 'Tiepolo's Empire of Flora', *Burl. Mag.*, 1957

170 'Two Paintings by Tiepolo from the Algarotti Collection', *Burl. Mag.*, 1960

171 LEVI, C. A. *Le collezione veneziane d'arte*, Venice 1900

172 LEWIS, L. *Connoisseurs and secret agents in 18th-century Rome*, London 1961

173 LEWIS, W. S. *Horace Walpole*, Washington 1961

174 LEWISOHN, S. *Is collecting an art?*, Parnassus 1934

175 LHOTZKY, A. 'Die Geschichte der Sammlungen des Kunsthistorischen Museums', *Festschrift des Kunsthistorischen Museums*, Vienna 1945

176 LIEB, N. *Die Fugger und die Kunst*, 2 vols, Munich 1952 and 1958

177 LILL, G. *Hans Fugger und die Kunst*, Leipzig 1908

178 LORENZ, S. 'Renovations of Museums in Poland', *Museum*, 1955

179 LUGT, F. 'Italiaansche Konstwerken in de Nederlandsche Verzamelingen van vroeger tiden', *Oud Holland*, 1936

180 *Répertoire des Catalogues des Ventes publiques*, 2 vols, The Hague 1938 and 1953

181 LULLIES, R. *Die kauernde Aphrodite*, Augsburg 1950

182 LUZIO, A. *La Galleria dei Gonzaga venduta all'Inghilterra nel 1627*, Milan 1913

183 MAEYER, M. DE *Albrecht, Isabella en de Schilderkunst*, Brussels 1955

184 MAHAFFY, J. P. *Greek Life from the Death of Alexander to the Roman conquest*, 2nd ed., London 1896

185 MAHON, D. 'Notes on the Dutch gift to Charles II', *Burl. Mag.*, 1949 and 1950

186 'Mazarin and Poussin', *Burl. Mag.*, 1960

187 MAISON, K. E. *Themes and Variations. Five centuries of master copies and interpretations*, London 1960

188 MANKOWSKI, T. *Galerie Stanislawa Augusta*, 3 vols, Lemberg 1932

189 MANN, J. 'The Founders of the Wallace Collection', *A General Guide to the Wallace Collection*, London 1961

190 MARILLIER, H. C. *Christies 1766–1925*, London 1926

191 MARQUET DE VASSELOT, J. J. 'Répertoire des Vues des Salles du Musée du Louvre', *Archives de l'Art Français*, 1946

192 MARTIN, K. *Grünewalds Kreuzigung der Karlsruher Kunsthalle in der Beschreibung von Joris Karl Huysmans*, Mainz 1947

193 'Zur Geschichte der Sammlung altdeutscher Meister des Hauses Wittelsbach', *Katalog II der Alten Pinakothek*, Munich 1963

194 MARTROYE, F. 'La destruction par les chrétiens des statues des divinités antiques', *Bulletin de la Société nationale des Antiquaires de France*, 1921

195 MASSON, D. *The British Museum*, Edinburgh 1850

196 MATHER, F. J. *The Collectors*, New York 1912

197 MAYOR, A. H. 'Collectors at home', *The Metropolitan Museum of Art Bulletin*, 1957

198 MICHAELIS, A. *Ancient Marbles in Great Britain*, Cambridge 1882

199 'Geschichte des Statuenhofs im Vatikanischen Belvedere', *Jahrbuch des Kaiserlich deutschen Archäologischen Instituts, Römische Abteilung*, 1891

200 'Storia della collezione Capitolina di Antichità', *Mitteilungen des Kaiserlichen deutschen Archäologischen Instituts*, 1890

201 MICHEL, M. R. 'From the Museum to the Musée du Louvre', *Burl. Mag.*, 1963

202 MIROT, L. *L'hôtel et les collections du Connetable de Montmorency*, Paris 1920

203 MOLAJOLI, B. *Notizie su Capodimonte*, Naples 1960

204 MÜNTZ, E. *Les artes à la cour des Papes*, Paris 1879

205 *Les collections d'antiques formées par les Médicis au XVIe siècle*, Paris 1895

206 MURRAY, D. *Museums, their history and their use*, 3 vols, Glasgow 1904

207 NEICKEL, C. F. *Museographia*, Leipzig 1727

208 NETTER, M. 'Zur Restaurierung zweier Holbeinbilder im Kunstmuseum Basel', *Werkzeitschrift der Fabrik Geigy in Basel*, 1960

209 NOACK, F. 'Kunstpflege und Kunstbesitz der Familie Borghese', *Repertorium für Kunstwissenschafte*, 1929

210 NOGARA, B. *Origine e sviluppo dei Musei e Gallerie Ponteficie*, Rome 1948

211 NORRIS, C. 'The disaster at Flakturm Friedrichshain', *Burl. Mag.*, 1952

212 ORBAAN, J. A. F. 'Deutsche Kunstsammlungen um 1600', *Museumskunde*, 1917

213 OULMONT, C. *Les lunettes de l'amateur d'objets d'art*, Paris 1926

214 PACH, W. *The Art Museum in America*, New York 1948

215 PEACHAM, H. *Compleat Gentleman*, 2nd ed., London 1634

216 PEVSNER, N. *Academies of Art, Past and Present*, Cambridge 1940

217 PFEFFER, A. 'Die Wurzacher Truchsessen-Galerie', *Oberrheinische Kunst*, 1942

218 PIETRANGELI, C. *Scavi e scoperte di Antichità nella Roma di Pio VI*, Rome 1942

219 'Storia dei Musei Capitolini', *Guida dei Musei Capitolini*, Rome 1961

220 PÖNSGEN, G. 'Die Begegnung Goethes mit der Sammlung Boisserée in Heidelberg', *Ruperto-Carola, Mitteilungen der Freunde der Universität Heidelberg*, 1960

221 POSSE, H. *Die Gemäldegalerie zu Dresden*, Dresden 1937

222 PREVITALI, G. 'Collezionisti di primitivi nel Settecento', *Paragone*, 1959

223 PUYVELDE, L. VAN 'Margarethe von Österreich', *Alte und moderne Kunst*, 1962

224 QUINCY, Q. DE *Lettres sur le Projet d'enlever les monuments de l'Italie*, Paris 1796

225 RAVE, P. O. *Art Dictatorship in the Third Reich*, London 1949

226 'Geschichtlicher Sinn und Historische Museen', *Schriften des Historischen Museums IX*, Frankfurt 1958

227 'Berliner Museen einst und jetzt', *Jahrbuch der Berliner Museen*, 1962

228 RÉAU, L. 'Musées américains', *Revue archéologique*, 1911

229 'Le Jardin Elysée du Musée Lenoir', *Beaux Arts, Revue d'Information artistique*, 1924

230 *Catherine la Grande de Russie, inspiratrice d'art*, Paris 1930

231 'L'art français du XVIIIe siècle dans la collection Stroganoff', *Arts et Artistes*, 1931

232 *Histoire du Vandalisme*, 2 vols, Paris 1959

233 REDE, B. 'William Frizell and the Royal Collection', *Burl. Mag.*, 1947

234 REDFORD, G. *Art Sales*, 2 vols, London 1888

235 REINACH, S. *L'Album de Pierre Jaques*, Paris 1902

236 REITLINGER, G. *The Economics of Taste. The rise and fall of picture prices 1760–1960*, 2 vols, London 1961 and 1963

237 REVILLE, J. B. *Vues pittoresques des Salles du Musée des Monuments français*, Paris 1816

238 RHEIMS, M. *Art on the market*, London 1961

239 RIAUT, P. E. D. 'Les dépouilles religieuses enlevées à Constantinople au XIIIe siècle', *Mémoires de la Société nationale des Antiquaires de France*, 1875

240 RICCI, C. *La Pinacoteca di Brera*, Bergamo 1901

241 RICCI, G. 'Relazioni artistico-commerciali tra Roma e la Grecia', *Antichità*, 1950

242 RIEGL, A. 'Über antike und moderne Kunstfreunde', *Kunstgeschichtliches Jahrbuch der kaiserlich-königlichen Zentralkommission, Beiblatt für Denkmalpflege*, 1907

243 RIS, L. C. DE *Les amateurs d'autrefois*, Paris 1887

244 RODENWALDT, G. 'Goethes Besuch im Museum Maffeianum in Verona', *Winckelmannsprogramm der Archäologischen Gesellschaft zu Berlin*, 1942

245 ROLFS, W. 'Der Neapeler Pferdekopf', *Jahrbuch der Preussischen Kunstsammlungen*, 1908

246 RORIMER, J. R. *The Cloisters*, New York 1946

247 ROSS, M. 'The Rubens Vase, its history and date', *Journal of the Walters Art Gallery*, 1943

248 ROSSI, F. *Il Museo del Bargello a Firenze*, Milan 1952

249 *Art Treasures of the Uffizi and Pitti*, London 1957

250 ROTHENSTEIN, J. *The Tate Gallery*, London 1958

251 ROTT, H. 'Strassburger Kunstkammern im 17. und 18. Jahrhundert', *Zeitschrift für die Geschichte des Oberrheins*, 1931

252 ROVELLI, L. *L'opera storica ed artistica di Paolo Giovio. Il Museo di ritratti*, Como 1928

253 ROXAN, D. and WANSTALL, K. *The Jackdaw of Linz: the story of Hitler's art thefts*, London 1964

254 SAARINEN, A. *The Proud Possessors. The lives, times and tastes of some adventurous American art collectors*, New York 1958

255 SALERNO, L. 'The Picture Gallery of Vincenzo Giustiniani', *Burl. Mag.*, 1960

256 SALET, F. 'Histoire de la collection Du Sommerard', *Guide du Musée de Cluny*, Paris 1949

257 SALIS, A. VON *Antike und Renaissance*, Zürich 1947

258 SALM, C. VON 'Joseph von Lassberg als Kunstsammler', *Joseph von Lassberg, Sammelwerk, herausgegeben von K. S. Bader*, Stuttgart 1955

259 SANCHEZ CANTON, F. J. *The Prado*, London 1964

260 SAVAGE, G. *Forgeries, Fakes and Reproductions*, London 1963

261 SAUNIER, C. *Les conquêtes artistiques de la Révolution et de l'Empire*, Paris 1902

262 SCHERER, V. *Deutsche Museen*, Jena 1913

263 SCHLOSSER, J. VON *Die Kunst- und Wunderkammern der Spätrenaissance*, Leipzig 1908

264 SCHMIDT, E. *Archaistische Kunst in Griechenland und Rom*, Munich 1922

265 SCHMIDT, P. 'Umtaufe antiker Gemmen in christliche Kunstwerke', *Stimmen der Zeit*, 1947–48

266 SCHREIBER, T. *Antike Bildwerke der Villa Ludovisi*, Leipzig 1880

267 SCHUDT, L. *Italienreisen im 17. und 18. Jahrhundert*, Vienna 1959

268 SCHÜLLER, S. *Forgers, dealers, experts*, London 1961

269 SCOTT-ELLIOT, A. H. 'The statues from Mantua in the Collection of King Charles I', *Burl. Mag.*, 1959

270 SEILERN, A. VON *Flemish Paintings and Drawings at 56 Princes Gate*, London 1955

271 SELIGMAN, G. *Merchants of Art: 1880–1960*, New York 1961

272 SELING, H. *Die Entstehung des Kunstmuseums als Aufgabe der Architektur* (Dissertation, Freiburg 1952)

273 SHAW, W. A. *Three Inventories of Pictures in the Collections of Henry VIII and Edward VI*, London 1937

274 SICHEL, E. *Johann Christian Mannlich*, Munich 1932

275 SICKLER, F. K. L. *Geschichte der Wegführung vorzüglicher Kunstwerke aus den eroberten Ländern*, Gotha 1803

276 SIEBENHÜNER, H. 'Der Palazzo Farnese in Rom', *Wallraf-Richartz-Jahrbuch*, 1952

277 *Das Kapitol in Rom*, Munich 1954

278 SIEBMACHER, J. *De Pinacothecis*, Leipzig 1658

279 SIMON, E. *Die Portlandvase*, Mainz 1957

280 SIREN, O. 'Trecento Pictures in American Collections', *Burl. Mag.*, 1908

281 SIZER, T. 'James Jackson Jarves', *New England Quarterly*, 1933

282 SMITH, A. H. 'Lord Elgin', *Journal of Hellenic Studies*, 1916

283 SMITH, R. *Bibliography of Museums and Museum Work*, Washington 1928

284 SOMBART, W. *Luxus und Kapitalismus*, Munich 1922

285 SPETH-HOLTERHOFF, S. 'A Flemish Picture Gallery by Gilles van Tilborgh', *Register of the Museum of Art of the University of Kansas*, 1955

286 *Les Peintres Flamands de Cabinets d'Amateurs au XVIIIe siècle*, Brussels 1957

287 'Trois amateurs d'art flamand au XVIIe siècle', *Revue belge d'Archéologie et d'histoire de l'art*, 1958

288 STÄHLIN, K. *Aus den Papieren Jakob von Stählins*, Königsberg 1926

289 STANGE, A. *Alte Bilderrahmen*, Darmstadt 1958

290 STIX, A. *Die Aufstellung der Kaiserlichen Gemäldegalerie in Wien im 18. Jahrhundert*, Vienna 1929

291 *Die Fürstlich Liechtensteinsche Gemäldegalerie in Wien*, Vienna 1938

292 STRAHAN, E. *The Art Treasures of America*, Philadelphia 1880

293 STUART-JONES, H. *The Sculptures of the Museo Capitolino*, London 1912

294 STÜBEL, M. *Christian Ludwig von Hagedorn, ein Diplomat und Sammler des 18. Jahrhunderts*, Leipzig 1912

295 'Deutsche Galeriewerke und Kataloge des 18. Jahrhunderts', *Monatshefte für Bücherfreunde*, 1925

296 SUTTON, D. 'Thomas Howard, Earl of Arundel, as a collector of drawings', *Burl. Mag.*, 1947

297 *Christie's since the War (1949–59)*, London 1959

298 SWARZENSKI, G. *Museumsfragen*, Frankfurt 1928

299 'Art and Forgery', *Magazine of Art*, 1948

300 TAMARO, B. F. 'La fortuna della scultura greca nel gusto veneziano del Cinquecento', *Studi Vasariani*, 1952

301 TAMBRONI, F. 'Il commercio delle opere d'arte in Roma antica', *Atti del decimo Congresso Romano*, 1929

302 TAYLOR, F. H. *Babel's Tower – the dilemma of the Modern Museum*, New York 1945

303 *The Taste of Angels*, Boston 1954

304 *Pierpont Morgan as collector and patron*, New York 1957

305 THIEME, G. *Der Kunsthandel in den Niederlanden im 17. Jahrhundert*, Cologne 1959

306 THODE, H. *Die Antiken in den Stichen Marcantons*, Leipzig 1881

307 TIETZE, H. *Genuine and False*, London 1948

308 'The European Art Museum', *Beiträge für Georg Swarzenski*, Berlin 1951

309 *Treasures of the Great National Galleries*, London 1955

310 TORMO, E. *Os Desenhos das Antigualhas que vio Francisco d'Ollanda 1539–40*, Madrid 1940

311 TOURNEUX, M. 'Les galeries privées en Amérique', *GBA*, 1908

312 VALENTINI, M. B. *Musaeum Musaeorum*, 3 vols, Frankfurt 1704–14

313 VANBESELAERE, W. 'Notice historique sur le Musée des Beaux-Arts Anvers', *Catalogue des Maîtres Anciens*, Antwerp 1958

314 VENTURI, A. 'Zur Geschichte der Kunstsammlungen Rudolfs II', *Repertorium für Kunstwissenschaft*, 1885

315 VENTURI, L. *Italian paintings in America*, 3 vols, Milan 1931–33

316 *Il gusti dei primitivi*, Bologna 1926

317 VEY, H. 'Die Gemäldesammlung des Kurfürsten Clemens August von Köln', *Wallraf-Richartz-Jahrbuch*, 1963

318 VOLLARD, A. *Souvenirs d'un marchand de tableaux*, Paris 1937

319 VORDERWINKLER, J. *Die Kunstkammer des Grafen Joachim von Windberg im Jahre 1666* (Dissertation, Vienna 1951)

320 WAAGEN, G. F. *Treasures of Art in Great Britain*, 3 vols, London 1854

321 'Taste of collectors in England', *The Crayon*, 1855

322 WACKERNAGEL, M. *Der Lebensraum des Künstlers in der florentinischen Renaissance*, Leipzig 1938

323 WALDMANN, E. *Sammler und ihresgleichen*, Berlin 1920

324 WALPOLE, H. *Anecdotes of Painting in England*, London 1782

325 WATERHOUSE, E. K. 'British collecting of Italian pictures in the later XVIIth Century', *Burl. Mag.*, 1960

326 WATSON, F. J. P. 'On the early history of collecting in England', *Burl. Mag.*, 1944

327 WEGNER, W. *Kurfürst Carl Theodor von der Pfalz als Kunstsammler*, Mannheim 1960

328 WEHLE, H. B. *Art Treasures of the Prado*, London 1954

329 WEIGERT, R. A. 'Les collections antiques de Mazarin', *Catalogue de l'exposition 'Mazarin'*, Paris 1961

330 WEIZSÄCKER, H. 'Michelangelo im Statuenhof des Belvedere', *Jahrbuch der Preussischen Kunstsammlungen*, 1942–43

331 WILDE, J. 'Wiedergefundene Gemälde aus der Sammlung des Erzherzogs Leopold Wilhelm', *Jahrbuch der Kunsthistorischen Sammlungen in Wien*, 1930

332 WILDENSTEIN, G. 'Fragonard et la formation des collections du Musée du Louvre', *GBA*, 1959

333 WINKLER, J. K. *Morgan the Magnificent*, New York 1930

334 WITTLIN, A. S. *The Museum and its tasks in Education*, London 1949

335 WÜTHRICH, L. H. *Christian von Mechel*, Basle 1956

336 YATES, R. F. *Antique Fakes and their detection*, New York 1950

337 YRIARTE, C. 'Sabbioneta', *GBA*, 1893

338 ZAHN, A. VON 'Historische Kunstsammlungen', *Archiv für die zeichnenden Künste*, 1859

339 ZOCCA, E. *Annuario dei Musei e Gallerie d'Italia*, Rome 1950

List of Illustrations

99 Sebastiano del Piombo. Christopher Columbus. *c.* 1530. Metropolitan Museum of Art, New York

100 Leonardo da Vinci. Mona Lisa. 1503–6. Louvre, Paris. *Photo Giraudon*

101 Gemma Augustea. Onyx cameo. Greek, *c.* AD 12. Kunsthistorisches Museum, Vienna

102 Hieronymus Bosch. Last Judgment. Panel. *c.* 1504. Gemäldesammlung der Akademie der bildenden Künste, Vienna

103 Titian (Tiziano Vecelli). Jupiter and Antiope (Pardo Venus). *c.* 1530–40. Louvre, Paris. *Photo Girandon*

104 Etruscan Chimaera. Bronze. Sixth century BC (?), slightly modified *c.* 1560. Museo Archaeologico, Florence. *Photo Mansell-Alinari*

105 Rape of the Sabine Woman. Small bronze replica of Giovanni da Bologna's marble original of 1583. Late sixteenth century. Bayerisches Nationalmuseum, Munich

106 The courtyard of the Palazzo Valle-Capranica. Print from a drawing. Dutch, *c.* 1536. Bibliothek, Heidelberg

107 Ascribed to Sebastian Vranck. Back of the Medici villa in Rome. *c.* 1600. Museo e Gallerie Nazionali di Capodimonte, Naples

108 Unknown painter. The Tribuna in the Uffizi. Probably French, *c.* 1830. Collection Mitchell R. Basker, U.S.A. *Photo Charles Uht*

109 Benvenuto Cellini. Ganymede. Marble, incorporating fragments of an antique statue. *c.* 1560. Museo del Bargello, Florence. *Photo Mansell-Alinari*

110 Jacopo Tintoretto. The Miracle of St Mark. *c.* 1570. Pinoteca di Brera, Milan. *Photo Mansell-Alinari*

111 Gallery in Sabbioneta. Built *c.* 1570. *Photo Mansell-Alinari*

112 John Scarlett Davis. The Uffizi Gallery. 1834. District Bank, Manchester. *Photo Colnaghi*

113 Jacopo de Strada. The 'Antiquarium' in Munich. Built 1570, alterations 1586–1600, restored after the Second World War. *Photo Direktion der Staatlichen Schlösser*

114 Lucas Cranach. Venus. Panel. 1532. Städelsches Kunstinstitut, Frankfurt

115 In the style of Dürer. Crucifixion. Panel. *c.* 1590. Reserves of the Staatlichen Kunstsammlungen, Dresden

116 In the style of Dürer. The Virgin and Child (Madonna with the Iris). Panel. *c.* 1590. National Gallery, London

117 Frans Franken the Younger. Kunstkammer. Panel. Early seventeenth century. Städtische Museen, Frankfurt

118 Credence vessel. Silver and fossilized shark-teeth. Late sixteenth century. Kunsthistorisches Museum, Vienna

119 Giuseppe Arcimboldo. Allegory of Fire. 1566. Kunsthistorisches Museum, Vienna

120 Headdress of Emperor Montezuma. Featherwork. Mexican, *c.* 1515. Museum für Völkerkunde, Vienna

121 Bowl. Porcelain. Chinese, *c.* 1550–80. German silver base added *c.* 1600. Landesmuseum, Stuttgart

122 Egidius Sadler. Wenceslas Hall in the Imperial Palace in Prague. Copper engraving. 1607. British Museum, London. *Photo John Freeman*

123 Ilioneus. Marble. Possibly Greek Hellenistic, second century BC. Glyptothek, Munich

124 Correggio (Antonio Allegri). Jupiter and Io. *c.* 1532. Kunsthistorisches Museum, Vienna

125 Tintoretto. The Origin of the Milky Way. *c.* 1578. National Gallery, London

126 Adriaen de Vries. The Emperor Rudolph II. Bronze. *c.* 1600. Kunsthistorisches Museum, Vienna

127 Wolfgang Heimbach. Christina of Sweden. Panel. *c.* 1650. Herzog Anton Ulrich-Museum, Brunswick

128 Bamberg Reliquary. Onyx set with jewels. Upper part dating from late classical times, setting between the tenth and thirteenth century. Statens Historiska Museum, Stockholm

129 Dürer. Eve. Panel. 1507. Prado, Madrid

130 Correggio. Leda and the Swan. *c.* 1532. Berlin Museums

131 Daniel Mytens, or van Somer. Thomas Howard, Earl of Arundel in his Galleries. *c.* 1617. Collection Duke of Norfolk, Arundel Castle. *Photo Royal Academy of Arts*

132 Hans Holbein. Sir Thomas More. Drawing. Royal Library, Windsor Castle. Reproduced by gracious permission of Her Majesty the Queen

133 Leonardo da Vinci. Neptune and Sea Horses. Drawing. Royal Library, Windsor Castle. Reproduced by gracious permission of Her Majesty the Queen

134 Francesco Parmigianino. Two Saints in Conversation. Pen and ink drawing. *c.* 1525. Ashmolean Museum, Oxford

135 Paolo Veronese. Rebecca at the Well. 1550. National Gallery, Washington, Samuel H. Kress Collection

136 Peter Paul Rubens. Apotheosis of the Duke of Buckingham. Tempera on wood. 1635–40. National Gallery, London

137 Georg Petel. Venus and Amor. Ivory. *c.* 1625. Ashmolean Museum, Oxford

138 Titian. Woman in a Fur. 1536. Kunsthistorisches Museum, Vienna

139 Dürer. Self-portrait. Panel. 1498. Prado, Madrid

140 Cranach. Cuspinian. Tempera on wood. Early sixteenth century. Oscar Reinhart Collection, Winterthur (Switzerland)

141 van Eyck. The Virgin and Child. Centre panel of the Giustiniani Altarpiece. 1437. Staatliche Kunstsammlungen, Dresden. *Photo Mansell-Alinari*

142 Rubens. Landscape with Gallows. Panel. Berlin Museums

143 Rembrandt van Rijn. Self-portrait. 1659. National Gallery, Washington, Mellon Collection

144 Willem van Haecht. Van Geest's Gallery. Collection van Berg, New York

145 Anthony van Dyck. Cornelius van der Geest. Before 1620. National Gallery, London

146 Frans Francken the Younger. Rubens' Studio in Antwerp. Tempera on wood. After 1640. Count Harrach Art Gallery, Vienna

147 Peter Thys. Archduke Leopold Wilhelm. *c.* 1650–55. Kunsthistorisches Museum, Vienna

148 van Eyck. Cardinal Albergati. Panel. 1431–32. Kunsthistorisches Museum, Vienna

149 Frans Francken the Younger. Friends and Enemies of Art. Panel. Pinakothek, Munich

150 Frans Francken the Younger. Jan Snellinck's Shop. Musées Royaux des Beaux Arts, Brussels

151 David Vinckeboons. Dutch Market. *c.* 1620–25. Herzog Anton Ulrich-Museum, Brunswick

152 Bartholomäus Sarburgh. Copy of *Burgomaster Meyer's Madonna* by Holbein. *c.* 1637. Staatliche Kunstsammlungen, Dresden. *Photo Alinari*

153 Rembrandt. Sketch of Raphael's portrait of Balthasar Castiglione. 1639. Graphische Sammlung, Albertina, Vienna

154 Rembrandt. Abraham Francken. Etching. *c.* 1656. Print Room, Rijksmuseum, Amsterdam

155 Rembrandt. Aristotle Contemplating the Bust of Homer. 1653. Metropolitan Museum of Art, New York

156 Joseph Heintz II. Cabinet of Curiosities. *c.* 1650. Kunsthalle, Hamburg

157 Joseph Arnold. The Kunstkammer of an unknown Citizen in Ulm. 1668. Städtisches Museum, Ulm

158 Reliquary. Copper-gilt and enamel on wooden frame; statuettes of ivory or walrus-tusk. Made in Cologne, *c.* 1175. Dankwarderode Palace, Brunswick

159 Royal gold Cup of the Kings of France and England. Gold and enamel. French, 1380. British Museum, London

160 The wall of an antique sculpture room in the Uffizi. Drawing. 1700–20. Print Department, Uffizi, Florence

161 Giovanni Lorenzo Bernini. Head of Medusa. Marble. Musei Capitolini, Rome

162 Rubens. Head of Medusa. Kunsthistorisches Museum, Vienna

163 Farnese Hercules. Marble. Roman copy of Greek Hellenistic original. Museo Nazionale, Naples. *Photo Mansell-Anderson*

164 Annibale Carracci. Courtyard of the Palazzo Farnese with the Farnese Hercules. Drawing. Early seventeenth century. Städelsches Kunstinstitut, Frankfurt

165 Jacques Blanchard. François Duquesnoy. *c.* 1625. Count Czernin Collection (on loan to the Residenz-galerie, Salzburg)

166 Bernini. Cardinal Scipione Borghese. Marble. *c.* 1625. Galleria Borghese Rome. *Photo Mansell-Alinari*

167 Giovanni Paolo Pannini. Cardinal Valenti-Gonzaga in the Picture Gallery of an imaginary Palace. 1749. Wadsworth Atheneum, Hartford, Conn. *Photo Gabinetto Fotografico Nazionale*

168 Picture gallery in the palace of Prince Colonna in Rome. Built 1654–1703. *Photo Mansell-Anderson*

169 Exhibition held in the Louvre in 1699. Engraving. Städelsches Kunstinstitut, Frankfurt

170 Bernini. Louis XIV. Bronze. 1665–66. National Gallery, Washington, Samuel H. Kress Collection

171 Francesco Solimena. Presentation of the inventory of the imperial picture gallery to the Emperor Charles VI. Preliminary sketch in oil. 1727–28. Kunsthistorisches Museum, Vienna

172 Ferdinand Storffer. A wall of the imperial picture gallery. Miniature on parchment. 1718–20. Kunsthistorisches Museum, Vienna

173 Salomon Kleiner. Part of the gallery of Count Schön-born in the castle of Pommersfelden. Engraving. *c.* 1730. Graphische Sammlung, Munich

174 Johann Bretschneider. The imperial gallery in Prague. 1714. Germanisches National-Museum, Nuremberg

175 Johann Georg Platzer. Interior of a house belonging to a Viennese artist. *c.* 1750. Art Museum, Breslau, Silesia *Photo Deutscher Kunstverlag GmbH*

176 Pieter van den Berghe. Prince Eugen selecting paintings. Pen and ink drawing. *c.* 1720. Print Department, Rijks-museum, Amsterdam

177 Balthasar Permoser. Apotheosis of Prince Eugen. Marble. *c.* 1730. Barockmuseum, Vienna

178 Rubens. Venus and Adonis. 1630–40. Metropolitan Museum of Art, New York (Gift of Harry Payne Bing-ham, 1937)

179 Augustus III. Mezzotint. *c.* 1750. Print Department, Staatliche Kunstsammlungen, Dresden

180 Bernardo Bellotto. The Neumarkt in Dresden, seen from the Jüdenhof. 1749. Staatliche Kunstsammlungen Dresden. *Photo Deutsche Fotothek*

181 (Jean) Antoine Watteau. L'Enseigne de Gersaint. 1720. Berlin Museums

182 Raphael. Sistine Madonna. 1516–17. Staatliche Kunst-sammlungen, Dresden

183 Giovanni Battista Tiepolo. The Banquet of Cleopatra. *c.* 1740–45. National Gallery of Victoria, Melbourne

184 Holbein. Hans Wedigh. Tempera and oil on wood. 1532. Metropolitan Museum of Art, New York

185 Carlo Dolci. St Catherine reading a Book. Residenz-Galerie, Salzburg

186 Per Hilleström. The gallery of ancient sculpture in the royal palace in Stockholm. 1792–93 (?). Nationalmu-seum, Stockholm

187 Apollo Belvedere. Marble. Roman copy of Greek origi-nal of fourth century BC. *c.* 200 BC. Vatican Museums, Rome. *Photo Mansell-Anderson*

188 Pompeo Girolamo Batoni. Prince Carl William Ferdi-nand of Brunswick. *c.* 1765. Herzog Anton Ulrich-Museum, Brunswick

189 Main room in the Cassel Gallery in 1936. Built 1749

190 Rembrandt. Jacob's Blessing. 1656. Staatliche Kunst-sammlungen, Cassel

191 Rembrandt. Nikolaes Bruyningh. 1652. Staatliche Kunstsammlungen, Cassel

192 Rembrandt. Landscape with Ruins. *c.* 1650. Staatliche Kunstsammlungen, Cassel

193 Jean Baptiste Siméon Chardin. Still-life with a Glass Bottle. Kunsthalle, Karlsruhe

194 Charles Nicolas Cochin. Art-lovers viewing paintings and drawings before an auction. Engraving. 1744. Albertina, Vienna

195 Baudouin. An auction of paintings and drawings. Engraving. 1765. Victoria and Albert Museum, London. *Photo Brompton Studio*

196 Vermeer van Delft. The Music Lesson. *c.* 1655. Royal Collection, Buckingham Palace. Reproduced by gracious permission of Her Majesty the Queen

197 The Portland Museum. Copper engraving. 1786. *Photo Courtesy of the Trustees of the British Museum, London*

198 Room in Wilton House, Salisbury. *Photo B. Matthews Ltd*

199 Anton van Maron. Prince Frederick Franz of Anhalt-Dessau. *c.* 1770. Germanisches National-Museum, Nu-remberg

200 Ferdinand Dietz. Seated Chinese figure with a dragon. Faience. *c.* 1755. Bayerisches Nationalmuseum, Munich

201 Priest. Porcelain. Chinese, early eighteenth century. Staatliche Kunstsammlungen, Cassel

202 Christian Stöcklin. A private collection in Frankfurt. *c.* 1760. Stadtgeschichtliches Museum, Frankfurt

203 Rembrandt. Christ the Saviour. 1661. Pinakothek, Munich

204 Daniel Nicolas Chodowiecki. Art-lovers admiring Dutch paintings. Copper-engraving. *c.* 1770. Staatliche Gra-phische Sammlung, Munich

205 Herm of Bacchus. Marble. Italian. *c.* 1770. Villa Bor-ghese Museum, Rome. *Photo Mansell-Alinari*

206 Apollo. Marble. Roman copy of a Greek original, probably of the fourth century BC. Exterior wall of Villa Albani, Rome. *Photo Mansell-Alinari*

207 Antonio Canova. Rondanini Medusa. Marble. Copy of first century AD original. Museo Nazionale, Naples. *Photo Mansell-Alinari*

208 Psyche. Marble. Greek copy of original of fourth or third century BC. Museo Nazionale, Naples. *Photo Mansell-Anderson*

209 Duplessis Berteaux and Robert Daudet II. Transfer of the statues from Portici to the Palazzo de' Studi in Naples. Engraving. From Richard St Non: *Descriptions des Royaumes de Naples et de Sicile*, Vol. II, *p.* 54, Paris 1782. *Photo British Museum*

210 The Niobids room in the Uffizi. Built by Paoletti, *c.* 1780. *Photo Mansell-Alinari*

211 Room V on the main floor of the Museo Capitolino, Rome. Built *c.* 1740. *Photo Mansell-Anderson*

212 A wall of the great salon of the Villa Borghese, Rome. Rebuilt by Asprucci 1782. *Photo Mansell-Alinari*

213 Sala d'Ingresso of the Villa Borghese, Rome. Rebuilt by Asprucci 1782. *Photo Mansell-Alinari*

214 The Sala Rotonda of the Museo Pio-Clementino, Vatican. Built by Simonetti 1790–95. *Photo Mansell-Anderson*

215 Giovanni Volpato. Sculpture gallery in the Museo Pio-Clementino, Vatican. Built 1790–95. Pen and wash drawing. Library of the Verwaltung der Staatlichen Schlösser und Gärten, West-Berlin

216 Pierre Gabriel Berthault. Entrée triomphale des Monuments (6 February 1798). Engraving from a drawing by Girardet. Department of Prints and Drawings, British Museum, London

217 Benjamin Zix. Napoleon visiting the antique sculpture rooms at night. Drawing. *c.* 1810. Cabinet des Dessins, Louvre, Paris

218 Benjamin Zix. The Imperial Cortège. Drawing. 1810. Musée Céramique, Sèvres

219 Rubens. Triumph of the Victor. *c.* 1613. Gemäldegalerie, Cassel

220 Hubert Robert. Plan for top-lighting the Grande Galerie in the Louvre. *c.* 1800. Collection Cailleux & Cie, Paris

221 Benjamin Zix. Vivant Dominique Denon. Drawing. *c.* 1813. Cabinet des Dessins, Louvre

222 Pinacoteca Vaticana. Engraving. 1821–22. Staatliche Graphische Sammlung, Munich

223 Titian. Jacopo Pesaro and Pope Alexander VI before St Peter. *c.* 1503. Koninklijk Museum voor Schone Kunsten, Antwerp. *Photo A. C. L.*

224 Correggio. Mercury instructing Cupid before Venus. *c.* 1530. National Gallery, London

225 Marbles in the third room on the east side of the British Museum. From *Marbles in the British Museum*, Vol. II, London, 1812. *Photo Thames and Hudson Archives*

226 Colossal head of Rameses II. Stone. *c.* 1280 BC. British Museum, London

227 John Zoffany. Townley with his friends. *c.* 1805. Townley Art Gallery, London. *Photo Gabinetto Fotografico Nazionale*

228 Glyptothek, Munich. Built by Leo von Klenze 1816–30. *Photo Lengauer*

229 Head of a warrior. Marble. Greek, *c.* 490 BC. Glyptothek, Munich

230 Raphael. Bindo Altiviti. 1520–25. National Gallery, Washington. Samuel H. Kress Collection. *Photo Pinakothek Munich*

231 Heinrich Maria von Hess. Young Italian Girl. *c.* 1825. St Annen-Museum, Lübeck

232 Piero di Cosimo. Venus and Mars. *c.* 1485–90. Berlin Museums

233 Klenze. Plan for a room on the ground floor of the Hermitage. Watercoloured drawing. 1847–49. Staatliche Graphische Sammlung, Munich

234 Braccio Nuovo of the Vatican Museums. Engraving. 1818–20. Staatliche Graphische Sammlung, Munich

235 Part of a room in the Museo Egizio in the Vatican. Engraving. *c.* 1835. Staatliche Graphische Sammlung, Munich

236 Sacred lion of the god Thot. Basalt. Egyptian, *c.* 300 BC. Museo Egizio, Vatican. *Photo Mansell-Alinari*

237 Vase. Mixture of Greek and Egyptian styles. *c.* 1780. Present whereabouts unknown. *Photo Bildarchiv Marburg*

238 The Gallery, Strawberry Hill. Engraving. From Horace Walpole: *Description of Strawberry Hill*, London, *c.* 1780. *Photo British Museum*

239 Abbot Suger's chalice. Gold and precious stones. French, *c.* 1140 partly Graeco-Roman. National Gallery, Washington

240 Diana d'Anet. Fountain designed by Jean Goujon. Limestone. *c.* 1550. Louvre, Paris. *Photo Giraudon*

241 Charles Percier. Michelangelo's Slaves. Engraving after a drawing by Lenoir of the Michelangelo original. From *Musée des Monuments Français*, Vol. III, Pl. 96. Paris 1805. *Photo John Freeman*

242 Hubert Robert. Garden of the Musée des Monuments Français. *c.* 1800. Kunsthalle, Bremen

243 Hubert Robert. One of the rooms of the Musée des Monuments Français. *c.* 1800. Kunsthalle, Bremen

244 The fourteenth-century room of the Musée des Monuments Français. Engraving. From J. P. Bres: *Souvenir du Musée des Monuments Français*, Pl. 18, Paris 1821

245 Charles Percier. Clovis and Clotilda. Engraving of Romanesque sculptures. From *Musée des Monuments Français*, vol. V, Pl. 206, Paris 1805

246 Old Testament King from St Denis. Limestone. French, *c.* 1180. The Cloisters, Metropolitan Museum of Art, New York

247 Stained-glass window from the refectory of St Germain des Prés. French, 1235–40. The Cloisters, Metropolitan Museum of Art, New York

248 Rogier van der Weyden. Portrait of a Lady. *c.* 1460. National Gallery, Washington, Mellon Collection

249 Hans Burgkmair. Hans Schellenberger. Panel. *c.* 1510. Wallraf-Richartz Museum, Cologne

250 Hermann. Lamentation. Panel. *c.* 1780. Reserves of the Pinakothek, Munich

251 Franz Wolfgang Rohrich. Head of Christ. Panel. *c.* 1800. Reserves of the Pinakothek, Munich

252 Rohrich. Duchess and Child. Panel. *c.* 1820. Reserves of the Pinakothek, Munich

253 Grünewald (Mathis Neithardt-Gothardt). Mary in Prayer. Drawing. *c.* 1515. Ashmolean Museum, Oxford

254 Master Bertram of Minden. Passion Altar. Tempera on wood. *c.* 1395. Landesmuseum, Hanover

255 Carlo Crivelli. The Annunciation, with St Emidius. 1486. National Gallery, London

256 Georg Karl Hoff. Dürer and Raphael kneeling before the Throne of Art. Etching from a drawing by Franz Pforr. *c.* 1810. Print department of the Berlin Museums

257 Cimabue. Madonna with Angels. Tempera on wood. *c.* 1300. Louvre, Paris. *Photo Giraudon*

258 Giunta Pisano or school of. Christ on the Cross. Tempera on wood. *c.* 1270. Wallraf-Richartz Museum, Cologne

259 Clock made for Philip the Good of Burgundy. *c.* 1430. Germanisches Nationalmuseum, Nuremberg

260 John Scarlett Davis. The Gallery of the Farnese Palace at Parma. 1839. Colnaghi's, London

261 John Scarlett Davis. An exhibition and gallery room of the British Institution, Pall Mall, in 1829. *Photo Birmingham Museum*

262 Eugène Louis Lami. The Grande Galerie of the Louvre. Engraving. 1841. Author's collection

263 Honoré Daumier. A dealer showing a client a picture. *c.* 1840. Boymans-van Beuningen Museum, Rotterdam

264 R. Thew, after Hiram Powers. An exhibition of the work of Düsseldorf artists held in New York. Engraving. 1857. *Photo New York Public Library*

265 Carl Goebel. The main sculpture room in the Lower Belvedere, Vienna. Watercolours. *c.* 1860. Library of the Kunsthistorisches Museum, Vienna

266 After Scopas. Head of Aphrodite. Marble. Greek, *c.* 200 BC. Museum of Fine Arts, Boston

267 Venus de Milo. Marble. Greek, *c.* 200 BC. Louvre, Paris

268 Nike of Samothrace. Marble. Greek. *c,* 300 BC. Louvre, Paris. *Photo Hirmer*

269 Head of Asclepius. Marble. Greek, *c.* 300 BC. British Museum, London

270 Portrait bust of a Roman. Terracotta. Roman, *c.* 50 BC. Museum of Fine Arts, Boston

271 Trebonianus Gallus. Marble. Roman, fourth century AD. Metropolitan Museum of Art, New York

272 Domenico Ghirlandaio. Portrait of Giovanna Tornabuoni. Panel. 1488. Thyssen Collection, Lugano

273 Mino da Fiesole. Florentine merchant. Marble. *c.* 1480. Berlin Museums

274 Velazquez. Portrait of Maria Anna, Queen of Spain. *c.* 1660. Nelson Gallery, Atkins Museum (Nelson Fund), Kansas City, Missouri, U.S.A.

275 Giovanni Battista Tiepolo. Rinaldo and Armida. *c.* 1750. Pinakothek, Munich

276 Main room of the Museo Stibbert in Florence, *c.* 1870. *Photo Mansell-Alinari*

277 Sword. Steel with silver inlay. German, *c.* 1575. Landesmuseum, Zürich

278 William Burgess. Painted sideboard. 1858. Reserves of the Victoria and Albert Museum, London

279 William L. Casey. A room in the Museum of Ornamental Art. Watercolour. 1856. Library of the Victoria and Albert Museum, London

280 Console. Gilded wood. Japanese, eighteenth century. Museum für Ostasiatische Kunst, Cologne. *Photo Bildarchiv Marburg*

281 Vase with dragon design. Porcelain. Chinese, fourteenth century. Musée Guimet, Paris

282 Deity of Wealth and Guardian of the North. Wood. Japanese, eleventh century. Museum of Fine Arts, Boston

283 Tree spirit. Limestone. North Indian, second century AD Victoria and Albert Museum, London

284 Dancing Shiva. Bronze. South Indian, second century AD. Musée Guimet, Paris. *Photo Bulloz*

285 Wu Wei. Hsi Wang-mu, legendary queen of the west, with a phoenix. Painting on silk. Chinese, *c.* 1500. British Museum, London

286 Head of a princess. Brown sandstone. Egyptian, fourteenth century BC. Berlin Museums. *Photo Bildarchiv Marburg*

287 Torso of a goddess. Black granite. Egyptian, seventh century BC. Kunsthistorisches Museum, Vienna

288 Head of Queen Nefertiti. Painted limestone. Egyptian, *c.* 1375 BC. Berlin Museums

289 El Greco (Domenikos Theotocopoulos). Annunciation. *c.* 1604. Museo del Arte, São Paulo, Brazil. *Photo Bildarchiv Marburg*

290 El Greco. Christ driving the Traders from the Temple. *c.* 1600. National Gallery, London. *Photo Thames and Hudson Archives*

291 El Greco. Christ on the Cross with Landscape. *c.* 1580. Cleveland Museum of Art, Gift of Hanna Fund

292 El Greco. Mater Dolorosa. 1594–97. Musée des Beaux-Arts, Strasbourg

293 Alessandro Magnasco. The Shipwreck. Phillips Collection, Washington. *Photo Thames and Hudson Archives*

294 Francisco de Goya. 'The Bewitched', a scene from 'El hechizado por fuerza'. Before 1798. National Gallery, London. *Photo Thames and Hudson Archives*

295 Joos de Momper. Imaginary Landscape. Panel. Berlin Museums

296 Jacopo Tintoretto. Moses striking Water from the Rock. *c.* 1555. Städelsches Kunstinstitut, Frankfurt. *Photo Thames and Hudson Archives*

297 Paul Gauguin. Nevermore. 1897. Courtauld Institute Galleries, London

298 Franz Marc. The Bewitched Mill. 1913. Art Institute of Chicago, Arthur Jerome Eddy Memorial Collection

299 Kukailimoku, god of war. Wood. Hawaiian, *c.* 1800. British Museum, London

300 Ancestor-figures. Wood. West Sudanese, Mali tribe, nineteenth century. Museum Rietberg, Zürich

301 King of Benin. Ivory pendant mask, with a tiara of miniature heads of Portuguese. Sixteenth century. British Museum, London. *Photo Thames and Hudson Archives*

302 Emil Nolde. Stil-Life. 1913-14. Landesgalerie, Hanover

303 Mask from an assembly-house. Wood. New Guinean, nineteenth century. Reiss-Museum, Mannheim

304 Aristocles. Stele from the tomb of Aristion. Marble. Greek, *c.* 510 BC. National-Museum, Athens

305 Coin with Athena represented as an owl. Silver. Greek, sixth century BC. Present whereabouts unknown

306 Relief of a Maenad's head. Clay tile. Graeco-Etruscan, sixth century BC. Landesmuseum, Karlsruhe

307 'Lady of Elche'. Limestone. Graeco-Phoenician, fifth century BC. Prado Museum, Madrid. *Photo Alinari*

308 Antefix from the Temple of Apollo. Clay tile. Graeco-Etruscan, late sixth century BC. Museo Nazionale di Villa Giulia, Rome

309 The Capitoline She-Wolf. Small bronze replica. Sienese, *c.* 1480. National Gallery, Washington, Samuel H. Kress Collection

310 Portrait of a woman. Encaustic on panel. Hellenistic, first century BC. National Gallery of Canada, Ottawa

311 Head of Eutropius, an official. Limestone. Asia Minor, fifth century AD. Kunsthistorisches Museum, Vienna

312 Georges Rouault. The Holy Shroud. 1937–38, Private Collection

313 Head of Christ. Panel. Byzantine-Russian, twelfth century. State Tretyakov Gallery, Moscow. *Photo Bildarchiv Marburg*

314 St John the Evangelist from the Echternach Gospels. Miniature on parchment. German, *c.* AD 1020. Germanisches National-Museum, Nuremberg

315 Christ giving commission to apostles. Ivory panel, from the former Ottonian Altarpiece of the cathedral at Magdeburg. German, late tenth century. City of Liverpool Museums

316 Martyrdom of St Sebastian. Painted wood. German, *c.* 1500. Annenmuseum, Lübeck

317 St George slaying the Dragon. Bronze cast of original by Bernt Notke made in 1489. Annenmuseum, Lübeck (now on loan to the church of St Catherine, Lübeck)

318 Virgin. Gilded, polychromed sandstone. French, *c.* 1250. The Cloisters, Metropolitan Museum of Art, New York

319 Christ and St John. Wood carving. South German, *c.* 1280. Cleveland Museum of Art, J. H. Wade Collection

320 Tomb of Armengol VII, Count of Urgel. Limestone. Spanish (Catalan, school of Lerida), 1299–1314. The Cloisters, Metropolitan Museum of Art, New York

321 Tilman Riemenschneider. St Lawrence. Painted and gilded lindenwood. German, *c.* 1502. Cleveland Museum of Art, Purchase, Leonhard C. Hanna, Jr., Bequest

322 Nicolas Lancret. La Camargo Dancing. *c.* 1740. National Gallery, Washington, Mellon Collection

323 Rembrandt. Portrait of a Lady with an Ostrich-Feather Fan. *c.* 1660. National Gallery, Washington, Widener Collection

324-6 Two sculpture halls and the façade of the National Gallery, Washington. Built by John Russell Pope, 1937–40

327-9 Three rooms in the Musée National d'Art Moderne, Paris. Built 1935–37

330 Altar of Zeus from Pergamum. Reconstruction, marble. Greek Hellenistic, *c.* 180 BC. Berlin Museums

List of Colour Plates

393

Index

Numbers in italics refer to black and white illustrations. Roman numbers refer to colour plates.
Important museums and collections are listed under their locations.